The News from Whitechapel

## LOCALITY OF THE SEVEN UNDISCOVERED MURDERS.

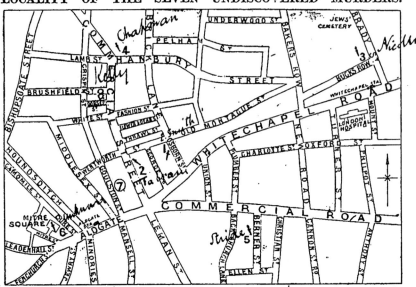

The above chart represents the locality within which, since April last, seven women of the unfortunate class have been murdered. The precise spot where each crime was committed is indicated by a dagger and a numeral.

1. April 3.—Emma Elizabeth Smith, forty-five, had a stake or iron instrument thrust through her body, near Osborn-street, Whitechapel.

2. Aug. 7.—Martha Tabram, thirty-five, stabbed in thirty-nine places, at George-yard-buildings, Commercial-street, Spitalfields.

3. Aug. 31.—Mary Ann Nicholls, forty-seven, had her throat cut and body mutilated, in Buck's-row, Whitechapel.

4. Sept. 8.—Annie Chapman, forty-seven, her throat cut and body mutilated, in Hanbury-street, Spitalfields.

5. Sept. 30.—A woman, supposed to be Elizabeth Stride, but not yet identified, discovered with her throat cut, in Berner-street, Whitechapel.

6. Sept 30.—A woman, unknown, found with her throat cut and body mutilated, in Mitre-square, Aldgate.

Figure 7 (encircled) marks the spot in Goulston-street where a portion of an apron belonging to the woman murdered in Mitre-square was picked up by a Metropolitan police-constable.

Figure 8. Nov. 9.—Mary Jane Kelly, 24, her throat cut and body terribly mutilated, in Miller's-court, Dorset-street.

# The News from Whitechapel

## Jack the Ripper in
## *The Daily Telegraph*

Alexander Chisholm,
Christopher-Michael DiGrazia *and*
Dave Yost

*Foreword by* PAUL BEGG

McFarland & Company, Inc., Publishers
*Jefferson, North Carolina, and London*

**Frontispiece:** A map of the East End of London showing locations of the various Whitechapel Murders, published in the *Daily Telegraph* of 10 November 1888 (courtesy of Evans/Skinner Crime Archive).

**Library of Congress Cataloguing-in-Publication Data**

The news from Whitechapel : Jack the Ripper in *The Daily Telegraph* / [transcribed and annotated by] Alexander Chisholm, Christopher-Michael DiGrazia and Dave Yost ; foreword by Paul Begg.
     p.    cm.
   Includes bibliographical references and index.
   ISBN 0-7864-1385-9 (softcover : 50# alkaline paper) ∞
   1. Jack, the Ripper.   2. Serial murders—England—London—History—19th century—Sources.   3. Whitechapel (London, England)—History—Sources.   I. Chisholm, Alexander, 1959–   II. DiGrazia, Christopher-Michael, 1963–   III. Yost, Dave, 1962–   IV. Daily telegraph (London, England)
HV6535.G73L664   2002
364.15'23'092—dc21               2002006089

British Library cataloguing data are available

*Cover photograph:* Church Passage, Aldgate (Evans/Skinner Crime Archive)

Manufactured in the United States of America

*McFarland & Company, Inc., Publishers*
  *Box 611, Jefferson, North Carolina 28640*
   *www.mcfarlandpub.com*

For Stewart Evans

# ACKNOWLEDGMENTS

When setting out to write about Jack the Ripper, the first thing an author learns is that he doesn't know nearly as much as he thought. Fortunately, there are the "Ripperati"—a coterie of researchers and writers devoted to uncovering and preserving the truth about those bloody events of 1888, without whose assistance this book could not have been completed. We are pleased to call them colleagues and friends and are deeply in debt to them all.

Grateful thanks to Stewart P. Evans for the generous gift of his time, patience and resources—most especially photographs and documents from his unparalleled collection—as well as for reading the early draft of this manuscript and saving us from untold blunders. Thanks as well to Paul Begg for his vetting of this book, his gentlemanly encouragement, and his contribution of a charming foreword.

We are indebted to Andy Aliffe and Adrian Phypers for their knowledge of London geography, Bernard Brown of the Metropolitan Police History Society for identifying obscure policemen, the organizers and staff of the Casebook Press Project for making our trawl through thousands of lines of newsprint immeasurably easier, Ivor Edwards for a monetary conversion table, Martin Fido, Neal Shelden, Keith Skinner and Philip Sugden for permission to quote from their books, Chris Payne at the British Newspaper Library for cheerful, prompt service over the years, and Jessica Stitson of the Woburn Public Library for finding obscure tomes.

In the personal sphere, we are grateful to Eric and Irene for their enduring support and encouragement and to Margaret for patiently enduring the Ripper as a constant, uninvited houseguest. They have borne the whole project with extraordinary good humor.

And, finally, thanks to Stephen Ryder and John Piper, creators of the *Casebook: Jack the Ripper* website, without which the authors would never have met.

Alexander Chisholm
Christopher-Michael DiGrazia
Dave Yost
*Drybridge, Scotland; Bradford, Massachusetts; and Burgettstown, Pennsylvania*
*April 2002*

# TABLE OF CONTENTS

## *Chapter 3—Elizabeth Stride*          87

## *Chapter 4—Catherine Eddowes*          140

# FOREWORD

## *by Paul Begg*

Be careful. The book you are holding is a time machine. It is the nearest you will ever get to the pavements of the East End of London in that dreadful autumn of 1888 when Jack the Ripper stalked his victims and sent a shiver of terror throughout London and far, far beyond.

Although many books have been written about Jack the Ripper, they are a distillation of the source material available to their respective authors. As such they present the story through the author's eyes—through the information that mattered to the author—and you are therefore receiving it second-hand. This book is different. In this book you are reading exactly what you would have read if you were living in the autumn of 1888.

Imagine you are seated at the table in your breakfast room. Outside, beyond the net curtains and the small and neat front lawn, horses' hooves and the iron-rimmed wheels of a cart clatter down the poorly surfaced road. Your bacon, eggs and devilled kidneys are on a plate on the linen tablecloth, nut-brown tea steams in a teacup, and next to it is the folded *Daily Telegraph*. You open the newspaper, set-

tling down to eat and absorb the news of a world largely dominated by the British Empire, and your eyes come to rest on…

Well, they come to rest on exactly what you are about to read in this book— the story of the horrible Ripper crimes as it unfolded, warts and blemishes of misreporting and all. Here are all the false leads. All the raised and dashed hopes. Here are the voices of the people who were there, voices carrying across time to speak to you, as they would have spoken to you if you'd been seated in that breakfast room.

One of the joys of writing books is that ideally you get to see all the files, papers, original newspaper reports and so on. You manage to get a real "feel" for the period. The reader doesn't get this. The reader just gets what the writer decides to give him.

That doesn't apply with this book. Here the reader get the original reports, unfiltered, unexpurgated, unedited. Back in the 1950s there was a famous cop show on television called *Dragnet* in which the main character's catch-phrase was "Just the facts, ma'am." Well, that's what you get here. Just the facts.

But there is a downside for the writer. Yes, he gets to read all that lovely colorful source material that his readers never see, but he doesn't know what a lot of it means. Who are these people named in the newspaper reports? Who is this mysterious Home Office mandarin called Lushington? What part did this policeman called Monro play? Who was Matthews? Is Anderson, whoever he may be, trustworthy? Again, this book gives you the edge, because the authors have provided footnoted explanations for all those bits you might not know about.

And you have the advantage over original readers of the newspapers because the authors have taken considerable pains to provide all the latest research and theories, so from time to time they tell you the latest thinking, being careful not to show whatever their own biases might be.

So, close your eyes for two minutes until you can maybe hear the horse-drawn hansom cab rattling by outside, then open this book and begin reading... It's 1888 and the newspaper seller down the street is crying out: "'Orrible murder! 'Nother 'orrible murder... Get yer *Telegraph* 'ere. 'Orrible murder."

And what better paper in which to read an account of those terrible crimes than the *Daily Telegraph*.

The *Daily Telegraph* was launched on 29th June 1855. A few days later the Stamp Act was repealed, opening the way for cheap, mass-circulation newspapers. The Stamp Act, by the way, was a tax imposed on British newspapers in 1712. It reached as high as 4d a copy, which made newspapers hugely expensive and well beyond the means of the average person. By the 1830s, when a campaign to abolish the tax was begun by several radical publishers, it was regarded as "a tax on knowledge." In 1836 the 4d tax was reduced to 1d. However, it was not until 1855 that it was abolished altogether.

Recognizing that this opened the way to create a newspaper for the masses, the *Daily Telegraph* seized the opportunity and on 20th September relaunched itself as the first 1d morning newspaper.

Called *The Daily Telegraph & Courier*, it was founded by Colonel Arthur Sleigh as a vehicle to air a personal grievance against the Duke of Cambridge, the future Commander-in-Chief of the British Army. It was printed by Joseph Moses Levy, proprietor of the *Sunday Times*, but when Sleigh proved unable to pay the printing bill, Levy took over the newspaper.

In 1855 there were ten newspapers published in London. The *Times* cost sevenpence, was by far the most expensive, and enjoyed a circulation of 10,000. The *Daily News* and the *Morning Post* cost fivepence. These were expensive items. Imagine paying £10 or $15 for a newspaper. That's what it was like. So Levy's penny paper soon outstripped the competition. Soon Levy was using the slogan: "the largest, best, and cheapest newspaper in the world." The *Daily Telegraph*'s circulation soared. Within a year or so it was outselling the *Times* with a circulation of 27,000—not bad considering that illiteracy was still quite high!

Levy's son, Edward Levy-Lawson, became editor of the newspaper along with Thornton Leigh Hunt and they hired an impressive team of journalists, among them George Augustus Sala, J. M. Le Sage, and T. P. Connor. They were also greatly inspired by the *New York Herald*, run by James Gordon Bennett—he whose son, James Gordon-Bennet Jnr., gave his name to the exasperated cry "Gordon Bennett!"—which leaned towards sensationalism and the unusual or bizarre. Some examples of early headlines used by the newspaper included *"A Child Devoured by Pigs," "Extraordinary Discovery of Man-Woman in Birmingham"* and *"Shocking Occurrence: Five Men Smothered in a Gin Vat."*

From the beginning, though, the *Telegraph* devoted considerable column inches to crime reporting. In 1856 its coverage of one crime story alone filled a quarter of the newspaper! And in 1881 the *Telegraph* made newspaper history when it published the first portrait block to appear in any newspaper. It was a picture of Percy Lefroy, who had murdered a wealthy businessman named William Gold on the London to Brighton train. As a result of the picture, 29 different men were arrested, among them Lefroy, who was later convicted and executed for the crime. Little surprise, then, that the *Daily Telegraph* should have given full coverage to the Jack the Ripper murders in 1888.

The growth of newspapers was phenomenal. The abolition of the "tax on knowledge," improvements in newspaper technology (leading to cheaper production costs and quicker reporting) and growing literacy due to improved education for the masses, led to not only an increase in the circulation of newspapers but in the number of newspapers—there were 14 daily newspapers in Britain in 1846; by 1880 the number had grown to 156.

And so there developed a circulation war, a battle for the "new" readers—the clerks and commuters—who sought information but also entertainment and in some cases ready-made opinion. The press turned its attention to the habits of the rich and famous and to commenting on and criticizing politicians. By the 1880s, Lord Salisbury, the Prime Minister, felt so oppressed by the intrusions of journalists that he magisterially complained: "it is really quite intolerable ... these vermin are omnipresent and it is hopeless to attempt to escape observation."

It was the birth of investigative journalism. *The Daily Telegraph* led the way—Hunt's death in 1873 having led to the editorship passing to Edwin Arnold, who began outspokenly questioning the policies of William Gladstone's government—but it was the *Pall Mall Gazette*, under the editorship of W.T. Stead (who was destined to die aboard the *Titanic*) that defined the new press by creating a heady mixture of social investigation with sensationalism. So by the 1880s there was a rather explosive mixture bubbling away that with the right spark could ignite the press into an orgy of sensationalist reporting as papers battled for their circulation.

Then in 1888, when the *Telegraph* achieved a circulation of about 300,000, Jack the Ripper provided that spark. And he couldn't have provided it in any place better than in the teeming warren of decaying houses that was London's East End. For this was a complex period of considerable social change. Complacent Londoners, wallowing in the wealth of being at the center of the greatest empire the world had ever known, were suddenly hit by a downturn in the economy which caused widespread unemployment (a word actually coined in 1888). The poor and starving had staged a march on the West End which some claimed turned into a riot. It was put down by the authorities with a heavy hand, but curious eyes turned towards the home of the unemployed, the East End. And as those eyes gazed upon that stage of infamy and vice, from the wings strode a lone madman, a shadow in the night upon whom someone, probably a journalist, bestowed the chilling soubriquet "Jack the Ripper."

This book tells the story of Jack the Ripper as it was reported in *The Daily Telegraph*. It is an important book because it allows you to read the unfolding drama as it was played out, day by day in 1888. So sit back, put your feet up, make sure you have a cup of strong, nut-brown tea close to hand, and travel back to the past, to a land of hansom cabs, flickering yellow gaslight, narrow alleys, and—Jack the Ripper.

# PREFACE

It has been over 100 years since the first victim of Jack the Ripper fell bleeding to the slutchy, verminous streets of Whitechapel. What can possibly be left for anyone to say? Haven't there been enough theories, enough resifting of evidence, enough claims to a "final solution?" In short, what possible reason can there be for anyone to add yet another title to the wearying plethora of Ripper books?

Valid questions, all. And they are posed time and again by dozens of authors, all pleading their own place in this well-ploughed field, all hastening to assure the reader that *this book* is worthy of their hard-earned money. Here at last is a new, valid suspect; here is a fresh retelling of the familiar story; here is the old finally made new. Sometimes—a rare sometimes—these declarations are true. More often, however, they amount to fresh wrapping around a spoilt package. The veteran reader soon casts a jaundiced eye on claims to originality.

Having said that, it is more than presumptuous of us to bring forth the same stale description again—and yet, it is true. This is a *new sort* of Ripper book. Within these pages you will not find some new suspect unearthed from long-forgotten files. You will not find a fresh case made

stronger against an old suspect. Secret plots, black magic and government conspiracies have no place here. What you are about to read is the real story of Jack the Ripper.

We have presented the Whitechapel Murders as they were reported by the *Daily Telegraph*, the world's largest-selling daily newspaper in 1888. You will read what men and women throughout the Empire read during that evil time, and with them watch as the killings grow from obscurity to the greatest mystery of the 19th century. It is Jack the Ripper as it happened.

We have structured this work in order to allow a constant narrative while providing explanation where needed. Each chapter is devoted to one of the Ripper's canonical victims through transcripts of the *Telegraph* coverage of her murder, its investigation and subsequent inquest. Interspersed with the transcripts are footnotes; the contents of these are drawn from Home Office and Metropolitan Police files, past and present Ripper books, other contemporary newspaper reports and our own researches. They are designed to correct what the newspapers got wrong, expand on certain points or at times merely explain to the reader things the

Victorians would have taken for granted. Each chapter opens with a short summing-up of its particular murder, allowing the accumulation of a store of knowledge while proceeding through the book.

There are also certain areas of the Ripper case which require a detailed discussion, as they are often traps for the novice and misinterpreted by other authors. Such topics as the reality of the Lusk Kidney or whether it was truly Mary Kelly who died in Miller's Court will be referenced in the victim chapters, but we feel they are also deserving of fuller explanation than footnoting can provide, and so we have labelled these and other brief essays as "Commentary."

Owing to space limitations, of course, what is presented in these pages can only be a sampler of some of the best *Telegraph* prose, and we have only briefly been able to touch upon how perceptions of both Whitechapel and its murders were shaped by a sensationalist press—a topic which is much more fully discussed in L. Perry Curtis, Jr.'s fascinating *Jack the Ripper and the London Press*. We wish we had more room to tell you about the arrest of John Pizer, so nearly lynched as "Leather Apron," for example, or about the tragicomic fate of a Miss Milligan, frightened to death by a man who leaped out at her and shouted, "I'm Jack the Ripper!" But we hasten to assure you that we have omitted nothing of real importance in press reports.

Over the last two decades, research into the Whitechapel Murders—frequently a catchall area for cranks and hucksters with only the rare sane voice—has moved towards books with detailed sourcing and extensive footnoting, such as Philip Sugden's *The Complete History of Jack the Ripper*, or Stewart Evans and Keith Skinner's *The Ultimate Jack the Ripper Sourcebook*, volumes whose thickness is often intimidating to the tyro. While we applaud this approach, we also realize its drawbacks, and here again we hope to offer something new.

This collection is designed for all students of the Ripper, at whatever level. The novice can read the *Telegraph* stories and see the crimes through our great-grandparents' eyes. The serious researcher can access footnotes and commentary in order to use this work as a reference for deeper forays into the world of the Great Victorian Mystery. We hope that, whatever your interest, *The News from Whitechapel: Jack the Ripper in* The Daily Telegraph will find a place in your library.

# Chapter 1

# MARY ANN NICHOLS

*—found murdered Friday, 31 August 1888*

Early yesterday morning a horrible murder was discovered in Buck's-row,
a narrow passage running out of Thames-street, Whitechapel.
—*Daily Telegraph*, Saturday, 1 September 1888

The name "Jack the Ripper"—bestowed on an otherwise unknown 19th century killer—is so deeply embedded in popular consciousness as a synonym for brutal, unreasoning murder that it is commonly used as a catchphrase by people who have only the vaguest notion of the truth behind his crimes. Because he was never caught, thus remaining an elusive chimera in the court of Justice, his chilling cognomen finds itself attached to any number of serial killers—Peter Kürten, the "Düsseldorf Ripper," Gordon Cummins, the "Blackout Ripper," Peter Sutcliffe, the "Yorkshire Ripper"—even obliquely in the 1960s to an anonymous London murderer of prostitutes dubbed "Jack the Stripper."

Fiction has ever found the Ripper a dark protagonist, but good fiction is not always good history. Much of what is "known" about Saucy Jack—his appearance, his motives, his identity—owes its origin more to the writer's inkwell than the policeman's files. Yet blame cannot be laid entirely at the door of the purveyors

of modern fiction. Some of the fantasy was present at the beginning, in the autumn of 1888, within the pages of some of London's biggest newspapers—the *Times*, the *Star*, the *Pall Mall Gazette* and the *Daily Telegraph*.

By the late summer of 1888, the *Telegraph* could boast of having the largest daily circulation in the world, with average sales of 250,000 copies per day at a time when those of its main established London rival, the *Times*, were 50,000 daily and falling. As a result, the *Telegraph*'s comprehensive reporting of Whitechapel murder—what historian Philip Sugden has called "the single best coverage"—reached the widest possible audience, and so played a significant role in the shaping of popular perceptions of Jack the Ripper.

The figure of the Ripper, however, was to be a late entrant onto the East End stage, with short curtain-raisers before the featured attraction. The first Whitechapel Murder—one only later attributed to him—occurred on Tuesday, 3 April 1888, when Emma Elizabeth Smith, a 45-year-old widow returning home along White-chapel Road about 1:30 in the morning, was attacked, robbed and raped. She somehow managed to stagger back to her lodgings and was taken to the London Hospital, where she died of peritonitis the next day.

Three months later, Martha Tabram was found butchered on the first-floor steps of George Yard Buildings, White-chapel, in the early hours of 7 August. At the time of her death, the unfortunate Tabram's fate was not deemed significant enough to merit attention in the pages of the *Telegraph*, although the paper did cover the second, final session of her inquest on 23 August. The jury returned a soon all-too-familiar verdict that the deceased had been murdered by "some person or persons unknown."

Martha Tabram's killer was destined to remain a person unknown, a fate which might well have befallen Tabram herself were it not for the fact that she was about to be cast amongst the predecessors of Mary Ann Nichols. And it was Mary Ann Nichols who, in the unfolding legend of Jack the Ripper, occupied the unusual position of being presented as the third victim in a series of crimes which her own death caused to be created. It was only following Nichols' demise that the phrase "The Whitechapel Murders" found its place in the language of infamy, and this unfortunate became unknowingly instrumental in the creation of a historical pageant where she would feature as but a simple, poor player.

It is to that history we must now turn.

---

# THE DAILY TELEGRAPH
## LARGEST CIRCULATION IN THE WORLD

THE SALE OF
THE DAILY TELEGRAPH
AMOUNTS TO AN AVERAGE
WHICH, IF TESTED
WILL SHOW AN
EXCESS OF HALF A MILLION
COPIES WEEKLY
OVER ANY OTHER MORNING
PAPER

London, Saturday, September 1, 1888

Page 3
MYSTERIOUS MURDER IN
WHITECHAPEL

Early yesterday morning a horrible murder was discovered in Buck's-row,[1] a narrow passage running out of Thames-street, Whitechapel. About a quarter-past four[2] in the morning, as Police-constable John Neil was walking down that thoroughfare, he came upon the body of a woman lying at the side of the street[3] with her throat cut right open from ear to ear. The wound was about two inches wide. The body was immediately conveyed to the Whitechapel Mortuary,[4] where it was found that, besides the wound in the throat, there were many other fearful injuries in other parts of the body.[5] The

---

[1]Buck's Row is now Durward Street. It was renamed after the Nichols murder in order to frustrate morbid sightseers.

[2]This is incorrect by half an hour; Nichols' body was discovered by PC Neil at approximately 3:45am (ref. HO 144/221/A49301C, ff. 6–10).

[3]Nichols was lying in the gateway leading to Brown's stableyard (ref. Neil's inquest testimony, 3 September).

[4]The parish of Whitechapel did not have its own mortuary. The "mortuary" referred to both here and during the Chapman murder investigation was, according to the researches of James Tully, a small brick shed in Stone Yard, off of Old Montague Street and the Whitechapel Road (Tully, pp. 364–367).

[5]See 3 September for a fuller description of Nichols' injuries.

Buck's Row (now Durward Street), Whitechapel. The site of the Nichols murder was on the pavement at the open garage door (courtesy of Evans/Skinner Crime Archives).

hands and face were bruised and bore evidence of there having been a severe struggle. The constable at once alarmed the people living in the house next to the stable-yard, which is occupied by a carman, named Green, and his family,[6] and also knocked up Mr Walter Perkins [Purkess], the resident manager at the Essex Wharf, on the opposite side of the road. Neither Mr. Perkins nor any of the Green family, although the latter were sleeping within a few yards of where the body was discovered, had heard any sound of a struggle. Dr. Llewellyn,[7] who lives only a short distance away, in Whitechapel-road, was at once sent for, and promptly arrived on the scene. He found the body lying on its back across the gateway, and the briefest possible examination was sufficient to prove that life was extinct. Death had not long taken place, because the extremities were still warm. With the assistance of Police-sergeant Kirby [*sic*] and Police-constable Thane [*sic*] the body was removed to the mortuary, and it was not until the unfortunate woman's clothes were removed that the horrible nature of the attack which had been made upon her was fully revealed. The instrument with which the wounds were inflicted must have been as sharp as a razor, and used with the utmost ferocity.

The murdered woman was about forty-five years of age,[8] and 5ft 2in in height. She had a dark complexion, brown

---

[6]Emma Green, who lived in New Cottage, Buck's Row, adjacent to the stableyard, was a widow with a daughter and two sons (Begg, Fido, Skinner [hereafter "BFS"], pp. 149). It is possible that one of the sons was mistaken for the head of the household.

[7]Rees Ralph Llewellyn (1849–1921), Medical Officer to the East and East Central police districts as well as the City Mission (BFS, pp. 254–255).

[8]Nichols was just 43, born 26 August 1845 (HO 144/221/A49301C [8a], ff. 129–134).

eyes and brown hair (turning grey). At the time of her death she was wearing a brown ulster,[9] fastened with seven large metal buttons, with the figure of a horse and a man standing by its side stamped thereon. She had on a brown linsey[10] frock and a grey woollen petticoat, with flannel underclothing, close ribbed brown stays,[11] black woollen stockings, side-spring boots, and black straw bonnet trimmed with black velvet. The mark "Lambeth Workhouse, R.R.,"[12] was found stamped on the petticoat bands, and a hope is entertained that by this the deceased's identity may be established. A photograph of the body has been taken, and this will be circulated amongst the workhouse officials.[13]

A general opinion is now entertained that the spot where the body was found was not the scene of the murder.[14] Buck's-row runs through from Thomas-street to Brady-street, and in the latter street what appeared to be blood stains were found at irregular distances on the footpaths on either side of the way. Occasionally a larger splash was visible, and from the manner in which the marks were scattered it seems as though the person carrying the muti-lated body had hesitated where to deposit his ghastly burden, and had gone from one side of the road to the other until the obscurity of Buck's-row afforded the shelter sought for. The street had been crossed twice within the space of about 120 yards. The point at which the stains were first visible is in front of the gateway to Honey's-mews,[15] in Brady-street, about 150 yards from the point where Buck's-row commences.[16] Several persons living in Brady-street state that early in the morning they heard screams, but this is a by no means uncommon incident in the neighbourhood, and, with one exception, nobody seems to have paid any attention to what was probably the death struggle of the unfortunate woman.

The exception referred to was a Mrs. Colville,[17] who lives only a short distance from the foot of Buck's-row. According to her statement she was awakened by her children, who said someone was trying to get into the house. She listened, and heard a woman screaming "Murder, Police!" five or six times. The voice faded away, as though the woman was going in the direction of Buck's-row, and all became

---

[9]A long loose overcoat.

[10]Cloth made of a mixture of linen and wool; also known as "linsey-woolsey."

[11]A lace underbodice or cheap corset stiffened with strips of whalebone, metal or wood.

[12]This is a misprint. The *Illustrated Police News* of 8 September records the mark "bearing the words 'Lambeth Workhouse, P.R.' (Prince's-road)"; this is confirmed by the *Telegraph* of 4 September.

[13]Presumably the extant photograph of Nichols used to illustrate most standard books on the Whitechapel Murders.

[14]The absence of any noise and apparent lack of blood at the murder scene raised some questions as to whether Nichols might have been killed somewhere else and her body left in Buck's Row. It was determined, however, that her clothing, hair and abdominal cavity had soaked up a large enough amount of blood to explain its relative absence in the street. The lack of noise may have been due to the severing of Nichols' windpipe; or alternatively, in view of the Ripper's presumed M.O., due to strangulation.

[15]"Mews" were stables or carriage-houses.

[16]It is difficult to know how seriously to take this passage. Certainly Inspector Spratling reported finding no bloodstains in Brady Street at 6:00 that morning (see 4 September), and Inspector Helson found nothing out of the ordinary at 8:00am, as noted later in this news story. There were a large number of slaughterhouses in the neighborhood of Buck's Row, and it is tempting to assign the various "splashes" to the clothing or knives of workers going about their business or who gathered to see the body. As well, a bit of wishful thinking may have accompanied the sight of any dark puddle or stain soon after the discovery of Nichols' murder (ref. MEPO 3/140, f. 241).

[17]Sarah Colwell. Despite her dramatic statement, the police discounted her tale and no corroborating witness to what she heard came forward.

quiet. She only heard the steps of one person. It is almost needless to point out that a person suffering from such injuries as deceased had inflicted upon her would be unable to traverse the distance from Honey's-mews to the gateway in Buck's-row, which is about 120 yards from Brady-street, making a total distance of at least 270 yards. Therefore the woman must have been carried or dragged there, and here the mystery becomes all the more involved. Even supposing that with the other wounds upon her she had sufficient strength left to call out in the tones which Mrs. Colville asserts she heard, the deceased's throat could not have been cut at the spot where she was found lying dead, as that would have caused a considerably heavier flow of blood than was found there. As a matter of fact but a very small quantity of blood was to be seen at this spot, or found in Buck's-row at all.

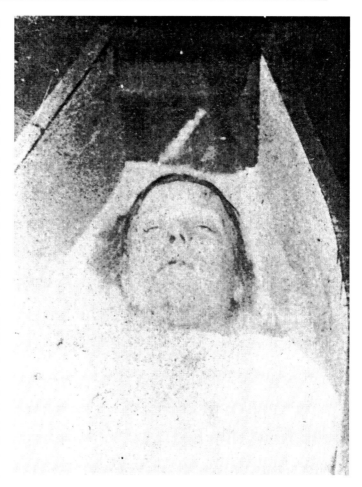

**Mortuary photograph of Mary Ann Nichols (courtesy of Evans/Skinner Crime Archives).**

On the other hand, if the murderer had cut the woman's throat at the onset, the deceased could not have uttered a single cry afterwards. Mrs. Colville's statement, looked at in the light of these circumstances, by no means totally clears up the mystery as to the exact locality which the murderer selected for the completion of his dreadful deed. Police-constable Neil traversed Buck's-row about three-quarters of an hour before the body was discovered, so it must have been deposited there soon after he had patrolled that thoroughfare.[18] Mrs. Green, Mr. and Mrs. Perkins, and the watchmen in Schneider's cap factory and a wool depot, which are both situated in Buck's-row, agree that the night was an unusually quiet one for the neighbourhood. Shortly after midday some men who were searching the pavement in Buck's-row above the gateway found two spots of

[18]According to Neil, he was last in Buck's Row approximately ½ hour before Nichols' body was discovered, i.e., near 3:15am. She was found by Charles Cross and Robert Paul (see 18 September) at about 3:40am, and by their report, she may have been dying at that time. If we assume Cross frightened away Nichols' killer— and this is quite likely—a time of 3:30–3:35am for the murder is probable.

blood in the roadway. They were some feet away from the gate, and they might have dropped from the hands or clothing of the murderer as he fled away.[19] The stableyard and the vicinity have been carefully searched in the hope of finding the weapon with which the crime was committed, but so far without success. A bridge over the Great Eastern Railway is close at hand, and the railway line was also fruitlessly searched for some distance.

Owing to the frequency of crimes in this locality of the most brutal character the inhabitants are becoming excited and alarmed. Some few months ago a woman was barbarously murdered near Whitechapel Church by being stabbed with a stick,[20] and on the night of the last Bank Holiday a woman named Turner[21] was found dead in George-yard, Whitechapel, with thirty stabs on her body.[22] In both cases no clue to the perpetrator of the deed was ever discovered.

Dr. Llewellyn has made the following statement: "I was called to Buck's-row about five minutes to four this morning by Police-constable Thane, who said a woman had been murdered. I went to the place at once, and found deceased lying on the ground in front of the stable-yard door. She was lying on her back, with her legs out straight, as though she had been laid down. Police-constable Neil told me that the body had not been touched. The throat was cut from ear to ear, and the woman was quite dead. On feeling the ex-

tremities of the body I found that they were still warm, showing that death had not long taken place. A crowd was now gathering, and as it was undesirable to make a further examination in the street I ordered the removal of the body to the mortuary, telling the police to send for me again if anything of importance transpired. There was a very small pool of blood on the pathway, which had trickled from the wound in the throat—not more than would fill two wine-glasses, or half a pint at the outside. This fact, and the way in which the deceased was lying, made me think at the time that it was at least probable that the murder was committed elsewhere, and the body conveyed to Buck's-row.[23] There were no marks of blood on deceased's thighs, and at the time I had no idea of the fearful abdominal wounds which had been inflicted upon the body.

At half-past five I was summoned to the mortuary by the police, and was astonished at finding the other wounds. I have seen many terrible cases, but never such a brutal affair as this. From the nature of the cuts on the throat it is probable that they were inflicted with the left hand. There is a mark at the point of the jaw on the right side of deceased's face, as though made by a person's thumb, and a similar bruise on the left side, as if the woman's head had been pushed back and her throat then cut. There is a gash under the left ear reaching nearly to the centre of the throat, and another cut apparently

---

[19]It is also possible that the blood came from the hands or clothing of nearby slaughtermen who came to see Nichols' body shortly after she was discovered; additionally, the spots may have been residual splashes from the work of Emma Green's son, James, who washed away the blood in Buck's Row after Nichols was removed (BFS, p. 149).

[20]This refers to Emma Smith. Confusion over Smith's fate and even her identity will recur throughout press coverage of the Whitechapel Murders.

[21]Martha Tabram, also known as Martha Turner. See Sugden, pp. 14–35, for a full account of her murder.

[22]Actually thirty-nine stab wounds (ref. *Times*, 10 August).

[23]Some imaginative writers have taken Llewellyn's "two wine-glasses" estimate as evidence that Nichols was murdered somewhere other than Buck's Row without taking the entire sense of the doctor's remarks into consideration. The slight amount of blood is easily explained by recalling that much of it had soaked into her hair and clothes, and Llewellyn is already admitting here to modifying his initial impression.

starting from the right ear. The neck is severed back to the vertebrae, which are also slightly injured. Deceased's clothes were loose, and the wounds could have been inflicted while she was dressed."[24]

Inspector Helson,[25] who has charge of the case, is making every effort to trace the murderer, but there is so little to guide the police that at present there does not seem much likelihood of success. The theory that the murder is the work of a lunatic, who is also the perpetrator of the other two murders of women which have occurred in Whitechapel during the last six months, meets with very general acceptance amongst the inhabitants of the district, the female portion of which are greatly alarmed. The more probable theory is that the murder has been committed by one or more of a gang of men who are in the habit of frequenting the streets at late hours of the night and levying blackmail on women. No money was found on deceased, and all she had in the pocket of her dress was a handkerchief, a small comb, and a piece of looking glass.

Another account states: "After the body was removed to the mortuary, steps were taken to secure, if possible, identification, but at first with little prospect of success. As the news of the murder spread, however, first one woman and then another came forward to view the body, and at length it was found that a person answering the description of the murdered woman had lodged in a common lodging-house, 18, Thrawle [*sic*]-street, Spitalfields. Women from that place were fetched, and they identified the deceased as 'Polly,' who had shared a room with three other females in the place on the usual terms of such houses—nightly payment of 4d each—each having a separate bed. It was gathered that the deceased had lodged in the house only for about three weeks past. Nothing more was known of her by them, but that when she presented herself for her lodging on Thursday night she was turned away by the deputy because she had not the money. She was then the worse for drink but not drunk, and went away laughing, saying, 'I'll soon get my "doss" money;[26] see what a jolly bonnet I've got now.' She was wearing a bonnet which she had not been seen with before, and left the lodging-house door. A woman of the neighbourhood, saw her later, she told the police—even as late as 2:30 on Friday morning—in Whitechapel-road, opposite the church, and at the corner of Osborne-street; and at a quarter to four she was found within 500 yards of the spot murdered.[27] The people of the lodging-house knew her as 'Polly,' but at about half-past

---

[24]An initial reading of this account would lead one to imagine Llewellyn is proposing a killer who stood behind Nichols, held her jaw with his right hand and cut her throat with his left. However, this tidy explanation is immediately complicated by the doctor's mention of a "gash under the left ear reaching nearly to the centre of the throat"—which would appear to indicate an assailant standing *in front* of Nichols—as well as his 1 September inquest testimony that "the wounds were from left to right and might have been done by a left-handed person." BFS, 2nd edition, concisely summarizes the confusion: "The M.O. proposed is clumsy, would be almost impossible to carry out silently and would probably rip the murderer's own sleeve" (pp. 306–307). It is difficult to believe that Llewellyn meant this awkward assault seriously, and he may have pictured the "gash" as inflicted after Nichols was laid down rather than during the course of a standing attack. The doctor appears never to have been questioned on his theory, and so we cannot be certain exactly how he envisioned Nichols' death. However, in a 19 October report (HO 144/221/A49301C, ff. 129–134), Inspector Donald Swanson wrote: "At first the doctor was of opinion that the wounds were caused by a left handed person but he is now doubtful," so presumably Llewellyn changed his earlier opinion.

[25]Joseph Henry Helson, warrant no. 51389. Local Inspector, CID, J (Bethnal Green) Division (BFS, pp. 160–161).

[26]Slang for bed money; lodging houses were also called "doss houses."

[27]The "woman" was Emily Holland; this was the last known sighting of Nichols before her death.

seven last evening a female named Mary Ann Monk, at present an inmate of Lambeth Workhouse, was taken to the mortuary, and, identified the body as that of Mary Ann Nicholls, also called 'Polly' Nicholls.[28] She knew her, she said, as they were inmates of the Lambeth Workhouse together in April and May last. On May 12, according to Monk, Nicholls left the workhouse to take a situation as servant at Ingleside, Wandsworth-common. It afterwards became known that Nicholls betrayed her trust as domestic servant by stealing £3 from her employer and absconding. From that time she had been wandering about. Monk met her, she said, about six weeks ago and drank with her. She was sure the deceased was 'Polly' Nicholls, and having twice viewed the features as the body lay in a shell maintained her opinion.

So far the police have satisfied themselves, but as to getting a clue to the murderer they express little hope. It has been stated that blood could be traced in thick spots and small pools from the spot where the body was found far down Buck's-row to a lateral thoroughfare called Brady-street. The police deny that statement. Inspector Helson states that he walked carefully over the ground soon after eight o'clock in the morning, and beyond the discolourations ordinarily found on pavements there was no sign of stain. Viewing the spot where the body was found, how-

ever, it seems difficult to believe that the woman received her death wounds there. The body must have been nearly drained of blood, but that found in Buck's-row was small in quantity. The police have no theory with respect to the matter, except that a sort of 'High Rip' gang exists in the neighbourhood, which, blackmailing women of the same class as the deceased, takes vengeance on those who do not find money for them.[29] They base that surmise on the fact that within twelve months two other women have been murdered in the district by almost similar means, and left in the gutter of the street in the early hours of the morning. The other theory is that the woman was murdered in a house, and killed whilst undressed, her clothes being then huddled on the body, which was afterwards conveyed out, to be deposited in the street. Colour is lent to this by the small quantity of blood found on the clothes, and by the fact that they are not cut.[30] The inquest is fixed for today."

---

# THE DAILY TELEGRAPH

Monday, September 3, 1888

Page 3
THE WHITECHAPEL MURDER
[*First Session of Inquest*]

On Saturday Mr. Wynne E. Baxter,[31]

---

[28]In the 19th century, "Polly" was a common diminutive of the name "Mary" (Baring-Gould, p. 153). Nichols' surname was continually spelled with two "L"s during the period of the Whitechapel Murders and in many writings afterwards.

[29]See also the *Daily News* of 1 September and Fido, *The Crimes, Detection and Death of Jack the Ripper*, pp. 18–25, regarding this surmise. Despite the asseverations of the *Telegraph*, it is debatable how seriously the "blackmailing gang" was taken by the police.

[30]See Spratling's inquest testimony, 4 September, for a refutation of the nude theory. The testimony of Charles Cross and Robert Mann (18 September) addresses the seemingly mysterious lack of cuts in the clothes.

[31]Wynne Edwin Baxter (1844–1920), coroner for the South-Eastern Division of London (BFS, pp. 37–39). In addition to the Nichols inquiry, he also chaired the inquests over canonical Ripper victims Annie Chapman and Elizabeth Stride as well as those of Rose Mylett, Alice McKenzie and Frances Coles. Baxter's clashes with the Metropolitan Police and his tendency towards self-aggrandizement have made him a polarizing figure among Ripper researchers. Frequent illustration of his concerns, theorizing and prejudices will be evident throughout the course of this book.

the coroner for South-East Middlesex, opened an inquiry at the Working Lads' Institute, Whitechapel-road,[32] into the circumstances surrounding the death of a woman supposed to be Mary Ann Nicholls, who was discovered lying dead on the pavement in Buck's-row, Baker's-row, Whitechapel, early on Friday morning. Her throat was cut, and she had other terrible injuries.

Inspector Helston [*sic*], who has the case in hand, attended, with other officers, on behalf of the Criminal Investigation Department.

**Edward Walker** deposed: I live at 15, Maidwell-street, Albany-road, Camberwell, and have no occupation. I was a smith when I was at work, but I am not now. I have seen the body in the mortuary, and to the best of my belief it is my daughter; but I have not seen her for three years. I recognise her by her general appearance and by a little mark she has had on her forehead since she was a child. She also had either one or two teeth out, the same as the woman I have just seen. My daughter's name was Mary Ann Nicholls, and she had been married twenty-two years.[33] Her husband's name is William Nicholls, and he is alive. He is a machinist. They have been living apart about seven or eight years.[34] I last heard of her before Easter. She was forty-two years of age.

THE CORONER: How did you see her?

WITNESS: She wrote to me.

THE CORONER: Is this letter in her handwriting?

WITNESS: Yes, that is her writing.

The letter, which was dated April 17, 1888,[35] was read by the Coroner,[36] and referred to a place which the deceased had gone to at Wandsworth.

THE CORONER: When did you last see her alive?

WITNESS: Two years ago last June.[37]

THE CORONER: Was she then in a good position?

WITNESS: I don't know. I was not on speaking terms with her. She had been living with me three or four years previously, but thought she could better herself, so I let her go.

THE CORONER: What did she do after she left you?

---

[32]The building which housed the Institute still stands opposite the London Hospital, but is now a second-hand clothing shop.

[33]Nichols had been married twenty four years, wedding William Nichols on 16 January 1864 at St. Bride's Parish Church, Fleet Street (Shelden, p. 3).

[34]William and Mary Ann parted ways around Easter of 1880, due to her alcoholism (ref. 4 September and also MEPO 3/140, ff. 235–238).

[35]This reported date cannot be correct, as from 16 April to 12 May, Nichols was resident at the Lambeth Workhouse. Begg, Evans & Skinner, Rumbelow, Shelden and Sugden all agree that Nichols' term of service with Samuel and Sarah Cowdry was from 12 May to 12 July. This is also corroborated by the testimony of Mary Ann Monk on 31 August, the *Daily News* of 3 September, Nichols' father here, and by Inspector Abberline's 19 September report on the Nichols and Chapman murders (MEPO 3/140, ff. 244–246). The *Times* of 3 September does not report a date for this letter, only giving the vague time of "around Easter." Easter Sunday fell on 1 April in 1888.

[36]Nichols' letter read: "I just write to say you will be glad to know that I am settled in my new place and going all right up to now. My people went out yesterday and have not returned so I am left in charge. It is a grand place with trees and gardens back and front. All has been newly done up. They are teetotallers and very religious so I ought to get on. They are very nice people and I have not much to do. I do hope you are all right and the boy has work. So goodbye now for the present. Yours Truly Polly. Answer soon please and let me know how you are" (Shelden, p. 6). The "boy" is a reference to Nichols' eldest son, Edward, who was living with Walker.

[37]5 June 1886, at the funeral of Nichols' brother Edward Walker, Jr. He had burned to death from a paraffin lamp explosion (Shelden, p. 5).

WITNESS: I don't know.

THE CORONER: This letter seems to suggest that she was in a decent situation.

WITNESS: She had only just gone there.

THE CORONER: Was she a sober woman?

WITNESS: Well, at times she drank, and that was why we did not agree.

THE CORONER: Was she fast?

WITNESS: No, I never heard of anything of that sort. She used to go with some young women and men that she knew, but I never heard of anything improper.

THE CORONER: Have you any idea what she has been doing lately?

WITNESS: I have not the slightest idea.

THE CORONER: She must have drunk heavily for you to turn her out of doors?

WITNESS: I never turned her out. She had no need to be like this while I had a home for her.

THE CORONER: How is it that she and her husband were not living together?

WITNESS: When she was confined her husband took on with the young woman who came to nurse her, and they parted, he living with the nurse, by whom he has another family.[38]

THE CORONER: Have you any reasonable doubt that this is your daughter?

WITNESS: No, I have not. I know nothing about her acquaintances, or what she had been doing for a living. I had no idea she was over here in this part of town. She has had five children, the eldest being twenty-one years old and the youngest eight or nine years.[39] One of them lives with me, and the other four are with their father.

THE CORONER: Has she ever lived with anybody since she left her husband?

WITNESS: I believe she was once stopping with a man in York-street, Walworth. His name was Drew, and he was a smith by trade.[40] He is living there now, I believe. The parish of Lambeth summonsed her husband for the keep of the children, but the summons was dismissed, as it was proved she was then living with another man. I don't know who that man was.

THE CORONER: Was she ever in the workhouse?

WITNESS: Yes, sir; Lambeth Workhouse, in April last, and went from there to a situation at Wandsworth.

BY THE JURY: The husband resides at Coburg-road, Old Kent-road. I don't know if he knows of her death.[41]

CORONER: Is there anything you know of likely to throw any light upon this affair?

WITNESS: No; I don't think she had any enemies, she was too good for that.

**John Neil**, police-constable, 97J, said: Yesterday morning I was proceeding down Buck's-row, Whitechapel, going towards Brady-street. There was not a soul about.

---

[38]This was in December 1876, at the birth of Eliza Nichols. Walker intimates here that William Nichols left Mary Ann for the nurse at the time of their daughter's birth, but this is not strictly true. While the couple were separated in February 1877, they reconciled and had another child together in 1878 before finally parting in 1880. William's affair preceded the Nichols' separation, but it was not apparently the immediate cause of it.

[39]Edward John (1865/66), Percy George (1868), Alice Esther (1870), Eliza Sarah (1876) and Henry Alfred (1878) (Shelden, pp. 3–4).

[40]Thomas Stuart Drew, blacksmith, living at York Mews, 15 York Street, Walworth. Nichols lived with him sometime between 1884 and October 1888 (BFS, p. 107).

[41]At the time of the murder, William Nichols' address was 37 Coburg Street, Old Kent Road (MEPO 3/140, ff. 244–246). He knew of her death by this time, having seen her body in the mortuary on the evening of 1 September.

I had been round there half an hour previously, and I saw no one then. I was on the right-hand side of the street, when I noticed a figure lying in the street. It was dark at the time, though there was a street lamp shining at the end of the row. I went across and found deceased lying outside a gateway, her head towards the east. The gateway was closed. It was about nine or ten feet high, and led to some stables. There were houses from the gateway eastward, and the School Board school occupies the westward. On the opposite side of the road is Essex Wharf. Deceased was lying lengthways along the street, her left hand touching the gate. I examined the body by the aid of my lamp, and noticed blood oozing from a wound in the throat. She was lying on her back, with her clothes disarranged.[42] I felt her arm, which was quite warm from the joints upwards. Her eyes were wide open. Her bonnet was off and lying at her side, close to the left hand.

I heard a constable passing Brady-street, so I called him.[43] I did not whistle. I said to him, "Run at once for Dr. Llewellyn," and, seeing another constable[44] in Baker's row, I sent him for the ambulance.[45] The doctor arrived in a very short time. I had, in the meantime, rung the bell at Essex Wharf, and asked if any disturbance had been heard. The reply was "No." Sergeant Kirby came after, and he knocked. The doctor looked at the woman and said, "Move her to the mortuary. She is dead, and I will make a further examination of her." We placed her on the ambulance, and moved her there. Inspector Spratley[46] came to the mortuary, and while

taking a description of the deceased turned up her clothes, and found that she was disembowelled. This had not been noticed by any of them before. On the body was found a piece of comb and a bit of looking-glass. No money was found, but an unmarked white handkerchief was found in her pocket.

THE CORONER: Did you notice any blood where she was found?

WITNESS: There was a pool of blood just where her neck was lying. It was running from the wound in her neck.

THE CORONER: Did you hear any noise that night?

WITNESS: No; I heard nothing. The farthest I had been that night was just through the Whitechapel-road and up Baker's-row. I was never far away from the spot.

THE CORONER: Whitechapel-road is busy in the early morning, I believe. Could anybody have escaped that way?

WITNESS: Oh yes, sir. I saw a number of women in the main road going home. At that time any one could have got away.

THE CORONER: Some one searched the ground, I believe?

WITNESS: Yes; I examined it while the doctor was being sent for.

INSPECTOR SPRATLEY: I examined the road, sir, in daylight.

A JURYMAN (TO WITNESS): Did you see a trap in the road at all?

WITNESS: No.

A JURYMAN: Knowing that the body was warm, did it not strike you that it might just have been laid there, and that the woman was killed elsewhere?

---

[42]When discovered by Charles Cross and Robert Paul, Nichols' skirts had been pushed up to her waistline by her killer. They pulled them down slightly to preserve her modesty, but in the process covered up her abdominal mutilations.

[43]PC 96J John Thain.

[44]PC 55H Jonas Mizen.

[45]A small wheeled and covered cart used for transporting bodies.

[46]Inspector John Spratling (1840–c. 1934), warrant 53457, divisional inspector J (Bethnal Green) Division. (BFS, p. 423, also *Ripperologist* No. 29, June 2000, pp. 10–12).

WITNESS: I examined the road, but did not see the mark of wheels.[47] The first to arrive on the scene after I had discovered the body were two men who work at a slaughterhouse opposite.[48] They said they knew nothing of the affair, and that they had not heard any screams. I had previously seen the men at work. That would be about a quarter-past three, or half an hour before I found the body.

**Henry** [*sic*] **Llewellyn**, surgeon, said: On Friday morning I was called to Buck's-row about four o'clock. The constable told me what I was wanted for. On reaching Buck's-row I found the deceased woman lying flat on her back in the pathway, her legs extended. I found she was dead, and that she had severe injuries to her throat. Her hands and wrists were cold, but the body and lower extremities were warm. I examined her chest and felt the heart. It was dark at the time.[49] I believe she had not been dead more than half-an-hour. I am quite certain that the injuries to her neck were not self-inflicted. There was very little blood round the neck. There were no marks of any struggle or of blood, as if the body had been dragged. I told the police to take her to the mortuary, and I would make another examination. About an hour later I was sent for by the Inspector to see the injuries he had discovered on the body. I went, and saw that the ab-

domen was cut very extensively. I have this morning made a post-mortem examination of the body.

I found it to be that of a female of about forty or forty-five years. Five of the teeth are missing, and there is a slight laceration of the tongue. On the right side of the face there is a bruise running along the lower part of the jaw. It might have been caused by a blow with the fist or pressure by the thumb. On the left side of the face there was a circular bruise, which also might have been done by the pressure of the fingers. On the left side of the neck, about an inch below the jaw, there was an incision about four inches long and running from a point immediately below the ear. An inch below on the same side, and commencing one inch in front of it, was a circular incision terminating at a point about three inches below the right jaw. This incision completely severs all the tissues down to the vertebrae. The large vessels of the neck on both sides were severed. The incision is about eight inches long. These cuts must have been caused with a long-bladed knife, moderately sharp, and used with great violence. No blood at all was found on the breast either of the body or the clothes.[50] There were no injuries about the body till just about the lower part of the abdomen. Two or three inches from the left side was a wound running in a jagged manner. It was a very deep

---

[47]Unofficial records of the Royal Meteorological Society at St. Luke's recorded a 0.01" rainfall for 31 August (RMC Weather Records, Meteorological Library and Archives). There was thus insufficient moisture to allow for mud on the cobblestones of Buck's Row to reveal the presence of any type of cart or carriage. Presumably Neil may also have looked for horse excrement to reveal whether any vehicle had stopped to deposit Nichols' body.

[48]Henry Tomkins and James Mumford, employed by Barber's Knacker's Yard, Winthrop Street (BFS, p. 56).

[49]Dawn arrived at 4:37am on 1 September; sunrise was at 5:12am (US Naval Observatory).

[50]Although this sentence posits strangulation as the primary cause of death, it also supports the theory that Nichols' throat was cut after her killer laid her down. Llewellyn's 1 September remark that "a very small pool of blood … trickled from the wound in the throat" would seem to bolster this conclusion, but it should be remembered that much blood had been soaked up by Nichols' clothes. It is interesting to note that as late as 19 September, Llewellyn still believed that Nichols' abdomen had been ripped open *before* her throat was cut (MEPO 3/140, ff. 242–256).

wound, and the tissues were cut through. There were several incisions running across the abdomen. On the right side there were also three or four similar cuts running downwards. All these had been caused by a knife, which had been used violently and been used downwards. The wounds were from left to right, and might have been done by a left-handed person. All the injuries had been done by the same instrument.

The inquiry was adjourned till to-morrow.

Up to a late hour last night the police had no clue whatever to the mystery, and had made no arrests.

# THE DAILY TELEGRAPH
Tuesday, September 4, 1888

Page 2
THE WHITECHAPEL MURDER
[*Second Session of Inquest*]

Mr. Wynne E. Baxter, the coroner for South-East Middlesex, yesterday resumed his inquiry at the Working Lads' Institute, Whitechapel-road, into the circumstances attending the death of the woman Mary Ann Nicholls, who was discovered lying dead on the pavement in Buck's-row, Baker's-row, Whitechapel, early on Friday morning last.

Inspectors Helston [*sic*] and Aberline [*sic*] attended for the police; whilst Detective-sergeant Enright, of Scotland-year [*sic*], was also in attendance.[51]

**Inspector John Spratling,** J Division, deposed that he first heard of the murder about half-past four on Friday morning, while he was in Hackney-road. He proceeded to Buck's-row, where he saw Police-constable Thain, who showed him the place where the deceased had been found. He noticed a blood stain on the footpath. The body of deceased had been removed to the mortuary in Old Montague-street, where witness had an opportunity of preparing a description.[52] The skin presented the appearance of not having been washed for some time previous to the murder. On his arrival Dr. Llewellyn made an examination of the body which lasted about ten minutes. Witness said he next saw the body when it was stripped.

DETECTIVE-SERGEANT ENRIGHT: That was done by two of the workhouse officials.[53]

THE CORONER: Had they any authority to strip the body?

WITNESS: No, sir; I gave them no instructions to strip it. In fact, I told them to leave it as it was.[54]

THE CORONER: I don't object to their stripping the body, but we ought to have evidence about the clothes.

---

[51]Frederick George Abberline (1843–1929). Warrant number 43519. Scotland Yard Central Office Detective Inspector (first-class) involved in, and in charge of, enquiries in the Whitechapel Murders from September 1888 to March 1889. Patrick Enright (b. 1849), warrant number 58207, Detective Sergeant serving in the J (Bethnal Green) division of the Metropolitan Police at the time of the Whitechapel Murders (Evans & Skinner, p. 675, BFS, p. 128).

[52]This "description" may be identical with that contained in a 19 October summary report on the Nichols murder submitted by Chief Inspector Donald Swanson (HO 144/221/A49301C, ff. 129–34).

[53]Robert Mann and James Hatfield, pauper inmates of the Whitechapel Union Workhouse (BFS, p. 160).

[54]Both Mann and Hatfield remarked they had not been told to leave Nichols' body alone, Hatfield noting they stripped her clothes in order to have her ready for the doctor. Both men were elderly, with Mann noted to suffer from fits and Hatfield with a bad memory. On 17 September, Hatfield testified that he heard "the doctor" was coming, and it seems the two tried to be helpful by preparing Nichols against his arrival. It is interesting in this context to note that when Annie Chapman's body was brought to the mortuary shed on 8 September, Mann testified he stayed with the body but did not touch it; the undressing was done by two infirmary nurses.

Sergeant Enright, continuing, said the clothes, which were lying in a heap in the yard, consisted of a reddish-brown ulster, with seven large brass buttons, and a brown dress, which looked new. There were also a woollen and a flannel petticoat, belonging to the workhouse. Inspector Helson had cut out pieces marked "P.R., Princes-road," with a view to tracing the body. There was also a pair of stays, in fairly good condition, but witness did not notice how they were adjusted.

The Coroner said he considered it important to know the exact state in which the stays were found.

On the suggestion of Inspector Aberline [sic], the clothes were sent for.

The Foreman of the jury asked whether the stays were fastened on the body.

Inspector Spratling replied that he could not say for certain. There was blood on the upper part of the dress body, and also on the ulster, but he only saw a little on the under-linen, and that might have happened after the removal of the body from Buck's-row. The clothes were fastened when he first saw the body. The stays did not fit very tightly, for he was able to see the wounds without unfastening them.

About six o'clock that day he made an examination of Buck's-row and Brady-street, which ran across Baker's-row, but he failed to trace any marks of blood. He subsequently examined, in company with Sergeant Godley,[55] the East London and District Railway lines and embankment, and also the Great Eastern Railway yard, without, however, finding any traces. A watchman of the Great Eastern Railway,

whose box was fifty or sixty yards from the spot where the body was discovered, heard nothing particular on the night of the murder.[56]

Witness also visited half a dozen persons living in the same neighbourhood, none of whom had noticed anything at all suspicious. One of these, Mrs. Purkiss, had not gone to bed at the time the body of deceased was found, and her husband was of opinion that if there had been any screaming in Buck's-row they would have heard it. A Mrs. Green, whose window looked out upon the very spot where the body was discovered, said nothing had attracted her attention on the morning of Friday last.

Replying to a question from one of the jury, witness stated that Constable Neil was the only one whose duty it was to pass through Buck's-row, but another constable[57] passing along Broad-street from time to time would be within hearing distance.

In reply to a juryman, witness said it was his firm belief that the woman had her clothes on at the time she was murdered.

**Henry Tomkins**, horse-slaughterer, 12, Coventry-street, Bethnal-green, was the next witness. He deposed that he was in the employ of Messrs. Barber, and was working in the slaughterhouse, Winthrop-street, from between eight and nine o'clock on Thursday evening till twenty minutes past four on Friday morning. He and his fellow workmen usually went home upon finishing their work, but on that morning they did not do so. They went to see the dead woman, Police-constable Thain having passed the slaughterhouse at about a quarter-past four, and told them that a

---

[55]Detective Sergeant George Godley (1858–1941), Metropolitan Police warrant number 61230, serving in J (Bethnal Green) Division of the CID during the Whitechapel Murders (BFS, pp. 143–144).

[56]In the *Times* of 4 September, this man is described as "a constable who was on duty at the gate of the Great Eastern Railway yard." All other press sources, however, name him a "watchman."

[57]PC Thain.

murder had been committed in Buck's-row. Two other men, James Mumford and Charles Britten [*sic*], had been working in the slaughterhouse. He (witness) and Britten left the slaughterhouse for one hour between midnight and one o'clock in the morning, but not afterwards till they went to see the body. The distance from Winthrop-street to Buck's-row was not great.[58]

THE CORONER: Is your work noisy?

WITNESS: No, sir, very quiet.

THE CORONER: Was it quiet on Friday morning, say after two o'clock?

WITNESS: Yes, sir, quite quiet. The gates were open and we heard no cry.

THE CORONER: Did anybody come to the slaughterhouse that night?

WITNESS: Nobody passed except the policeman.

THE CORONER: Are there any women about there?

WITNESS: Oh! I know nothing about them, I don't like 'em.

THE CORONER: I did not ask you whether you like them; I ask you whether there were any about that night.

WITNESS: I did not see any.

THE CORONER: Not in Whitechapel-road?

WITNESS: Oh, yes, there, of all sorts and sizes; its [*sic*] a rough neighbourhood, I can tell you. Witness, in reply to further questions, said the slaughter-house was too far away from the spot where deceased was found for him to have heard if anybody had called for assistance. When he arrived at Buck's-row the doctor and two or three policemen were there. He believed that two other men, whom he did not know, were also there. He waited till the body was taken away, previous to which about a dozen men came up. He heard no statement as to how the deceased came to be in Buck's-row.

THE CORONER: Have you read any statement in the newspapers that there were two people, besides the police and doctor, in Buck's-row, when you arrived?[59]

WITNESS: I cannot say, sir.[60]

THE CORONER: Then you did not see a soul from one o'clock on Friday morning till a quarter-past four, when the policeman passed your slaughterhouse?

WITNESS: No, sir.

A JURYMAN: Did you hear any vehicle pass the slaughterhouse?—No, sir.

Would you have heard it if there had been one?—Yes, sir.

Where did you go between twenty minutes past twelve and one o'clock?—I and my mate went to the front of the road.

Is not your usual hour for leaving off work six o'clock in the morning, and not four?—No; it is according to what we have to do. Sometimes it is one time and sometimes another.

What made the constable come and tell you about the murder?—He called for his cape.[61]

---

[58]Approximately 160 yards by walking along Winthrop Street and round the Board School into Buck's Row.

[59]Baxter may be referring here to a story in the *Times* of 3 September where PC Neil is quoted as saying it was not true "that he was called to the body by two men." See also Charles Cross' testimony below.

[60]A more poignant version from the *East London Advertiser* of 8 September gives Tomkins' reply as "I can't read, sir."

[61]It was common for police to leave an awkward or restricting cape or overcoat—if not required because of inclement weather—at a premises on their beat with workers they were friendly with. Barber's slaughterhouse may well have been a tea-stop, and patrolling officers no doubt got friendly with the workers by calling in while on night patrol. Obviously the garment would have to be retrieved when needed and certainly before finishing a tour of duty. This was a common enough practice that Thain would probably not have been disciplined for it. However, in this instance it would appear that the slaughterhouse was slightly off his assigned beat (he did not approach nearer than Brady Street), and he was careful to say that the cape had been deposited by a "brother officer," presumably Neil (see 18 September). Although Barber's was not far off Thain's route, it was a disciplinary offense for him to stray (personal correspondence, Stewart P. Evans).

**Inspector Jos. Helson** deposed that he first received information about the murder at a quarter before seven on Friday morning. He afterwards went to the mortuary, where he saw the body with the clothes still on it. The dress was fastened in front, with the exception of a few buttons, the stays, which were attached with clasps, were also fastened. He noticed blood on the hair, and on the collars of the dress and ulster, but not on the back of the skirts. There were no cuts in the clothes, and no indications of any struggle having taken place. The only suspicious mark discovered in the neighbourhood of Buck's-row was in Broad-street, where there was a stain which might have been blood. Witness was of the opinion that the body had not been carried to Buck's-row, but that the murder was committed on the spot.

**Police-constable Mizen** said that at a quarter to four o'clock on Friday morning he was at the crossing, Hanbury-street, Baker's-row, when a carman[62] who passed by in company with another man informed him that he was wanted by a policeman in Buck's-row, where a woman was lying.[63] When he arrived there Constable Neil sent him for the ambulance. At that time nobody but Neil was with the body.

**Chas. Andrew Cross**, carman, said he had been in the employment of Messrs. Pickford and Co. for over twenty years. About half-past three on Friday he left his home to go to work, and he passed through Buck's-row. He discerned on the opposite side something lying against the gateway, but he could not at once make out what it was. He thought it was a tarpaulin sheet. He walked into the middle of the road, and saw that it was the figure of a woman. He then heard the footsteps of a man going up Buck's-row, about forty yards away, in the direction that he himself had come from. When he came up witness said to him, "Come and look over here; there is a woman lying on the pavement." They both crossed over to the body, and witness took hold of the woman's hands, which were cold and limp. Witness said, "I believe she is dead." He touched her face, which felt warm. The other man, placing his hand on her heart, said, "I think she is breathing, but very little if she is."

Witness suggested they should give her a prop, but his companion refused to touch her. Just then they heard a policeman coming. Witness did not notice that her throat was cut, the night being very dark. He and the other man left the deceased, and in Baker's-row they met the last witness, whom they informed that they had seen a woman lying in Buck's-row. Witness said, "She looks to me to be either dead or drunk; but for my part I think she is dead." The policeman said, "All right," and then walked on. The other man left witness soon after.[64] Witness had never seen him before.

Replying to the coroner, witness denied having seen Police-constable Neil in Buck's-row. There was nobody there when he and the other man left. In his opinion, deceased looked as if she had been outraged and gone off in a swoon; but he had no idea that there were any serious injuries.[65]

---

[62]Carman: one who drives a cart.

[63]Charles Cross with Robert Paul. See Cross' testimony below.

[64]At Corbett's Court, near the corner of Hanbury Street (ref. *Times*, 4 September). See 18 September for Paul's testimony.

[65]There is some slight confusion here. Cross told Baxter he did not see Neil in Buck's Row, but only moments before, while relating his discovery of Nichols' body, he is reported as having said he and Paul heard a policeman coming. Cross does say further on that he was late to work, but even so, it seems odd he and Paul would leave Nichols if they thought a policeman was coming their way in order to proceed on to work and hope to meet a constable during their journey. One is tempted to believe Cross was misheard or *(cont.)*

THE CORONER: Did the other man tell you who he was?

WITNESS: No, sir; he merely said that he would have fetched a policeman, only he was behind time. I was behind time myself.

A JURYMAN: Did you tell Constable Mizen that another constable wanted him in Buck's-row?

WITNESS: No, because I did not see a policeman in Buck's-row.

**Wm. Nicholls**, printer's machinist, Coburg-road, Old Kent-road, said deceased was his wife, but they had lived apart for eight years. He last saw her alive about three years ago, and had not heard from her since. He did not know what she had been doing in the meantime.

A JURYMAN: It is said that you were summoned by the Lambeth Union for her maintenance, and you pleaded that she was living with another man. Was he the blacksmith whom she had lived with?

WITNESS: No; it was not the same; it was another man.[66] I had her watched.

Witness further deposed that he did not leave his wife, but that she left him of her own accord. She had no occasion for so doing. If it had not been for her drinking habits they would have got on all right together.

**Emily Holland**, a married woman, living at 18, Thrawl-street, said deceased had stayed at her lodgings for about six weeks, but had not been there during the last ten days or so. About half-past two on Friday morning witness saw deceased walking down Osborne-street, Whitechapel-road. She was alone, and very much the worse for drink. She informed witness that where she had been living they would not allow her to return because she could not pay for her room. Witness persuaded her to go home. She refused, adding that she had earned her lodging money three times that day. She then went along the Whitechapel-road. Witness did not know in what way she obtained a living. She always seemed to her to be a quiet woman, and kept very much to herself. In reply to further questions witness said she had never seen deceased quarrel with anybody. She gave her the impression of being weighed down by some trouble. When she left the witness at the corner of Osborne-street, she said she would soon be back.

**Mary Ann Monk** was the last witness examined. She deposed to having seen deceased about seven o'clock entering a public house in the New Kent-road. She had seen her before in the workhouse, and had no knowledge of her means of livelihood.

The inquiry was then adjourned until Sept. 17.

# THE DAILY TELEGRAPH
Friday, September 7, 1888

Page 5
THE WHITECHAPEL MURDER
[*Burial of Mary Ann Nichols*]

No arrest has yet been made in connection with the murder of Mary Ann Nicholls. Her remains were buried yesterday afternoon. The body, enclosed in a solid-looking coffin, was conveyed by hearse to Ilford Cemetery, where it was interred.[67]

---

misreported by the *Telegraph*, as a search of contemporary newspapers does not reveal any reference to Cross and Paul hearing a policeman in Buck's Row.

[66]The identity of this man is not known.

[67]Nichols is buried in public grave 49500, square 318, Memorial Gardens, City of London Cemetery, Manor Park, London (*Ripperana* No. 14, October 1995). Her surname there is misspelled as "Nicholls" and her age incorrectly given as 42.

# THE DAILY TELEGRAPH

Tuesday, September 18, 1888

Page 2
WHITECHAPEL MURDERS
THE BUCK'S ROW TRAGEDY
[*Third Session of Inquest*]

Yesterday, at the Working Lads' Institute, Whitechapel-road, Mr. Wynne Baxter, coroner for the North-Eastern [*sic*] District of Middlesex, resumed his inquiry relative to the death of Mary Ann Nicholls, the victim of the Buck's-row tragedy, on Friday morning, Aug. 31.

**Dr. Llewellyn**, recalled, said he had re-examined the body and there was no part of the viscera missing.[68]

**Emma Green**, who lives in the cottage next to the scene of the murder in Buck's-row, stated that she had heard no unusual sound during the night.

BY THE JURY: Rough people often passed through the street, but she knew of no disorderly houses in Buck's-row, all the houses being occupied by hardworking folk.

**Thomas Ede**, a signalman in the employ of the East London Railway Company, said he saw a man with a knife on the morning of the 8th.

The coroner was of the opinion that this incident could have no reference to the present inquiry, as the 8th was the day of the Hanbury-street murder. He would, however, accept the evidence.

WITNESS THEN SAID: On Saturday, the 8th inst., at noon, I was coming down the Cambridge-heath-road, and when near the Forester's Arms, I saw a man on the other side of the street. His peculiar appearance made me take notice of him. He seemed to have a wooden arm. I watched him until level with the Forester's Arms, and then he put his hand to his trouser's [*sic*] pocket, and I saw about four inches of a knife. I followed him, but he quickened his pace, and I lost sight of him.

Inspector Helson, in reply to the coroner, stated that the man had not been found.[69]

Witness described the man as 5 ft. 8 in. high, about thirty-five years of age, with a dark moustache and whiskers. He wore a double-peaked cap, a short dark brown jacket, and a pair of clean white overalls over dark trousers. The man walked as though he had a stiff knee, and he had a fearful look about the eyes. He seemed to be a mechanic.

BY THE JURY: He was not a muscular man.

**Walter Purkess** [Purkiss], manager, residing at Essex Wharf, deposed that his house fronted Buck's-row, opposite the gates where deceased was discovered. He slept in the front room on the second floor[70] and had heard no sound, neither had his wife.

**Alfred Malshaw**,[71] a night watchman in Winthorpe [*sic*]-street, had also heard no cries or noise. He admitted that he sometimes dozed.

THE CORONER: I suppose your watching is not up to much?

---

[68]Presumably this statement was made in light of Annie Chapman's killer having removed her uterus, upper portion of the vagina and posterior two-thirds of the bladder during her murder on 8 September.

[69]The "man" was Henry Jacobs, a harmless lunatic.

[70]Third floor, to Americans.

[71]Patrick Mulshaw, a night porter and watchman employed by the Whitechapel Board of Works (BFS, p. 308).

THE WITNESS: I don't know. It is thirteen long hours for 3s and find your own coke. (Laughter.)

BY THE JURY: In a straight line I was about thirty yards from the spot where the deceased was found.[72]

Police-constable John Thail [*sic*] stated that the nearest point on his beat to Buck's-row was Brady-street. He passed the end every thirty minutes on the Thursday night, and nothing attracted his attention until 3.45 a.m., when he was signalled by the flash of the lantern of another constable (Neale [*sic*]).[73] He went to him, and found Neale standing by the body of the deceased, and witness was despatched for a doctor. About ten minutes after he had fetched the surgeon he saw two workmen[74] standing with Neale. He did not know who they were. The body was taken to the mortuary, and witnessed [*sic*] remained on the spot. Witness searched Essex Wharf, the Great Eastern Railway arches, the East London Railway line, and the District Railway as far as Thames-street, and detected no marks of blood or anything of a suspicious character.

BY THE JURY: When I went to the horse-slaughterer's for my cape I did not say that I was going to fetch a doctor, as a murder had been committed. Another constable had taken my cape there.[75]

**Robert Baul** [*sic*], 30, Forster [*sic*]-street, Whitechapel, carman, said as he was going to work at Cobbett's-court, Spitalfields, he saw in Buck's-row a man standing in the middle of the road. As witness drew closer he walked towards the pavement, and he (Baul [*sic*]) stepped in the roadway to pass him. The man touched witness on the shoulder and asked him to look at the woman, who was lying across the gateway. He felt her hands and face, and they were cold. The clothes were disarranged, and he helped to pull them down. Before he did so he detected a slight movement as of breathing, but very faint. The man walked with him to Montague-street, and there they saw a policeman. Not more than four minutes had elapsed from the time he first saw the woman. Before he reached Buck's-row he had seen no one running away.

**Robert Mann**, the keeper of the mortuary, said the police came to the workhouse, of which he was an inmate. He went, in consequence, to the mortuary at five a.m. He saw the body placed there, and then locked the place up and kept the keys. After breakfast witness and Hatfield, another inmate of the workhouse, undressed the woman.

The police were not present?—No; there was no one present. Inspector Helson was not there.

Had you been told not to touch it?—No.

Did you see Inspector Helson?—I can't say.

Was he present?—I can't say.

I suppose you do not recollect whether the clothes were torn?—They were not torn or cut.

You cannot describe where the blood was?—No, sir; I cannot.

---

[72]Winthrop Street ran parallel to Buck's Row from Brady Street at its upper end to the Board School, where it converged with Buck's Row. Mulshaw's "straight line" presumably meant from his location over to the next street.

[73]At the time of the Nichols murder, police were generally instructed not to use their whistles at night except in cases of emergency such as fire, so as not to rouse nearby sleepers (Fido, *A History of British Serial Killing*, p. 14).

[74]Tomkins and Mumford.

[75]As noted earlier, this appears to be Thain's attempt to avoid disciplinary action for straying from his beat.

How did you get the clothes off?—Hatfield had to cut them down the front.

A JURYMAN: Was the body undressed in the mortuary or in the yard?—In the mortuary.

THE CORONER: It appears the mortuary-keeper is subject to fits, and neither his memory nor statements are reliable.

**James Hatfield**, an inmate of the Whitechapel Workhouse, said he accompanied Mann, the last witness, to the mortuary, and undressed the deceased. Inspector Helson was not there.

Who was there?—Only me and my mate.

What did you take off first?—An ulster, which I put aside on the ground. We then took the jacket off, and put it in the same place. The outside dress was loose, and we did not cut it. The bands of the petticoats were cut, and I then tore them down with my hand. I tore the chemise down the front. There were no stays.

Who gave you instructions to do all this?—No one gave us any. We did it to have the body ready for the doctor.

Who told you a doctor was coming?—I heard someone speak about it.

Was any one present whilst you were undressing the body?—Not as I was aware of.

Having finished, did you make the post-mortem examination?—No, the police came.[76]

Oh, it was not necessary for you to go on with it! The police came?—Yes, they examined the petticoats, and found the words "Lambeth Workhouse" on the bands.

It was cut out?—I cut it out.

Who told you to do it?—Inspector Helson.

Is that the first time you saw Inspector Helson on that morning?—Yes; I arrived at about half-past six.

Would you be surprised to find that there were stays?—No.

A JURYMAN: Did you not try the stays on in the afternoon to show me how short they were.—I forgot it.

THE CORONER: He admits that his memory is bad.

WITNESS: Yes.

THE CORONER: We cannot do more. (TO THE POLICE): There was a man who passed down Buck's-row when the doctor was examining the body.[77] Have you heard anything of him?

INSPECTOR ABBERLINE: We have not been able to find him.

**Inspector Spratley** [sic], J Division, stated he had made inquiries in Buck's-row, but not at all of the houses.

THE CORONER: Then that will have to be done.

Witness added that he made inquiries at Green's, the wharf, Snider's factory, and also at the Great Eastern wharf, and no one had heard anything unusual on the morning of the murder. He had not called at any of the houses in Buck's-row, excepting at Mrs. Green's. He had seen the Board School keeper.

THE CORONER: Is there not a gentleman at the G.E. Railway? I thought we should have had him here.[78]

WITNESS: I saw him that morning, but he said he had heard nothing.

The witness added that when at the

---

[76]Baxter's irritation at the mentally-wandering Mann and Hatfield as well as the seemingly haphazard procedures concurrent with Whitechapel post-mortems is evident here.

[77]See Commentary 1 regarding this man.

[78]This was the "watchman" previously mentioned on 4 September as being approximately 50–60 yards from the murder site yet hearing nothing.

mortuary he had given instructions that the body was not to be touched.[79]

THE CORONER: Is there any other evidence?

INSPECTOR HELSON: No, not at present.

The Foreman thought that, had a reward been offered by the Government after the murder in George-yard, very probably the two later murders would not have been perpetrated.[80] It mattered little into whose hands the money went so long as they could find out the monster in their midst, who was terrorising everybody and making people ill. There were four horrible murders remaining undiscovered.[81]

The Coroner considered that the first one was the worst, and it had attracted the least attention.

The Foreman intimated that he would be willing to give £25 himself, and he hoped that the Government would offer a reward. These poor people had souls like anybody else.

The Coroner understood that no rewards were now offered in any case. It mattered not whether the victims were rich or poor. There was no surety that a rich person would not be the next.

THE FOREMAN: If that should be, then there will be a large reward.

Inspector Helson, in reply to the coroner, said rewards had been discontinued for years.[82]

The inquiry was then adjourned until Saturday.

# THE DAILY TELEGRAPH
## Monday, September 24, 1888

### THE WHITECHAPEL MURDERS
*[Fourth and Final Session of Nichols Inquest]*

On Saturday Mr. Wynne E. Baxter resumed the inquest upon the body of Mary Ann Nicholls, aged forty-seven, the victim in the Buck's-row murder, one of the series of Whitechapel tragedies. The inquiry was held at the Working Lads' Institute. Signalman Eades was recalled to supplement his previous evidence to the effect that he had seen a man named John James carrying a knife near the scene of the murder. It transpired, however, that this man is a harmless lunatic who is well known in the neighborhood.

**The Coroner** then summed up. Having reviewed the career of the deceased from the time she left her husband, and reminded the jury of the irregular life she had led for the last two years, Mr. Baxter then proceeded to point out that the unfortunate woman was last seen alive at half-past two o'clock on Saturday morning, Sept. 1, by Mrs. Holland, who knew her well. Deceased was at that time much the worse for drink, and was endeavouring to walk eastward down Whitechapel. What her exact movements were after this it is impossible to say; but in less than an hour and a quarter her dead body was discovered at a spot rather under three-quarters

---

[79]Whether Spratling really ordered that Nichols not be touched until Llewellyn's arrival or was attempting an alibi in view of Baxter's obvious petulance is not known.

[80]This will not be the last time in the course of the Whitechapel murders that such a sentiment is voiced.

[81]Smith, Tabram, Nichols and, since 8 September, Chapman.

[82]The persistent refusal by the Home Office to sanction a reward in the Ripper case baffled and infuriated contemporary observers. There were, however, sound precedents for this, as long and bitter experience—particularly during the eighteenth century—had seen scores of innocent people framed by "thief-takers" in order to collect rewards, or allowed to commit crimes unhindered until the monies offered for their capture grew to the largest sum allowable under Parliamentary law. Home Secretary Henry Matthews had good arguments to offer against establishing a reward, but maddeningly refused to explain his stance publicly, and thereby needlessly angered the press and public. See also Sugden, pp. 138–140.

of a mile distant. The time at which the body was found cannot have been far from 3:45 a.m., as it is fixed by so many independent data.[83] The condition of the body appeared to prove conclusively that the deceased was killed on the exact spot in which she was found. There was not a trace of blood anywhere, except at the spot where her neck was lying, this circumstance being sufficient to justify the assumption that the injuries to the throat were committed when the woman was on the ground, whilst the state of her clothing and the absence of any blood about her legs suggested that the abdominal injuries were inflicted whilst she was still in the same position.

Coming to a consideration of the perpetrator of the murder, the Coroner said: It seems astonishing at first thought that the culprit should have escaped detection, for there must surely have been marks of blood about his person. If, however, blood was principally on his hands, the presence of so many slaughter-houses in the neighbourhood would make the frequenters of this spot familiar with blood-stained clothes and hands, and his appearance might in that way have failed to attract attention while he passed from Buck's-row in the twilight into Whitechapel-road, and was lost sight of in the morning's market traffic.

We cannot altogether leave unnoticed the fact that the death that you have been investigating is one of four presenting many points of similarity, all of which have occurred within the space of about five months, and all within a very short distance of the place where we are sitting.

All four victims were women of middle age, all were married, and had lived apart from their husbands in consequence of intemperate habits, and were at the time of their death leading an irregular life, and eking out a miserable and precarious existence in common lodging-houses. In each case there were abdominal as well as other injuries.[84] In each case the injuries were inflicted after midnight, and in places of public resort, where it would appear impossible but that almost immediate detection should follow the crime, and in each case the inhuman and dastardly criminals are at large in society. Emma Elizabeth Smith, who received her injuries in Osborn-street on the early morning of Easter Tuesday, April 3, survived in London Hospital for upwards of twenty-four hours, and was able to state that she had been followed by some men, robbed and mutilated, and even to describe imperfectly one of them. Martha Tabram was found at three a.m. on Tuesday, Aug. 7, on the first floor landing of George-yard-buildings, Wentworth-street, with thirty-nine punctured wounds on her body.[85]

In addition to these, and the case under your consideration, there is the case of Annie Chapman, still in the hands of another jury. The instruments used in the two earlier cases are dissimilar. In the first it was a blunt instrument, such as a walking-stick; in the second, some of the woulds were thought to have been made by a dagger; but in the two recent cases the instruments suggested by the medical witnesses are not so different. Dr. Llewellyn says the injuries on Nicholls could have been produced by a strong bladed instru-

[83]Baxter is referring primarily to Neil and Kirby's earlier patrols down Buck's Row at 3:15am and the discovery of Nichols by Cross and Paul (ref. MEPO 3/140, f. 142, and Begg, p. 42).
[84]This is technically true, in that Emma Smith's assailants rammed a blunt instrument into her vagina. Otherwise, that bestial assault (which does not seem to have been intended as murder) bears no resemblance to the abdominal stabs inflicted on Tabram, Nichols and Chapman (ref. Evans & Skinner, pp. 3–7).
[85]Tabram's body was found at 4:45am by John Saunders Reeves; Baxter may be thinking of the testimony of Alfred Crow, who saw a body (presumably Tabram) on the landing at 3:30am (ref. *Times*, 10 August).

ment, moderately sharp. Dr. Phillips is of opinion that those on Chapman were by a very sharp knife, probably with a thin, narrow blade, at least six to eight inches in length, probably longer. The similarity of the injuries in the two cases is considerable. There are bruises about the face in both cases; the head is nearly severed from the body in both cases; there are other dreadful injuries in both cases; and those injuries, again, have in each case been performed with anatomical knowledge. Dr. Llewellyn seems to incline to the opinion that the abdominal injuries were first and caused instantaneous death; but, if so, it seems difficult to understand the object of such desperate injuries to the throat, or how it comes about that there was so little bleeding from the several arteries, that the clothing on the upper surface was not stained, and, indeed, very much less bleeding from the abdomen than the neck. Surely it may well be that, as in the case of Chapman, the dreadful wounds to the throat were inflicted first and the others afterwards.

This is a matter of some importance when we come to consider what possible motive there can be for all this ferocity. Robbery is out of the question; and there is nothing to suggest jealousy; there could not have been any quarrel, or it would have been heard. I suggest to you as a possibility that these two women may have been murdered by the same man with the same object, and that in the case of Nicholls the wretch was disturbed before he had accomplished his object, and having failed in the open street he tries again, within a week of his failure, in a more secluded place. If this should be correct, the audacity and daring is equal to its maniacal fanaticism and abhorrent wickedness. But this surmise may or may not be correct, the suggested motive may be the wrong one; but one thing is very clear—that a murder of a most atrocious character has been committed.

The jury, after a short consultation, returned a verdict of willful murder against some person or persons unknown. A rider was added expressing the full coincidence of the jury with some remarks made by the coroner as to the need of a mortuary for Whitechapel.

# Mary Ann Nichols— Commentary

## DAVE YOST

### 1. Patrick Mulshaw and What He Saw

When watchman Patrick Mulshaw testified at the 17 September installment of the Nichols inquest, the *Telegraph* noted he amused the jury with a complaint about his working conditions, answering Coroner Wynne Baxter's dismissal of his abilities as "not up to much" with the truculent reply, "I don't know. It is thirteen long hours for 3s and find your own coke." Yet the *Times*, in its reporting, additionally noted two items of interest:

Patrick Mulshaw, a night porter in the employ of the Whitechapel District Board of Works, living at 3, Rupert-street, Whitechapel, said on the night of this occurrence he was at the back of the Working Lads' Institute in Winthorpe-street. He went on duty about a quarter to 5 in the afternoon, and remained until about five minutes to 6 the next morning, when he was relieved. He was watching some sewage works. He dozed at times during the night, but was not asleep between 3 and 4 o'clock. He did not see any one about during that period, and did not hear any cries for assistance, or any other noise. The slaughterhouse was about 70 yards away from where he was. Another man then passed by, and said, "Watchman, old man, I believe somebody is murdered down the street." Witness then went to Buck's-row, and saw the body of deceased lying on the ground. Three or four police-men and five or six working men were there.

By the CORONER.—...He did not often see the police there. During the night he saw two constables, including Constable Neil. He was unable to say what time he saw that officer [*Times*, 18 September, p. 12].

The reference to "another" man has puzzled later researchers, and is a tanta-lising loose end in the Ripper case, since he was apparently never identified and we cannot say what his connection with the Nichols murder might have been. So who, then, might have been Mulshaw's myste-rious communicant—the killer or an in-nocent passerby?

Let us try to see if we can determine whom Mulshaw might have meant by the comment, "another man." Between 3:00 and 4:00am, he testified, he neither saw nor heard anything. During that period, PC Thain traveled north through Brady Street during his patrol. PC Neil's patrol included Winthrop Street, and Sergeant Kirby passed through Buck's Row. Paul and Cross walked down Buck's Row and found Nichols' body at about 3:40am. Ap-proximately five minutes later, Neil redis-covered the body; a short time later, he sent Thain to fetch Dr. Llewellyn, who lived at 152 Whitechapel Road, two doors west of Brady Street and Whitechapel Road on the north side of the street (Begg, p. 42, *Telegraph*, 3 September, p. 3, 18 Sep-tember, p. 2).

In carrying out his errand, Thain had three possible directions to travel; either round the junction into Winthrop Street, south down Wood's Buildings and then east onto Whitechapel Road, or round the junction into Winthrop, down Winthrop and then south onto Brady Street, or by the most direct route, back down Buck's Row and south onto Brady. Yet Thain most likely traversed Winthrop and Brady Streets—his patrol included Brady Street, and he informed Henry Tomkins (a local slaughterer) about the murder, which could only have happened if Thain were in Winthrop Street. Mulshaw himself al-ludes to this—"During the night he [Mul-shaw] saw two constables, including Con-stable Neil. He was unable to say what time he saw that officer" (*Telegraph*, 4 Sep-tember, p. 2, 18 September, p. 2; *Times*, 18 September, p. 12).

When Mulshaw arrived upon the murder scene, he noted that "[t]hree or four policemen and five or six working men were there." Hence, his arrival could only have been after that of the slaughter-men. These events indicate that Mul-shaw's "another man" was most likely PC Thain, who was in the process of fetching Dr. Llewellyn. But if Mulshaw's "another man" was Thain, then who *first* informed him about the murder? Mulshaw never in-dicated that anyone at the scene was his "another man" or his informant. This might indicate that neither the informant nor the "another man" was at the scene; al-beit, in this instance, we might forbear making such a conclusion; Mulshaw never explicitly stated that PC Neil was at the murder scene either, and he was a consta-ble who *was* undoubtedly there and whom Mulshaw knew!

The statement made to Mulshaw might provide an indication as to who said it: "Watchman, old man, I believe some-body is murdered down the street." Now, had it been PC Thain who spoke thusly, very likely Mulshaw would have indicated it was a constable who informed him, sim-ilar to what Henry Tomkins stated to the court on 3 September: "Police-constable Thain having passed the slaughterhouse at about a quarter-past four, and told them [Tomkins, et al] that a murder had been committed in Buck's-row" (*Telegraph*, 4 September, p. 2). Additionally, Thain would have specified that a murder had been committed, as he did to the slaughterers. It is very doubtful that he would have traveled down Winthrop Street casually informing people about the murder—he had only done so with the slaughterers while in process of retrieving his cape.

Upon being informed, Mulshaw "went to Buck's-row, and saw the body of deceased lying on the ground." As previously mentioned, Mulshaw arrived at the scene after the slaughterers Tomkins, Brittain and Mumford, yet all three of those men did not remain at the scene. Brittain did indeed join Tomkins and Mumford at the scene soon after 4:20am, yet no other testimony directly mentions his presence; only that several workmen from near-by were at the scene, one of whom might or might not have been Brittain (the others were workmen and watchmen from the neighboring buildings who had arrived upon the scene out of curiosity). It is possible that Brittain informed Mulshaw about the murder in passing, after his departure from the scene and while on his way home, though as Brittain's address is currently unknown, this can be only speculation.

## 2. Interruption or Cessation?

A discussion about darkness and what Cross and Paul might have seen leads into a more enticing aspect about the Nichols murder—whether or not her killer was disturbed, or ceased his mutilations of his own volition. Like the modern researcher, Wynne Baxter had definite thoughts about this topic: "in the case of Nichols the wretch was disturbed before he had accomplished his object" (*Telegraph*, 24 September, p. 3).

But was the killer actually disturbed, or is this a myth created by Baxter's remarks? In order to answer this question, several conflicting points require clarification beforehand:

*Timing in Evidence—Robert Paul:* At the inquest, Paul stated that he "left home about a quarter to 4 on the Friday morning." Yet PC Neil discovered the body at 3:45am. Neil's timing of discovery is accepted as more accurate, because of its relationship to other events. Paul's residence at 30 Foster Street would indicate that he had left for work at approximately 3:35am (MEPO 3/140, f. 239; *Times*, 18 September, p. 12).

*Timing in Evidence—PC Mizen:* On 3 September, PC Mizen stated how and when Cross and Paul notified him of the murder:

> Police-constable Mizen said that at a quarter to four o'clock on Friday morning he was at the crossing, Hanbury-street, Baker's-row, when a carman who passed in company with another man informed him that he was wanted by a policeman in Buck's-row, where a woman was lying. When he arrived there Constable Neil sent him for the ambulance. At that time nobody but Neil was with the body [*Telegraph*, 4 September, p. 2].
> Constable G. Mizen, 56 H, stated that at a quarter past 4 on Friday morning he was in Hanbury-street, Baker's-row, and a man passing said "You are wanted in Baker's-row." The man, named Cross, stated a woman had been found there. In going to the spot he saw Constable Neil, and by the direction of the latter he went for the ambulance. When Cross spoke to witness he was accompanied by another man, and both of them afterwards went down Hanbury-street. Cross simply said he was wanted by a policeman, and did not say anything about a murder having been committed. He denied that before he went to Buck's-row he continued knocking people up [*Times*, 4 September, p. 8].

Cross and Paul would have initially come across the body at approximately 3:40am, and it would not have taken very long for them to travel from the murder scene to the junction of Hanbury Street and Baker's Row.

By the CORONER.—The morning was rather a chilly one. Witness and the other man walked on together until they met a policeman at the corner of Old Montagu [sic]-street, and told him what they had seen. Up to that time not more than four minutes had elapsed from the time he saw the body. He had not met any one before he reached Buck's-row, and did not see any one running away [Times, 18 September, p. 12].

PC Mizen would have been informed of the body at about the time that PC Neil discovered it. This correlates to the timing of the other events that followed the body's discovery. In this particular instance, the Times reporter mis-recorded Mizen's time as c.4:15am, instead of the correct c.3:45am, which is corroborated by several statements:

I [Neil] heard a constable [Thain] passing Brady-street, so I called him. I did not whistle. I said to him, "Run at once for Dr. Llewellyn," and, seeing another constable in Baker's-row [Mizen], I sent him for the ambulance [Telegraph, 3 September, p. 3].
On Friday morning I [Dr. Llewellyn] was called to Buck's-row about four o'clock [Telegraph, 3 September, p. 3].

The times for these events could only occur if PC Mizen was informed of the murder by Cross and Paul at approximately 3:45am. This ties into Nichols' time of death, which is typically estimated as being shortly before the arrival of Cross and Paul, and is commonly used to indicate that the killer was disturbed, in accordance with Baxter's earlier comment. However, the statements provided by those who were first at or nearest to the scene indicate quite the opposite:

—At 3:15am, PC Neil traveled easterly through Buck's Row, seeing nothing:

Yesterday morning I [Neil] was proceeding down Buck's-row, Whitechapel, going towards Brady-street. There was not a soul about. I had been round there half an hour previously [3:15am], and I saw no one then [Telegraph, 3 September, p. 3].

—At c.3:20am, Sergeant Kirby traveled easterly through Buck's Row, seeing nothing: "P.C. [Neil] states he passed through Buck's Row at 3.15. Am. And P.S. 10 Kirby about the same time [3:20am], but the woman was not there" (MEPO 3/140, f. 240; Begg, p. 42).

—At c.3:40am, Cross and Paul came upon the body:

[Cross:]—About half-past three on Friday he left his home to go to work, and he passed through Buck's-row. He discerned on the opposite side something lying against the gateway, but he could not at once make out what it was. He thought it was a tarpaulin sheet. He walked into the middle of the road, and saw that it was the figure of a woman. He then heard the footsteps of a man [Paul] going up Buck's-row, about forty yards away, in the direction that he himself had come from [Brady Street] [Telegraph, 4 September, p. 2].
All the time he did not think the woman had been murdered. Witness did not hear any sounds of a vehicle, and believed that had any one left the body after he got into Buck's-row he must have heard him [Times, 4 September, p. 8].

[Paul:]—He saw in Buck's-row a man [Cross] standing in the middle of the road. As witness drew closer he walked towards the pavement, and he [Paul] stepped in the roadway to pass him [Cross]. The man touched witness on the shoulder and asked him to look at the woman, who was lying across the gateway. He felt her hands and face, and they were cold. The clothes were disarranged, and he helped to pull them down. Before he did so he detected a slight movement as of breathing, but very faint. The man walked with him to Montague-street, and there they saw a policeman. Not more than four minutes had elapsed from the time he first saw the woman. Before he reached Buck's-row he had seen no one running away [*Telegraph*, 18 September, p. 2].

They [Cross and Paul] looked to see if there was a constable, but one was not to be seen... He [Paul] had not met any one before he reached Buck's-row, and did not see any one running away [*Times*, 18 September, p. 12].

Cross and Paul neither saw nor heard anyone at or departing from the scene prior their arrival.

*—At 3:45am, PC Neil came upon the body:*

Yesterday morning I [Neil] was proceeding down Buck's-row, Whitechapel, going towards Brady-street. There was not a soul about. I had been round there half an hour previously [3:15am], and I saw no one then... I heard a constable passing Brady-street, so I called him...

THE CORONER: Did you hear any noise that night?

WITNESS: No; I heard nothing. The farthest I had been that night was just through the Whitechapel-road and up Baker's-row. I was never far away from the spot.

THE CORONER: Whitechapel-road is busy in the early morning, I believe. Could anybody have escaped that way?

WITNESS: Oh yes, sir. I saw a number of women in the main road going home. At that time any one could have got away....

A JURYMAN (TO WITNESS): Did you see a trap in the road at all?

WITNESS: No.

...

WITNESS: I examined the road, but did not see the mark of wheels. The first [nonpolicemen] to arrive on the scene after I had discovered the body were two men who work at a slaughterhouse opposite. They said they knew nothing of the affair, and that they had not heard any screams. I had previously seen the men at work. That would be about a quarter-past three, or half an hour before I found the body [*Telegraph*, 3 September, p. 3].

PC Neil neither saw nor heard anyone or anything at or departing from the scene. Even though Neil intimated that the killer most likely escaped into Whitechapel Road, this does not indicate that the killer was disturbed.

*—At 3:45am, PC Thain was signaled by PC Neil:*

The nearest point on his [Thain's] beat to Buck's-row was Brady-street. He passed the end every thirty minutes on the Thursday night, and nothing attracted his attention until 3:45 a.m., when he was signalled by the flash of the lantern of another constable [Neil]. He went to him, and found Neale [*sic*] standing by the body of the deceased, and witness was despatched for a doctor [*Telegraph*, 18 September, p. 2].

*—At c.3:45am, PC Neil sent PC Mizen for an ambulance:*

I [Neil] said to him [Thain], "Run at once for Dr. Llewellyn," and, seeing another constable [ Mizen] in Baker's-row, I sent him for the ambulance (*Telegraph*, 3 September, p. 3).

*—At 4:00am, Dr. Llewellyn was called to the scene:*

I [Llewellyn] was called to Buck's-row about four o'clock (*Telegraph*, 3 September, p. 3).

*—At c.4:10am, Dr. Llewellyn arrived at the scene:*

About ten minutes after he [PC Thain] had fetched the surgeon he saw two workmen standing with Neale [*sic*] [*Telegraph*, 18 September, p. 2].

On reaching Buck's-row I [Llewellyn] found the deceased woman... I believe she had not been dead more than half-an-hour [*Telegraph*, 3 September, p. 3].

Dr. Llewellyn's time of death, "not been dead more than half-an-hour," indicates that he believed Nichols died no earlier than 3:40am. Additionally, he stated that the injuries could have been inflicted within four minutes. Dr. Llewellyn erred, however, on several salient points regarding Nichols' death. He intimated that Nichols was killed while standing up, even though no blood was found on the front of her clothes. He originally believed that her killer was left-handed, even though all wounds ran from the victim's left to right (in fairness, he did eventually doubt the left-handed notion). And, most notably, he opined that the abdominal injuries came first and could have caused instantaneous death. While interesting in theory, the body *in situ* clearly shows that not only was Nichols killed where found, but that she was killed while lying down and that the throat wound caused death and preceded the abdominal injuries (*Times*, 24 September, p, 3; HO 144/221/A49301C [8a], f. 129; BFS [2nd ed.], pp. 306–307).

Nevertheless, Dr. Llewellyn's information suggests that Nichols died at approximately 3:40am with the killer taking about four minutes to mutilate her. This is not possible, since Cross and Paul were upon the body at c.3:40 and PC Neil rediscovered the body at 3:45am. Taking this into account with respect to Llewellyn's statements, then Nichols could have died at about 3:35am with the killer being interrupted by Cross' entry into Buck's Row.

However, gauging time of death by rigor mortis is, at best, a guess, as we will see when trying to determine the times of death for Annie Chapman and Mary Kelly. And it is certain that Nichols died no later than 3:35am. PC Neil even indicated that it was possible to hear someone in Brady Street while standing at the murder scene—"*I heard a constable passing Brady-street*"—but no witness heard or saw anyone at or departing from the scene. This suggests that Nichols' time of death is closer to 3:30am than to 3:35am, with the killer ceasing the mutilations on his own rather then being scared off.

*Chapter 2*

# ANNIE CHAPMAN

*—found murdered Saturday, 8 September 1888*

Another most horrible murder has been perpetrated in Whitechapel. At an early hour on Saturday morning, the body of a woman was found lying in the corner of a yard in Hanbury-street, a low thoroughfare, not far from Buck's-row, the scene of a similar tragedy ten days ago.
*—Daily Telegraph*, Monday, September 10, 1888

On 8 September, the *East London Advertiser* printed an unknowingly prophetic editorial: "The murderer must creep out from somewhere, he must patrol the streets in search of his victims ... three successful murders will have the effect of whetting his appetite still further, and unless a watch of the strictest be kept, the murder of Thursday will certainly be followed by a fourth."

Even as these words were being set in type, the eviscerated body of 47-year-old Eliza Anne Chapman was discovered in the backyard of a tumbledown rooming-house at 29 Hanbury Street. Now there *was* a fourth murder—"latest of the series," as the *Telegraph* proclaimed it—and the East End was plunged into a hysterical frenzy. On the evening of 8 September, hundreds of people choked the Whitechapel avenues, moving from Buck's Row to Hanbury Street and on to the police stations, watching the comings and goings of investigators while hoping for a glimpse

of any suspects brought in for questioning. The Gentlemen of the Press, not allowed access to the new crime scene, let loose a flood of speculation, self-satisfied crowing and breathless prose:

There can be no shadow of a doubt now that our original theory was correct and that the Whitechapel murderer, who has now four ... victims to his knife, is one man and that man a murderous maniac [*Star*, 8 September].

Some officers also consider that the latest Whitechapel mystery is the fourth of a series of similar crimes ... and that one person alone is responsible for these awful deaths [*Telegraph*, 10 September].

This neighbourhood is in a state of wild excitement, bordering on panic, for the other cases are fresh in everybody's memory, and nobody has been brought to justice for any one of the crimes... [*Pall Mall Gazette*, 8 September].

Smith, Tabram, Nichols and Chapman were now definitively linked as a series of slayings, and all laid at the door of the yet-to-be-named Ripper. In such an atmosphere—where rumor and half-truth garnered massive headlines and papers routinely printed double or triple versions of the Chapman murder in a single issue, differentiating them only by the heading "another account"—it was inevitable that suspicion must sooner or later fall on some luckless person. The Whitechapel Murderer had to be found, even if the naming were to prove abortive.

The dubious honor would fall on the shoulders of a Jewish boot-finisher named John Pizer. He would be arrested, saddled with the nick-name "Leather Apron" (which was, at the moment, the *nom de meutre* of the mysterious killer), and ultimately cleared of all complicity at the Chapman inquest. His case is interesting for the buildup in the tabloid press when he was intangible and the somewhat muted response when Pizer actually materialised.

During the search for Nichols' assassin, the names of John Pizer and Leather Apron were first coupled, as Whitechapel prostitutes spoke of being assaulted and subjected to extortion. The police were privately anxious to locate Pizer, if only to remove him from suspicion, but somehow the more sensationalist newspapers got hold of the story. Many of the London dailies seized on the opportunity for sales that Leather Apron presented, but the *Star* outdid them all. Calling him a "noiseless midnight terror," their articles were a nauseating blend of fraud, anti–Semitism and blood libel which was representative of the public mood and of much more to come. Realising that he stood a good chance of being lynched in such an atmosphere, Pizer went to ground, eventually to be arrested. At the Leman Street police station, Pizer provided an alibi for the Nichols and Chapman murders which was accordingly checked on by the police.

Now that "Leather Apron" had assumed bodily form, the lurid coverage was somewhat modified:

> It is not yet possible to say whether Piser [*sic*] is the "Leather Apron" who is believed to have perpetrated the latest outrages, but his remarkable likeness to the suspected individual is held to justify the most searching investigation [*Telegraph*, 11 September].
>
> It is thought that if he is not actually implicated in the murder, or murders, he may still be able to throw some light on the affair [*Pall Mall Gazette*, 11 September].

A far cry from the *Star*'s bogeyman throwing "Universal Fear Among the Women"!

The police being satisfied as to his movements, Pizer was brought to Chapman's inquest on 12 September in order to be publicly exonerated. In contrast to what had gone before, the *Telegraph* summary of his appearance was remarkably laconic: "John Piser [*sic*], otherwise 'Leather Apron,' … satisfactorily accounted for his whereabouts not only on Saturday morning but some days previously, and the coroner remarked that his statements had been corroborated." The *East London Observer*, though giving Pizer a somewhat forbidding physical description in keeping with his "Leather Apron" status, noted: "He displayed not the slightest symptoms of insanity and chatted freely and affably … until the adjournment of the inquiry." And then it was over. John Pizer returned home and Leather Apron returned to his incorporeal state.

A nightmare had been created and then took physical form. The phantasm sold papers; the mortal proved to be an innocent man whose news value quickly dissipated. The lesson seemed clear: "Leather Apron"—or someone very like him—would be profitable only so long as he could not be found. We must keep this in mind when the name "Jack the Ripper" is at last penned.

# THE DAILY TELEGRAPH
Monday, September 10, 1888

Page 3
THE WHITECHAPEL MURDERS—
LATEST OF THE SERIES

Early on Saturday morning a ghastly murder was perpetrated near Spitalfields Market, under circumstances which have led the police to the belief that the author of the diabolical outrage was the same person who ten days ago cruelly killed Mary Ann Nicholls, in Buck's-row. Some officers also consider that the latest Whitechapel mystery is the fourth of a series of similar crimes which have taken place in the neighbourhood during the present year, and that one person alone is responsible for these awful deaths. In each case the victim was a woman, belonging, there is every reason to suppose, to the class of unfortunates who infest the locality. The first murder at Christmas[1] passed without much notice, and no evidence of identification was adduced at the inquest. A

wholly satisfactory explanation of the cause of death was not forthcoming, but in some respects the nature of the injuries sustained had a resemblance to those which were inflicted upon the three other women who have since succumbed to violence of a most revolting character. In August, near to the scene of the first tragedy, a Mrs. Turner was discovered upon the landing of some model dwellings in George-yard, and it was ascertained that she had received no fewer than thirty-six

**The front of 29 Hanbury Street, Spitalfields. The site of the Chapman murder was in the rear yard, accessed through the left-hand door (courtesy of Evans/Skinner Crime Archive).**

---

[1]Later news reports make explicit reference to Emma Smith as the first victim. Extensive research has failed to identify any woman being murdered in the Whitechapel district at Christmas 1887. The closest match yet seems to be Margaret Hames, a fellow lodger of Smith, who was attacked—though not killed—on 8 December 1887 and released from hospital on 28 December. This mythical "first victim" would later be given the imaginary name of "Fairy Fay" by journalist Terence Robertson in 1950. For the confusion this invention has caused later historians, see Connell & Evans, pp. 14–19.

stabbing wounds. The still more recent and very horrible murder of Mary Ann Nicholls in Buck's-row, which is within a very short distance of George-yard, has been more than paralleled by the latest deed of ferocity which has thrown White-chapel into a state of panic. This last crime was committed in Hanbury-street, not far removed from Buck's-row. The woman, now lying dead at the mortuary in Mon-tague-street, awaiting the inquest of to-day, has been identified as Annie Chap-man, well known as one of the frequenters of a common lodging-house in Dorset-street.[2] Her past history is to some extent known, but her relatives—the mother, sis-ter, and brother-in-law—have not been found. The manner in which Chapman came to her end corresponds almost in every detail with the mode in which Nicholls was brutally done to death by an unknown assailant. She seems to have been decoyed by a man in the early hours of the morning into a place where he might effect his purpose unobserved. The woman's clothes, when her corpse was found, were thrown up and her body ex-posed. Her throat was cut and the mur-derer, yielding to the impulse of a maniac, had then disembowelled the corpse. With so much cunning was the horrifying deed carried out that apparently no clue would seem to have been left which may serve to unearth the criminal. No knife or weapon of any sort was picked up; no one saw the murderer; and the outrage was without conceivable motive. Altogether this entire absence thus far alike of personal testi-mony and circumstantial evidence have very naturally contributed greatly to alarm the inhabitants throughout the district.

Hanbury-street is a narrow thor-oughfare, having Commercial-street at the western end and Baker's-row, Whitecha-pel, at the eastern extremity. It bisects Brick-lane, which runs between Bethnal-green-road and Whitechapel-road. The District Railway line, which has its termi-nus at Mile-end, opposite the London Hospital, is situate to the eastwards, and it divides Buck's-row from Hanbury-street, which was lately called Brown-lane. This neighbourhood is described as a very rough one, and respectable people are ac-customed to avoid it. It is inhabited by dock labourers, market porters, the ten-ants of common lodging-houses, and a certain number of cabinet-makers who supply the furniture establishments of Curtain-road. Leather aprons and knives are, therefore, by no means uncommonly to be seen in the district. In these squalid parts of the metropolis aggravated as-saults, attended by flesh wounds from knives, are frequently met with, and men and women become accustomed to scenes of violence. The people do not appear, however, to interfere with each other's affairs, unless provoked. Late at night there are many scenes of degradation and immorality, and with these the man now sought by the police was evidently famil-iar. It is this information which enabled him to commit murder unperceived and to escape without detection. The houses in Hanbury-street are seldom more than two or three storeys [sic] in height. No. 29 has two rooms on the ground-floor, with a cel-lar below. Above there are two floors, the front rooms each having two windows, and there is an attic, with one large win-dow, of the character to indicate that the house was originally occupied by silk weavers. The window of the ground-floor room in the front has a pair of green shut-ters, and the apartment is used as a cat's-meat shop. On the right of this shop there is a narrow door opening into a passage

---

[2]Crossingham's at 35 Dorset Street, not to be confused with Crossingham's other lodging-house directly across from 26 Dorset Street.

about 3 ft. wide and 20 ft. long, leading down two stone steps into a yard at the back. The flooring of this passage is bare and rough: the doors, at each end, have no locks; and there is nothing to prevent any one knowing the ways of the place to walk from the street into the yard. This yard is of small dimensions, about fifteen feet square. It contains a shed, in which packing cases are made, and is separated from the adjoining properties by fences about five feet high. No outlet exists at the rear whatever, and the theory has been formed that the murderer and his victim entered the yard by the ordinary ingress, and that the way of escape led in the same direction. Not a sound was heard to fix any time when either event could have occurred. On Saturday the sun rose at twenty-three minutes past five; for half an hour previously the light would be such as to render it difficult for any one to distinguish even near objects.[3] At a quarter before five o'clock John Richardson, of 2, St. John-street, son of the landlady of 29, Hanbury-street, the proprietor of the packing-case business, as usual went to his mother's to see if everything was right in the back yard. A short while before there had been a burglary in this place. Richardson sat down on the steps to cut a piece of leather from his boot. The door would then partially hide the corner between the house and the fence.[4] This man is quite clear that he saw nothing to attract his attention before he left. About twenty-five minutes past five Albert Cadosch, living at No. 31 [*sic* #27], the next house on the left hand side, entered the yard adjoining that of No. 29. He states that he heard some talk-

ing on the other side of the palings, and he distinguished the word "No."[5] There was then, he fancied, a slight scuffle, with the noise of something falling, but he took no notice, thinking that it was from his neighbours. Half an hour later, at six o'clock, one of the lodgers at No. 29, John Davis, before going to his work, walked along the passage into the yard. He was horrified to discover, near to the steps, close to the fence, the recumbent body of the woman Chapman, covered with blood, the head towards the wall and the knees drawn up, with the clothing disarranged. Her throat had been cut, and there were frightful gashes and hideous mutilations of the body. At once Davis ran to the Commercial-street Police-station,[6] giving the alarm on his way to some men who were waiting to begin work. Fifteen persons sleep in the house behind which the discovery was made, and most of them saw the dreadful sight. It is the opinion of Mrs. Richardson that the deceased had not moved an inch after she was struck, but had died instantly. The blood had flowed to the doorstep, and the witness believes that the murderer must have gone away with blood marks upon his clothing. A pan of water stood in the yard, but it had not been used. Adam Osborne, of 31, Hanbury-street, looking over the fence, also saw the corpse which had been left in such a frightful condition. Evidently the work of mutilation had been undertaken with a most determined purpose; but although the offence was of a far more ghastly character than any which had preceded it, and which rumour has ascribed to the same hand, it may be stated that several reports

---

[3]Dawn broke at 4:51am with the sun rising at 5:25am. There was enough light to sufficiently "distinguish even near objects." (RMC Weather Records, Meteorological Library & Archives).

[4]The door would not have blocked Richardon's view. See Commentary 3.

[5]See Cadoche's testimony, 20 September, and Commentary 3.

[6]Davis did eventually go to Commercial Street Police Station, but not until he, Kent, Green, and Holland viewed the body.

The Courtyard where the body was first discovered

**A contemporary sketch of the rear yard of 29 Hanbury Street. Chapman's body was discovered at the foot of the steps (courtesy of Evans/Skinner Crime Archive).**

ear, and then, with a large and keen weapon, to rip the body from groin to breast-bone, throwing the organs thus exposed under one arm. In order not to lose any evidence of value, the post-mortem examination was conducted without delay at the mortuary,[7] to which the body had been removed by the police divisional surgeon,[8] who, upon advice, reserves his description of the injuries until the inquest. It is, however, this gentleman's opinion, as communicated to his chiefs, that death had taken place some two or three hours prior to the first examination of the corpse, shortly after its discovery.[9] If that view of the medical aspect of the case be correctly stated, the time of the murder must have been earlier than four in the morning, which seems difficult to reconcile with the statements of other witnesses.

which have been published possess sensational features not warranted by the facts. All that appears to have been done by the miscreant was first to silence the woman by cutting her throat, almost from ear to

Some of the evidence as to the actual hour of the commission of the crime has been already mentioned. There is other testimony of importance upon this point, but it is necessary first to refer to the

---

[7]The autopsy was conducted at 2:00 that afternoon.

[8]Dr. George Bagster Phillips (1834–1897), police surgeon for H (Whitechapel) division. He saw the bodies of Chapman, Stride and Kelly *in situ* and attended the Eddowes post-mortem (BFS, pp. 346–355).

[9]See Phillips' testimony on 14 September and Commentary 3 regarding time of death.

matter of identification. The body was that of a woman forty-five years of age[10] and five feet high, who in lifetime was well-formed and of good looks. The complexion was fair, the hair of a wavy brown, the nose large and strongly marked, and the colour of the eyes blue. From the third finger of the left hand rings had been wrenched off, and the hands and arms were much bruised. Deceased wore laced-up boots and striped stockings, two cotton petticoats, and was otherwise respectably, though poorly, dressed. In the pockets there were a handkerchief, two small combs, and an envelope with the seal of the Sussex Regiment. There were also found two farthings polished brightly, and, according to some, these coins had been passed off as half-sovereigns upon the deceased by her murderer.[11] It was also assumed that she was of questionable character, and that she had accompanied the man into the yard of her own accord. That this might have happened without disturbing the sleepers in the house may be seen from the statement of Mrs. Richardson, who has been the occupier of the house for fifteen years, some of her lodgers having been with her as long as twelve. She says: "They mostly work at the fish market or in the Spitalfields Market. Some of the carmen leave home as early as one a.m., while others go out at four and five, so that the place is open all night, and any one can get in. It is certain that the deceased came voluntarily into the yard, as if there had been any struggle it must have been heard. Several persons sleep at the back of the house, and some had their windows open, but no noise was heard

from the yard. One of my lodgers, a carman, named Thompson, employed at Goodson's, in Brick-lane, went out at four o'clock in the morning. He did not go into the yard, but he did not notice anything particular in the passage. My son John came in at ten minutes to five, and he gave a look round before he went to market. He walked into the yard, but no one was there then, and everything was right. Just before six o'clock, when Mr. Davis, another of my lodgers, came down, he found the deceased lying in the corner of the yard, close to the house, and by the side of the step. The only possible clue that I can think of is that Mr. Thompson's wife met a man about a month ago lying on the stairs, about four o'clock in the morning. He spoke with a foreign accent. When asked what he was doing there he replied he was waiting to do a 'doss' before the market opened. He slept on the stairs that night, and I believe on other nights also."

When the news of the crime was noised abroad the dead woman was first identified by a man who had known her as Annie "Sivey." On inquiry being made it was learned from the deputy of a lodging house at 30, Dorset-street, that she had stopped there with a man known as Jack Sivey, a sieve-maker. She had the character of a quiet woman, and from the same source of information it was gleaned that she had had two children—one, the boy, a cripple, being maintained at a charitable school, and the other, a girl, getting a living in France.[12] According to another statement this girl is employed in a French circus. A little later in the day, at ten o'clock, the police were put in possession

---

[10]Chapman was born "in about September 1840/41," making her approximately 47 (Shelden, p. 11).

[11]No official report mentions coins at the scene. See Commentary 1 and Tully, pp. 384–386.

[12]Annie and John Chapman had three children: Emily Ruth (1870), Annie Georgina (1873) and John Alfred (1880) (Shelden, pp. 12–13). Annie Georgina is described both in 1888 and in current reference works as either having been placed in a French institution after the death of her father, or as part of a performing troupe traveling with a circus in France. In *Jack the Ripper Victim Annie Chapman: A Short Biography*, Shelden writes that these rumors "are dismissed entirely as a myth by her family."

A previously unseen photograph of Annie and John Chapman, circa 1869 (reproduced courtesy of Neal Shelden and Annie Chapman's descendants).

of more complete information. Amelia Farmer, who had occupied the next bed to that of deceased, in another lodging-house in Dorset-street, which they had lately put up, stated that she had known Chapman for a considerable time. She was taken to the mortuary and immediately recognised her friend. Subsequently she said that Annie Chapman, who was the wife of a veterinary surgeon at Windsor,[13] had for a long time been separated from her husband by mutual agreement, and had been allowed 10s a week by him for her maintenance. The money had been sent by Post-office Order, made payable at the Commercial-street Post-office, and had always come regularly. About eighteen months ago the installments suddenly ceased, and, upon inquiry being made, it was found that the husband had died.[14] Annie Chapman had two children, but where they were she could not say. The deceased had a mother and sister, who were living in the neighbourhood of Brompton or Fulham. Farmer had been in the habit of writing letters for her friend. She could not remember the exact address of the mother or sister, but thought it was near the Brompton Hospital.[15] Last Monday Chapman had intimated her intention of communicating with her sister, saying, "If I can get a pair of boots from my sister I shall go hop-picking." Another relative, a brother-in-law of the deceased, lived somewhere in or near Oxford-street.[16] Farmer asserted that her murdered friend was apparently a sober, steady-going sort of woman, and one who seldom took any drink.[17] For some time past she had been living occasionally with a man named Ted Stanley, who had been in the militia, but was now working at some neighbouring brewery.[18] Ted Stanley was a good-tempered man, rather tall, about 5 ft. 10 in., fair, and of florid complexion. He was the last man in the world to have quarrelled with Chapman, nor would he have injured her in any way. At the beginning of the week the deceased had been rather severely knocked about in the breast and face by another woman of the locality through jealousy in connection with Ted Stanley, and had been obliged to go to the casual ward or infirmary.[19] As a regular means of livelihood she had not been in the habit of frequenting the streets, but had made antimacassars[20] for sale. Sometimes she would buy flowers or matches with which to pick up a living. Farmer was perfectly certain that on Friday night the murdered woman had worn three rings, which were not genuine, but were imitations, otherwise she would not have troubled to go out and find money for her lodgings.[21] The police, on the statement of Farmer, are making a vigilant search for the mother, sister, and brother-in-law. A man named Chapman, from Oxford-street, has been found, but he proves to be no relation.

It has been ascertained that the deceased woman did wear two rings at the time of her death. They were of brass. One was a wedding ring, and the other a keeper

---

[13]This may have been a fable told by Annie; John Chapman worked as a coachman and domestic servant, but apparently never as a veterinary surgeon (BFS, pp. 78–79).

[14]John Chapman died 25 December 1886 from cirrhosis of the liver, ascites and dropsy (Shelden, p. 15).

[15]According to the 1881 and 1891 censuses, Chapman's mother and sister were living at 29 Montpelier Place, Knightsbridge.

[16]None of Chapman's three sisters is known to have married. The *Times* of 11 September has "relative" in place of "brother-in-law."

[17]This characterization is not accurate. See testimonies of Amelia Palmer and Timothy Donovan, 11 September.

[18]Ted Stanley, also known as "The Pensioner," was a bricklayer who pretended to be an ex-soldier from the Essex Regiment. He would later reluctantly have to admit his fabrications.

[19]The fight was with fellow-lodger Eliza Cooper (ref. 20 September). Although Chapman did obtain medication, pills and lotion, no record has yet surfaced showing that she was in an infirmary, casual ward, or hospital.

[20]Knitted or crocheted pieces of cloth placed over chairs to prevent gentlemen's hair oils from spoiling the upholstery.

[21]"Imitations" means that Chapman's rings were brass rather than gold.

*Left:* A previously unseen photograph of Emily Ruth Chapman, Annie's eldest daughter, circa 1877–78 (reproduced courtesy of Neal Shelden and Annie Chapman's descendants). *Right:* A previously unseen photograph of Annie Georgina Chapman, Annie's second daughter, circa 1879–81 (reproduced courtesy of Neal Shelden and Annie Chapman's descendants).

of fancy pattern. Both are missing, and the police are still searching for them. It was believed on Saturday night that an important clue had been obtained, a pawnbroker having detained rings of the same description which were offered in pledge, but the incident has no reference to the murder, as investigation has showed. With regard to the deceased's movements on the night preceding her death, it has been learned that she came out of an infirmary on the Friday morning, and that on the night of the same day she returned to the lodging-house, at 35, Dorset-street, the deputy of which, Timothy Donovan, states that Chapman stayed there on the previous Saturday night. She had been in the habit of coming there for the past four months. She was a quiet woman, and gave no trouble. He had heard her say she wished she was as well off as her relatives, but she never told him who her friends were or where they lived. A pensioner or a soldier usually came to the lodging-house with her on Saturday nights, and generally he stayed until the Monday morning.[22] He

---

[22]This is generally read as referring to Ted Stanley, but see 14 September for some confusion between Stanley and "The Pensioner."

would be able to identify the man instantly if he saw him. After the man left on Monday, deceased would usually remain in the room for some days longer, the charge being eightpence per night. The man stayed at the house from Saturday to Monday last, and when he went the deceased went with him. She was not seen at the place again until Friday night about half-past eleven o'clock, when she passed the doorway, and Donovan, calling out, asked her where she had been since Monday, and why she had not slept there, to which she replied, "I have been in the infirmary." Then she went on her way in the direction of Bishopsgate-street. About 1:40a.m. on Saturday morning she came again to the lodging-house, and asked for a bed. The message was brought upstairs to him, and he sent downstairs to ask for the money. The woman replied, "I haven't enough now, but keep my bed for me. I sha'n't be long." Then as she was going away she said to John Evans, the watchman, "Brummy, I won't be long. See that Jim [*sic*] keeps my bed for me." She was the worse for drink at the time,[23] and was eating some baked potatoes. He saw nothing of her again until he was called to the mortuary yesterday morning, when he identified the deceased by her features and her wavy hair, which was turning grey. After the deceased left on Monday last he found two large bottles in the room, one containing medicine, and labelled as follows: "St. Bartholomew's Hospital. Take two tablespoonfuls three times a day." The other bottle contained a milky lotion, and was labelled "St. Bartholomew's Hospital. The lotion. Poison." This, he thought, confirmed her statement that she had been

under medical treatment. But there is no proof that the bottles really belonged to Chapman. According to the statement of Simpson and Stevens, two young men who knew the deceased at Dorset-street, she returned to the lodging-house at twelve o'clock, saying that she had been to see some friends at Vauxhall. There are several reports of deceased having been seen in the company of a man early on Saturday morning, but little reliance is placed upon them… Similar statements to those which follow have been supplied to the police, who are investigating them in the hope that they may furnish a clue of value; but it has to be borne in mind that the inhabitants of the district have been in an excited state of mind, and they might easily be mistaken in the appearance of the supposed blood-stains.[24]

# THE DAILY TELEGRAPH
Tuesday, September 11, 1888

Page 3
THE WHITECHAPEL MURDER
INQUEST AND ARRESTS
A REWARD OFFERED
[*First Session of Inquest*]

Our Windsor correspondent telegraphs: From inquiries made by Superintendent Hayes, of the Windsor police, there is every reason to believe that the murdered woman was the widow of a coachman named Chapman, formerly in the service of a gentleman living near the Royal borough, and not of a veterinary surgeon, as stated. Her husband held a most excellent position, but she appears to

---

[23]Although Chapman appeared drunk to many who saw her the night of her death, Dr. Phillips was convinced she had not had any "strong alcohol" that night. She was suffering from a "disease of the membranes of the brain," and it may have been this condition that manifested itself as drunkenness. See Phillips' testimony, 14 September, and Frederick Stevens' testimony, 20 September.

[24]"Blood-stains" would be common enough due to the number of slaughterhouses in the area.

have become very dissipated while with him, and he was at last reluctantly obliged to disassociate himself from her. She lived for a time at Windsor, and eventually quitted that town for London. One of her children, a girl, was educated at a highly-respectable ladies' school in the Royal borough,[25] the cost of her tuition being defrayed by the victim's sister. Chapman was taken ill two years ago, when the remittances sent to his wife seem to have ceased. During his sickness a wretched-looking woman, having the appearance of a tramp, called at the Merry Wives of Windsor, in the Spital-road, and inquired where he was living. She said that she was his wife, and that she had walked down from London, and had slept at a lodging house in Colnbrook. On her way she also stated that, having been told that her husband, who had discontinued sending her 10s a week, was ill, she had come to Windsor to ascertain if the report was true, and not merely an excuse for failing to send her the money as usual. The woman quitted the house shortly afterwards, and the landlord did not see her again. Chapman died over eighteen months ago, and there is little doubt that since his decease the unfortunate woman has had to depend upon her own resources for a livelihood.

At the Working Lads' Institute, Whitechapel-road, yesterday morning, Mr. Wynne Baxter opened an inquiry into the circumstances attending the death of Annie Chapman, a widow, whose body was found horribly mutilated in the back yard of 29, Hanbury-street, Spitalfields, early on Saturday morning. The jury viewed the corpse at the mortuary in Montague-street, but all evidences of the outrage to which the deceased had been subjected were concealed. The clothing was also in-spected, and subsequently the following evidence was taken.

**John Davies** [Davis] deposed: I am a carman employed at Leadenhall Market. I have lodged at 29, Hanbury-street for a fortnight, and I occupied the top front room on the third floor with my wife and three sons, who live with me. On Friday night I went to bed at eight o'clock, and my wife followed about half an hour later. My sons came to bed at different times, the last one at about a quarter to eleven. There is a weaving shed window, or light across the room. It was not open during the night. I was awake from three a.m. to five a.m. on Saturday, and then fell asleep until a quarter to six, when the clock at Spitalfields Church struck. I had a cup of tea and went downstairs to the back yard. The house faces Hanbury-street, with one window on the ground floor and a front door at the side leading into a passage which runs through into the yard. There is a back door at the end of this passage opening into the yard. Neither of the doors was able to be locked, and I have never seen them locked. Any one who knows where the latch of the front door is could open it and go along the passage into the back yard.

THE CORONER: When you went into the yard on Saturday morning was the yard door open or shut?—I found it shut. I cannot say whether it was latched—I cannot remember. I have been too much upset. The front street door was wide open and thrown against the wall. I was not surprised to find the front door open, as it was not unusual. I opened the back door, and stood in the entrance.

Will you describe the yard?—It is a large yard. Facing the door, on the opposite side, on my left as I was standing,

---

[25]It is not known which of Chapman's two daughters this refers to.

there is a shed, in which Mrs. Richardson keeps her wood. In the right-hand corner there is a closet.[26] The yard is separated from the next premises on both sides by close wooden fencing, about 5 ft. 6 in. high.

THE CORONER: I hope the police will supply me with a plan. In the country, in cases of importance, I always have one.

INSPECTOR HELSON: We shall have one at the adjourned hearing.

THE CORONER: Yes; by that time we shall hardly require it.

EXAMINATION RESUMED: There was a little recess on the left. From the steps to the fence is about 3 ft. There are three stone steps, unprotected, leading from the door to the yard, which is at a lower level than that of the passage. Directly I opened the door I saw a woman lying down in the lefthand recess, between the stone steps and the fence. She was on her back, with her head towards the house and her legs towards the wood shed. The clothes were up to her groins. I did not go into the yard, but left the house by the front door, and called the attention of two men to the circumstances. They work at Mr. Bailey's, a packing-case maker, of Hanbury-street. I do not know their names, but I know them by sight.[27]

THE CORONER: Have the names of these men been ascertained?

INSPECTOR CHANDLER: I have made inquiries, but I cannot find the men.

THE CORONER: They must be found.

WITNESS: They work at Bailey's; but I could not find them on Saturday, as I had my work to do.

THE CORONER: Your work is of no consequence compared with this inquiry.

WITNESS: I am giving all the information I can.

THE CORONER (TO WITNESS): You must find these men out, either with the assistance of the police or of my officer.

EXAMINATION RESUMED: Mr. Bailey's is three doors off 29, Hanbury-street, on the same side of the road. The two men were waiting outside the workshop. They came into the passage, and saw the sight. They did not go into the yard, but ran to find a policeman. We all came out of the house together. I went to the Commercial-street Police-station to report the case. No one in the house was informed by me of what I had discovered. I told the inspector at the police-station, and after a while I returned to Hanbury-street, but did not re-enter the house. As I passed I saw constables there.

Have you ever seen the deceased before?—No.

Were you the first down in the house that morning?—No; there was a lodger named Thompson, who was called at half-past three.[28]

Have you ever seen women in the passage?—Mrs. Richardson has said there have been. I have not seen them myself. I have only been in the house a fortnight.

Did you hear any noise that Saturday morning?—No, sir.

**Amelia Palmer**, examined, stated: I live at 35, Dorset-street, Spitalfields, a common lodging-house. Off and on I have stayed there three years. I am married to Henry Palmer, a dock labourer. He was foreman, but met with an accident at the beginning of the year. I go out charing [*sic*]. My husband gets a pension, having been in the Army Reserve. I knew the deceased very well, for quite five years. I saw the body on Saturday at the mortuary, and

---

[26]Closet: a water-closet; an outhouse.

[27]James Green and James Kent (BFS, p. 99).

[28]Thompson's first name is not known. He was a carman employed by Goodson's of Brick Lane (BFS, p. 450).

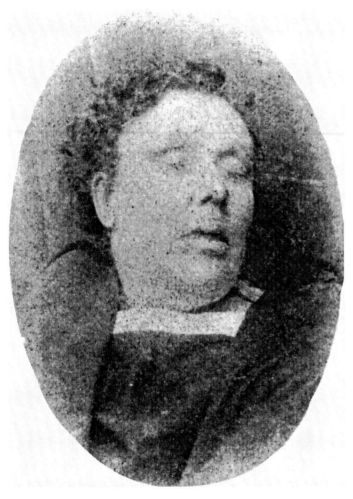

Mortuary photograph of Annie Chapman (courtesy of Evans/Skinner Crime Archive).

am quite sure that it is that of Annie Chapman. She was a widow, and her husband, Frederick Chapman, was a veterinary surgeon in Windsor. He died about eighteen months ago. Deceased had lived apart from him for about four years or more. She lived in various places, principally in common lodging-houses in Spitalfields. I never knew her to have a settled home.

Has she lived at 30, Dorset-street?— Yes, about two years ago, with a man who

made wire sieves, and at that time she was receiving 10s a week from her husband by post-office order, payable to her at the Commercial-road. This payment stopped about eighteen months ago, and she then found, on inquiry of some relative, that her husband was dead. I am under the impression that she ascertained this fact either from a brother or sister of her husband in Oxford-street, Whitechapel. She was nicknamed, Mrs. Sivvy," because she lived with the sievemaker. I know the man perfectly well, but don't know his name.[29] I saw him last about eighteen months ago, in the City, and he told me that he was living at Notting-hill. I saw deceased two or three times last week. On Monday she was standing in the road opposite 35, Dorset-street. She had been staying there, and had no bonnet on. She had a bruise on one of her temples—I think the right. I said, "How did you get that?" She said, "Yes, look at my chest." Opening her dress, she showed me a bruise. She said, "Do you know the woman?" and gave some name, which I do not remember.[30] She made me understand that it was a woman who goes about selling books. Both this woman and the deceased were acquainted with a man called "Harry the Hawker." Chapman told me that she was with some other man, Ted Stanley, on Saturday, Sept. 1. Stanley is a

---

[29]Palmer means that she knows him by sight only. It is unknown whether Chapman's paramour was only nicknamed "Jack Sivvy" (or "Sievey") or whether such was, in fact, his real name.

[30]This refers to the Chapman-Cooper fight.

very respectable man. Deceased said she was with him at a beer-shop,[31] 87, Commercial-street, at the corner of Dorset-street, where "Harry the Hawker" was with the woman. This man put down a two shilling piece and the woman picked it up and put down a penny. There was some feeling in consequence and the same evening the book-selling woman met the deceased and injured her in the face and chest. When deceased told me this, she said she was living at 35, Dorset-street. On the Tuesday afternoon I saw Chapman again near to Spitalfields Church.[32] She said she felt no better, and she should go into the casual ward for a day or two. I remarked that she looked very pale, and asked her if she had had anything to eat. She replied, "No, I have not had a cup of tea to-day." I gave her two-pence to get some, and told her not to get any rum, of which she was fond. I have seen her the worse for drink.

What did she do for a living?—She used to do crochet work, make antimaccassars, and sell flowers. She was out late at night at times. On Fridays she used to go to Stratford to sell anything she had. I did not see her from the Tuesday to the Friday afternoon, 7th inst., when I met her about five o'clock in Dorset-street. She appeared to be perfectly sober. I said, "Are you going to Stratford to-day?" She answered, "I feel too ill to do anything." I left her immediately afterwards, and returned about ten minutes later, and found her in the same spot. She said, "It is of no use my going away. I shall have to go somewhere to get some money to pay my lodgings."[33] She said no more, and that

was the last time that I saw her. Deceased stated that she had been in the casual ward, but did not say which one. She did not say she had been refused admission. Deceased was a very industrious woman when she was sober. I have seen her often the worse for drink. She could not take much without making her drunk. She had been living a very irregular life during the whole time that I have known her. Since the death of her husband she has seemed to give way altogether. I understood that she had a sister and mother living at Brompton, but I do not think they were on friendly terms. I have never known her to stay with her relatives even for a night. On the Monday she observed: "If my sister will send me the boots, I shall go hopping." She had two children—a boy and a girl. They were at Windsor until her husband's death, and since then they have been in a school. Deceased was a very respectable woman, and never used bad language. She has stayed out in the streets all night.

Do you know of any one that would be likely to have injured her?—No.

THE CORONER (having read a communication handed to him by the police): It seems to be very doubtful whether the husband was a veterinary surgeon. He may have been a coachman.

**Timothy Donovan,** 35, Dorset-street, Spitalfields, said: I am the deputy of a common lodging house. I have seen the body of the deceased, and have identified it as that of a woman who stayed at my house for the last four months. She was not there last week until Friday afternoon,

---

[31]The Britannia, known colloquially as "Ringer's" after its landlords, Walter and Matilda Ringer. It stood at the eastern end of Dorset Street (ref. "The Whitechapel Dossier: Dorset Street and Miller's Court," *Ripper Notes*, April 2001, pp. 20–23).

[32]Christ Church at the corner of Commercial and Church streets, built 1711–1729 by the architect Nicholas Hawksmoor.

[33]This has also been reported as, "It's no good my *giving way…*" (BFS, pp. 338–339).

between two and three o'clock. I was coming out of the office after getting up, and she asked me if she could go down in the kitchen, and I said "Yes," and asked her where she had been all the week. She replied that she had been in the infirmary, but did not say which.

A police-officer stated that the deceased had been in the casual ward.

WITNESS RESUMED: Deceased went down in the kitchen, and I did not see her again until half-past one or a quarter to two on Saturday morning. At that time I was sitting in the office, which faces the front door. She went into the kitchen. I sent the watchman's wife, who was in the office with me, downstairs to ask her husband about the bed. Deceased came upstairs to the office and said, "I have not sufficient money for my bed. Don't let it. I shan't be long before I am in."

How much was it?—Eightpence for the night. The bed she occupied, No. 29, was the one that she usually occupied. Deceased was then eating potatoes, and went out. She stood in the door two or three minutes, and then repeated, "Never mind, Tim; I shall soon be back. Don't let the bed." It was then about ten minutes to two a.m. She left the house, going in the direction of Brushfield-street. John Evans, the watchman, saw her leave the house. I did not see her again.

Was she the worse for drink when you saw her last?—She had had enough; of that I am certain. She walked straight. Generally on Saturdays she was the worse for drink. She was very sociable in the kitchen. I said to her, "You can find money for your beer, and you can't find money for your bed." She said she had been only to the top of the street—where there is a public-house.

Did you see her with any man that night?—No, sir.

Where did you think she was going to get the money from?—I did not know. She used to come and stay at the lodging-house on Saturdays with a man—a pensioner—of soldierly appearance, whose name I do not know.[34]

Have you seen her with other men?—At other times she has come with other men, and I have refused her.

You only allow the women at your place one husband?—The pensioner told me not to let her a bed if she came with any other man. She did not come with a man that night. I never saw her with any man that week.

In answer to the jury witness said the beds were double at 8d per night, and as a rule deceased occupied one of them by herself.

THE CORONER: When was the pensioner last with deceased at the lodging-house?—On Sunday, Sept. 2. I cannot say whether they left together. I have heard the deceased say, "Tim, wait a minute. I am just going up the street to see if I can see him." She added that he was going to draw his pension. This occurred on Saturday, Aug. 25, at three a.m.

In reply to the Coroner, the police said nothing was known of the pensioner.

EXAMINATION CONTINUED: I never heard deceased call the man by any name. He was between forty and forty-five years of age, about 5 ft. 6 in. or 5 ft. 8 in. in height. Sometimes he would come dressed as a dock labourer; at other times he had a gentlemanly appearance. His hair was rather dark. I believe she always used to find him at the top of the street. Deceased

---

[34]Baxter and Donovan probably knew perfectly well how Chapman was going to find money at that late hour, but Donovan was likely to be circumspect in light of the 1858 Act regarding "disorderly houses." A similar situation arose in the case of victim Catherine Eddowes, her lover John Kelly and lodging-house deputy Frederick Williamson. See Donovan's recalled testimony, 14 and 20 September, and Chapter 4.

was on good terms with the lodgers. About Tuesday, Aug. 28, she and another woman had a row in the kitchen. I saw them both outside. As far as I know she was not injured at that time. I heard from the watchman that she had had a clout. I noticed a day or two afterwards, on the Thursday, that she had a slight touch of a black eye. She said, "Tim, this is lovely," but did not explain how she got it. The bruise was to be seen on Friday last. I know the other woman, but not her name. Her husband hawks laces and other things.

**John Evans** testified: I am night watchman at 35, Dorset-street, and have identified the deceased as having lived at the lodging-house. I last saw her there on Saturday morning, and she left at about a quarter to two o'clock. I was sent down in the kitchen to see her, and she said she had not sufficient money. When she went upstairs I followed her, and as she left the house, I watched her go through a court called Paternoster-street, into Brushfield-street, and then turn towards Spitalfields Church. Deceased was the worse for drink, but not badly so. She came in soon after twelve (midnight), when she said she had been over to her sister's in Vauxhall. She sent one of the lodgers for a pint of beer,[35] and then went out again, returning shortly before a quarter to two. I knew she had been living a rough night life. She associated with a man, a pensioner, every Saturday, and this individual called on Saturday at 2:30 p.m. and inquired for the deceased. He had heard something about her death, and came to see if it was true. I do not know his name or address. When I told him what had occurred he went straight out, without saying a word, towards Spitalfields Church. I did not see

deceased and this man leave the house last Sunday week.

Did you see the deceased and another woman have a row in the kitchen?—Yes, on Thursday, Aug. 30. Deceased and a woman known as "Eliza," at 11:30 a.m., quarrelled about a piece of soap, and Chapman received a blow in the chest. I noticed that she had a slight black eye. There are marks on the body in a similar position.

BY THE JURY: I have never heard any one threaten her, nor express any fear of any one. I have never heard any one of the women in the lodging-house say that they had been threatened.

At this stage the inquiry was adjourned until tomorrow (Wednesday).

---

# THE DAILY TELEGRAPH
Wednesday, September 12, 1888

Page 3
THE WHITECHAPEL MURDER— IMPORTANT CLUE
[*Bloodstains Discovered in Hanbury Street*]

A discovery which, it is believed, throws considerable light upon the movements of the murderer immediately after the committal of the crime was made yesterday afternoon. A little girl happened to be walking in the back garden or yard of the house, 25, Hanbury-street, the next house but one to the scene of the murder, when her attention was attracted to peculiar marks on the wall and on the garden path. She communicated the discovery to Detective-Inspector Chandler, who had just called at the house in order to make a plan of the back premises of the three houses for the use of the Coroner at the inquest, which will be resumed to-day. The whole of the yard was then carefully

---

[35]This was most likely William Stevens.

examined, with the result that a bloody trail[36] was found distinctly marked for a distance of five or six feet in the direction of the back door of the house.

Further investigation left no doubt that the trail was that of the murderer, who, it was evident, after finishing his sanguinary work, had passed through or over the dividing fence between Nos. 29 and 27, and thence into the garden of No. 25. On the wall of the last house there was found a curious mark, between a smear and a sprinkle, which had probably been made by the murderer, who, alarmed by the blood-soaked state of his coat, took off that garment and knocked it against the wall. Abutting on the end of the yard at No. 25 are the works of Mr. Bailey, a packing-case maker. In the yard of this establishment, in an out-of-the-way corner, the police yesterday afternoon found some crumpled paper, almost saturated with blood. It was evident that the murderer had found the paper in the yard of No. 25, and had wiped his hands with it afterwards, throwing it over the wall into Bailey's premises.[37]

The house No. 25, like most of the dwellings in the street, is let out in tenements direct from the owner, who does not live on the premises,[38] and has no representative therein. The back and front doors are therefore always left either on the latch or wide open, the tenant of each room looking after the safety of his own particular premises. The general appearance of the bloody trail and other indications seem to show that the murderer in-

tended to make his way as rapidly as possible into the street through the house next door but one, being frightened by some noise or light in No. 29 from retreating by the way which he came. On reaching the yard of No. 25 he, it is believed, made for the back door, and then, suddenly remembering his bloodstained appearance, he must have hesitated a moment, and then, catching sight of the pieces of paper lying about, doubtless retraced his steps to the end of the yard, and there sought to remove the bloodstains.[39] He might have had some thought of retreating by way of Bailey's premises, but the height of the walls made such a course somewhat perilous, and he finally elected to get into Hanbury-street by way of the house.

---

# THE DAILY TELEGRAPH
Thursday, September 13, 1888

Page 3
THE WHITECHAPEL MURDER—
EVIDENCE OF
"LEATHER APRON"
[*Second Session of Inquest*]

Mr. Wynne Baxter yesterday resumed the inquiry into the circumstances attending the death of Annie Chapman, whose body was found brutally mutilated in the back yard of 29, Hanbury-street, Spitalfields, at six o'clock on the morning of Saturday last.

The Police were represented by Inspector Abberline, of the Criminal Inves-

---

[36]The little girl was Laura Sickings; the "blood spots" ultimately proved to be "sewage," or urine (BFS, p. 412).

[37]While the *Telegraph*'s scenario of the Ripper wiping his hands on a piece of paper and casually tossing it over the fence is possible, it seems more likely that this paper was used as a makeshift bandage by one of the packing-case workers in Bailey's yard.

[38]Note the owner was not Mrs. Richardson; she was merely the landlady, or house-deputy. It is currently unknown who actually owned the house.

[39]This is a commonly proposed scenario; however, it neglects the medical opinion that the killer would not be covered in blood (ref. Phillips' testimony, 14 September).

tigation Department, and Inspector Helson, J Division.

**Fontain** [Fountain] **Smith**, printer's warehouseman, stated: I have seen the body in the mortuary, and recognise it as that of my eldest sister, Annie, the widow of John Chapman, who lived at Windsor, a coachman. She had been separated from her husband for about three years. Her age was forty-seven. I last saw her alive a fortnight ago, in Commercial-street, where I met her promiscuously.[40] Her husband died at Christmas, 1886. I gave her 2s; she did not say where she was living nor what she was doing. She said she wanted the money for a lodging.

Did you know anything about her associates?—No.

**James Kent**, 20, Drew's Blocks, Shadwell, a packing-case maker, said: I work for Mr. Bayley, 23A, Hanbury-street, and go there at six a.m. On Saturday I arrived about ten minutes past that hour.[41] Our employer's gate was open, and there I waited for some other men. Davis, who lives two or three doors away, ran from his house into the road and cried, "Men, come here." James Green and I went together to 29, Hanbury-street, and on going through the passage, standing on the top of the back door steps, I saw a woman lying in the yard between the steps and the partition between the yard and the next. Her head was near the house, but no part of the body was against the wall. The feet were lying towards the back of Bayley's premises. (Witness indicated the precise position

upon a plan produced by the police-officers). Deceased's clothes were disarranged, and her apron was thrown over them. I did not go down the steps, but went outside and returned after Inspector Chandler[42] had arrived. I could see that the woman was dead. She had some kind of handkerchief around her throat which seemed soaked in blood. The face and hands were besmeared with blood, as if she had struggled. She appeared to have been on her back and fought with her hands to free herself. The hands were turned toward her throat. The legs were wide apart, and there were marks of blood upon them. The entrails were protruding, and were lying across her left side. I got a piece of canvass [*sic*] from the shop to throw over the body, and by that time a mob had assembled, and Inspector Chandler was in possession of the yard. The foreman gets to the shop at ten minutes to six every morning, and he was there before us.

**James Green**, of Ackland-street, Burdett-road, a packing-case maker, in the same employ as last witness, said: I arrived in Hanbury-street at ten minutes past six on Saturday morning, and accompanied Kent to the back door of No. 29. I left the premises with him. I saw no one touch the body.

**Amelia Richardson**, 29, Hanbury-street, deposed: I am a widow, and occupy half of the house—*i.e.*, the first floor, ground floor,[43] and workshops in the cellar. I carry on the business of a packing-

---

[40]Here "promiscuously" means "by chance."

[41]This timing appears to be in error. Although Kent and Green testified to not arriving in Hanbury Street until 6:10am, the testimonies of John Davis (11 September), Amelia Richardson and Harriet Hardiman (13 September) and Inspector Chandler (14 September) all point to Chapman's body being found at about 6:00am.

[42]Joseph Luniss Chandler (b. 1850), warrant no. 56638. The duty Inspector for H (Whitechapel) division at the time of the Chapman murder (BFS, p. 74).

[43]Second and first floors, respectively, to Americans.

case maker there, and the shops are used by my son John, aged thirty-seven, and a man Francis Tyler, who have worked for me eighteen years. The latter ought to have come at six a.m., but he did not arrive until eight o'clock, when I sent for him. He is often late when we are slack. My son lives in John-street, Spitalfields, and he works also in the market on market mornings. At six a.m. my grandson, Thomas Richardson, aged fourteen, who lives with me, got up. I sent him down to see what was the matter, as there was so much noise in the passage.[44] He came back and said, "Oh, grandmother, there is a woman murdered." I went down immediately, and saw the body of the deceased lying in the yard. There was no one there at the time, but there were people in the passage. Soon afterwards a constable came and took possession of the place. As far as I know the officer was the first to enter the yard.

Which room do you occupy?—The first floor front, and my grandson slept in the same room on Friday night. I went to bed about half-past nine, and was very wakeful half the night. I was awake at three a.m., and only dozed after that.

Did you hear any noise during the night?—No.

Who occupies the first floor back?—Mr. Walker, a maker of lawn-tennis boots. He is an old gentleman, and he sleeps there with his son, twenty-seven years of age. The son is weak-minded and inoffensive. On the ground floor there are two rooms. Mrs. Hardman [sic] occupies them with her son, aged sixteen. She uses the front room as a cats' meat shop.[45] In the front room on the first floor on Friday night I had a prayer meeting, and before I went to bed I locked the door of this room, and took the key with me. It was still locked in the morning. John Davies and his family tenant the third floor front, and Mrs. Sarah Cox has the back room on the same floor. She is an old lady I keep out of charity. Mr. Thompson and his wife, with an adopted little girl, have the front room on the second floor. On Saturday morning I called to Thompson at ten minutes to four o'clock. I heard him leave the house. He did not go into the back yard. Two unmarried sisters[46] reside in the second floor back. They work at a cigar factory. When I went down all the tenants were in the house except Mr. Thompson and Mr. Davies. I am not the owner of the house.

Were the front and back doors always left open?—Yes, you can open the front and back doors of any of the houses about there. They are all let out in rooms. People are coming in or going out all the night.

Did you ever see anyone in the passage?—Yes, about a month ago I heard a man on the stairs. I called Thompson, and the man said he was waiting for market.[47]

At what time was this?—Between half-past three and four o'clock. I could hear anyone going through the passage. I did not hear any one going through on Saturday morning.

You heard no cries?—None.

Supposing a person had gone through at half-past three, would that have attracted your attention?—Yes.[48]

---

[44]The "noise" was most likely Davis, Kent, Green and Holland viewing the body.

[45]A shop where horseflesh was ground and sold as food for domestic cats.

[46]There is some slight confusion here. These "sisters" are called "Mr. and Mrs. Copsey" in the *Times* of 13 September and BFS, p. 89 but the "Misses Cooksley" in the *Eastern Post* of 15 September. Sugden calls them "two unmarried sisters," noting their surname was variously transcribed as "Cooksley, Copsey and Huxley" and considers the *Times* to be in error (pp. 83 and 487).

[47]Waiting for the Spitalfields market to open, likely in order to get a day-laborer's job.

[48]Baxter asked this question in relation to Emily Walter's statement (ref. 10 September).

You always hear people going to the back-yard?—Yes; people frequently do go through.

People go there who have no business to do so?—Yes; I daresay they do.

On Saturday morning you feel confident no one did go through?—Yes; I should have heard the sound.

They must have walked purposely quietly?—Yes; or I should have heard them.

BY THE JURY: I should not allow any stranger to go through for an immoral purpose if I knew it.

**Harriett Hardiman**, living at 29, Hanbury-street, catsmeat saleswoman, the occupier of the ground-floor front room, stated: I went to bed on Friday night at half-past ten. My son sleeps in the same room. I did not wake during the night. I was awakened by the trampling through the passage at about six o'clock. My son was asleep, and I told him to go to the back as I thought there was a fire. He returned and said that a woman had been killed in the yard. I did not go out of my room. I have often heard people going through the passage into the yard, but never got up to look who they were.

**John Richardson**, of John-street, Spitalfields, market porter, said: I assist my mother in her business. I went to 29, Hanbury-street, between 4:45 a.m. and 4:50 a.m. on Saturday last. I went to see if the cellar was all secure, as some while ago there was a robbery there of some tools. I have been accustomed to go on market mornings since the time when the cellar was broken in.

Was the front door open?—No, it was closed. I lifted the latch and went through the passage to the yard door.

Did you go into the yard?—No, the yard door was shut. I opened it and sat on the doorstep, and cut a piece of leather off my boot with an old table-knife, about five inches long. I kept the knife upstairs at John-street. I had been feeding a rabbit with a carrot that I had cut up, and I put the knife in my pocket. I do not usually carry it there. After cutting the leather off my boot I tied my boot up, and went out of the house into the market. I did not close the back door. It closed itself. I shut the front door.

How long were you there?—About two minutes at most.

Was it light?—It was getting light, but I could see all over the place.

Did you notice whether there was any object outside?—I could not have failed to notice the deceased had she been lying there then. I saw the body two or three minutes before the doctor came. I was then in the adjoining yard. Thomas Pierman had told me about the murder in the market. When I was on the doorstep I saw that the padlock on the cellar door was in its proper place.

Did you sit on the top step?—No, on the middle step; my feet were on the flags of the yard.

You must have been quite close to where the deceased was found?—Yes, I must have seen her.

You have been there at all hours of the night?—Yes.

Have you ever seen any strangers there?—Yes, plenty, at all hours—both men and women. I have often turned them out. We have had them on our first floor as well, on the landing.

Do you mean to say that they go there for an immoral purpose?—Yes, they do.

At this stage witness was despatched by the coroner to fetch his knife.

**Mrs. Richardson**, recalled, said she had never missed anything, and had such confidence in her neighbours that she had left the doors of some rooms unlocked. A saw and a hammer had been taken from the cellar a long time ago. The padlock was broken open.

Had you an idea at any time that a part of the house or yard was used for an immoral purpose?—Witness (emphatically): No, sir.

Did you say anything about a leather apron?—Yes, my son wears one when he works in the cellar.

THE CORONER: It is rather a dangerous thing to wear, is it not?

WITNESS: Yes. On Thursday, Sept. 6, I found my son's leather apron in the cellar mildewed. He had not used it for a month. I took it and put it under the tap in the yard, and left it there. It was found there on Saturday morning by the police, who took charge of it. The apron had remained there from Thursday to Saturday.

Was this tap used?—Yes, by all of us in the house. The apron was on the stones. The police took away an empty box, used for nails, and the steel out of a boy's gaiter.[49] There was a pan of clean water near to the tap when I went in the yard at six o'clock on Saturday. It was there on Friday night at eight o'clock, and it looked as if it had not been disturbed.

Did you ever know of strange women being found on the first-floor landing?— No.

Your son had never spoken to you about it?—No.[50]

**John Piser** [Pizer] was then called. He said: I live at 22, Mulberry-street,

Commercial-road East. I am a shoe-maker.

Are you known by the nickname of "Leather Apron?"—Yes, sir.[51]

Where were you on Friday night last?—I was at 22, Mulberry-street. On Thursday, the 6th inst. I arrived there.

From where?—From the west end of town.

THE CORONER: I am afraid we shall have to have a better address than that presently. What time did you reach 22, Mulberry-street?—Shortly before eleven p.m.

BY THE CORONER: Who lives at 22, Mulberry-street?—My brother and sister-in-law and my stepmother. I remained indoors there.

BY THE CORONER: Until when?— Until I was arrested by Sergeant Thicke [*sic*],[52] on Monday last at nine a.m.

BY THE CORONER: You say you never left the house during that time?—I never left the house.

BY THE CORONER: Why were you remaining indoors?—Because my brother advised me.

BY THE CORONER: You were the subject of suspicion?—I was the object of a false suspicion.

[By the Coroner] You remained on the advice of your friends?—Yes; I am telling you what I did.

THE CORONER: It was not the best advice that you could have had.[53] You have been released, and are not now in custody?—I am not.

---

[49]A filth or injury protection for the ankle and foot or entire lower leg, usually made from cloth or leather.

[50]Mrs. Richardson's answer is not wholly unexpected in light of the "Disorderly House Act" of 1858.

[51]This is not the same thing as being *the* "Leather Apron," about whom so much was published by the press; see testimony of Sergeant Thick below.

[52]Sergeant William Thick (1845–1930), warrant no. 49889. Member of H (Whitechapel) division and nicknamed "Johnny Upright" in tribute either to his probity or ability to find a suspect to fit a crime. In the case of Pizer, cynicism leans towards the latter explanation (BFS, p. 448).

[53]Probably not, but considering the wild stories of "Leather Apron" in the press, the association of Pizer with them and a not-unreasonable fear that he could be seriously injured were he to go on the streets, Pizer no doubt felt safer hiding with his family than throwing himself on the none-too-tender mercies of the police. The interested reader is directed to Sugden, pp. 57–76.

PISER: I wish to vindicate my character to the world at large.

THE CORONER: I have called you in your own interests, partly with the object of giving you an opportunity of doing so. Can you tell us where you were on Thursday, Aug. 30?

WITNESS (AFTER CONSIDERING): In the Holloway-road.

BY THE CORONER: You had better say exactly where you were. It is important to account for your time from that Thursday to the Friday morning.

BY PIZER: What time, may I ask?

THE CORONER: It was the week before you came to Mulberry-street.

WITNESS: I was staying at a common lodging-house called the Round House, in the Holloway-road.[54]

BY THE CORONER: Did you sleep the night there?—Yes.

BY THE CORONER: At what time did you go in?—On the night of the London Dock fire.[55] I went in about two or a quarter-past. It was on the Friday morning.

BY THE CORONER: When did you leave the lodging-house?—At eleven a.m. on the same day. I saw on the placards, "Another Horrible Murder."

BY THE CORONER: Where were you before two o'clock on Friday morning?—At eleven p.m. on Thursday I had my supper at the Round House.

BY THE CORONER: Did you go out?—Yes, as far as the Seven Sisters-road, and then returned towards Highgate way, down the Holloway-road. Turning, I saw the reflection of a fire. Coming as far as the church in the Holloway-road I saw two constables and the lodging-housekeeper talking together. There might have been one or two constables, I cannot say which.

I asked a constable where the fire was, and he said it was a long way off. I asked him where he thought it was, and he replied: "Down by the Albert Docks." It was then about half-past one, to the best of my recollection. I went as far as Highbury Railway Station on the same side of the way, returned, and then went into the lodging house.

BY THE CORONER: Did any one speak to you about being so late?—No: I paid the night watchman. I asked him if my bed was let, and he said: "They are let by eleven o'clock. You don't think they are to let to this hour." I paid him 4d for another bed. I stayed up smoking on the form of the kitchen, on the right hand side near the fireplace, and then went to bed.

BY THE CORONER: You got up at eleven o'clock?—Yes. The day man came, and told us to get up, as he wanted to make the bed.[56] I got up and dressed, and went down into the kitchen.

BY THE CORONER: Is there anything else you want to say?—Nothing.

BY THE CORONER: When you said the West-end of town did you mean Holloway?—No; another lodging house in Peter-street, Westminster.

THE CORONER: It is only fair to say that the witness's statements can be corroborated.

**William Thicke** [*sic*], detective sergeant, deposed: Knowing that "Leather Apron" was suspected of being concerned in the murder, on Monday morning I arrested Piser at 22, Mulberry-street. I have known him by the name of "Leather Apron" for many years.

BY THE CORONER: When people in

---

[54]Another name for Crossman's lodging-house (Eddleston, p. 193).

[55]This burned the night of 30–31 August at Shadwell Dry Dock and Gowland's Coal Wharf (BFS, p. 136).

[56]Despite the price paid by Pizer, which was common for a single bed, this demonstrates that more than one person might occupy a bed in a typical lodging-house.

the neighbourhood speak of the "Leather Apron" do they mean Piser?—They do.

BY THE CORONER: He has been released from custody?—He was released last night at 9:30.

**John Richardson** (recalled) produced the knife—a much-worn dessert knife—with which he had cut his boot. He added that as it was not sharp enough he had borrowed another one at the market.

BY THE JURY: My mother has heard me speak of people having been in the house. She has heard them herself.[57]

THE CORONER: I think we will detain this knife for the present.

**Henry John Holland**, a boxmaker, stated: As I was passing 29, Hanbury-street, on my way to work in Chiswell-street, at about eight minutes past six on Saturday. I spoke to two of Bayley's [sic] men. An elderly man came out of the house and asked us to have a look in his back yard. I went through the passage and saw the deceased lying in the yard by the back door. I did not touch the body. I then went for a policeman in Spitalfields Market. The officer told me he could not come. I went outside and could find no constable. Going back to the house I saw an inspector run up with a young man, at about twenty minutes past six o'clock. I had told the first policeman that it was a similar case to Buck's-row, and he referred me to two policemen outside the market, but I could not find them. I afterwards complained of the policeman's conduct at the Commercial-street police station the same afternoon.[58]

THE CORONER: There does not seem to have been much delay. The inspector says there are certain spots where constables are stationed with instructions not to leave them. Their duty is to send some one else.

THE FOREMAN OF THE JURY: That is the explanation.

THE CORONER: The doctor will be here first thing tomorrow.

This afternoon the inquiry will be resumed.

Yesterday the supposed bloodstains upon the wall of No. 25, Hanbury-street, were closely examined by the divisional police surgeon and the officers engaged in the case, and the opinion was then formed that they were some kind of sewage deposit. The colour was such as to mislead any but the eye of an expert. Renewed investigation showed that similar discolouration was apparent on the other side of the wall, proceeding from the same cause, apparently; and this fact, taken in conjunction with the medical opinion, was held to render a chemical analysis unnecessary.

A woman named Mrs. Durrell[59] made a statement yesterday to the effect that at about half-past five o'clock on the morning of the murder of Mrs. Chapman she saw a man and a woman conversing outside No. 29, Hanbury-street, the scene of the murder, and that they disappeared very suddenly. Mrs. Durrell was taken to the mortuary, and identified the body of Chapman as that of the woman whom she saw in Hanbury-street. If this identification can be relied upon, it is obviously an important piece of evidence, as it fixes

---

[57]Based on Richardson's previous statements, this would seem to be correct, and his mother was most likely unwilling to publicly acknowledge that the house was a favored trysting-place for prostitutes.

[58]The policeman Holland encountered was on "fixed-point" duty and insisted he could not leave his area under any circumstances. Due to the Whitechapel Murders, such strict interpretation of the rules was subsequently relaxed.

[59]Actually Mrs. Elizabeth Long—some modern accounts still list or view Mrs. Durrell (or Darrell) as a separate person (ref. Long's testimony, 20 September).

with tolerable precision the time at which the murder was committed, and corroborates the statement of John Richardson, who went into the yard at a quarter to five, and has persistently declared that the body was not then on the premises. Davis, the man who first saw the corpse, went into the yard shortly after six o'clock.[60] Assuming, therefore, that the various witnesses have spoken the truth, which there is no reason to doubt, the murder must have been committed between half-past five and six o'clock, and the murderer must have walked through the streets in almost broad daylight. This has naturally strengthened the belief of many of those engaged in the case that the man had not far to go to reach his lodgings.

# THE DAILY TELEGRAPH
Friday, September 14, 1888

Page 3
THE WHITECHAPEL MURDER—
EXTRAORDINARY
REVELATIONS
[*Third Session of Inquest*]

Yesterday Mr. Wynne Baxter, coroner, resumed, at the Working Lads' Institute, Whitechapel-road, his adjourned inquiry relative to the death of Annie Chapman, who was murdered in the back yard of 29, Hanbury-street, on Saturday morning last.

The police were represented by Inspectors Abberline, Helson, and Chandler.

**Joseph Chandler,** Inspector H Division Metropolitan Police, deposed: On Saturday morning, at ten minutes past six,[61] I was on duty in Commercial-street. At the corner of Hanbury-street I saw several men running. I beckoned to them. One of them said, "Another woman has been murdered." I at once went with him to 29, Hanbury-street, and through the passage into the yard. There was no one in the yard. I saw the body of a woman lying on the ground on her back. Her head was towards the back wall of the house, nearly two feet from the wall, at the bottom of the steps, but six or nine inches away from them. The face was turned to the right side, and the left arm was resting on the left breast. The right hand was lying down the right side. Deceased's legs were drawn up, and the clothing was above the knees. A portion of the intestines, still connected with the body, were lying above the right shoulder, with some pieces of skin. There were also some pieces of skin on the left shoulder. The body was lying parallel with the fencing dividing the two yards. I remained there and sent for the divisional surgeon, Mr. Phillips, and to the police-station for the ambulance and for further assistance. When the constables arrived I cleared the passage of people, and saw that no one touched the body until the doctor arrived. I obtained some sacking to cover it before the arrival of the surgeon, who came at about half-past six o'clock, and he, having examined the body, directed that it should be removed to the mortuary. After the body had been taken away I examined the yard, and found a piece of coarse muslin, a small tooth comb, and a pocket hair comb in a case. They were lying near the feet of the woman. A portion

---

[60]Rather, Davis' testimony combined with that of Mrs. Richardson, Hardiman and Chandler suggests he was in the yard at or just before 6:00am. See Commentary 3.

[61]Chandler's timing corresponds more closely with that of Mrs. Richardson, John Davis, Dr. Phillips and Mrs. Hardiman than with James Green, James Kent, or Henry Holland. Chandler's timing is more preferred in this case because of his 8 September police report, which tallies with his inquest testimony.

of an envelope was found near her head, which contained two pills.

What was on the envelope?—On the back there was a seal with the words, embossed in blue, "Sussex Regiment." The other part was torn away. On the other side there was a letter "M" in writing.

A man's handwriting?—I should imagine so.

Any postage stamp?—No. There was a postal stamp "London, Aug. 3, 1888." That was in red. There was another black stamp, which was indistinct.

Any other marks on the envelope?—There were also the letters "Sp" lower down, as if some one had written "Spitalfields." The other part was gone. There were no other marks.[62]

Did you find anything else in the yard?—There was a leather apron, lying in the yard, saturated with water. It was about two feet from the water tap.

Was it shown to the doctor?—Yes. There was also a box, such as is commonly used by casemakers for holding nails. It was empty. There was also a piece of steel, flat, which has since been identified by Mrs. Richardson as the spring of her son's leggings.

Where was that found?—It was close to where the body had been. The apron and nail box have also been identified by her as her property. The yard was paved roughly with stones in parts; in other places it was earth.

Was there any appearance of a struggle there?—No.

Are the palings strongly erected?—No; to the contrary.

Could they support the weight of a man getting over them?—No doubt they might.

Is there any evidence of anybody having got over them?—No. Some of them in the adjoining yard have been broken since. They were not broken then.

You have examined the adjoining yard?—Yes.

Was there any staining as of blood on any of the palings?—Yes, near the body.

Was it on any of the other yards?—No.

Were there no other marks?—There were marks discovered on the wall of No. 25. They were noticed on Tuesday afternoon. They have been seen by Dr. Phillips.

Were there any drops of blood outside the yard of No. 29?—No; every possible examination has been made, but we could find no trace of them. The bloodstains at No. 29 were in the immediate neighbourhood of the body only. There were also a few spots of blood on the back wall, near the head of the deceased, 2ft from the ground. The largest spot was of the size of a sixpence. They were all close together. I assisted in the preparation of the plan produced, which is correct.

Did you search the body?—I searched the clothing at the mortuary. The outside jacket—a long black one, which came down to the knees—had bloodstains round the neck, both upon the inside and out, and two or three spots on the left arm. The jacket was hooked at the top, and buttoned down the front. By the appearance of the garment there did not seem to have been any struggle. A large pocket was worn under the skirt (attached by strings), which I produce. It was torn down the front and also at the side, and it was empty. Deceased wore a black skirt. There was a little blood on the outside. The two petticoats were stained very little; the two bodices were stained with blood round the neck, but they had not been damaged. There was no cut in the clothing at all. The boots were on the feet of deceased.

[62]See Commentary 2 regarding the envelope piece.

They were old. No part of the clothing was torn. The stockings were not blood-stained.

Did you see John Richardson?—I saw him about a quarter to seven o'clock. He told me he had been to the house that morning about a quarter to five. He said he came to the back door and looked down to the cellar, to see if all was right, and then went away to his work.

Did he say anything about cutting his boot?—No.

Did he say that he was sure the woman was not there at that time?—Yes.

BY THE JURY: The back door opens outwards into the yard, and swung on the left hand to the palings where the body was. If Richardson were on the top of the steps he might not have seen the body. He told me he did not go down the steps.[63]

THE FOREMAN OF THE JURY: Reference has been made to the Sussex Regiment and the pensioner. Are you going to produce the man Stanley?

WITNESS: We have not been able to find him as yet.

THE FOREMAN: He is a very important witness. There is evidence that he has associated with the woman week after week. It is important that he should be found.

WITNESS: There is nobody that can give us the least idea where he is. The parties were requested to communicate with the police if he came back. Every inquiry has been made, but nobody seems to know anything about him.

THE CORONER: I should think if that pensioner knows his own business he will come forward himself.

**Sergeant Baugham** [Badham], 31 H, stated that he conveyed the body of the deceased to the mortuary on the ambulance.

Are you sure that you took every portion of the body away with you?—Yes.

Where did you deposit the body?—In the shed, still on the ambulance. I remained with it until Inspector Chandler arrived. Detective-Sergeant Thicke viewed the body, and I took down the description. There were present two women, who came to identify the body, and they described the clothing. They came from 35, Dorset-street.[64]

Who touched the clothing?—Sergeant Thicke. I did not see the women touch the clothing nor the body. I did not see Sergeant Thicke touch the body.

**Inspector Chandler**, recalled, said he reached the mortuary a few minutes after seven. The body did not appear to have been disturbed. He did not stay until the doctor arrived. Police-constable 376 H[65] was left in charge, with the mortuary keeper.

**Robert Marne** [Mann], the mortuary keeper and an inmate of the Whitechapel Union Workhouse, said he received the body at seven o'clock on Saturday morning. He remained at the mortuary until Dr. Phillips came. The door of the mortuary was locked except when two nurses from an infirmary came and undressed the body. No one else touched the corpse. He gave the key into the hands of the police.

THE CORONER: The fact is that Whitechapel does not possess a mortuary. The place is not a mortuary at all. We have no right to take a body there. It is simply a shed belonging to the workhouse officials.

[63]By not going "down the steps," Richardson meant that he did not literally walk into the yard. See also Commentary 3.

[64]One of the women is Amelia Palmer (ref. Palmer's testimony 11 September).

[65]PC Barnes (Begg, p. 64).

Juries have over and over again reported the matter to the District Board of Works. The East-end, which requires mortuaries more than anywhere else, is most deficient. Bodies drawn out of the river have to be put in boxes, and very often they are brought to this workhouse arrangement all the way from Wapping. A workhouse inmate is not the proper man to take care of a body in such an important matter as this.

The foreman of the jury called attention to the fact that a fund to provide a reward had been opened by residents in the neighbourhood, and that Mr. Montagu, M.P., had offered a reward of £100. If the Government also offered a reward some information might be forthcoming.

THE CORONER: I do not speak with any real knowledge, but I am told that the Government have determined not to give any rewards in future, not with the idea to economise but because the money does not get into right channels.

TO WITNESS: Were you present when the doctor was making his post-mortem?—Yes.

Did you see the doctor find the handkerchief produced?—It was taken off the body. I picked it up from off the clothing, which was in the corner of the room. I gave it to Dr. Phillips, and he asked me to put it in some water, which I did.

Did you see the handkerchief taken off the body?—I did not. The nurses must have taken it off the throat.

How do you know?—I don't know.

Then you are guessing?—I am guessing.

THE CORONER: That is all wrong, you know. (To the jury). He is really not the proper man to have been left in charge.[66]

**Timothy Donovan**, the deputy of the lodging-house, 35, Dorset-street, was recalled.

You have seen that handkerchief?—I recognise it as one which the deceased used to wear. She bought it of [*sic*] a lodger, and she was wearing it when she left the lodging-house. She was wearing it three-corner ways, placed round her neck, with a black woollen scarf underneath. It was tied in front with one knot.

THE FOREMAN OF THE JURY: Would you recognise Ted Stanley, the pensioner?

A JURYMAN: Stanley is not the pensioner.

THE CORONER (TO WITNESS): Do you know the name of Stanley?

WITNESS: No.

THE FOREMAN: He has been mentioned, and also "Harry the Hawker."

WITNESS: I know "Harry the Hawker."

THE CORONER, HAVING REFERRED TO THE EVIDENCE, SAID: It may be an inference—there is no actual evidence—that the pensioner was called Ted Stanley.

The Foreman said he referred to the man who came to see the deceased regularly. The man ought to be produced.

THE CORONER (TO WITNESS): Would you recognise the pensioner?—Yes.

When did you see him last?—On Saturday.

Why did you not then send him to the police?—Because he would not stop.

THE FOREMAN: What was he like?—He had a soldierly appearance. He dressed differently at times—sometimes gentlemanly.

A JUROR: He is not Ted Stanley.

**Mr. George Baxter** [Bagster] **Phillips**, divisional-surgeon of police, said: On Saturday last I was called by the police at 6:20 a.m. to 29, Hanbury-street, and arrived at half-past six. I found the body of

---

[66]From his experiences during the Nichols inquest, Baxter was already familiar with Robert Mann and the mortuary set-up.

the deceased lying in the yard on her back, on the left hand of the steps that lead from the passage. The head was about 6in in front of the level of the bottom step, and the feet were towards a shed at the end of the yard. The left arm was across the left breast, and the legs were drawn up, the feet resting on the ground, and the knees turned outwards. The face was swollen and turned on the right side, and the tongue protruded between the front teeth, but not beyond the lips; it was much swollen. The small intestines and other portions were lying on the right side of the body on the ground above the right shoulder, but attached. There was a large quantity of blood, with a part of the stomach above the left shoulder. I searched the yard and found a small piece of coarse muslin, a small-tooth comb, and a pocket-comb, in a paper case, near the railing. They had apparently been arranged there. I also discovered various other articles, which I handed to the police. The body was cold, except that there was a certain remaining heat, under the intestines, in the body. Stiffness of the limbs was not marked, but it was commencing. The throat was dissevered deeply. I noticed that the incision of the skin was jagged, and reached right round the neck. On the back wall of the house, between the steps and the palings, on the left side, about 18in from the ground, there were about six patches of blood, varying in size from a sixpenny piece to a small point, and on the wooden fence there were smears of blood, corresponding to where the head of the deceased laid, and immediately above the part where the blood had mainly flowed from the neck, which was well clotted. Having received instructions soon after two o'clock on Saturday afternoon, I went to the labour-yard of the Whitechapel Union for the purpose of further examining the body and making the usual post-mortem investigation. I was surprised to find that the body had been stripped and was laying ready on the table. It was under great disadvantage I made my examination. As on many occasions I have met with the same difficulty, I now raise my protest, as I have before, that members of my profession should be called upon to perform their duties under these inadequate circumstances.

THE CORONER: The mortuary is not fitted for a post-mortem examination. It is only a shed. There is no adequate convenience, and nothing fit, and at certain seasons of the year it is dangerous to the operator.

THE FOREMAN: I think we can all endorse the doctor's view of it.

THE CORONER: As a matter of fact there is no public mortuary from the City of London up to Bow. There is one at Mile-end, but it belongs to the workhouse, and is not used for general purposes.

EXAMINATION RESUMED: The body had been attended to since its removal to the mortuary, and probably partially washed. I noticed a bruise over the right temple. There was a bruise under the clavicle, and there were two distinct bruises, each the size of a man's thumb, on the fore part of the chest. The stiffness of the limbs was then well-marked. The finger nails were turgid. There was an old scar of long standing on the left of the frontal bone. On the left side the stiffness was more noticeable, and especially in the fingers, which were partly closed. There was an abrasion over the bend of the first joint of the ring finger, and there were distinct markings of a ring or rings—probably the latter. There were small sores on the fingers. The head being opened showed that the membranes of the brain were opaque and the veins loaded with blood of a dark character. There was a large quantity of fluid between the membranes and the substance of the brain. The brain substance was unusually firm, and its cavities also contained a large amount of fluid. The throat had been severed. The incisions of the skin indicated that they had been made from the left side of the neck on a line with the angle of the jaw, carried entirely round and again in front of the neck, and ending at a point about midway between the jaw and the sternum or breast bone on the right hand. There were two distinct clean cuts on the body of the vertebrae on the left side of the spine. They were parallel to each other, and separated by about half an inch. The muscular structures between the side processes of bone of the vertebrae had an appearance as if an attempt had been made to separate the bones of the neck. There are various other mutilations of the body, but I am of opinion that they occurred subsequently to the death of the woman and to the large escape of blood from the neck. The witness, pausing, said: I am entirely in your hands, sir, but is it necessary that I should describe the further mutilations. From what I have said I can state the cause of death.

THE CORONER: The object of the inquiry is not only to ascertain the cause of death, but the means by which it occurred. Any mutilation which took place afterwards may suggest the character of the man who did it. Possibly you can give us the conclusions to which you have come respecting the instrument used.

THE WITNESS: You don't wish for details. I think if it is possible to escape the details it would be advisable. The cause of death is visible from injuries I have described.

THE CORONER: You have kept a record of them?

WITNESS: I have.

THE CORONER: Supposing any one is charged with the offence, they would have to come out then, and it might be a matter of comment that the same evidence was not given at the inquest.

WITNESS: I am entirely in your hands.

THE CORONER: We will postpone that for the present. You can give your opinion as to how the death was caused.

WITNESS: From these appearances I am of opinion that the breathing was interfered with previous to death, and that death arose from syncope, or failure of the heart's action, in consequence of the loss of blood caused by the severance of the throat.

Was the instrument used at the throat the same as that used at the abdomen?—Very probably. It must have been a very sharp knife, probably with a thin, narrow blade, and at least six to eight inches in length, and perhaps longer.

Is it possible that any instrument used by a military man, such as a bayonet, would have done it?—No; it would not be a bayonet.

Would it have been such an instrument as a medical man uses for postmortem examinations?—The ordinary post-mortem case perhaps does not contain such a weapon.

Would any instrument that slaughterers employ have caused the injuries?—Yes; well ground down.

Would the knife of a cobbler or of any person in the leather trades have done?—I think the knife used in those trades would not be long enough in the blade.

Was there any anatomical knowledge displayed?—I think there was. There were indications of it. My own impression is that that anatomical knowledge was only less displayed or indicated in consequence of haste. The person evidently was hindered from making a more complete dissection in consequence of the haste.

Was the whole of the body there?—No; the absent portions being from the abdomen.

Are those portions such as would require anatomical knowledge to extract?—

I think the mode in which they were extracted did show some anatomical knowledge.

You do not think they could have been lost accidentally in the transit of the body to the mortuary?—I was not present at the transit. I carefully closed up the clothes of the woman. Some portions had been excised.

How long had the deceased been dead when you saw her?—I should say at least two hours, and probably more; but it is right to say that it was a fairly cold morning, and that the body would be more apt to cool rapidly from its having lost the greater portion of its blood.[67]

Was there any evidence of any struggle?—No; not about the body of the woman. You do not forget the smearing of blood about the palings.

In your opinion did she enter the yard alive?—I am positive of it. I made a thorough search of the passage, and I saw no trace of blood, which must have been visible had she been taken into the yard.

You were shown the apron?—I saw it myself. There was no blood upon it. It had the appearance of not having been unfolded recently.

You were shown some staining on the wall of No. 25, Hanbury-street?—Yes; that was yesterday morning. To the eye of a novice I have no doubt it looks like blood. I have not been able to trace any signs of it. I have not been able to finish my investigation. I am almost convinced I shall not find any blood.

We have not had any result of your examination of the internal organs. Was there any disease?—Yes. It was not important as regards the cause of death. Disease of the lungs was of long standing, and there was disease of the membranes of the brain. The stomach contained a little food.

Was there any appearance of the deceased having taken much alcohol?—No. There were probably signs of great privation. I am convinced she had not taken any strong alcohol for some hours before her death.

Were any of these injuries self-inflicted?—The injuries which were the immediate cause of death were not self-inflicted.

Was the bruising you mentioned recent?—The marks on the face were recent, especially about the chin and sides of the jaw. The bruise upon the temple and the bruises in front of the chest were of longer standing, probably of days. I am of opinion that the person who cut the deceased's throat took hold of her by the chin, and then commenced the incision from left to right.

Could that be done so instantaneously that a person could not cry out?

WITNESS: By pressure on the throat no doubt it would be possible.

THE FOREMAN: There would probably be suffocation.

THE CORONER: The thickening of the tongue would be one of the signs of suffocation?—Yes. My impression is that she was partially strangled.

Witness added that the handkerchief produced was, when found amongst the clothing, saturated with blood. A similar article was round the throat of the deceased when he saw her early in the morning at Hanbury-street.

It had not the appearance of having been tied on afterwards?—No.

**Sarah Simonds,**[68] a resident nurse at the Whitechapel Infirmary, stated that, in

---

[67]See Commentary 3 regarding time of death.
[68]The *Times* of 14 September calls her "Mary Elizabeth Simonds."

company of the senior nurse,[69] she went to the mortuary on Saturday, and found the body of the deceased on the ambulance in the yard. It was afterwards taken into the shed, and placed on the table. She was directed by Inspector Chandler to undress it, and she placed the clothes in a corner. She left the handkerchief round the neck. She was sure of this. They washed stains of blood from the body. It seemed to have run down from the throat. She found the pocket tied round the waist. The strings were not torn. There were no tears or cuts in the clothes.

INSPECTOR CHANDLER: I did not instruct the nurses to undress the body and to wash it.

The inquiry was adjourned until Wednesday.

# THE DAILY TELEGRAPH
Saturday, September 15, 1888

Page 3
WHITECHAPEL MURDERS—
STATEMENT BY
"THE PENSIONER"
[*Ted Stanley Speaks;
Burial of Annie Chapman*]

The police were yesterday in communication with the pensioner Edward Stanley, who is known to have been frequently in the company of the murdered woman, Chapman. Last night Stanley, who is a man of forty-seven years of age, attended at the Commercial-street Police-station, and made a statement, which was taken down by Inspector Helson. His explanation of his proceedings is regarded as perfectly satisfactory, and as affording no possible ground for associating him in any way with the recent outrage. In view of his relations with the deceased woman, Stanley felt considerable diffidence in coming forward, but after the expressions of opinion by the coroner at the inquest on Thursday, he placed himself in indirect communication with the police. It was by arrangement that he subsequently proceeded to Commercial-street Police Station.

Stanley has given the police a full account of his whereabouts since he last saw the deceased woman, which was on the Sunday preceding the murder. Since then he has been following his usual employment, and has taken no steps to conceal his movements. The man is described as superior to the ordinary run of those who frequent the lodging-houses of Spitalfields. He states that he has known Chapman for about two years, and denies that she was of a quarrelsome disposition. So far as he is aware there was no man with whom she was on bad terms, or who would have any reason for seeking her life. Stanley will attend the inquest when the proceedings are resumed, though his evidence is not expected to throw much light on the tragedy. Yesterday morning a telegram was received from the police at Brentford, stating that a pensioner there answered the description of Stanley, and a detective was at once despatched to make inquiries. When, however, the real Stanley had appeared further investigation was abandoned.[70]

In respect to the pieces of newspaper discovered in Bayley's yard on Tuesday afternoon, where they had been, it was supposed, thrown by the murderer, who had first wiped his hands upon them when

---

[69]Frances Wright (BFS, p. 413).

[70]During the inquest, Stanley acknowledged the nickname, "the pensioner"; however, he did not corroborate that he was the man known by Donovan (ref. Donovan's testimonies, 11 and 14 September, and testimonies of Stanley and Donovan, 20 September).

standing in the yard of No. 25, Hanbury-street, it has been alleged that they have been subjected to analysis, and the stains upon them proved to be those of human blood. On inquiry at the surgery of Mr. Phillips it was stated that these pieces of paper have not been examined as reported, and the doctor was so satisfied of the real nature of the other so-called bloodstains upon the wall that he has not thought it necessary to analyse the matter submitted to him. Mr. Phillips personally has hitherto withheld information from reporters upon conscientious grounds, and Inspector Abberline himself says that the surgeon has not told him what portions of the body were missing.[71] From independent testimony[72] it has been gathered that the description of them would enable the jury, if not the public, to form some idea of the motive of the singular crime, and at the same time it would perhaps enable the police to pursue their investigations on a wider basis,[73] and probably with the object of showing that the guilty man moves in a more respectable rank of life than that to which the larger proportion of the inhabitants of Spitalfields and Whitechapel belong.

The funeral of Annie Chapman took place early yesterday morning, the utmost secrecy having been observed, and none but the undertaker, police, and relatives of the deceased knew anything about the arrangements. Shortly after seven o'clock a hearse drew up outside the mortuary in Montague-street, and the body was quickly removed. At nine o'clock a start was made for Manor Park Cemetery. No coaches followed, as it was desired that public atten-

tion should not be attracted. Mr. Smith and other relatives met the body at the cemetery. The black-covered elm coffin bore the words "Annie Chapman, died Sept. 8, 1888, aged 48 years."[74]

# THE DAILY TELEGRAPH
Thursday, September 20, 1888

Page 2
THE WHITECHAPEL MURDERS
[*Fourth Session of Inquest*]

In the Whitechapel Working Lads' Institute, yesterday afternoon, Mr. Wynne E. Baxter, Coroner for East Middlesex, resumed his inquiry respecting the death of Mrs. Annie Chapman, who was found dead in the yard of the house 29, Hanbury-street, Whitechapel, her body dreadfully cut and mutilated, early on the morning of Saturday, the 8th inst. The following evidence was called:

**Eliza Cooper:** I am a hawker, and lodge in Dorset-street, Spitalfields. Have done so for the last five months. I knew the deceased, and had a quarrel with her on the Tuesday before she was murdered. The quarrel arose in this way: On the previous Saturday she brought Mr. Stanley into the house where I lodged in Dorset-street, and coming into the kitchen asked the people to give her some soap. They told her to ask "Liza"—meaning me. She came to me, and I opened the locker and gave her some. She gave it to Stanley, who went outside and washed himself in the lavatory. When she came back I asked for the

---

[71]This does not demonstrate a lack of knowledge on his part. Contemporary police policy prohibited Abberline from giving out such information.

[72]Contemporary version of the public opinion poll.

[73]This is an erroneous belief which has been carried into modern times. While a full account would be most useful to researchers, the contemporary police already possessed such information.

[74]Chapman is buried in public grave 78, square 148, City of London Cemetery, Manor Park, London (*Ripperana* no. 14, October 1995).

soap, but she did not return it. She said, "I will see you by and bye." Mr. Stanley gave her two shillings, and paid for her bed for two nights. I saw no more of her that night. On the following Tuesday I saw her in the kitchen of the lodging-house. I said, "Perhaps you will return my soap." She threw a halfpenny on the table, and said, "Go and get a halfpennyworth of soap." We got quarrelling over this piece of soap, and we went out to the Ringers Public-house and continued the quarrel. She slapped my face, and said, "Think yourself lucky I don't do more." I struck her in the left eye, I believe, and then in the chest. I afterwards saw that the blow I gave her had marked her face.

When was the last time you saw her alive?—On the Thursday night, in the Ringers.

Was she wearing rings?—Yes, she was wearing three rings on the middle finger of the left hand. They were all brass.

Had she ever a gold wedding ring to your knowledge?—No, not since I have known her. I have known her about fifteen months. I know she associated with Stanley, "Harry the Hawker," and several others.

THE FOREMAN: Are there any of those with whom she associated missing?—I could not tell.

A JURYMAN: Was she on the same relations with them as she was with Stanley?—No, sir. She used to bring them casually into the lodging-house.[75]

**Dr. Phillips**, divisional surgeon of the metropolitan police, was then recalled.

THE CORONER, BEFORE ASKING HIM TO GIVE EVIDENCE, SAID: Whatever may be your opinion and objections, it appears to me necessary that all the evidence that you ascertained from the post-mortem ex-

amination should be on the records of the Court for various reasons, which I need not enumerate. However painful it may be, it is necessary in the interests of justice.

DR. PHILLIPS: I have not had any notice of that. I should have been glad if notice had been given me, because I should have been better prepared to give the evidence; however, I will do my best.

THE CORONER: Would you like to postpone it?

DR. PHILLIPS: Oh, no. I will do my best. I still think that it is a very great pity to make this evidence public. Of course, I bow to your decision; but there are matters which have come to light now which show the wisdom of the course pursued on the last occasion, and I cannot help reiterating my regret that you have come to a different conclusion. On the last occasion, just before I left the court, I mentioned to you that there were reasons why I thought the perpetrator of the act upon the woman's throat had caught hold of her chin. These reasons were that just below the lobe of the left ear were three scratches, and there was also a bruise on the right cheek. When I come to speak of the wounds on the lower part of the body I must again repeat my opinion that it is highly injudicious to make the results of my examination public. These details are fit only for yourself, sir, and the jury, but to make them public would simply be disgusting.

THE CORONER: We are here in the interests of justice, and must have all the evidence before us. I see, however, that there are several ladies and boys in the room, and I think they might retire. (Two ladies and a number of newspaper messenger boys accordingly left the court.)

DR. PHILLIPS AGAIN RAISED AN OBJECTION TO THE EVIDENCE, REMARKING: In giving these details to the public I

---

[75]While researchers view Chapman as a habitual prostitute, Cooper's testimony might indicate it was only a part-time profession.

believe you are thwarting the ends of justice.

THE CORONER: We are bound to take all the evidence in the case, and whether it be made public or not is a matter for the responsibility of the press.

THE FOREMAN: We are of opinion that the evidence the doctor on the last occasion wished to keep back should be heard. (Several Jurymen: Hear, hear.)

THE CORONER: I have carefully considered the matter and have never before heard of any evidence requested being kept back.

DR. PHILLIPS: I have not kept it back; I have only suggested whether it should be given or not.

THE CORONER: We have delayed taking this evidence as long as possible, because you said the interests of justice might be served by keeping it back; but it is now a fortnight since this occurred, and I do not see why it should be kept back from the jury any longer.

DR. PHILLIPS: I am of opinion that what I am about to describe took place after death, so that it could not affect the cause of death, which you are inquiring into.

THE CORONER: That is only your opinion, and might be repudiated by other medical opinion.

DR. PHILLIPS: Very well. I will give you the results of my post-mortem examination. Witness then detailed the terrible wounds which had been inflicted upon the woman, and described the parts of the body which the perpetrator of the murder had carried away with him.[76] He added: I am of opinion that the length of the weapon with which the incisions were inflicted was at least five to six inches in length—probably more—and must have been very sharp. The manner in which they had been done indicated a certain amount of anatomical knowledge.

THE CORONER: Can you give any idea how long it would take to perform the incisions found on the body?

DR. PHILLIPS: I think I can guide you by saying that I myself could not have performed all the injuries I saw on that woman, and effect them, even without a struggle, under a quarter of an hour. If I had done it in a deliberate way, such as would fall to the duties of a surgeon, it would probably have taken me the best part of an hour. The whole inference seems to me that the operation was performed to enable the perpetrator to obtain possession of these parts of the body.

THE CORONER: Have you anything further to add with reference to the stains on the wall?

DR. PHILLIPS: I have not been able to obtain any further traces of blood on the wall.

THE FOREMAN: Is there anything to indicate that the crime in the case of the woman Nicholls was perpetrated with the same object as this?

THE CORONER: There is a difference in this respect, at all events, that the medical expert[77] is of opinion that, in the case of Nicholls, the mutilations were made first.

THE FOREMAN: Was any photograph of the eyes of the deceased taken, in case they should retain any impression of the murderer.[78]

---

[76]Phillips' post-mortem notes have been lost, and no official inquest transcript now exists. The press did not print detailed descriptions of Chapman's abdominal injuries, though the historian can reconstruct what was probably said from a perusal of the *Lancet*, Vol. II, 29 September 1888, and Chief Inspector Swanson's Home Office report of 15 October (HO 144/221/A49301C, ff. 137–145).

[77]Dr. Llewellyn.

[78]There was a popular belief in the 19th century that the eyes of a deceased person retained in their retinas the last image seen before death. The suggestion that Chapman's eyes be photographed was raised (*cont.*)

DR. PHILLIPS: I have no particular opinion upon that point myself. I was asked about it very early in the inquiry, and I gave my opinion that the operation would be useless, especially in this case. The use of a blood-hound was also suggested. It may be my ignorance, but the blood around was that of the murdered woman, and it would be more likely to be traced than the murderer. These questions were submitted to me by the police very early. I think within twenty-four hours of the murder of the woman.

THE CORONER: Were the injuries to the face and neck such as might have produced insensibility?

THE WITNESS: Yes; they were consistent with partial suffocation.

**Mrs. Elizabeth Long** said: I live in Church-row, Whitechapel, and my husband, James Long, is a cart minder. On Saturday, Sept. 8, about half past five o'clock in the morning, I was passing down Hanbury-street, from home, on my way to Spitalfields Market. I knew the time, because I heard the brewer's clock strike half-past five just before I got to the street. I passed 29, Hanbury-street. On the right-hand side, the same side as the house, I saw a man and a woman standing on the pavement talking. The man's back was turned towards Brick-lane, and the woman's was towards the market. They were standing only a few yards nearer Brick-lane from 29, Hanbury-street. I saw the woman's face. Have seen the deceased in the mortuary, and I am sure the woman that I saw in Hanbury-street was the deceased. I did not see the man's face, but I noticed that he was dark. He was wearing a brown low-crowned felt hat. I think he had on a dark coat, though I am not certain. By the look of him he seemed to me a man over forty years of age. He appeared to me to be a little taller than the deceased.

Did he look like a working man, or what?—He looked like a foreigner.

Did he look like a dock labourer, or a workman, or what?—I should say he looked like what I should call shabby-genteel.

Were they talking loudly?—They were talking pretty loudly. I overheard him say to her "Will you?" and she replied, "Yes." That is all I heard, and I heard this as I passed. I left them standing there, and I did not look back, so I cannot say where they went to.

Did they appear to be sober?—I saw nothing to indicate that either of them was the worse for drink.

Was it not an unusual thing to see a man and a woman standing there talking?—Oh no. I see lots of them standing there in the morning.

At that hour of the day?—Yes; that is why I did not take much notice of them.

You are certain about the time?—Quite.

What time did you leave home?—I got out about five o'clock, and I reached the Spitalfields Market a few minutes after half-past five.

THE FOREMAN OF THE JURY: What brewer's clock did you hear strike half-past five?—The brewer's in Brick-lane.[79]

**Edward [Ted] Stanley**, Osborn-place, Osborn-street, Spitalfields, deposed: I am a bricklayer's labourer.

THE CORONER: Are you known by the name of the Pensioner?—Yes.

by the *Star* of 13 September, and Home Secretary Matthews asked if an attempt had been made to photograph the eyes of Elizabeth Stride after her death. Walter Dew also claimed an attempt had been made to photograph the eyes of Mary Kelly, but this cannot be corroborated (ref. Kelly and Sharp, pp. 33–38, and Sugden, pp. 137–138).
[79]See Cadoche's testimony and Baxter's summation, 20 September, and also Commentary 3.

Did you know the deceased?—I did.

And you sometimes visited her?—Yes.

At 35, Dorset-street?—About once there, or twice, something like that. Other times I have met her elsewhere.

When did you last see her alive?—On Sunday, Sept. 2, between one and three o'clock in the afternoon.

Was she wearing rings when you saw her?—Yes, I believe two. I could not say on which finger, but they were on one of her fingers.[80]

What sort of rings were they—what was the metal?—Brass, I should think by the look of them.

Do you know any one she was on bad terms with?—No one, so far as I know. The last time I saw her she had some bruises on her face—a slight black eye, which some other woman had given her. I did not take much notice of it. She told me something about having had a quarrel. It is possible that I may have seen deceased after Sept. 2, as I was doing nothing all that week. If I did see her I only casually met her, and we might have had a glass of beer together. My memory is rather confused about it.

THE CORONER: The deputy of the lodging-house said he was told not to let the bed to the deceased with any other man but you?—It was not from me he received those orders. I have seen it described that the man used to come on the Saturday night, and remain until the Monday morning. I have never done so.

THE FOREMAN: You were supposed to be the pensioner.

THE CORONER: It must be some other man?

WITNESS: I cannot say; I am only speaking for myself.

Are you a pensioner?—Can I object to answer that question, sir? It does not touch on anything here.

CORONER: It was said the man was with her on one occasion when going to receive his pension?

WITNESS: Then it could not have been me. It has been stated all over Europe that it was me, but it was not.

THE CORONER: It will affect your financial position all over Europe when it is known that you are not a pensioner?—It will affect my financial position in this way, sir, in that I am a loser by having to come here for nothing, and may get discharged for not being at my work.

Were you ever in the Royal Sussex Regiment?—Never, sir. I am a law-abiding man, sir, and interfere with no person who does not interfere with me.

THE CORONER: Call the deputy.

**Timothy Donovan**, deputy of the lodging-house, who gave evidence on a previous occasion, was then recalled.

THE CORONER: Did ever you see that man (pointing to Stanley) before?—Yes.

Is he the man you call "the pensioner"?—Yes.

Was it he who used to come with the deceased on Saturday and stay till Monday?—Yes.

Was it he who told you not to let the bed to the deceased with any other man?—Yes; on the second Saturday he told me.

How many times have you seen him there?—I should think five or six Saturdays.

When was he last there?—On the Saturday before the woman's death. He stayed until Monday. He paid for one night, and the woman afterwards came down and paid for the other.

THE CORONER: What have you got to say to that, Mr. Stanley?

---

[80]See Cooper's testimony (20 September) and Palmer's statement to the press (10 September).

STANLEY: You can cross it all out, sir.

Cross your evidence out, you mean?— Oh, no; not mine, but his. It is all wrong.[81] I went to Gosport on Aug. 6 and remained there until Sept. 1.

THE CORONER: Probably the deputy has made a mistake.[82]

A JUROR (TO STANLEY): Had you known deceased at Windsor at all?—No; she told me she knew some one about Windsor, and that she once lived there.

You did not know her there?—No; I have only known her about two years. I have never been to Windsor.

Did you call at Dorset-street on Saturday, the 8th, after the murder?—Yes; I was told by a shoeblack it was she who was murdered, and I went to the lodging-house to ask if it was the fact. I was surprised, and went away.

Did you not give any information to the police that you knew her? You might have volunteered evidence, you know?—I did volunteer evidence. I went voluntarily to Commercial-street Police-station, and told them what I knew.

THE CORONER: They did not tell you that the police wanted you?—Not on the 8th, but afterwards. They told me the police wanted to see me after I had been to the police.

**Albert Cadosch** [Cadoche] deposed: I live at 27, Hanbury-street, and am a carpenter. 27 is next door to 29, Hanbury-street. On Saturday, Sept. 8, I got up about a quarter past five in the morning, and went into the yard. It was then about twenty minutes past five, I should think. As I returned towards the back door I heard a voice say "No" just as I was going through the door. It was not in our yard, but I should think it came from the yard of No. 29. I, however, cannot say on which side it came from. I went indoors, but returned to the yard about three or four minutes afterwards. While coming back I heard a sort of a fall against the fence which divides my yard from that of 29. It seemed as if something touched the fence suddenly.[83]

THE CORONER: Did you look to see what it was?—No.

Had you heard any noise while you were at the end of your yard?—No.

Any rustling of clothes?—No. I then went into the house, and from there into the street to go to my work. It was about two minutes after half-past five as I passed Spitalfields Church.

Do you ever hear people in these yards?—Now and then, but not often.

BY A JURYMAN: I informed the police the same night after I returned from my work.

THE FOREMAN: What height are the palings?—About 5 ft. 6 in. to 6 ft. high.

And you had not the curiosity to look over?—No, I had not.

It is not usual to hear thumps against the palings? They are packing-case makers, and now and then there is a great case goes up against the palings. I was thinking about my work, and not that there was anything the matter, otherwise most likely I would have been curious enough to look over.

THE FOREMAN OF THE JURY: It's a pity you did not.

By the Coroner.—I did not see any

---

[81]In the *Times* of 20 September, Stanley followed this declaration with the unintentionally humourous statement, "When you talk to me, Sir, you talk to an honest man."

[82]Donovan might have confused his dates, but Stanley was clearly unwilling to acknowledge himself as the man Donovan knew as "the pensioner." It is, of course, possible that an embarrassed Stanley simply did not want to admit to more of a relationship with Chapman than he could get away with.

[83]See Long's testimony (20 September), Baxter's summation (27 September) and Commentary 3.

man and woman in the street when I went out.

**William Stevens**, 35, Dorset-street, stated: I am a painter. I knew the deceased. I last saw her alive at twenty minutes past twelve on the morning of Saturday, Sept. 8. She was in the kitchen. She was not the worse for drink.

Had she got any rings on her fingers?— Yes. Shown a piece of an envelope, witness said he believed it was the same as she picked up near the fireplace. Did not notice a crest, but it was about that size, and it had a red postmark on it. She left the kitchen, and witness thought she was going to bed. Never saw her again. Did not know any one that she was on bad terms with.

This was all the evidence obtainable.

A JURYMAN: Is there any chance of a reward being offered by the Home Secretary?

THE FOREMAN: There is already a reward of £100 offered by Mr. Samuel Montagu, M.P.[84] There is a committee getting up subscriptions, and they expect to get about £200. The coroner has already said that the Government are not prepared to offer a reward.

A JUROR: There is more dignity about a Government reward, and I think one ought to be offered.

THE FOREMAN OF THE JURY: There are several ideas of rewards, and it is supposed that about £300 will be got up. It will all be done by private individuals.

THE CORONER: As far as we know, the case is complete.

THE FOREMAN OF THE JURY: It seems to be a case of murder against some person or persons unknown.

It was then agreed to adjourn the inquiry until next Wednesday before deciding upon the terms of the verdict.

# THE DAILY TELEGRAPH
Thursday, September 27, 1888

Page 2
## THE WHITECHAPEL MURDERS—IMPORTANT STATEMENT
[*Fifth and Final Session of Chapman Inquest*]

Yesterday afternoon Mr. Wynne Baxter, coroner for East Middlesex, concluded his inquiry, at the Whitechapel Working Lads' Institute, relative to the death of Mrs. Annie Chapman, whose body was found dreadfully cut and mutilated in the yard of 29, Hanbury-street, Whitechapel, early on the morning of Saturday, the 8th inst.

The Coroner inquired if there was any further evidence to be adduced.

Inspector Chandler replied in the negative.

**The Coroner** then addressed the jury. He said: I congratulate you that your labours are now nearly completed. Although up to the present they have not resulted in the detection of any criminal, I have no doubt that if the perpetrator of this foul murder is eventually discovered, our efforts will not have been useless. The evidence is now on the records of this court, and could be used even if the witnesses were not forthcoming; while the publicity given has already elicited further information, which I shall presently have to mention, and which, I hope I am not sanguine in believing, may perhaps be of the utmost importance. We shall do well to recall the important facts.

The deceased was a widow, forty-seven years of age, named Annie Chapman. Her husband was a coachman living

---

[84]Samuel Montagu (1832–1911), later Lord Swaythling. MP for the Whitechapel division of Tower Hamlets, 1885–1900 (BFS, pp. 302–303).

at Windsor. For three or four years before his death she had lived apart from her husband, who allowed her 10s a week until his death at Christmas, 1886. Evidently she had lived an immoral life for some time, and her habits and surroundings had become worse since her means had failed. Her relations were no longer visited by her, and her brother had not seen her for five months, when she borrowed a small sum from him. She lived principally in the common lodging houses in the neighbourhood of Spitalfields, where such as she herd like cattle, and she showed signs of great deprivation, as if she had been badly fed. The glimpses of life in these dens which the evidence in this case discloses is sufficient to make us feel that there is much in the nineteenth century civilisation of which we have small reason to be proud; but you who are constantly called together to hear the sad tale of starvation, or semi-starvation, of misery, immorality, and wickedness which some of the occupants of the 5,000 beds in this district have every week to relate to coroner's inquests, do not require to be reminded of what life in a Spitalfields lodging-house means. It was in one of these that the older bruises found on the temple and in front of the chest of the deceased were received, in a trumpery quarrel, a week before her death. It was in one of these that she was seen a few hours before her mangled remains were discovered.

On the afternoon and evening of Friday, Sept. 7, she divided her time partly in such a place at 35, Dorset-street, and partly in the Ringers public-house, where she spent whatever money she had; so that between one and two on the morning of Saturday, when the money for her bed is demanded, she is obliged to admit that she is without means, and at once turns out into the street to find it. She leaves there at 1:45 a.m., is seen off the premises by the night watchman, and is observed to turn down Little Paternoster-row into Brushfield-street, and not in the more direct route to Hanbury-street. On her wedding finger she was wearing two or three rings, which appear to have been palpably of base metal, as the witnesses are all clear about their material and value. We now lose sight of her for about four hours, but at half-past five, Mrs. Long is in Hanbury-street[85] on her way from home in Church-street, Whitechapel, to Spitalfields Market. She walked on the northern side of the road going westward, and remembers having seen a man and woman standing a few yards from the place where the deceased is afterwards found. And, although she did not know Annie Chapman, she is positive that that woman was deceased. The two were talking loudly, but not sufficiently so to arouse her suspicions that there was anything wrong. Such words as she overheard were not calculated to do so. The laconic inquiry of the man, "Will you?" and the simple assent of the woman, viewed in the light of subsequent events, can be easily translated and explained. Mrs. Long passed on her way, and neither saw nor heard anything more of her, and this is the last time she is known to have been alive. There is some conflict in the evidence about the time at which the deceased was despatched. It is not unusual to find inaccuracy in such details, but this variation is not very great or very important. She was found dead about six o'clock. She was not in the yard when Richardson was there at 4:50 a.m. She was talking outside the house at half-past five when Mrs. Long passed them. Cadosh says it was about 5:20 when he was in the backyard of the adjoining house, and heard a voice say

---

[85]Baxter gives the erroneous implication that Mrs. Long saw the couple at precisely 5:30am, but see Long's testimony on 20 September and also Commentary 3.

"No," and three or four minutes afterwards a fall against the fence; but if he is out of his reckoning but a quarter of an hour,[86] the discrepancy in the evidence of fact vanishes, and he may be mistaken, for he admits that he did not get up till a quarter past five, and that it was after the half-hour when he passed Spitalfields clock. It is true that Dr. Phillips thinks that when he saw the body at 6:30 the deceased had been dead at least two hours, but he admits that the coldness of the morning and the great loss of blood may affect his opinion; and if the evidence of the other witnesses be correct, Dr. Phillips has miscalculated the effect of those forces. But many minutes after Mrs. Long passed the man and woman cannot have elapsed before the deceased became a mutilated corpse in the yard of 29, Hanbury-street, close by where she was last seen by any witness.

This place is a fair sample of a large number of houses in the neighbourhood. It was built, like hundreds of others, for the Spitalfields weavers, and when handlooms were driven out by steam and power, these were converted into dwellings for the poor. Its size is about such as a superior artisan would occupy in the country, but its condition is such as would to a certainty leave it without a tenant. In this place seventeen persons were living, from a woman and her son sleeping in a cat's-meat shop on the ground floor to Davis and his wife and their three grown-up sons, all sleeping together in an attic. The street door and the yard door were never locked, and the passage and yard appear to have been constantly used by people who had no legitimate business there. There is little

doubt that the deceased knew the place, for it was only 300 or 400 yards from where she lodged. If so, it is quite unnecessary to assume that her companion had any knowledge[87]—in fact, it is easier to believe that he was ignorant both of the nest of living beings by whom he was surrounded, and of their occupations and habits. Some were on the move late at night, some were up long before the sun. A carman, named Thompson, left the house for his work as early as 3:50 a.m.; an hour later John Richardson was paying the house a visit of inspection; shortly after 5:15 Cadosh, who lived in the next house, was in the adjoining yard twice.[88]

Davis, the carman, who occupied the third floor front, heard the church clock strike a quarter to six, got up, had a cup of tea, and went into the back yard, and was horrified to find the mangled body of deceased. It was then a little after six a.m.— a very little, for at ten minutes past the hour Inspector Chandler had been informed of the discovery[89] while on duty in Commercial-street. There is nothing to suggest that the deceased was not fully conscious of what she was doing. It is true that she had passed through some stages of intoxication, for although she appeared perfectly sober to her friend who met her in Dorset-street at five o'clock the previous evening, she had been drinking afterwards; and when she left the lodging-house shortly before two o'clock the night watchman noticed that she was the worse for drink, but not badly so, while the deputy asserts that, though she had evidently been drinking, she could walk straight, and it was probably only malt

[86]Baxter preferred Long's timing over Cadoche's, because she allegedly saw the killer. See Commentary 3.
[87]Baxter's astute observation points out that each victim most likely led her murderer to the place where she was killed.
[88]Even though Baxter did not necessarily accept Cadoche's timing, he did believe Cadoche's testimony of hearing "no" and a noise against the fence.
[89]Baxter here recognized the conflict between the time of "after six a.m." for Davis finding the body and the time of Inspector Chandler being notified.

liquor that she had taken, and its effects would pass off quicker than if she had taken spirits. Consequently it is not surprising to find that Mrs. Long saw nothing to make her think that the deceased was the worse for drink. Moreover, it is unlikely that she could have had the opportunity of getting intoxicants. Again the post-mortem examination shows that while the stomach contained a meal of food there was no sign of fluid and no appearance of her having taken alcohol, and Dr. Phillips is convinced that she had not taken any alcohol for some time. The deceased, therefore, entered the yard in full possession of her faculties; although with a very different object from her companion. From the evidence which the condition of the yard affords and the medical examination discloses, it appears that after the two had passed through the passage and opened the swing-door at the end, they descended the three steps into the yard. On their left hand side there was a recess between those steps and the palings. Here a few feet from the house and a less distance from the paling they must have stood. The wretch must have then seized the deceased, perhaps with Judas-like approaches. He seized her by the chin. He pressed her throat, and while thus preventing the slightest cry, he at the same time produced insensibility and suffocation. There is no evidence of any struggle. The clothes are not torn. Even in these preliminaries, the wretch seems to have known how to carry out efficiently his nefarious work. The deceased was then lowered to the ground, and laid on her back; and although in doing so she may have fallen slightly against the fence, this movement was probably effected with care. Her throat was then cut in two places with sav-

age determination, and the injuries to the abdomen commenced. All was done with cool impudence and reckless daring; but, perhaps, nothing is more noticeable than the emptying of her pockets, and the arrangement of their contents with business-like precision in order near her feet.

The murder seems, like the Buck's-row case, to have been carried out without any cry. Sixteen people were in the house.[90] The partitions of the different rooms are of wood. Davis was not asleep after three a.m., except for three-quarters of an hour, or less, between five and 5:45. Mrs. Richardson only dozed after three a.m., and heard no noise during the night. Mrs. Hardman, who occupies the front ground-floor room, did not awake until the noise succeeding the finding of the body had commenced, and none of the occupants of the houses by which the yard is surrounded heard anything suspicious. The brute who committed the offence did not even take the trouble to cover up his ghastly work, but left the body exposed to the view of the first comer. This accords but little with the trouble taken with the rings, and suggests either that he had at length been disturbed, or that as the daylight broke a sudden fear suggested the danger of detection that he was running. There are two things missing. Her rings had been wrenched from her fingers and have not been found, and the uterus has been removed. The body has not been dissected, but the injuries have been made by some one who had considerable anatomical skill and knowledge.[91] There are no meaningless cuts. It was done by one who knew where to find what he wanted, what difficulties he would have to contend against, and how he should use his knife, so as to abstract the organ without injury

---

[90]Seventeen people lived in the house, but Thompson had left for work prior Chapman's death.

[91]Baxter over-emphasized Phillips' 14 September comments regarding the skill of Chapman's killer, perhaps as groundwork for the theory he was soon to advance.

to it. No unskilled person could have known where to find it, or have recognised it when it was found. For instance, no mere slaughterer of animals could have carried out these operations.[92] It must have been some one accustomed to the post-mortem room.

The conclusion that the desire was to possess the missing part seems overwhelming. If the object were robbery, these injuries were meaningless, for death had previously resulted from the loss of blood at the neck. Moreover, when we find an easily accomplished theft of some paltry brass rings and such an operation, after, at least, a quarter of an hour's work, and by a skilled person, we are driven to the deduction that the mutilation was the object, and the theft of the rings was only a thin-veiled blind, an attempt to prevent the real intention being discovered. Had not the medical examination been of a thorough and searching character, it might easily have been left unnoticed. The difficulty in believing that this was the real purport of the murderer is natural. It is abhorrent to our feelings to conclude that a life should be taken for so slight an object; but, when rightly considered, the reasons for most murders are altogether out of proportion to the guilt. It has been suggested that the criminal is a lunatic with morbid feelings. This may or may not be the case; but the object of the murderer appears palpably shown by the facts, and it is not necessary to assume lunacy, for it is clear that there is a market for the object of the murder. To show you this, I must mention a fact which at the same time proves the assistance which publicity and the newspaper press afford in the detection of crime.

Within a few hours of the issue of the morning papers containing a report of the medical evidence given at the last sitting of the Court, I received a communication from an officer of one of our great medical schools, that they had information which might or might not have a distinct bearing on our inquiry. I attended at the first opportunity, and was told by the sub-curator of the Pathological Museum that some months ago an American had called on him, and asked him to procure a number of specimens of the organ that was missing in the deceased. He stated his willingness to give £20 for each, and explained that his object was to issue an actual specimen with each copy of a publication on which he was then engaged. Although he was told that his wish was impossible to be complied with, he still urged his request. He desired them preserved, not in spirits of wine, the usual medium, but in glycerine, in order to preserve them in a flaccid condition, and he wished them sent to America direct. It is known that this request was repeated to another institution of a similar character. Now, is it not possible that the knowledge of this demand may have incited some abandoned wretch to possess himself of a specimen. It seems beyond belief that such inhuman wickedness could enter into the mind of any man, but unfortunately our criminal annals prove that every crime is possible. I need hardly say that I at once communicated my information to the Detective Department at Scotland-yard. Of course I do not know what use has been made of it, but I believe that publicity may possibly further elucidate this fact, and, therefore, I have not withheld from you my knowledge. By means of the press some further explanation may be forthcoming from America if not from here.

---

[92]Baxter's judgment on this matter was made too quickly, but was done so in light of Phillips' opinion of the killer's skill and of an individual who, "some months ago," requested uteri samples from the Pathological Museum.

I have endeavoured to suggest to you the object with which this offence was committed, and the class of person who must have perpetrated it.[93] The greatest deterrent from crime is the conviction that detection and punishment will follow with rapidity and certainty, and it may be that the impunity with which Mary Ann Smith and Anne Tabram were murdered suggested the possibility of such horrid crimes as those which you and another jury have been recently considering. It is, therefore, a great misfortune that nearly three weeks have elapsed without the chief actor in this awful tragedy having been discovered. Surely, it is not too much even yet to hope that the ingenuity of our detective force will succeed in unearthing this monster. It is not as if there were no clue to the character of the criminal or the cause of his crime. His object is clearly divulged. His anatomical skill carries him out of the category of a common criminal, for his knowledge could only have been obtained by assisting at post-mortems, or by frequenting the post-mortem room. Thus the class in which search must be made, although a large one, is limited. Moreover it must have been a man who was from home, if not all night, at least during the early hours of Sept. 8. His hands were undoubtedly blood-stained, for he did not stop to use the tap in the yard as the pan of clean water under it shows. If the theory of lunacy be correct— which I very much doubt—the class is still further limited; while, if Mrs. Long's memory does not fail, and the assumption be correct that the man who was talking to the deceased at half-past five was the culprit, he is even more clearly defined. In addition to his former description, we should know that he was a foreigner of dark complexion, over forty years of age, a little taller than the deceased, of shabby-genteel appearance, with a brown deerstalker hat on his head, and a dark coat on his back.

If your views accord with mine, you will be of opinion that we are confronted with a murder of no ordinary character, committed not from jealousy, revenge, or robbery, but from motives less adequate than the many which still disgrace our civilisation, mar our progress, and blot the pages of our Christianity. I cannot conclude my remarks without thanking you for the attention you have given to the case, and the assistance you have rendered me in our efforts to elucidate the truth of this horrible tragedy.

**The Foreman**: We can only find one verdict—that of wilful murder against some person or persons unknown. We were about to add a rider with respect to the condition of the mortuary, but that having been done by a previous jury it is unnecessary.

A verdict of wilful murder against a person or persons unknown was then entered.

# Annie Chapman— Commentary

## DAVE YOST

### 1. The Mysterious Coins

The alleged coins found by Annie Chapman's body might be viewed as an important myth associated with the case, because the presence of these supposed relics have given theorists sufficient

---

[93]Baxter was tentatively, if not overtly, suggesting that a doctor committed the crimes for the purpose of obtaining uteri. However, the *Lancet* (29 September) and the *British Medical Journal* (6 October) openly criticized the suggestion.

motivations for their proposed suspects. So it must be asked—were the coins really there?

On 10 September, the *Telegraph* reported that coins were found at the Chapman murder scene:

> In the pockets there were a handkerchief, two small combs, and an envelope with the seal of the Sussex Regiment. There were also found two farthings polished brightly, and, according to some, these coins had been passed off as half-sovereigns upon the deceased by her murderer [10 September, p. 3].

> With regard to the bright farthings found on the deceased, a woman has stated that a man accosted her on Saturday morning and gave her two "half-sovereigns," but that, when he became violent, she screamed and he ran off. She discovered afterwards that the "half-sovereigns" were two brass medals. It is said that this woman did accompany the man, who seemed as if he would kill her, to a house in Hanbury-street, possibly No. 29, at 2.30 a.m. [10 September, p. 3].

> The hapless prostitute butchered on Saturday morning in the back-yard of No. 29, Hanbury-street, had in her pocket two bright farthings only—possibly passed off upon her as half-sovereigns... [10 September, p. 4].

But throughout the remainder of September, the *Telegraph* reported nothing else about these alleged coins, and there was no mention of them during the inquest. If they existed, it might be understandable why the police and Dr. Phillips never mentioned them at the inquest. Withholding a minor detail about a crime from the public is a common tactic used to distinguish the real culprit from people who merely confess without culpability. Yet, oddly, the coins are not mentioned in MEPO 3/140, the main Scotland Yard file; this alone would seem to be the best indication that neither Dr. Phillips nor Inspector Chandler discovered any type of coin at the murder scene.

Along with Chandler and Phillips, there were others at the scene or with the body who also did not discover any coins. Sergeant Badham conveyed the body to the mortuary; PC Barnes oversaw the body at the mortuary; Sergeant Thick viewed the body at the mortuary; and, there were two nurses—Sarah Simonds and Frances Wright—who stripped the body. There were simply too many people who never noted the coins' existence for such items to have been merely overlooked until a news reporter showed up.

Could the coins have been stolen? While anything is possible (such as a newspaper mixing two unrelated incidents), the answer would be most likely not. If the coins were stolen prior to Chandler's arrival, then there would be no basis for that part of the story. Additionally, there were too many witnesses watching the inspection of the yard, the examination of the body, and the conveyance of the body. Along with people gawking from adjoining yards and back windows, there were several hundred people in the street by the time the body was moved. Had anyone removed the coins from the scene, separately from the other items, chances are it would have been quickly noted. The idea that the coins might have been stolen after the body was removed from the back-yard would seem to be not very possible either, considering the thoroughness of Chandler and Phillips' examinations of yard and body.

The singular aspect of the *Telegraph*'s report on 10 September was presented on page 3, "a woman stated that a man accosted her ... and gave her two 'half-sovereigns.'" By all accounts, this woman is known as Emily Walter. She informed the police that she and a man were in the backyard of 29 Hanbury Street between 2.00–2.30 on the morning of Chapman's death. Some modern writers have a tendency to discount Walter's story, either because she did not testify at the inquest or because she was not mentioned in an official report. She cannot necessarily be dismissed out of hand, however, because the police published the description of the man who accosted her:

> At eight o'clock last night [9 September] the Scotland-yard authorities had come to a definite conclusion as to the description of the murderer of two, at least, of the hapless women found dead at the East-end, and the following is the official telegram despatched to every station throughout the metropolis and suburbs: "Commercial-street, 8:20 p.m.—Description of a man wanted, who entered a passage of the house at which the murder was committed with a prostitute, at two a.m. the 8th. Aged thirty-seven, height 5 ft. 7 in., rather dark, beard and moustache; dress, short dark jacket, dark vest and trousers, black scarf and black felt hat; spoke with a foreign accent" [*Telegraph*, 10 September, p. 3].

These details could only have come from Walter. She probably did not testify because her statement had no direct bearing on Chapman's death; yet the police were willing to follow every lead, which included sending dispatches about this description.

The mysterious vanishing coin aspect of the Chapman case stems from mixing two incidents which are unrelated to each other—Walter being accosted and Chapman's death. There were no coins at the Chapman murder scene, but Emily Walter was given two fake half-sovereigns for her troubles.

## 2. A Fragment of an Envelope

Unlike the mysterious coins, no doubt exists that a piece of envelope was at the murder scene. However, modern attempts to determine the envelope's author or recipient are even more hopeless now than they were for the contemporary police, who spent vain energy in trying to locate the original letter's author.

During the third day of the inquest, Inspector Chandler informed the court what was on the envelope piece:

> A portion of an envelope was found near her head, which contained two pills.
> What was on the envelope?—On the back there was a seal with the words, embossed in blue, "Sussex Regiment." The other part was torn away. On the other side there was a letter "M" in writing.
> A man's handwriting?—I should imagine so.
> Any postage stamp?—No. There was a postal stamp "London, Aug. 3, 1888." That was in red. There was another black stamp, which was indistinct.
> Any other marks on the envelope?—There were also the letters "Sp" lower down, as if some one had written "Spitalfields." The other part was gone. There were no other marks [*Telegraph*, 14 September, p. 3].

The Scotland Yard files bear out the *Telegraph*'s report, adding that a "2" preceded the "Sp." Yet the Sussex Regiment seal was more coincidental than confirmational, since the public could purchase Sussex Regiment envelopes and stationary (MEPO 3/140, ff. 15 and 19).

However, some disagreement exists over the postal stamp's date. The *Telegraph* of 14 September reported "Aug. 3," Home Office file HO144/221/A49301C (8a), ff. 137–146 states "23rd Augst," and the latest edition of the *Jack the Ripper A–Z* uses "28 August." A natural tendency would be to favor an official file over a news report; it is very possible that the reporter heard "third" instead of "twenty-third," and a misreading of "August 23" might easily produce "August 28." Nonetheless, does the postal date contain any significance for the modern researcher? Thursday, 23 August saw the second and last day of the Tabram inquest. The media did not play up this murder; in fact, the *Telegraph* did not even report the first day of her inquest, while the *Times* gave it minimal coverage compared to the canonical five. Despite the coincidence, nothing significant is forthcoming without many assumptions.

The text of the envelope piece offers very little with which to work in order to determine who sent it or who received it: "M," "2," and "Sp." Many will agree that "2 ... Sp" could refer to an address in Spitalfields. Without the street name, however, there is no way to properly ascertain to which, if any, part of Spitalfields the letter was originally sent. The "M" is generally accepted as the first letter in a name, but it is unknown which initial it represents—first, middle, or last. There are quite a few "M" names to review and compare to contemporary census records, but such a comparison would be fruitless, anyway, given the number of transient classes who might have been around in 1888 but not in 1881. Additionally, if the "M" referred to "Mr.," "Mrs." or "Miss," then the issue of identification is even more confounded. This difficulty was noted by Inspector Chandler on 15 September: "35 Dorset Street is a common lodging-house and frequented by a great many strangers" (MEPO 3/140, f. 20). In other words, given the transient nature of even the *permanent* locals, the discarded envelope could just as easily have been picked off the street by one of Chapman's fellow lodgers as it could have been dropped in the kitchen by an unknown who stayed for only one night. Additionally, the torn condition of the envelope piece would indicate that several people had taken advantage of its presence.

On 15 September, Chandler reported how Chapman came to possess the envelope piece and why. Four days later, on the fourth day of the inquest, William Stevens presented that information to the court:

> I last saw her alive at twenty minutes past twelve on the morning of Saturday, Sept. 8. She was in the kitchen. She was not the worse for drink... Shown a piece of an envelope, witness said he believed it was the same as she picked up near the fireplace. Did not notice a crest, but it was about that size, and it had a red postmark on it. She left the kitchen, and witness thought she was going to bed [*Telegraph*, 20 September, p. 2].

In addition to what Stevens testified in court, he previously informed the police that: "as she [Chapman] was handling the box [with two pills] it came to pieces. She took out the pills and picked up a piece of paper from the kitchen floor near the fireplace, and wrapped the pills up in it" (MEPO 3/140, ff. 19–20).

The envelope, sadly, is a happenstance. It has no bearing on Chapman's death or her killer.

### 3. Time of Death

Even though Chapman's time of death is generally accepted as being at or around 5:30am, it is prudent to properly review the question, "When did Annie Chapman die?" Therefore, a detailed look will be given to Dr. Phillips' testimony, John Richardson's statements and information from Elizabeth Long and Albert Cadoche.

Dr. Phillips examined Chapman's body *in situ* at approximately 6:30am, and noted several aspects about its condition (all quotes from the *Telegraph* of 14 September, p. 3):

> The body was cold, except that there was a certain remaining heat, under the intestines, in the body. Stiffness of the limbs was not marked, but it was commencing ... on the wooden fence there were smears of blood, corresponding to where the head of the deceased laid, and immediately above the part where the blood had mainly flowed from the neck, which was well clotted.

The autopsy was conducted after 2:00pm that day, at which time Phillips noted the further advance of rigor mortis, along with the condition of Chapman's brain:

> The stiffness of the limbs was then well-marked. The finger nails were turgid... On the left side the stiffness was more noticeable, and especially in the fingers, which were partly closed.... The head being opened showed that the membranes of the brain were opaque and the veins loaded with blood of a dark character. There was a large quantity of fluid between the membranes and the substance of the brain. The brain substance was unusually firm, and its cavities also contained a large amount of fluid.

Phillips presented the bulk of his findings at the inquest on 13 September, giving his view regarding Chapman's time of death: "How long had the deceased been dead when you saw her?—I should say at least two hours, and probably more..."

This indicates that Chapman died at approximately 4:30am, or earlier; however, Phillips knew that such a judgment was not as an exact a science as some crime-fiction writers might portray: "...but it is right to say that it was a fairly cold morning, and that the body would be more apt to cool rapidly from its having lost the greater portion of its blood." Dr. Phillips' next statement qualifies much, because without proper liver or rectal temperatures, time of death via rigor mortis is guessing. Several factors can speed up a body's state of rigor, providing a false impression for estimating time of death: air temperature, physique, exposed organs, health, location, alcohol or drug ingestion, etc. While Phillips opined that Chapman may not have been the worse for drink— "I am convinced she had not taken any strong alcohol for some hours before her death"—there were other conditions that quickened Chapman's state of rigor:

1. *Disease*: "Disease of the lungs was of long standing, and there was disease of the membranes of the brain."
2. *Exposed Organs*: "The small intestines and other portions were lying on the right side of the body on the ground above the right shoulder, but attached."
3. *Loss of Blood*: "There was a large quantity of blood, with a part of the stomach above the left shoulder."
4. *Lack of Nutrition*: "There were probably signs of great privation... The stomach contained a little food."

Even though body size will play a role in how quickly rigor will set in (*i.e.,* quicker for a thin person; slower for a heavy-set person), the first-three hours will not see a significant difference based on the person's physique [Lane, *Encyclopedia of Forensic Science*, Headline Publishing, 1993, pp. 616–620].

The culmination of these factors worked to quicken Chapman's state of rigor; hence, she appeared to have been dead for longer than she was. Dr. Phillips implied that Chapman might not have died at approximately 4:30am—correct. She died after 4:30am. And it will be seen how other witnesses corroborate this view.

Like many others, the testimony of John Richardson is self-explanatory on one hand, and requires clarification on the other. There is little doubt as to when and why Richardson was in the backyard of 29 Hanbury Street:

> I went to 29, Hanbury-street, between 4:45 a.m. and 4:50 a.m. on Saturday last [8 Sep]. I went to see if the cellar was all secure, as some while ago there was a robbery there of some tools. I have been accustomed to go on market mornings since the

time when the cellar was broken in [*Telegraph*, 13 September, p. 3].

Richardson then described his movements from the time he arrived, to the time he departed:

[Coroner] Was the front door open?—No, it was closed. I lifted the latch and went through the passage to the yard door.
[Coroner] Did you go into the yard?—No, the yard door was shut. I opened it and sat on the doorstep, and cut a piece of leather off my boot with an old table-knife, about five inches long. I kept the knife upstairs at John-street. I had been feeding a rabbit with a carrot that I had cut up, and I put the knife in my pocket. I do not usually carry it there. After cutting the leather off my boot I tied my boot up, and went out of the house into the market. I did not close the back door. It closed itself. I shut the front door.
[Coroner] How long were you there?—About two minutes at most.
[Coroner] Was it light?—It was getting light, but I could see all over the place.
[Coroner] Did you notice whether there was any object outside?—I could not have failed to notice the deceased had she been lying there then. I saw the body two or three minutes before the doctor came. I was then in the adjoining yard. Thomas Pierman had told me about the murder in the market. When I was on the doorstep I saw that the padlock on the cellar door was in its proper place.
[Coroner] Did you sit on the top step?—No, on the middle step; my feet were on the flags of the yard.
[Coroner] You must have been quite close to where the deceased was found?—Yes, I must have seen her [*Telegraph*, 13 September, p. 3].

There would seem to be little to detract from these statements, unless a researcher is simply convinced that Richardson was merely lying. Yet some potential confusion does exist, because of Inspector Chandler's testimony at the inquest:

[Coroner] Did you see John Richardson?—I saw him about a quarter to seven o'clock. He told me he had been to the house that morning about a quarter to five. He said he came to the back door and looked down to the cellar, to see if all was right, and then went away to his work.
[Coroner] Did he say anything about cutting his boot?—No.
[Coroner] Did he say that he was sure the woman was not there at that time?—Yes.
BY THE JURY: The back door opens outwards into the yard, and swung on the left hand to the palings where the body was. If Richardson were on the top of the steps he might not have seen the body. He told me he did not go down the steps [*Telegraph*, 14 September, p. 3].

Based on Chandler's comments only, it would seem possible for Richardson to have missed a great deal. Someone could easily opine that Richardson opened the yard door sufficient for him to see the cellar door, turn around, then leave for work, never placing himself in a position to know if a body was there or not. Yet Richardson clarified what he meant by "not going into the yard"—he did not walk down the steps and literally walk into the yard; however, he did sit down on the middle step with his feet in the yard. From that position, he could not have missed seeing a five foot body that would have been only six to nine inches away from him. And there was sufficient light at the time for him to not only see if the cellar doors were still securely padlocked, but to notice a dead body, if it had been there—dawn broke at 4:51am and sunrise occurred at 5:25am. Additionally, a contemporary sketch from the *Penny Illustrated Paper and Illustrated Times* has recently surfaced showing the backyard as it was at the time of the murder. It readily shows an "awning" located above the cellar doors at such a height to confirm that Richardson would most likely had to have sat on the steps, as he claimed, in order to properly see the cellar door's padlock.

Inspector Chandler did not know the full story; hence, he could only relate some of the events. It was not until Coroner Baxter questioned Richardson that the real story came out. And Richardson's information clearly shows that Chapman's body was not in the back yard prior to 4:45am.

The last sightings of Chapman are known via the testimonies of Elizabeth Long and Albert Cadoche. Their information is important because it helps establish the chain of events with respect to Chapman's final movements and subsequent death. Yet, unfortunately, neither Long nor Cadoche's statements are as ironclad as a researcher would like. Long admitted that seeing such a couple was not unusual and that she did not pay very close attention to them:

> [Coroner] Were they talking loudly?—They were talking pretty loudly. I overheard him say to her "Will you?" and she replied, "Yes." That is all I heard, and I heard this as I passed. I left them standing there, and I did not look back, so I cannot say where they went to.
>
> [Coroner] Did they appear to be sober?—I saw nothing to indicate that either of them was the worse for drink.
>
> Was it not an unusual thing to see a man and a woman standing there talking?—Oh no. I see lots of them standing there in the morning.
>
> [Coroner] At that hour of the day?—Yes; that is why I did not take much notice of them [*Telegraph*, 20 September, p. 2].

Cadoche saw neither who nor what produced the noise about which he testified, and acknowledged that "thumps" against the fence were not uncommon:

> As I returned towards the back door I heard a voice say "No" just as I was going through the door. It was not in our yard, but I should think it came from the yard of No. 29. I, however, cannot say on which side it came from. I went indoors, but returned to the yard about three or four minutes afterwards. While coming back I heard a sort of a fall against the fence which divides my yard from that of 29. It seemed as if something touched the fence suddenly.
>
> THE CORONER: Did you look to see what it was?—No.
>
> [Coroner] Had you heard any noise while you were at the end of your yard?—No.
>
> Any rustling of clothes?—No. I then went into the house, and from there into the street to go to my work. It was about two minutes after half-past five as I passed Spitalfields Church.
>
> [Coroner] Do you ever hear people in these yards?—Now and then, but not often.
>
> BY A JURYMAN: I informed the police the same night after I returned from my work.
>
> THE FOREMAN: What height are the palings?—About 5 ft. 6 in. to 6 ft. high.
>
> [Coroner] And you had not the curiosity to look over?—No, I had not.
>
> [Coroner] It is not usual to hear thumps against the palings?—They are packing-case makers, and now and then there is a great case goes up against the palings [*Telegraph*, 20 September, p. 2].

Nevertheless, most students of the case agree that Long saw Chapman and accept that Cadoche overheard Chapman. But in so acknowledging these events as accurate, the differences between Long and Cadoche's statements have to be recognized also. These differences do not necessarily make either of them more important a witness than the other, because each one relates only part of the story. However, the primary difference does affect the manner in how the chain of events is viewed.

The times given by Long and by Cadoche clearly indicate that Cadoche would have overheard Chapman and the killer from the backyard (c.5:20) before

Long saw Chapman and the killer in the street [c.5:30]. This scenario is interesting but unlikely. Because Chapman was in the backyard to indulge in quick prostitution and obtain doss money, it is doubtful that she would have been there, haggled, and left, only to return again with the same man within a few minutes. Baxter recognized this "discrepancy" during the last day of the inquest:

> There is some conflict in the evidence about the time at which the deceased was despatched. It is not unusual to find inaccuracy in such details, but this variation is not very great or very important... She [Chapman] was talking outside the house at half-past five when Mrs. Long passed them. Cadosh says it was about 5:20 when he was in the backyard of the adjoining house, and heard a voice say "No," and three or four minutes afterwards a fall against the fence; but if he is out of his reckoning but a quarter of an hour, the discrepancy in the evidence of fact vanishes, and he may be mistaken, for he admits that he did not get up till a quarter past five, and that it was after the half-hour when he passed Spitalfields clock [*Telegraph*, 27 September, p. 2].

Baxter accepted Long's information as more important, because she saw Chapman with a man; hence, altering Cadoche's timing to coincide with Long's seemed to be the reasonable course of action. This means that Long saw Chapman, then Cadoche overheard Chapman, which is indeed reasonable (and generally accepted), but that is not the final solution. Other bits of information, which will build a more complete story, might negate part or all of Baxter's view.

During his coroner's summation, Baxter incorrectly reiterated when Long was near 29 Hanbury Street, noting it was "at half-past five when Mrs. Long passed them." This comment is understandable if we accept he might have recalled only the

first part of Long's testimony: "On Saturday, Sept. 8, about half past five o'clock in the morning, I was passing down Hanbury-street, from home, on my way to Spitalfields Market" (*Telegraph*, 20 September, p. 2). However, Long qualified the first part of her statement, saying, "I knew the time, because I heard the brewer's clock strike half-past five just before I got to the street." She told the court that it was *after* 5:30 when she passed Chapman and her killer. It would have taken Long about one minute to travel from the corner of Brick Lane and Hanbury Street to 29 Hanbury Street, indicating that she would have passed Chapman at about 5:31.

How does this information compare to Coroner Baxter's adjustment of Cadoche's time—"if he [Cadoche] is out of his reckoning but a quarter hour" (*Telegraph*, 20 September, p. 2)? Baxter placed Cadoche in the backyard at about 5:38–5:39am. This leaves about seven to eight minutes between Long and Cadoche's sightings, which is possible since Long never looked back to see what the couple did or where they went.

During the fourth day of the inquest, Dr. Phillips offered the following:

> The Coroner: Can you give any idea how long it would take to perform the incisions found on the body?
> Dr. Phillips: I think I can guide you by saying that I myself could not have performed all the injuries I saw on that woman, and effect them, even without a struggle, under a quarter of an hour. If I had done it in a deliberate way, such as would fall to the duties of a surgeon, it would probably have taken me the best part of an hour [*Telegraph*, 20 September, p. 2].

Adding Phillips' testimony into Baxter's equation, Chapman would have been killed at or about 5:39am, with the mutilations being complete no earlier than

5:54. Additionally, John Davis informed the Coroner's court on 10 September that: "I was awake from three a.m. to five a.m. on Saturday [8 Sep], and then fell asleep until a quarter to six, when the clock at Spitalfields Church struck. I had a cup of tea and went downstairs to the back yard."

Davis drank his tea while the killer mutilated Chapman, yet he never heard any sound in the passageway when he later took to the stairs. He did not hear the door of 29 Hanbury, which led to the street, open as he came down the stairs—"The front street door was wide open" (our emphasis on this comes from the view that the killer most likely would have shut the door as he entered that morning for privacy)—and he did not discover anyone along the way. While most likely correct in that Long saw before Cadoche heard, Baxter's view provides some discrepancies of its own by timing the events in such a manner whereby Davis could have come across the killer, which did not happen. Hence, a post–5:30 sighting by Long is not very likely. Fortunately, Long and Cadoche provide additional information.

Cadoche gave a time reference relating to when he would have left his residence that morning: "I then went into the house, and from there into the street to go to my work. It was about two minutes after half-past five as I passed Spitalfields Church" (*Telegraph*, 20 September, p. 2).

It would have taken him about four minutes to travel from 27 Hanbury Street to Spitalfields Church, which indicates that he left his residence at approximately 5:28am. This corresponds with the times he gave the court (ref. 1873 Whitechapel, 1894 Bethnal Green, and 1893 Shoreditch Old Ordnance Survey maps, Godfrey Edition).

Long provided a similar time reference: "I got out [left home] about five o'clock, and I reached the Spitalfields Market a few minutes after half-past five" (*Telegraph*, 20 September, p. 2).

It would take about fifteen minutes to walk from Church Row to the corner of Brick Lane and Hanbury Street. When Long noted the time, she was already past the clock, for it chimed just before she turned onto Hanbury Street. Long never stated nor indicated that she stopped anywhere along the way, and she did not verify the time by looking at the clock when she passed it. Hence, the time as she turned onto Hanbury Street was most likely 5:15, *not* 5:30. (While this does not correspond to her arrival time at the market, it suggests that she might have arrived at about 5:20am. Ref. 1873 Whitechapel, 1894 Bethnal Green, and 1893 Shoreditch Old Ordnance Survey maps, Godfrey Edition).

The relationship between the various statements and testimonies validates Coroner Baxter's main premise, *Long saw before Cadoche heard*, albeit Long saw shortly after 5:15 with Cadoche hearing at around 5:20. Dr. Phillips was correct in his assertion about estimating time of death via rigor mortis—"the body would be more apt to cool rapidly from its having lost the greater portion of its blood." It is also interesting to point out that the authorities took note of this, as well: "Evidence points to something between 5:30 and 6:—but medical evidence says about 4 o'cl." (HO 144/221/A49301C [8g], ff. 160–161). Based on the foregoing, we can say with a fair amount of certainty that Annie Chapman died at around 5:30am.

*Chapter 3*

# ELIZABETH STRIDE

*—found murdered Sunday, 30 September 1888*

Not yet recovered from its recent terror, Whitechapel was yesterday thrown into a state of excitement and alarm by the perpetration of another cold-blooded crime very near the scene of the notorious Lipski murder.

*—Daily Telegraph*, Monday, 1 October 1888

By the end of September, the Ripper scare—though not yet so named—was fading away. The lack of any new murders and the public clearing of John Pizer as a suspect reduced the press again to fruitless speculation, more column space, in fact, being devoted to schemes for slum clearance and affordable housing than to the Whitechapel Murders. What news there was came from coroner Wynne Baxter and his simultaneous inquests on Nichols and Chapman. As we have seen, the major results of his labored proceedings were graphic details of Chapman's mutilations, an odd notion of a mad medico stalking the streets and a determination to extract the maximum publicity from his investigations, all of which would prove treacherous for later researchers. Still, as the month drew to a close, the general consensus was that the Whitechapel Murderer had breathed his last. Events, however, would soon prove the consensus wrong.

September 30 is known to Ripper historians as "The Double Event," because of the concurrent murders of Elizabeth Stride and Catherine Eddowes within one mile and one hour of each other. Stride was a 45-year-old Swedish immigrant who had lived in England for 22 years. Known colloquially as "Long Liz," she was a charwoman, ex-coffee shop proprietress, fabulist and occasional prostitute, who since 1885 had lived with a bullying sot of a docker named Michael Kidney. The two had a stormy relationship; Stride would leave him from time to time, had had him brought up on charges of assault, and now—as he would testify at her inquest—Kidney had lately taken to locking her in each day as he went to work.

They had separated again in September, and Stride was living in a lodging-house. The last day of her life was spent in charring, for which she earned a few coins. She then tidied herself and set off into the night.

As the winding path of her last few hours gradually converged with that of Catherine Eddowes, Stride was seen in multiple locations with an assortment of men, possibly suggesting a busy night for trade. At last, however, she ended up in Berner Street, where a Hungarian immigrant named Israel Schwartz reported her being attacked by a man who threw her to the ground. That man then spat an anti-Semitic epithet at Schwartz, who timidly scurried away. Behind him, Stride's assailant dragged her into Dutfield's Yard and slit her throat.

It has been suggested that Stride's killer might not have been the murderer known as Jack the Ripper, but rather Kidney himself. This, of course, is an unanswerable question. But if she met her fate at the hands of the Whitechapel monster, however, he was unable to inflict his hallmark mutilations; Louis Diemschütz, a costume jewellry dealer, chose that moment to turn his cart into the yard, interrupting the Ripper—if such he were—before his work was done.

This was at about 1:00am. At the same time, Eddowes—arrested earlier for public drunkenness—was deemed sober enough to be released from police custody.

The horror was not yet complete.

# THE DAILY TELEGRAPH
Monday, October 1, 1888

Page 5
TWO MORE WOMEN
MURDERED IN WHITECHAPEL
AND ALDGATE
SAVAGE BUTCHERY
AND MUTILATION
THE CRIME IN WHITECHAPEL.

Not yet recovered from its recent terror, Whitechapel was yesterday thrown into a state of excitement and alarm by the perpetration of another cold-blooded crime very near the scene of the notorious Lipski murder.[1] The latest tragedy resembles those by which the neighbourhood has within the past few months been startled, in that the victim is a woman belonging to the unfortunate class, and that the motive for the fiendish deed is enshrouded in mystery. True, the atrocious act was not accompanied by mutilation, but that circumstance would seem to be due to the fact that the assassin was interrupted before completing his foul designs.

On the right side of Commercial-road East, about a quarter of a mile from Aldgate, is a somewhat narrow thoroughfare, called Berner-street, which is composed of small dwellings, occupied by tailors, shoe-makers, cigarette makers, and others—mostly Poles and Germans—who do their work at home. A stone's-throw down the street, facing one of the huge establishments belonging to the London School Board, is a house of three storeys, used as a club by the International Working Men's Education Society, which is affiliated with the foreign section of the Socialist's League, and which, though some Englishmen are enrolled as members, consists largely of foreign Jews. The main entrance to the club is in Berner-street, but ingress can also be obtained from a court which runs along the whole length of the club building. Three cottages stand on the opposite side of the yard, whilst at the end is a store or workshop in the possession of Messrs. Hindley and Co., sack manufacturers. The vacant space can be screened from the street by means of high double-doors, but the barriers are

[1]This refers to the murder of Miriam Angel by Israel Lipski on 28 June 1887. Subsequently, his surname entered briefly into the language as an anti-Semitic slur (ref. MEPO 3/140/221/A49301C, ff. 204–207, and Friedland, *The Trials of Israel Lipski*).

Berner Street (now Henriques Street), St. George's-in-the-East. Dutfield's Yard, site of the Stride murder, was located approximately behind the first lamppost in the picture (courtesy Evans/Skinner Crime Archive).

usually wide open. They were so on Saturday night and Sunday morning, and it was just inside the open doors—not more than three yards from the pavement of Berner-street—that the appalling crime took place.[2]

The members of the International Workmen's Club generally meet on Saturday nights to engage in discussion, finishing up with a concert and conviviality, the discussions being conducted alternately in German and in English. That course was pursued on Saturday last, when a debate on "Why Jews should be Socialists" was carried on in the German language. Nearly one hundred members attended, but on the approach of midnight the number dwindled down to thirty. Half an hour later a member named Joseph

Lave—a Russian Jew, who is a printer and photographer by trade, and is in England on a short stay from the United States—proceeded to the yard in order to momentarily escape the heat of the concert-room. He remained there five minutes, but nothing attracted his attention. The place was not well lighted, inasmuch as the occupants of the cottages opposite had retired to rest, and the only means of illumination was from an upper window of the club. The street was not noisy, heavy rain having recently fallen. Later still Morris Eagle, a young Russian Jew and a traveller in jewellery, also passed through the yard. He, too, was a member of the club, and had attended the concert, accompanied by his young woman. Leaving about midnight he saw his young lady home, and

---

[2]The site of Stride's murder is now within the grounds of the Harry Gosling Primary School. Berner Street is now called Henriques Street (ref. "The Whitechapel Dossier: Berner Street," *Ripper Notes*, January 2002).

returned at twenty minutes to one o'clock. Finding the front door locked, he passed through the court and entered the club by the side door, but he likewise failed to observe anything unusual. The steward is a Russian Jew, called Lewis Diemshitz [Diemschütz], he having held that position for six months. He follows the occupation of a traveller in common jewellery, and spent the greater part of Saturday at Westowhill Market, near the Crystal Palace,[3] with a pony and trap.

It was five minutes to one o'clock on Sunday morning when he reached the club, and as he drove through the gateway of the yard his pony shied slightly at an object near the dead wall on the right hand side. He bent his head down and observed something, but could not tell what, although he touched it with the handle of his whip. Jumping off the vehicle he struck a match, and an awful spectacle then met his gaze. Stretched out on the ground, with feet towards the street and face towards the wall, was the body of a woman, the throat terribly cut and blood trickling down the gutter in a stream. Stricken with horror, Diemshitz rushed into the club and raised an alarm, shouting out that something had happened, though not saying what. Then, accompanied by Eagle and another member, named Isaac Kozebrodski, a Polish Jew, he went back to the yard, and after another match had been struck the trio reassured themselves that a foul murder had been committed. In all haste Eagle and Kozebrodski ran out for the police, and after some delay found Constable Lamb, 252 H Division, in Commercial-road. On the arrival of that officer he perceived that the dead woman was lying on her left side, and was clutching some grapes in her right hand and sweetmeats in her left. In addition to the ghastly cut on the throat, there were scars on the left temple and cheek, the wounds being discoloured with dirt. The body was still warm. No signs of a scuffle could be discovered, but the idea of suicide was negatived by the absence of any weapon.

At once a messenger was despatched to the police-station in Leman-street, and some constables quickly arrived on the scene with an ambulance, the superintendent and an inspector of the H Division speedily following. The first precaution taken was to close the doors of the yard and the entrance of the club, the members of which were informed that they could not leave until each individual had been searched and his belongings examined—a process which occupied until nearly five o'clock in the morning, when the men were told that they were free to depart, no clue to the murder having been met with. Meanwhile Dr. Phillips, the divisional police surgeon, was fetched from his residence in Spital-square, and shortly after two o'clock that gentleman came upon the scene, accompanied by Drs. Blackwell and Kaye.[4] It was then obvious that the jugular vein and the windpipe had been severed; that the wound, which was nearly three inches long, and ran from left to right, had been caused by a very sharp instrument; and that death must have been instantaneous. The deceased appeared to be between thirty-five and forty years of age, and about 5 ft. 4 in. in height. She was of dark complexion, and her hair black and curly. She wore a short black jacket, which was open at the bosom, as was also her old black velveteen[5] bodice, thus exposing her

---

[3]The Crystal Palace was a giant glass and iron hall in Hyde Park built by Sir Joseph Paxton to house the Great Exhibition of 1851. Later moved to Sydenham Hill, it was destroyed by fire in 1936.

[4]See testimonies of Drs. Blackwell and Phillips, 3, 4 and 6 October.

[5]A fabric with the appearance or texture of velvet, but made of cotton.

stays and chemise.[6] Her dress, which was saturated with rain,[7] was of a common black material. She had on two petticoats, one made of a poor material resembling sacking, and white cotton stockings; but the clothes were in no way disarranged. Eventually the corpse was conveyed on an ambulance to the parish mortuary of St. George-in-the-East, where it remained in charge of the police. No ring or jewellery of any sort was on the deceased, but two handkerchiefs—one large and one small—were found in her pockets, together with a common brass thimble and a skein of black worsted. Part of an old evening newspaper was found crammed into her bonnet.[8] During the day several women of the unfortunate class saw the body, but failed to identify it, although some of them stated that the features of the poor creature seemed to be familiar to them.

Intelligence of the murder was telegraphed early to Scotland-yard, and the case was placed in the hands of Chief Inspector Swanson[9] and Inspector Abberline, the latter having been formerly stationed in the H Division. Later on Sir Charles Warren,[10] Chief Commissioner of Metropoli-

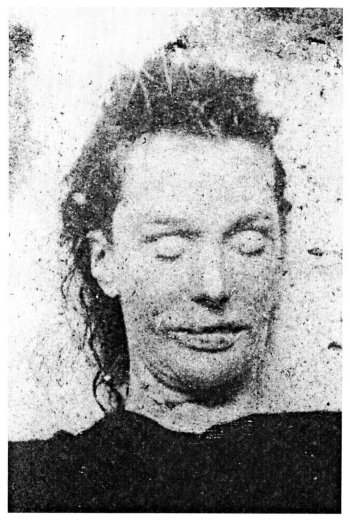

**Mortuary photograph of Elizabeth Stride (courtesy Evans/ Skinner Crime Archive).**

tan Police, also visited the scene of the murder. Up to the present time, however, no clue has been discovered that is likely to lead to the detection of the crime, although a description has been given of a

---

[6]See Edward Johnston's testimony, 4 October.

[7]However, Dr. Blackwell noted "the clothes were not wet with rain" (ref. 3 October).

[8]This statement has never been corroborated.

[9]Chief Inspector Donald Sutherland Swanson (1848–1924), in charge of overall supervision of the Whitechapel Murders case (Evans & Skinner, p. 679).

[10]General Sir Charles Warren (1840–1927), Chief Commissioner of the Metropolitan Police. A career military man at a loss in detecting this new type of killer, or government stooge in charge of a cover-up, depending on an author's prejudices (Evans and Skinner, pp. 679–680).

man who was seen in the company of the deceased about midnight on Saturday. This individual is stated to have been about twenty-eight years of age, 5 ft. 8 in. in height, of dark complexion, but having no whiskers. He was attired in a black diagonal[11] coat, and had on a hard felt hat and a collar and tie. He was of respectable appearance, and carried a newspaper parcel.[12]

As soon as the news became generally known thousands of people of all classes flocked to Berner-street, but they were able to see little to gratify their curiosity. The double doors of the court yard were closed, and the approaches guarded by a dozen constables under the charge of an inspector. The police authorities observed a reticence which has now apparently become systematic, and any information procured was obtained in spite of them. After Dr. Phillips had seen the body they caused the blood which had flowed about the ground at the scene of the tragedy to be removed—a step the wisdom of which might well be questioned. Various theories have been started as to the manner in which the assassin accomplished his purpose, but the hypothesis which finds most favour is that the miscreant tempted his victim into the darkness of the courtyard, and at an opportune moment put his left arm round her neck, cutting her throat with his right. It is believed that no considerable interval elapsed between the committal of the murder and the discovery of the body, and, as previously stated, it is conjectured that the fiendish wretch was disturbed, and was obliged to decamp before completing his ghastly work. The obvious poverty of the woman and her total lack of valuables destroy the possibility of robbery having been contemplated, and the expedition with which the crime was effected demonstrates that it was the work of no ordinary hand. Indeed, though there is no positive proof, all the circumstances tend to strengthen the supposition that this murderer was also the perpetrator of the horrible deed subsequently committed within the precincts of the City. It is remarkable that the crime could have been done so silently; but a slight scream or cry of distress would probably have been drowned by the noise of the singing at the workmen's club.

It is understood that a post mortem examination has not been made, but it is officially announced that the inquest will be opened by Mr. Wynne E. Baxter, coroner for East Middlesex, at the Vestry Hall, Cable-street, St. George-in-the-East, at eleven o'clock this morning.

Statements have been made by several members of the International Workmen's Club. Lewis Diemshitz [sic], the steward, said: "I have been steward of the club six or seven months. I am also a traveller in common jewellery. I went yesterday to Westow-hill Market, a place I usually visit on Saturdays, and I came back about one o'clock this morning. My usual time for getting home from market is between one and two in the morning. I drove home in my own trap. My pony is rather shy, and as I turned into the yard it struck me that it bore too much to the left-hand side against the wall. I bent my head to see what it was that he was shying at, and I noticed that the ground was not level. I saw a little heap, which I thought might perhaps be some mud swept together. I touched the heap with the handle of my whip, and then I found that it was not mud. I jumped off the trap and struck a match, when I saw the body of a woman. I did not wait to see whether she was drunk or dead, but ran indoors and asked

[11]A thick twilled cotton coat with small cords running obliquely throughout.
[12]See PC William Smith's testimony, 6 October.

whether my wife was there. I did this because I knew she had rather a weak constitution.[13] I saw my wife was sitting downstairs, and I at once informed the members that something had happened in the yard. I did not tell them whether the woman was murdered or drunk, because I did not then know. A member named Isaacs went down into the yard with me, and we struck a match. We saw blood right from the gate up the yard. Then we both went for the police; but, unfortunately, it was several minutes before we could find a constable. At last another member of the club, named Eagle, who ran out after us and went in a different direction, found one somewhere in Commercial-road. This policeman blew his whistle, and several more policemen came up, and soon after the doctors arrived. The woman seemed to be about twenty-seven or twenty-eight years old. She was a little bit better dressed, I should say, than the woman who was last murdered. Her clothes were not disarranged. She had a flower in the bosom of her dress. In one hand she had some grapes,[14] and in the other some sweets. She was grasping them tightly. I had never seen her before. She was removed about a quarter to five to Cable-street Mortuary. When I first saw her she was lying on her left side two yards from the entrance, with her feet towards the street. I do not keep my trap in the yard, but I keep my goods at the club."

Mrs. Mortimer, living at 36, Berner-street, four doors from the scene of the tragedy, states: "I was standing at the door of my house nearly the whole time between half-past twelve and one o'clock this (Sunday) morning, and did not notice anything unusual.[15] I had just gone indoors and was preparing to go to bed when I heard a commotion outside, and immediately ran out, thinking that there was another row at the Socialists' Club close by. I went to see what was the matter, and was informed that another dreadful murder had been committed in the yard adjoining the club-house, and on going inside I saw the body of a woman lying huddled up just inside the gates, with her throat cut from ear to ear. A man touched her face, and said it was quite warm,[16] so that the deed must have been done while I was standing at the door of my house. There was certainly no noise made, and I did not observe any one enter the gates. It was just after one o'clock when I went out, and the only person whom I had seen pass through the street previously was a young man carrying a black shiny bag, who walked very fast from the direction of Commercial-road.[17] He looked up at the club, and then went round the corner by the Board School. I was told that the manager or steward of the club had discovered the woman on his return home in his pony-cart. He drove through the gates, and my opinion is that he interrupted the murderer, who must have made his escape immediately, under cover of the cart. If a man had come out of the yard before one o'clock I must have seen him."[18]

In an interview Dr. Blackwell made a statement, in which he said that about ten minutes past one he was called by a policeman to 40, Berner-street, where he found the corpse of the murdered woman. The body was perfectly warm, and life could not have been extinct for more than

---

[13]Diemschütz's reasoning is sometimes reported as his being uncertain if the woman he found was or was not his wife.
[14]See Commentary 1 regarding grapes.
[15]See Commentary 1 regarding Mortimer's timing.
[16]The "man" is Edward Spooner (ref. 3 October).
[17]This is Leon Goldstein (ref. HO 144/221/A49301C [8a] ff. 148–159).
[18]See Commentary 3 regarding Stride's canonical victim status.

# POLICE NOTICE.

## TO THE OCCUPIER.

On the mornings of Friday, 31st August, Saturday 8th, and Sunday, 30th September, 1888, Women were murdered in or near Whitechapel, supposed by some one residing in the immediate neighbourhood. Should you know of any person to whom suspicion is attached, you are earnestly requested to communicate at once with the nearest Police Station.

Metropolitan Police Office,
30th September, 1888.

Printed by M'Corquodale & Co. Limited, " The Armoury," Southwark.

Handbill distributed by the police in early October appealing to the public for information regarding the Ripper crimes (courtesy of Evans/Skinner Crime Archive). See also the *Telegraph* of 4 October.

knife. His belief was that as the woman held the sweets in her left hand her head was dragged back by means of a silk handkerchief which she wore round her neck, and that her throat was then cut. One of her hands was smeared with blood, and this was evidently done in the struggle. He had, however, no doubt that her windpipe being completely cut through, she was rendered unable to make any sound. It did not follow that the murderer would be bespattered with blood, for, as he was sufficiently cunning in other things, he could contrive to avoid coming in contact with it by reaching well forward.

At a late hour last night it was stated that the woman murdered in Berner-street had been identified. A female known as "One-armed Liz," living in Flower and Dean-street, is said to have accompanied Sergeant Thick to St. George's Mortuary, and recognised the body as that of Annie Morris, an unfortunate, residing in a common lodging house in the neighbourhood of Flower and Dean-street. Another account says: "The woman murdered in Berner-street has been identified as Elizabeth Stride, who, it seems, had been leading a gay life, and had resided latterly in Flower and Dean-street. She was identified by a sister living in Holborn."[19]

twenty minutes. It did not appear to him that the woman was a Jewess; she was more like an Irishwomen. He hastily examined her, and found no other injuries. He had no doubt that the same man committed both this murder and the one in the City. In his opinion the criminal is a maniac, and accustomed to use a heavy

[19]This "sister" is the troublesome Mrs. Mary Malcolm (ref. 3 October).

# THE DAILY TELEGRAPH
Tuesday, October 2, 1888

Page 3
## THE WHITECHAPEL CRIME.
*[First Session of Inquest]*

So far as the identity of the criminal who committed the murder in the court-yard of the International Working Men's Constitutional Club is concerned, the Whitechapel mystery remains in exactly the same state as on Sunday. Detectives have been drafted into the district from Scotland-yard, and additional constables from other divisions of the metropolitan area sent to augment the numbers in the East-end, but neither the old nor the new men have been able to elucidate a single fact likely to direct them to a capture of importance. In lieu of this, they have been able to arrest several persons of more or less suspicious appearance, who, after due examination, have given such explanations of their antecedents and occupations as to satisfy the officers that they have had nothing to do with the outrages. Detective-Inspector Reid,[20] who has charge of the case, has had a great deal of information volunteered to him by women of the class to which the victims belonged regarding men whom they allege to have threatened them with death. Each informant is firmly convinced that the man she saw was the Unknown, who is now so keenly searched for, but as the description varies in each case it is quite plain that they cannot refer to the same person.

In the neighbourhood of Berner-street the excitement of the inhabitants continues unabated, and during the whole of yesterday a large number of spectators took delight in gazing at the premises of the International Working Man's Constitutional Club, whose committee are making profit out of the notoriety the premises have acquired by charging curiosity-hunters a small sum for admission, the money thus obtained being devoted to the "propaganda fund" of Socialism. As all material traces of the tragedy have been removed, there is nothing to be seen, but many people seemed unsatisfied unless they were shown the exact spot where the body was found, and retold the story of the discovery of the ghastly object as it was narrated before the coroner. Notwithstanding the excitement which the occurrences have created, they have made no difference in the appearance of the streets of Whitechapel, except that there are more constables about than usual. The thoroughfares are as crowded as ever, even up to a late hour, and the same class of people as Annie Chapman and Elizabeth Stride can be seen flitting about the dark and ill-lighted alleys which abound in the district.

As to the last-named person—who was found at Berner-street—there is some doubt as to her identification. It is believed that she is the woman known as Elizabeth Stride, or more familiarly as "Long Liz,"[21] but this identity is not definitely established. The people who saw her in the lodging-house in Flower and Dean-street, Commercial-road, say there is no doubt she is Elizabeth, but relatives have not been found to identify her. Those who knew her state that she was a good-tempered, harmless woman, who sometimes worked as a charwoman, and only went out when she could find no employment. As indicating the intensity of the feeling of the inhabitants of Whitechapel it may

---

[20]Inspector Edmund John James Reid (1846–1917), warrant no. 56100, head of the local CID during the murders (BFS, pp. 368–370). See the Connell & Evans biography, *The Man Who Hunted Jack the Ripper.*
[21]Stride's nickname of "Long Liz" appears to have been a punning reference to her surname (BFS, p. 438).

be mentioned that when the police arrest any man, for no matter what offence, the cry is at once raised that he is the "Whitechapel murderer," and an immense crowd at once gathers around the supposed miscreant, hooting and jeering. The Vigilance Committee have again written to the Home Secretary, requesting him to offer a reward, and it has been arranged to hold an indignation meeting of the residents, at which it is expected Mr. Montagu, M.P., will preside.

Tuesday Morning (1:30 a.m.)

Upon inquiry at Scotland Yard and at the City Police Office this morning, it was stated that no additional information had been obtained, and that no further arrests were made. The bodies of the victims remain unidentified.

## *The Inquest*

Yesterday, at the Vestry Hall in Cable-street, St. George-in-the-East, Mr. Wynne E. Baxter, coroner for East Middlesex, opened an inquest on the body of the woman who was found dead, with her throat cut, at one o'clock on Sunday morning, in Berner-street, Commercial-road East. At the outset of the inquiry the deceased was described as Elizabeth Stride, but it subsequently transpired that she had not yet been really identified. A jury of twenty-four having been empanelled, they proceeded to view the body at the St. George's Mortuary.

Detective-Inspector Reid, H Division, watched the case on behalf of the police.

**William Wess** [West], who affirmed instead of being sworn, was the first wit-

ness examined, and, in reply to the coroner, he said: I reside at No. 2, William-street, Cannon-street-road, and am overseer in the printing office attached to No. 40, Berner-street, Commercial-road, which premises are in the occupation of the International Working Men's Education Society, whose club is carried on there. On the ground floor of the club is a room, the door and window of which face the street. At the rear of this is the kitchen, whilst the first floor consists of a large room which is used for our meetings and entertainments, I being a member of the club. At the south side of the premises is a courtyard, to which entrance can be obtained through a double door, in one section of which is a smaller one, which is used when the larger barriers are closed. The large doors are generally closed at night, but sometimes remain open. On the left side of the yard is a house, which is divided into three tenements, and occupied, I believe, by that number of families. At the end is a store or workshop belonging to Messrs. Hindley and Co., sack manufacturers. I do not know that a way out exists there. The club premises and the printing-office occupy the entire length of the yard on the right side. Returning to the club-house, the front room on the ground floor is used for meals. In the kitchen is a window which faces the door opening into the yard. The intervening passage is illuminated by means of a fanlight over the door. The printing-office, which does not communicate with the club, consists of two rooms, one for compositors and the other for the editor.[22] On Saturday the compositors finished their labours at two o'clock in the afternoon. The editor concluded earlier, but remained at the place until the discovery of the murder.

How many members are there in the

---

[22]The printing office housed the Yiddish radical newspaper *Der Arbeter Fraint* ("The Worker's Friend").

club?—From seventy-five to eighty. Working men of any nationality can join.

Is any political qualification required of members?—It is a political—a Socialist—club.

Do the members have to agree with any particular principles?—A candidate is proposed by one member and seconded by another, and a member would not nominate a candidate unless he knew that he was a supporter of Socialist principles. On Saturday last I was in the printing-office during the day and in the club during the evening. From nine to half-past ten at night I was away seeing an English friend home, but I was in the club again till a quarter-past midnight. A discussion was proceeding in the lecture-room, which has three windows overlooking the courtyard. From ninety to 100 persons attended the discussion, which terminated soon after half-past eleven, when the bulk of the members left, using the street door, the most convenient exit. From twenty to thirty members remained, some staying in the lecture-room and the others going downstairs. Of those upstairs a few continued the discussion, while the rest were singing. The windows of the lecture-room were partly open.

How do you know that you finally left at a quarter-past twelve o'clock?—Because of the time when I reached my lodgings. Before leaving I went into the yard, and thence to the printing-office, in order to leave some literature there, and on returning to the yard I observed that the double door at the entrance was open. There is no lamp in the yard, and none of the street lamps light it, so that the yard is only lit by the lights through the windows at the side of the club and of the tenements opposite. As to the tenements, I only observed lights in two first-floor windows. There was also a light in the printing-office, the editor being in his room reading.

Was there much noise in the club?—Not exactly much noise; but I could hear the singing when I was in the yard.

Did you look towards the yard gates?—Not so much to the gates as to the ground, but nothing unusual attracted my attention.

Can you say that there was no object on the ground?—I could not say that.

Do you think it possible that anything can have been there without your observing it?—It was dark, and I am a little shortsighted, so that it is possible. The distance from the gates to the kitchen door is 18 ft.

What made you look towards the gates at all?—Simply because they were open. I went into the club, and called my brother, and we left together by the front door.

On leaving did you see anybody as you passed the yard?—No.

Or did you meet any one in the street?—Not that I recollect. I generally go home between twelve and one o'clock.

Do low women frequent Berner-street?—I have seen men and women standing about and talking to each other in Fairclough-street.

But have you observed them nearer the club?—No.

Or in the club yard?—I did once, at eleven o'clock at night, about a year ago. They were chatting near the gates. That is the only time I have noticed such a thing, nor have I heard of it.

**Morris Eagle**, who also affirmed, said: I live at No. 4, New-road, Commercial-road, and travel in jewellery. I am a member of the International Workmen's Club, which meets at 40, Berner-street. I was there on Saturday, several times during the day, and was in the chair during the discussion in the evening. After the discussion, between half-past eleven and a quarter to twelve o'clock, I left the club to take my young lady home, going out through the front door. I returned about twenty minutes to one. I tried the front door, but, finding it closed, I went through the gateway into the yard, reaching the club in that way.

Did you notice anything lying on the ground near the gates?—I did not.

Did you pass in the middle of the gateway?—I think so. The gateway is 9 ft. 2 in. wide. I naturally walked on the right side, that being the side on which the club door was.

Do you think you are able to say that the deceased was not lying there then?—I do not know, I am sure, because it was rather dark. There was a light from the upper part of the club, but that would not throw any illumination upon the ground. It was dark near the gates.

You have formed no opinion, I take it, then, as to whether there was anything there?—No.

Did you see anyone about in Berner-street?—I dare say I did, but I do not remember them.

Did you observe any one in the yard?—I do not remember that I did.

If there had been a man and woman there you would have remembered the circumstance?—Yes; I am sure of that.

Did you notice whether there were any lights in the tenements opposite the club?—I do not recollect.

Are you often at the club late at night?—Yes, very often.

In the yard, too?—No, not in the yard.

And you have never seen a man and woman there?—No, not in the yard; but I have close by, outside the beershop, at the corner of Fairclough-street. As soon as I entered the gateway on Saturday night I could hear a friend of mine singing in the upstair [sic] room of the club. I went up to him. He was singing in the Russian language, and we sang together. I had been there twenty minutes when a member named Gidleman [Gilleman] came upstairs, and said "there is a woman dead in the yard." I went down in a second and struck a match, when I saw a woman lying on the ground in a pool of blood, near the gates. Her feet were towards the gates, about six or seven feet from them. She was lying by the side of and facing the club wall. When I reached the body and struck the match another member was present.

Did you touch the body?—No. As soon as I struck the match I perceived a lot of blood, and I ran away and called the police.

Were the clothes of the deceased disturbed?—I cannot say. I ran towards the Commercial-road, Dienishitz [sic], the club steward, and another member going in the opposite direction down Fairclough-street. In Commercial-road I found two constables at the corner of Grove-street. I told them that a woman had been murdered in Berner-street, and they returned with me.[23]

Was any one in the yard then?—Yes, a few persons—some members of the club and some strangers. One of the policemen turned his lamp on the deceased and sent me to the station for the inspector, at the same time telling his comrade to fetch a doctor. The onlookers seemed afraid to go near and touch the body. The constable, however, felt it.

Can you fix the time when the discovery was first made?—It must have been about one o'clock. On Saturday nights there is free discussion at the club, and among those present last Saturday were about half a dozen women, but they were those we knew—not strangers. It was not

---

[23]PC252H Henry Lamb (BFS, p. 235) and PC426H Albert Collins (personal correspondence, Bernard Brown). But see Collins' testimony, 6 October.

a dancing night, but a few members may have danced after the discussion.

If there was dancing and singing in the club you would not hear the cry of a woman in the yard?—It would depend upon the cry.

The cry of a woman in great distress—a cry of "Murder"?—Yes, I should have heard that.

**Lewis Dienishitz** [Diemschütz], having affirmed, deposed: I reside at No. 40 Berner-street, and am steward of the International Workmen's Club. I am married, and my wife lives at the club too, and assists in the management. On Saturday I left home about half-past eleven in the morning, and returned exactly at one o'clock on Sunday morning. I noticed the time at the baker's shop at the corner of Berner-street. I had been to the market near the Crystal Palace, and had a barrow like a costermonger's, drawn by a pony, which I keep in George-yard Cable-street. I drove home to leave my goods. I drove into the yard, both gates being wide open. It was rather dark there. All at once my pony shied at some object on the right. I looked to see what the object was, and observed that there was something unusual, but could not tell what. It was a dark object. I put my whip handle to it, and tried to lift it up, but as I did not succeed I jumped down from my barrow and struck a match. It was rather windy, and I could only get sufficient light to see that there was some figure there. I could tell from the dress that it was the figure of a woman.

You did not disturb it?—No. I went into the club and asked where my wife was. I found her in the front room on the ground floor.

What did you do with the pony?—I left it in the yard by itself, just outside the club door. There were several members in the front room of the club, and I told them all that there was a woman lying in the yard, though I could not say whether she was drunk or dead. I then got a candle and went into the yard, where I could see blood before I reached the body.

Did you touch the body?—No, I ran off at once for the police. I could not find a constable in the direction which I took, so I shouted out "Police!" as loudly as I could. A man whom I met in Grove-street returned with me, and when we reached the yard he took hold of the head of the deceased. As he lifted it up I saw the wound in the throat.

Had the constables arrived then?—At the very same moment Eagle and the constables arrived.

Did you notice anything unusual when you were approaching the club?—No.

You saw nothing suspicious?—Not at all.

How soon afterwards did a doctor arrive?—About twenty minutes after the constables came up. No one was allowed by the police to leave the club until they were searched, and then they had to give their names and addresses.

Did you notice whether the clothes of the deceased were in order?—They were in perfect order.

How was she lying?—On her left side, with her face towards the club wall.

Was the whole of the body resting on the side?—No, I should say only her face. I cannot say how much of the body was sideways. I did not notice what position her hands were in, but when the police came I observed that her bodice was unbuttoned near the neck. The doctor said the body was quite warm.

What quantity of blood should you think had flowed from the body?—I should say quite two quarts.

In what direction had it run?—Up the yard from the street. The body was about one foot from the club wall. The gutter of the yard is paved with large stones, and the centre with smaller irregular stones.

Have you ever seen men and women together in the yard?—Never.

Nor heard of such a thing?—No.

A JUROR: Could you in going up the yard have passed the body without touching it?—Oh, yes.

Any person going up the centre of the yard might have passed without noticing it?—I, perhaps, should not have noticed it if my pony had not shied. I had passed it when I got down from my barrow.

How far did the blood run?—As far as the kitchen door of the club.

Was any person left with the body while you ran for the police?—Some members of the club remained; at all events, when I came back they were there. I cannot say whether any of them touched the body.

INSPECTOR REID (INTERPOSING): When the murder was discovered the members of the club were detained on the premises, and I searched them, whilst Dr. Phillips examined them.

A JUROR: Was it possible for anybody to leave the yard between the discovery of the body and the arrival of the police?

WITNESS: Oh, yes—or, rather, it would have been possible before I informed the members of the club, not afterwards.

When you entered the yard, if any person had run out you would have seen them in the dark?—Oh, yes, it was light enough for that. It was dark in the gateway, but not so dark further in the yard.

THE CORONER: The body has not yet been identified?—Not yet.

THE FOREMAN: I do not quite understand that. I thought the inquest had been opened on the body of one Elizabeth Stride.

THE CORONER: That was a mistake. Something is known of the deceased, but she has not been fully identified. It would be better at present to describe her as a woman unknown. She has been partially identified. It is known where she lived. It was thought at the beginning of the inquest that she had been identified by a relative, but that turns out to have been a mistake.[24]

The inquiry was then adjourned till this (Tuesday) afternoon, at two o'clock.

# THE DAILY TELEGRAPH
Wednesday, October 3, 1888

Page 3
INQUEST—IDENTIFICATION OF THE BODY—A STRANGE STORY.
*[Second Session of Inquest]*

Yesterday afternoon, in the Vestry Hall of St. George-in-the-East, Cable-street, Mr. Wynne E. Baxter, coroner for East Middlesex, resumed the inquiry into the circumstances attending the death of the woman who was found with her throat cut in a yard adjoining the clubhouse of the International Working Men's Education Society, No. 40, Berner-street, Commercial-road East, at one o'clock on Sunday morning last.

**Constable Henry Lamb,** 252 H division, examined by the coroner, said: Last Sunday morning, shortly before one o'clock, I was on duty in Commercial-road, between Christian-street and Batty-street, when two men came running towards me and shouting. I went to meet

[24]This exchange singularly points out the difficulties encountered by the authorities during the case. The press did report as early as 1 October that the Berner Street victim was, though "not yet identified," Elizabeth Stride. Because Mary Malcolm claimed the victim as a blood relation—her sister—that identification took legal precedence until proven otherwise.

them, and they called out, "Come on, there has been another murder." I asked where, and as they got to the corner of Berner-street they pointed down and said, "There." I saw people moving some distance down the street. I ran, followed by another constable—426 H. Arriving at the gateway of No. 40 I observed something dark lying on the ground on the right-hand side. I turned my light on, when I found that the object was a woman, with her throat cut and apparently dead. I sent the other constable for the nearest doctor, and a young man who was standing by I despatched to the police station to inform the inspector what had occurred. On my arrival there were about thirty people in the yard, and others followed me in. No one was nearer than a yard to the body. As I was examining the deceased the crowd gathered round, but I begged them to keep back, otherwise they might have their clothes soiled with blood, and thus get into trouble.

Up to this time had you touched the body?—I had put my hand on the face.

Was it warm?—Slightly. I felt the wrist, but could not discern any movement of the pulse. I then blew my whistle for assistance.

Did you observe how the deceased was lying?—She was lying on her left side, with her left hand on the ground.

Was there anything in that hand?—I did not notice anything. The right arm was across the breast. Her face was not more than five or six inches away from the club wall.

Were her clothes disturbed?—No.

Only her boots visible?—Yes, and only the soles of them. There were no signs of a struggle. Some of the blood was in a liquid state, and had run towards the kitchen door of the club. A little—that nearest to her on the ground—was slightly congealed. I can hardly say whether any was still flowing from the throat. Dr.

Blackwell was the first doctor to arrive; he came ten or twelve minutes after myself, but I had no watch with me.

Did any one of the crowd say whether the body had been touched before your arrival?—No. Dr. Blackwell examined the body and its surroundings. Dr. Phillips came ten minutes later. Inspector Pinhorn arrived directly after Dr. Blackwell. When I blew my whistle other constables came, and I had the entrance of the yard closed. This was while Dr. Blackwell was looking at the body. Before that the doors were wide open. The feet of the deceased extended just to the swing of the gate, so that the barrier could be closed without disturbing the body. I entered the club and left a constable at the gate to prevent any one passing in or out. I examined the hands and clothes of all the members of the club. There were from fifteen to twenty present, and they were on the ground floor.

Did you discover traces of blood anywhere in the club?—No.

Was the steward present?—Yes.

Did you ask him to lock the front door?—I did not. There was a great deal of commotion. That was done afterwards.

THE CORONER: But time is the essence of the thing.

WITNESS: I did not see any person leave. I did not try the front door of the club to see if it was locked. I afterwards went over the cottages, the occupants of which were in bed. I was admitted by men, who came down partly dressed; all the other people were undressed. As to the waterclosets in the yard, one was locked and the other unlocked, but no one was there.

There is a recess near the dust-bin. Did you go there?—Yes, afterwards, with Dr. Phillips.

THE CORONER: But I am speaking of at the time.

WITNESS: I did it subsequently. I do not recollect looking over the wooden partition. I, however, examined the store belonging to Messrs. Hindley, sack manufacturers, but I saw nothing there.

How long were the cottagers in opening their doors?—Only a few minutes, and they seemed frightened. When I returned Dr. Phillips and Chief Inspector West[25] had arrived.

Was there anything to prevent a man escaping while you were examining the body?—Several people were inside and outside the gates, and I should think that they would be sure to observe a man who had marks of blood.

But supposing he had no marks of blood?—It was quite possible, of course, for a person to escape while I was examining the corpse. Every one was more or less looking towards the body. There was much confusion.

Do you think that a person might have got away before you arrived?—I think he is more likely to have escaped before than after.

DETECTIVE-INSPECTOR REID: How long before had you passed this place?

WITNESS: I am not on the Berner-street beat, but I passed the end of the street in Commercial-road six or seven minutes before.

When you were found what direction were you going in?—I was coming towards Berner-street. A constable named Smith[26] was on the Berner-street beat. He did not accompany me, but the constable who was on fixed-point duty between Grove-street and Christian-street in Commercial-road. Constables at fixed-points leave duty at one in the morning. I believe that is the practice nearly all over London.

THE CORONER: I think this is important. The Hanbury-street murder was discovered just as the night police were going off duty. (To witness): Did you see anything suspicious?—I did not at any time. There were squabbles and rows in the streets, but nothing more.

THE FOREMAN: Was there light sufficient to enable you to see, as you were going down Berner-street, whether any person was running away from No. 40?—It was rather dark, but I think there was light enough for that, though the person would be somewhat indistinct from Commercial-road.

THE FOREMAN: Some of the papers state that Berner-street is badly lighted; but there are six lamps within 700 feet, and I do not think that is very bad.

THE CORONER: The parish plan shows that there are four lamps within 350 feet, from Commercial-road to Fairclough-street.

WITNESS: There are three, if not four, lamps in Berner-street between Commercial-road and Fairclough-street. Berner-street is about as well lighted as other side streets. Most of them are rather dark, but more lamps have been erected lately.

THE CORONER: I do not think that London altogether is as well lighted as some capitals are.

WITNESS: There are no public-house lights in Berner-street. I was engaged in the yard and at the mortuary all the night afterwards.

**Edward Spooner**, in reply to the coroner, said: I live at No. 26, Fairclough-street, and am a horse-keeper with Messrs. Meredith, biscuit bakers. On Sunday morning, between half-past twelve and one o'clock, I was standing outside the Beehive Public-house, at the corner of Christian-street, with my young woman.

---

[25]Chief Inspector John West (b. 1842), with the Metropolitan Police from 1865 to 1891 (Evans & Skinner, p. 680). He is the protagonist in Pamela West's evocative 1987 novel, *Yours Truly, Jack the Ripper*.
[26]PC 452H William Smith (BFS, pp. 420–421).

We had left a public-house in Commercial-road at closing time, midnight, and walked quietly to the point named. We stood outside the Beehive about twenty-five minutes, when two Jews came running along, calling out "Murder" and "Police." They ran as far as Grove-street, and then turned back. I stopped them and asked what was the matter, and they replied that a woman had been murdered. I thereupon proceeded down Berner-street and into Dutfield's-yard, adjoining the International Workmen's Club-house, and there saw a woman lying just inside the gate.

Was any one with her?—There were about fifteen people in the yard.

Was any one near her?—They were all standing round.

Were they touching her?—No. One man struck a match, but I could see the woman before the match was struck. I put my hand under her chin when the match was alight.

Was the chin warm?—Slightly.

Was any blood coming from the throat?—Yes; it was still flowing. I noticed that she had a piece of paper doubled up in her right hand, and some red and white flowers pinned on her breast. I did not feel the body, nor did I alter the position of the head. I am sure of that. Her face was turned towards the club wall.

Did you notice whether the blood was still moving on the ground?—It was running down the gutter. I stood by the side of the body for four or five minutes, until the last witness arrived.

Did you notice any one leave the yard while you were there?—No.

Could any one have left without your observing it?—I cannot say, but I think there were too many people about. I believe it was twenty-five minutes to one o'clock when I arrived in the yard.

Have you formed any opinion as to whether the people had moved the body before you came?—No.

THE FOREMAN: As a rule, Jews do not care to touch dead bodies.

WITNESS: The legs of the deceased were drawn up, but her clothes were not disturbed. When Police-constable Lamb came I helped him to close the gates of the yard, and I left through the club.

INSPECTOR REID: I believe that was after you had given your name and address to the police?—Yes.

And had been searched?—Yes.

And examined by Dr. Phillips?—Yes.

THE CORONER: Was there no blood on your hands?—No.

Then there was no blood on the chin of the deceased?—No.

BY THE JURY: I did not meet any one as I was hastening through Berner-street.

**Mary Malcolm** was the next witness, and she was deeply affected while giving her evidence. In answer to the coroner she said: I live at No. 50, Eagle-street, Red Lion-square, Holborn, and am married. My husband, Andrew Malcolm, is a tailor. I have seen the body at the mortuary. I saw it once on Sunday and twice yesterday.

Who is it?—It is the body of my sister, Elizabeth Watts.

You have no doubt about that?—Not the slightest.

You did have some doubts about it at one time?—I had at first.

When did you last see your sister alive?—Last Thursday, about a quarter to seven in the evening.

Where?—She came to see me at No. 59, Red Lion-street, where I work as a trousermaker.

What did she come to you for?—To ask me for a little assistance. I have been in the habit of assisting her for five years.

Did you give her anything?—I gave her a shilling and a short jacket—not the jacket which is now on the body.

How long was she with you?—Only a few moments.

Did she say where she was going?—No.

Where was she living?—I do not know. I know it was somewhere in the neighbourhood of the tailoring Jews—Commercial-road or Commercial-street, or somewhere at the East-end.

Did you understand that she was living in lodging-houses?—Yes.

Did you know what she was doing for a livelihood?—I had my doubts.

Was she the worse for drink when she came to you on Thursday?—No, sober.

But she was sometimes the worse for drink, was she not?—That was, unfortunately, a failing with her. She was thirty-seven years of age last March.

Had she ever been married?—Yes.

Is her husband alive?—Yes, so far as I know. She married the son of Mr. Watts, wine and spirit merchant, of Walcot-street, Bath. I think her husband's Christian name was Edward. I believe he is now in America.

Did he get into trouble?—No.

Why did he go away?—Because my sister brought trouble upon him.

When did she leave him?—About eight years ago, but I cannot be quite certain as to the time. She had two children. Her husband caught her with a porter, and there was a quarrel.

Did the husband turn her out of doors?—No, he sent her to my poor mother, with the two children.

Where does your mother live?—She is dead. She died in the year 1883.

Where are the children now?—The girl is dead, but the boy is at a boarding school kept by his aunt.

Was the deceased subject to epileptic fits?—Witness (sobbing bitterly): No, she only had drunken fits.

Was she ever before the Thames police magistrate?—I believe so.

Charged with drunkenness?—Yes.

Are you aware that she has been let off on the supposition that she was subject to epileptic fits?—I believe that is so, but she was not subject to epileptic fits.

Has she ever told you of troubles she was in with any man?—Oh yes; she lived with a man.

Do you know his name?—I do not remember now, but I shall be able to tell you to-morrow. I believe she lived with a man who kept a coffee-house at Poplar.

INSPECTOR REID: Was his name Stride?—No; I think it was Dent, but I can find out for certain by to-morrow.

THE CORONER: How long had she ceased to live with that man?—Oh, some time. He went away to sea, and was wrecked on the Isle of St. Paul, I believe.

How long ago should you think that was?—It must be three years and a half; but I could tell you all about it by to-morrow, even the name of the vessel that was wrecked.

Had the deceased lived with any man since then?—Not to my knowledge, but there is some man who says that he has lived with her.

Have you ever heard of her getting into trouble with this man?—No, but at times she got locked up for drunkenness. She always brought her trouble to me.

You never heard of any one threatening her?—No; she was too good for that.

Did you ever hear her say that she was afraid of any one?—No.

Did you know of no man with whom she had relations?—No.

INSPECTOR REID: Did you ever visit her in Flower and Dean-street?—No.

Did you ever hear her called "Long Liz"?—That was generally her nickname, I believe.

Have you ever heard of the name of Stride?—She never mentioned such a name to me. I think that if she had lived with any one of that name she would have told me. I have heard what the man Stride has said, but I think he is mistaken.

THE CORONER: How often did your sister come to you?—Every Saturday, and I always gave her 2s. That was for her lodgings.

Did she come to you at all last Saturday?—No, I did not see her on that day.

The Thursday visit was an unusual one, I suppose?—Yes.

Did you think it strange that she did not come on the Saturday?—I did.

Had she ever missed a Saturday before?—Not for nearly three years.

What time in the day did she usually come to you?—At four o'clock in the afternoon.

Where?—At the corner of Chancery-lane. I was there last Saturday afternoon from half-past three till five, but she did not turn up.

Did you think there was something the matter with her?—On the Sunday morning when I read the accounts in the newspapers I thought it might be my sister who had been murdered. I had a presentiment that that was so. I came down to Whitechapel and was directed to the mortuary; but when I saw the body I did not recognise it as that of my sister.

How was that? Why did you not recognise it in the first instance?—I do not know, except that I saw it in the gaslight, between nine and ten at night. But I recognised her the next day.

Did you not have some special presentiment that this was your sister?—Yes.

Tell the jury what it was?—I was in bed, and about twenty minutes past one on Sunday morning I felt a pressure on my breast and heard three distinct kisses. It was that which made me afterwards suspect that the woman who had been murdered was my sister.

THE CORONER (TO THE JURY): The only reason why I allow this evidence is that the witness has been doubtful about her identification. (To witness) Did your sister ever break a limb?—No.

Never?—Not to my knowledge.

THE FOREMAN: Had she any special marks upon her?—Yes, on her right leg there was a small black mark.

THE CORONER: Have you seen that mark on the deceased?—Yes.

When did you see it?—Yesterday morning.

But when, before death, did you see it on your sister?—Oh not for years. It was the size of a pea. I have not seen it for 20 years.

Did you mention the mark before you saw the body?—I said that I could recognise my sister by this particular mark.

What was the mark?—It was from the bite of an adder. One day, when children, we were rolling down a hill together, and we came across an adder. The thing bit me first and my sister afterwards. I have still the mark of the bite on my left hand.

THE CORONER (EXAMINING THE MARK): Oh, that is only a scar. Are you sure that your sister, in her youth, never broke a limb?—Not to my knowledge.

Has your husband seen your sister?—Yes.

Has he been to the mortuary?—No; he will not go.

Have you any brothers and sisters alive?—Yes, a brother and a sister, but they have not seen her for years. My brother might recognise her. He lives near Bath. My sister resides at Folkestone. My sister (the deceased) had a hollowness in her right foot, caused by some sort of accident. It was the absence of this hollowness that made me doubt whether the deceased was really my sister. Perhaps it passed away in death. But the adder mark removed all doubt.

Did you recognise the clothes of the deceased at all?—No. (Bursting into tears). Indeed, I have had trouble with her. On one occasion she left a naked baby outside my door.

One of her babies?—One of her own.

One of the two children by her husband?—No, another one; one she had by a policeman, I believe. She left it with me, and I had to keep it until she fetched it away.

INSPECTOR REID: Is that child alive, do you know?—I believe it died in Bath.

THE CORONER: It is important that the evidence of identification should be unmistakable, and I think that the witness should go to the same spot in Chancery-lane on Saturday next, in order to see if her sister comes.

WITNESS: I have no doubt.

THE CORONER: Still, it is better that the matter should be tested.

WITNESS (IN REPLY TO THE JURY): I did not think it strange that my sister came to me last Thursday instead of the Saturday, because she has done it before. But on previous occasions she has come on the Saturday as well. When she came last Thursday she asked me for money, stating that she had not enough to pay for her lodgings, and I said, "Elizabeth, you are a pest to me."

THE CORONER: Has your sister been in prison?—Witness: Yes.

Has she never been in prison on a Saturday?—No; she has only been locked up for the night.

Never more?—No; she has been fined.

A JUROR: You say that before when she has come on the Thursday she has also come on the Saturday as well?—Always.

THE CORONER: So that the Thursday was an extra. You are quite confident now about the identity?—I have not a shadow of doubt.

**Mr. Frederick William Blackwell** deposed: I reside at No. 100, Commercial-road, and am a physician and surgeon. On Sunday morning last, at ten minutes past one o'clock, I was called to Berner-street by a policeman. My assistant, Mr. Johnston, went back with the constable, and I followed immediately I was dressed. I consulted my watch on my arrival, and it was 1:16 a.m. The deceased was lying on her left side obliquely across the passage, her face looking towards the right wall. Her legs were drawn up, her feet close against the wall of the right side of the passage. Her head was resting beyond the carriage-wheel rut, the neck lying over the rut. Her feet were three yards from the gateway. Her dress was unfastened at the neck. The neck and chest were quite warm, as were also the legs, and the face was slightly warm. The hands were cold. The right hand was open and on the chest, and was smeared with blood. The left hand, lying on the ground, was partially closed, and contained a small packet of cachous[27] wrapped in tissue paper. There were no rings, nor marks of rings, on her hands. The appearance of the face was quite placid. The mouth was slightly open. The deceased had round her neck a check silk scarf, the bow of which was turned to the left and pulled very tight. In the neck there was a long incision which exactly corresponded with the lower border of the scarf. The border was slightly frayed, as if by a sharp knife. The incision in the neck commenced on the left side, 2 inches below the angle of the jaw, and almost in a direct line with it, nearly severing the vessels on that side, cutting the windpipe completely in two, and terminating on the opposite side 1 inch below the angle of the right jaw, but without severing the vessels on that side. I could not ascertain whether the bloody hand had been moved. The blood was running down the gutter into the drain in the opposite direction from the

---

[27]A sort of sweetmeat used to freshen the breath. Pronounced "cashews," this has often led authors and theorists to mistakenly assert Stride was eating nuts at the time of her death.

feet. There was about 1lb of clotted blood close by the body, and a stream all the way from there to the back door of the club.

Were there no spots of blood about?—No; only some marks of blood which had been trodden in.

Was there any blood on the soles of the deceased's boots?—No.

No splashing of blood on the wall?—No, it was very dark, and what I saw was by the aid of a policeman's lantern. I have not examined the place since. I examined the clothes, but found no blood on any part of them. The bonnet of the deceased was lying on the ground a few inches from the head. Her dress was unbuttoned at the top.

Can you say whether the injuries could have been self-inflicted?—It is impossible that they could have been.

Did you form any opinion as to how long the deceased had been dead?—From twenty minutes to half an hour when I arrived. The clothes were not wet with rain. She would have bled to death comparatively slowly on account of vessels on one side only of the neck being cut and the artery not completely severed.

After the infliction of the injuries was there any possibility of any cry being uttered by the deceased?—None whatever. Dr. Phillips came about twenty minutes to half an hour after my arrival. The double doors of the yard were closed when I arrived, so that the previous witness must have made a mistake on that point.

A JUROR: Can you say whether the throat was cut before or after the deceased fell to the ground?—I formed the opinion that the murderer probably caught hold of the silk scarf, which was tight and knotted, and pulled the deceased backwards, cutting her throat in that way. The throat might have been cut as she was falling, or when she was on the ground. The blood would have spurted about if the act had been committed while she was standing up.

THE CORONER: Was the silk scarf tight enough to prevent her calling out?—I could not say that.

A hand might have been put on her nose and mouth?—Yes, and the cut on the throat was probably instantaneous.

The inquest was then adjourned till one o'clock today.

# THE DAILY TELEGRAPH
Thursday, October 4, 1888

Page 5
THE LONDON TRAGEDIES
THE WHITECHAPEL MURDER.
*[Third Session of Inquest]*

No success has yet attended the exertions of the detectives to unearth the perpetrator of the Berner-street murder, but the search is now becoming more systematic. A large staff of men have been told off to visit all the lodging-houses in the neighbourhood—of which the number is legion—to make thorough inquiry regarding all suspicious characters who take up their abode there or are known to the "deputies." Yesterday the police were busy all day distributing from house to house throughout the whole of the Whitechapel district a handbill to the following effect: "Police Notice.—To the occupier.—On the mornings of Friday, 31st August, Saturday, 8th, and Sunday, 30th Sept., 1888, women were murdered in Whitechapel, it is supposed by someone residing in the immediate neighbourhood. Should you know of any person to whom suspicion is attached, you are earnestly requested to communicate at once with the nearest police-station.—Metropolitan Police Office, 30th Sept., 1888."

INQUEST—
FURTHER IDENTIFICATION.
A KNIFE FOUND.

Yesterday, at St. George's Vestry Hall,

Cable-street, Mr. Wynne E. Baxter, coroner for East Middlesex, again resumed the inquiry into the circumstances attending the death of the woman who was found with her throat cut at one o'clock on Sunday morning last in a yard adjoining the International Working Men's Club, Berner-street, Commercial-road East.

**Elizabeth Tanner**, examined by the Coroner, said: I am deputy of the common lodging-house, No. 32, Flower and Dean-street, and am a widow. I have seen the body of the deceased at St. George's Mortuary, and recognise it as that of a woman who has lodged in our house, on and off, for the last six years.

Who is she?—She was known by the nick-name of "Long Liz."

Do you know her right name?—No.

Was she an English woman?—She used to say that she was a Swedish woman. She never told me where she was born. She said that she was married, and that her husband and children were drowned in the Princess Alice.[28]

When did you last see her alive?—Last Saturday evening, at half-past six o'clock.

Where was she then?—With me in a public-house, called the Queen's Head, in Commercial-street.

Did she leave you there?—She went back with me to the lodging-house. At that time she had no bonnet or cloak on. She never told me what her husband was.

Where did you actually leave her?— She went into the kitchen, and I went to another part of the building.

Did you see her again?—No, until I saw the body in the mortuary to-day.

You are quite certain it is the body of the same woman?—Quite sure. I recognise, beside the features, that the roof of her mouth is missing.[29] Deceased accounted for this by stating that she was in the Princess Alice when it went down, and that her mouth was injured.

How long had she been staying at the lodging-house?—She was there last week only on Thursday and Friday nights.

Had she paid for her bed on Saturday night?—No.

Do you know any of her male acquaintances?—Only of one.[30]

Who is he?—She was living with him. She left him on Thursday to come and stay at our house, so she told me.

Have you seen this man?—I saw him last Sunday.

DETECTIVE-INSPECTOR REID: He is present to-day.

WITNESS: I do not know that she was ever up at the Thames Police-court, or that she suffered from epileptic fits.[31] I am aware that she lived in Fashion-street, but not that she has ever resided at Poplar. I never heard of a sister at Red Lion-square. I never heard of any relative except her late husband and children.[32]

---

[28]Stride's story that she was associated with the *Princess Alice*, a pleasure craft which collided with the collier *Bywell Castle* in 1878, killing 527 passengers, has never been confirmed. Even though she told people her husband died in the disaster, their marriage did not break down until four years later; John Stride died two years after that in October 1884.

[29]But see Dr. Phillips' testimony, 6 October.

[30]Michael Kidney (b. 1852), a dock labourer often described as a drunken, brawling lout (BFS, pp. 222–223). Theorists who remove Stride from the Ripper's tally often attribute her murder to Kidney; Hinton, Wolf and a cautious Eddleston have endorsed this suggestion in print.

[31]To date, it is known that Stride was before the Thames Magistrates eight times for drunkenness during 1887–1888.

[32]Stride gave birth to a stillborn girl in 1865, after registering as a "prostitute" in Gothenburg, Sweden (Shelden, p. 19), but there is no evidence she had any other children. Much like Mary Kelly, Stride appears to have indulged in fabrications.

What sort of a woman was she?—Very quiet.

A sober woman?—Yes.

Did she use to stop out late at night?—Sometimes.

Do you know if she had any money?—She cleaned two rooms for me on Saturday, and I paid her 6d for doing it. I do not know whether she had any other money.

Are you able to say whether the two handkerchiefs now at the mortuary belonged to the deceased?—No.

Do you recognise her clothes?—Yes. I recognise the long cloak which is hanging up in the mortuary. The other clothes she had on last Saturday.

Did she ever tell you that she was afraid of any one?—No.

Or that any one had ever threatened to injure her?—No.

The fact of her not coming back on Saturday did not surprise you, I suppose?—We took no notice of it.

What made you go to the mortuary, then?—Because I was sent for. I do not recollect at what hour she came to the lodging-house last Thursday. She was wearing the long cloak then. She did not bring any parcel with her.

BY THE JURY: I do not know of any one else of the name of Long Liz. I never heard of her sister allowing her any money, nor have I heard the name of Stride mentioned in connection with her. Before last Thursday she had been away from my house about three months.[33]

THE CORONER: Did you see her during that three months?—Yes, frequently; sometimes once a week, and at other times almost every other day.

Did you understand what she was doing?—She told me that she was at work among the Jews, and was living with a man in Fashion-street.

Could she speak English well?—Yes, but she spoke Swedish also.

When she spoke English could you detect that she was a foreigner?—She spoke English as well as an English woman. She did not associate much with Swedish people. I never heard of her having hurt her foot, nor of her having broken a limb in childhood. I had no doubt that she was what she represented herself to be—a Swede.

**Catherine Lane**: I live in Flower and Dean-street, and am a charwoman and married. My husband is a dock labourer, and is living with me at the lodging house of which the last witness is deputy. I have been there since last February. I have seen the body of the deceased at the mortuary.

THE CORONER: Did you recognise it?—Yes, as the body of Long Liz, who lived occasionally in the lodging-house. She came there last Thursday.

Had you ever seen her before?—I have known her for six or seven months. I used to see her frequently in Fashion-street, where she lived, and I have seen her at our lodging-house.

Did you speak to her last week?—On Thursday and Saturday.

At what time did you see her first on Thursday?—Between ten and eleven o'clock.

Did she explain why she was coming back?—She said she had had a few words with the man she was living with.

When did you see her on Saturday?—When she was cleaning the deputy's room.

And after that?—I last saw her in the kitchen, between six and seven in the evening. She then had on a long cloak and a black bonnet.

Did she say where she was going?—No. I first saw the body in the mortuary on

---

[33]This is a good example of how transient even the locals could be.

Sunday afternoon, and I recognised it then.

Did you see her leave the lodging-house?—Yes; she gave me a piece of velvet as she left, and asked me to mind it until she came back. (The velvet was produced, and proved to be a large piece, green in colour.)

Had she no place to leave it?—I do not know why she asked me, as the deputy would take charge of anything. I know deceased had sixpence when she left; she showed it to me, stating that the deputy had given it to her.

Had she been drinking then?—Not that I am aware of.

Do you know of any one who was likely to have injured her?—No one.

Have you heard her mention any person but this man she was living with?—No. I have heard her say she was a Swede, and that at one time she lived in Devonshire-street, Commercial-road—never in Poplar.

Did you ever hear her speak of her husband?—She said he was dead. She never said that she was afraid, or that any one had threatened her life. I am satisfied the deceased is the same woman.

BY THE JURY: I could tell by her accent that she was a foreigner. She did not bring all her words out plainly.

Have you ever heard of her speaking to any one in her own language?—Yes; with women for whom she worked.[34] I never heard of her having a sister, or of her having left a child at her sister's door.

**Charles Preston** deposed: I live at No. 32, Flower and Dean-street, and I am

a barber. I have been lodging at my present address for eighteen months, and have seen the deceased there. I saw the body on Sunday last, and am quite sure it is that of Long Liz.

THE CORONER: When did you last see her alive?—On Saturday morning between six and seven o'clock.

Where was she then?—In the kitchen of the lodging-house.

Was she dressed to go out?—Yes, and asked me for a brush to brush her clothes with, but I did not let her have one.

What was she wearing?—The jacket I have seen at the mortuary, but no flowers in the breast. She had the striped silk handkerchief round her neck.

Do you happen to have seen her pocket-handkerchiefs?—No.

You cannot say whether she had two?—No.

Do you know anything about her?—I always understood that she was born at Stockholm, and came to England in the service of a gentleman.

Did she ever tell you her age?—She said once that she was thirty-five.

Did she ever tell you that she was married?—Yes; and that her husband and children went down in the Princess Alice—that she had been saved while they were lost.

Did she ever state what her husband was?—I have some recollection that she said he was a seafaring man, and that he had kept a coffee-house in Chrisp-street, Poplar.[35]

Did she ever tell you that she was taken to the Thames Police-court?—I only remember her having been taken into custody for being drunk and disorderly at the Ten Bells public-house, Commercial-

---

[34]As Stride was earlier mentioned as "working for the Jews," she might actually have been speaking Yiddish rather than Swedish; Kidney believed she spoke fluent Yiddish (BFS, p. 435).

[35]For further discussion of this detail, see Phypers, "Jack the Ripper and the Coffee Connection," *Ripper Notes*, December 2000, pp. 14–17.

street, one Sunday morning from four to five months ago.[36]

Do you know of any one who was likely to have injured her?—No.

Did she ever state that she was afraid of any one?—Never.

Did she say where she was going on Saturday?—No.

Or when she was coming back?—No.

Did she say whether she was coming back?—She never said anything about it. She always gave me to understand that her name was Elizabeth Stride.[37] She never mentioned any sister. She stated that her mother was still alive in Sweden. She apparently spoke Swedish fluently to people who came into the lodging-house.

**Michael Kidney** said: I live at No. 38, Dorset-street, Spitalfields, and am a waterside labourer. I have seen the body of the deceased at the mortuary.

THE CORONER: Is it the woman you have been living with?—Yes.

You have no doubt about it?—No doubt whatever.

What was her name?—Elizabeth Stride.

How long have you known her?—About three years.

How long has she been living with you?—Nearly all that time.

What was her age?—Between thirty-six and thirty-eight years.

Was she a Swede?—She told me that she was a Swede, and I have no doubt she was. She said she was born three miles from Stockholm, that her father was a farmer, and that she first came to England for the purpose of seeing the country; but I have grave doubts about that. She afterwards told me that she came to England in a situation with a family.

Had she got any relatives in England?—When I met her she told me she was a widow, and that her husband had been a ship's carpenter at Sheerness.

Did he ever keep a coffee-house?—She told me that he had.

Where?—In Chrisp-street, Poplar.

Did she say when he died?—She informed me that he was drowned in the Princess Alice disaster.

Was the roof of her mouth defective?—Yes.

You had a quarrel with her on Thursday?—I did not see her on Thursday.

When did you last see her?—On the Tuesday, and I then left her on friendly terms in Commercial-street. That was between nine and ten o'clock at night, as I was coming from work.

Did you expect her home?—I expected her home half an hour afterwards. I subsequently ascertained that she had been in and had gone out again, and I did not see her again alive.[38]

Can you account for her sudden disappearance? Was she the worse for drink when you last saw her?—She was perfectly sober.

You can assign no reason whatever for her going away so suddenly?—She would occasionally go away.

Oh, she has left you before?—During the three years I have known her she has

---

[36]The Ten Bells is one of the few remaining Ripper-era Whitechapel pubs and is one Mary Kelly was known to have frequented.

[37]Of those who lived at the lodging-house, Preston was apparently the only one who knew Stride's correct name. Ironically, despite her confiding in Preston, he refused to loan her a brush.

[38]Kidney implied that no disagreement took place between them, yet Stride supposedly told Catherine Lane that she and her man had "a few words," which has been described as a "row" in some accounts. There is no evidence, however, to suggest that Kidney assaulted Stride. While Kidney would obviously want to avoid a public disclosure of any argument under the circumstances, Stride, as can be seen, showed a propensity for exaggeration.

been away from me about five months altogether.

Without any reason?—Not to my knowledge. I treated her the same as I would a wife.

Do you know whether she had picked up with any one?—I have seen the address of the brother of the gentleman with whom she lived as a servant, somewhere near Hyde Park, but I cannot find it now.

Did she have any reason for going away?—It was drink that made her go on previous occasions. She always came back again. I think she liked me better than any other man. I do not believe she left me on Tuesday to take up with any other man.

Had she any money?—I do not think she was without a shilling when she left me. From what I used to give her I fancy she must either have had money or spent it in drink.

You know of nobody whom she was likely to have complications with or fall foul of?—No, but I think the police authorities are very much to blame, or they would have got the man who murdered her. At Leman-street Police-station, on Monday night, I asked for a detective to give information to get the man.[39]

What information had you?—I could give information that would enable the detectives to discover the man at any time.

Then will you give us your information now?—I told the inspector on duty at the police-station[40] that I could give information provided he would let me have a young, strange [sic] detective to act on it, and he would not give me one.

What do you think should be inquired into?—I might have given infor-

mation that would have led to a great deal if I had been provided with a strange young detective.[41]

INSPECTOR REID: When you went to Leman-street and saw the inspector on duty, were you intoxicated?—Yes; I asked for a young detective, and he would not let me have one, and I told him that he was uncivil. (Laughter.)

You have been in the army, and I believe have a good pension?—Only the reserve.

A JUROR: Have you got any information for a detective?—I am a great lover of discipline, sir. (Laughter.)

THE CORONER: Had you any information that required the service of a detective?—Yes. I thought that if I had one, privately, he could get more information than I could myself. The parties I obtained my information from knew me, and I thought someone else would be able to derive more from them.

INSPECTOR REID: Will you give me the information directly, if you will not give it to the coroner?—I believe I could catch the man if I had a detective under my command.

THE CORONER: You cannot expect that. I have had over a hundred letters making suggestions, and I dare say all the writers would like to have a detective at their service. (Laughter.)

WITNESS: I have information which I think might be of use to the police.

THE CORONER: You had better give it, then.

WITNESS: I believe that, if I could place the policeman myself, the man would be captured.

---

[39]Kidney's arrival at the police station on Monday night has been viewed as self-incriminating. However, *Lloyd's Weekly* printed an "Extra Special Edition" at 4:00am on Sunday morning with news of the "double event," and most daily papers publicised Stride's name as the Berner Street victim by Monday morning (ref. Curtis, pp. 141–143).

[40]Inspector Charles Pinhorn (personal correspondence, Bernard Brown). See also Brown, "The New Broom," *Ripperana* No. 35, January 2001.

[41]In this context, "strange young detective" is probably a misreport for a *strong* young detective.

THE CORONER: You must know that the police would not be placed at the disposal of a man the worse for drink.

WITNESS: If I were at liberty to place 100 men about this city the murderer would be caught in the act.

INSPECTOR REID: But you have no information to give to the police?

WITNESS: No, I will keep it to myself.[42]

A JUROR: Do you know of any sister who gave money to the deceased?—No. On Monday I saw Mrs. Malcolm, who said the deceased was her sister. She is very like the deceased.

Did the deceased have a child by you?—No.

Or by a policeman?—She told me that a policeman used to court her when she was at Hyde Park, before she was married to Stride. Stride and the policeman courted her at the same time, but I never heard of her having a child by the policeman. She said she was the mother of nine children, two of whom were drowned with her husband in the Princess Alice, and the remainder were either in a school belonging to the Swedish Church on the other side of London Bridge, or with the husband's friends. I thought she was telling the truth when she spoke of Swedish people. I understood that the deceased and her husband were employed on the Princess Alice.[43]

**Mr. Edward Johnson** [Johnston]: I live at 100, Commercial-road, and am assistant to Drs. Kaye and Blackwell. On Sunday morning last, at a few minutes past one o'clock, I received a call from Constable 436 H.[44] After informing Dr. Blackwell, who was in bed, of the case, I accompanied the officer to Berner-street, and in a courtyard adjoining No. 40 I was shown the figure of a woman lying on her left side.

THE CORONER: Were there many people about?—There was a crowd in the yard.

And police?—Yes.

Was any one touching the deceased?—No.

Was there much light?—Very little.

What light there was, where did it come from?—From the policeman's lantern. I examined the woman and found an incision in the throat.

Was blood coming from the wound?—No, it had stopped bleeding. I felt the body and found all warm except the hands, which were quite cold.

Did you undo the dress?—The dress was not undone when I came. I undid it to see if the chest was warm.

Did you move the head at all?—I left the body precisely as I found it. There was a stream of blood down to the gutter; it was all clotted. There was very little blood near the neck; it had all run away. I did not notice at the time that one of the hands was smeared with blood. The left arm was bent, away from the body. The right arm was also bent, and across the body.

Can you say whether any one had stepped into the stream of blood?—There was no mark of it.

Did you look for any?—Yes. I had no watch with me, but Dr. Blackwell looked at his when he arrived, and the time was 1:16 a.m. I preceded him by three or four

---

[42]The banter among Baxter, Reid and Kidney regarding this alleged information demonstrates an amateurish belief in being able to do something better than those who are trained to do it, *e.g.*, armchair detectives.

[43]As before, there is no evidence Stride had any children beyond a stillborn girl.

[44]Although both the *Telegraph* and the *Times* of 4 October have Johnston saying "436H," in light of PC Lamb's earlier testimony that he was accompanied to Berner Street by PC 426H and sent him "for the nearest doctor," it is probable this is a misprint. See 3 October.

minutes. The bonnet of the deceased was lying three or four inches beyond the head on the ground. The outer gates were closed shortly after I came.[45]

**Thomas Coram**: I live at No. 67, Plummer's-road, and work for a cocoanut dealer. On Monday shortly after midnight I left a friend's house in Bath-gardens, Brady-street. I walked straight down Brady-street and into Whitechapel-road towards Aldgate. I first walked on the right side of Whitechapel-road, and afterwards crossed over to the left, and when opposite No. 253 I saw a knife lying on the doorstep.[46]

What is No. 253?—A laundry. There were two steps to the front door, and the knife was on the bottom step.

The production of the knife created some sensation, its discovery not having been generally known. It was a knife such as would be used by a baker in his trade, it being flat at the top instead of pointed, as a butcher's knife would be. The blade, which was discoloured with something resembling blood, was quite a foot long and an inch broad, whilst the black handle was six inches in length, and strongly rivetted in three places.

WITNESS (CONTINUING): There was a handkerchief round the handle of the knife, the handkerchief having been first folded and then twisted round the blade. A policeman coming towards me, I called his attention to the knife, which I did not touch.

Did the policeman take the knife away?—Yes, to the Leman-street station, I accompanying him.

Were there many people passing at the time?—Very few. I do not think I passed more than a dozen from Brady-street to where I found the knife. The weapon could easily be seen; it was light there.

Did you pass any policeman between Brady-street and where the knife was?—I passed three policemen.

**Constable Joseph Drage**, 282 H Division: On Monday morning at half-past twelve o'clock I was on fixed point duty opposite Brady-street, Whitechapel-road, when I saw the last witness stooping down to pick up something about twenty yards from me. As I went towards him he beckoned with his finger, and said, "Policeman, there is a knife lying here." I then saw a long-bladed knife on the doorstep. I picked up the knife, and found it was smothered with blood.

Was it wet?—Dry. A handkerchief, which was also blood-stained, was bound round the handle and tied with a string. I asked the lad how he came to see it, and he said, "I was just looking around, and I saw something white." I asked him what he did out so late, and he replied, "I have been to a friend's in Bath-gardens." I took down his name and address, and he went to the police-station with me. The knife and handkerchief are those produced. The boy was sober, and his manner natural. He said that the knife made his blood run cold, adding, "We hear of such funny things nowadays." I had passed the step a quarter of an hour before. I could not be positive, but I do not think the knife was there then. About an hour earlier I stood near the door, and saw the landlady let out a woman. The knife was not there then. I

---

[45]Johnston's testimony, along with others (PC Smith, Dr. Blackwell and Dr. Phillips), is indicative that Stride was not killed at 1:00am.

[46]The knife was discovered approximately one hour after Stride's body was discovered and about fifteen minutes after Catherine Eddowes' body was found at what might be called a *non-related* location to the two murder sites, *i.e.*, near London Hospital (ref. testimonies of Drs. Phillips and Blackwell, 6 October).

handed the knife and handkerchief to Dr. Phillips on Monday afternoon.

**Mr. George Baxter** [Bagster] **Phillips**: I live at No. 2, Spital-square, and am surgeon of the H Division of police. I was called on Sunday morning last at twenty past one to Leman-street Police-station, and was sent on to Berner-street, to a yard at the side of what proved to be a club-house. I found Inspector Pinhorn and Acting-Superintendent West in possession of a body, which had already been seen by Dr. Blackwell, who had arrived some time before me. The body was lying on its left side, the face being turned towards the wall, the head towards the yard, and the feet toward the street. The left arm was extended from elbow, and a packet of cachous was in the hand. Similar ones were in the gutter. I took them from the hand and gave them to Dr. Blackwell. The right arm was lying over the body, and the back of the hand and wrist had on them clotted blood. The legs were drawn up, feet close to wall,[47] body still warm, face warm, hands cold, legs quite warm, silk handkerchief round throat, slightly torn (so is my note, but I since find it is cut). I produce the handkerchief. This corresponded to the right angle of the jaw. The throat was deeply gashed, and there was an abrasion of the skin, about an inch and a quarter in diameter, under the right clavicle.

On Oct. 1, at three p.m., at St. George's Mortuary, present Dr. Blackwell and for part of the time Dr. Reigate and Dr. Blackwell's assistant; temperature being about 55 degrees, Dr. Blackwell and I made a post-mortem examination, Dr. Blackwell kindly consenting to make the dissection, and I took the following note:

"Rigor mortis still firmly marked. Mud on face and left side of the head. Matted on the hair and left side. We removed the clothes. We found the body fairly nourished. Over both shoulders, especially the right, from the front aspect under colar [*sic*] bones and in front of chest there is a bluish discolouration which I have watched and seen on two occasions since. On neck, from left to right, there is a clean cut incision six inches in length; incision commencing two and a half inches in a straight line below the angle of the jaw. Three-quarters of an inch over undivided muscle, then becoming deeper, about an inch dividing sheath and the vessels, ascending a little, and then grazing the muscle outside the cartilages on the left side of the neck. The carotid artery on the left side and the other vessels contained in the sheath were all cut through, save the posterior portion of the carotid, to a line about 1-12th of an inch in extent, which prevented the separation of the upper and lower portion of the artery. The cut through the tissues on the right side of the cartilages is more superficial, and tails off to about two inches below the right angle of the jaw. It is evident that the haemorrhage which produced death was caused through the partial severance of the left carotid artery.[48] There is a deformity in the lower fifth of the bones of the right leg, which are not straight, but bow forward; there is a thickening above the left ankle. The bones are here straighter. No recent external injury save to neck.[49] The lower lobe of the ear was torn, as if by the forcible removing or wearing through of an earring, but it was thoroughly healed. The right ear was pierced for an earring, but had not been so injured, and the ear-

---

[47]Phillips is describing the fetal position.

[48]The incision ran from Stride's left to her right.

[49]The lack of other recent injuries precludes Stride having been assaulted earlier that week or having been attacked twice on 30 September. This also shows Kidney only argued with Stride, instead of assaulting her.

ring was wanting. On removing the scalp there was no sign of bruising or extravasation of blood between it and the skull-cap. The skull was about one-sixth of an inch in thickness, and dense in texture. The brain was fairly normal. Both lungs were unusually pale. The heart was small; left ventricle firmly contracted, right less so. Right ventricle full of dark clot; left absolutely empty. Partly digested food, apparently consisting of cheese, potato, and farinaceous edibles. Teeth on left lower jaw absent."

On Tuesday, at the mortuary, I found the total circumference of the neck 12 inches. I found in the pocket of the underskirt of the deceased a key, as of a padlock,[50] a small piece of lead pencil, a comb, a broken piece of comb, a metal spoon, half a dozen large and one small button, a hook, as if off a dress, a piece of muslin, and one or two small pieces of paper. Examining her jacket I found that although there was a slight amount of mud on the right side, the left was well plastered with mud.[51]

A JUROR: You have not mentioned anything about the roof of the mouth. One witness said part of the roof of the mouth was gone.—WITNESS: That was not noticed.

THE CORONER: What was the cause of death?—Undoubtedly the loss of blood from the left carotid artery and the division of the windpipe.[52]

Did you examine the blood at Berner-street carefully, as to its direction and so forth?—Yes. The blood near to the neck and a few inches to the left side was well clotted, and it had run down the waterway to within a few inches of the side entrance to the club-house.

Were there any spots of blood anywhere else?—I could trace none except that which I considered had been transplanted—if I may use the term—from the original flow from the neck. Roughly estimating it, I should say there was an unusual flow of blood, considering the stature and the nourishment of the body.[53]

BY A JUROR: I did notice a black mark on one of the legs of the deceased, but could not say that it was due to an adder bite.

Before the witness had concluded his evidence the inquiry was adjourned until Friday, at two o'clock.

# THE DAILY TELEGRAPH
Friday, October 5, 1888

Page 3
LONDON TRAGEDIES.
ARRESTS AND SEARCHES.
THE WHITECHAPEL MURDER.

The miscreant who butchered the woman Watts, better known as Stride, in Berner-street, Commercial-road East, in the early hours of Sunday last, is still at large, and, so far as can be ascertained, no clue has been discovered which is likely to lead to his capture. The excitement in the neighbourhood is as intense as ever, and during yesterday many thousands of people visited the scene of the crime, though very little was to be observed, the police on duty effectually keeping intruders away from the now notorious yard adjoining the

---

[50]It has been suggested that Stride used this key to let herself out when Kidney tried to lock her in.

[51]The amount of mud on Stride's jacket suggests that she was not lying on her back, but on her left side as she died, which was how she was found.

[52]At an adjourned date of the inquest, it was wondered why little noise was made when Stride was killed. Dr. Phillips answered that question with his statement about the windpipe being severed.

[53]By "unusual flow," Phillips meant that the blood flowed more readily than what might have been expected from someone of Stride's size and physical condition.

International Working Men's Club. Further arrests have been made, but in every instance the captives have been released.

Late on Wednesday night a man rushed out of a public-house in Aldgate, followed by a woman, who loudly declared that he had threatened her. Hastily entering a cab the man was driven off, but a hue and cry being raised by a mob the vehicle was stopped and its occupant soon found himself at Leman-street Police-station. He was detained during the night pending inquiries. While in the cell he became defiant, and with an American accent frequently used the word "boss," contained in the letter of "Jack the Ripper."[54] No special importance was attached to this, however, and shortly after nine o'clock the man was discharged, sobered by his incarceration.

Just before ten o'clock on Wednesday night a second arrest was effected in Ratcliff-highway. Hearing a woman screaming for help in a court, Sergeant Adams, H Division, went in the direction whence the cries proceeded, and met a foreigner leaving the place. The man was captured, and it was observed that he bore some resemblance to the individual who was last seen in the company of the murdered woman in Berner-street. The stranger volunteered the information that he was a Scandinavian, and was about to sail for America, but the officer, deeming his conduct suspicious, marched him to the police-station. At Leman-street he was searched, but no weapons were found upon him, and in the course of a few hours he was liberated. A third arrest took place in Cable-street the same night, but the prisoner gave a satisfactory account of himself and was speedily released.

# THE DAILY TELEGRAPH
Saturday, October 6, 1888

Page 3
LONDON TRAGEDIES.
BERNER-STREET INQUEST.
*[Fourth Session of Inquest]*

Yesterday afternoon at the Vestry Hall of St. George-in-the-East, Cable-street, Mr. Wynne E. Baxter, coroner for East Middlesex, resumed the inquiry concerning the death of the woman who was found early on Sunday last with her throat cut, in a yard adjoining the International Working Men's Club, Berner-street, Commercial-road East.

**Dr. Phillips**, surgeon of the H Division of police, being recalled, said: On the last occasion I was requested to make a re-examination of the body of the deceased, especially with regard to the palate, and I have since done so at the mortuary, along with Dr. Blackwell and Dr. Gordon Brown. I did not find any injury to, or absence of, any part of either the hard or the soft palate. The Coroner also desired me to examine the two handkerchiefs which were found on the deceased. I did not discover any blood on them, and I believe that the stains on the larger handkerchief are those of fruit. Neither on the hands nor about the body of the deceased did I find grapes, or connection with them. I am convinced that the deceased had not swallowed either the skin or seed of a grape within many hours of her death.[55] I have stated that the neckerchief which she had on was not torn, but cut. The abrasion which I spoke of on the right side of the neck was only

---

[54]See Chapter 4 (4 October) for the full particulars of this letter.

[55]The reference to grapes here with Phillips and further on during Dr. Blackwell's testimony is likely in response both to a story in the *Evening News* of 4 October, which detailed the imaginative ruminations of Matthew Packer—who claimed to have sold grapes to Stride and her escort the night of her death—and to the subsequent discovery of a grape-stalk in Dutfield's Yard by private detectives Grand and Batchelor. See Sugden, pp. 219–228.

apparently an abrasion, for on washing it it was removed, and the skin found to be uninjured. The knife produced on the last occasion was delivered to me, properly secured, by a constable, and on examination I found it to be such a knife as is used in a chandler's shop, and is called a slicing knife. It has blood upon it, which has characteristics similar to the blood of a human being. It has been recently blunted, and its edge apparently turned by rubbing on a stone such as a kerbstone. It evidently was before a very sharp knife.

THE CORONER: Is it such as knife as could have caused the injuries which were inflicted upon the deceased?—Such a knife could have produced the incision and injuries to the neck, but it is not such a weapon as I should have fixed upon as having caused the injuries in this case; and if my opinion as regards the position of the body is correct, the knife in question would become an improbable instrument as having caused the incision.

What is your idea as to the position the body was in when the crime was committed?—I have come to a conclusion as to the position of both the murderer and the victim, and I opine that the latter was seized by the shoulders and placed on the ground, and that the murderer was on her right side when he inflicted the cut. I am of opinion that the cut was made from the left to the right side of the deceased, and taking into account the position of the incision it is unlikely that such a long knife inflicted the wound in the neck.

The knife produced on the last occasion was not sharp pointed, was it?—No, it was rounded at the tip, which was about an inch across. The blade was wider at the base.

Was there anything to indicate that the cut on the neck of the deceased was made with a pointed knife?—Nothing.

Have you formed any opinion as to the manner in which the deceased's right

hand became stained with blood?—It is a mystery. There were small oblong clots on the back of the hand. I may say that I am taking it as a fact that after death the hand always remained in the position in which I found it—across the body.

How long had the woman been dead when you arrived at the scene of the murder, do you think?—Within an hour she had been alive.

Would the injury take long to inflict?—Only a few seconds—it might be done in two seconds.

Does the presence of the cachous in the left hand indicate that the murder was committed very suddenly and without any struggle?—Some of the cachous were scattered about the yard.

THE FOREMAN: Do you not think that the woman would have dropped the packet of cachous altogether if she had been thrown to the ground before the injuries were inflicted?—That is an inference which the jury would be perfectly entitled to draw.

THE CORONER: I assume that the injuries were not self-inflicted?—I have seen several self-inflicted wounds more extensive than this one, but then they have not usually involved the carotid artery. In this case, as in some others, there seems to have been some knowledge where to cut the throat to cause a fatal result.

Is there any similarity between this case and Annie Chapman's case?—There is very great dissimilarity between the two. In Chapman's case the neck was severed all round down to the vertebral column, the vertebral bones being marked with two sharp cuts, and there had been an evident attempt to separate the bones.

From the position you assume the perpetrator to have been in, would he have been likely to get bloodstained?—Not necessarily, for the commencement of the wound and the injury to the vessels would be away from him, and the stream of blood—for stream it was—would be directed away from him, and towards the gutter in the yard.

Was there any appearance of an opiate or any smell of chloroform?—There was no perceptible trace of any anaesthetic or narcotic. The absence of noise is a difficult question under the circumstances of this case to account for, but it must not be taken for granted that there was not any noise. If there was an absence of noise I cannot account for it.

THE FOREMAN: That means that the woman might cry out after the cut?—Not after the cut.

But why did she not cry out while she was being put on the ground?—She was in a yard, and in a locality where she might cry out very loudly and no notice be taken of her. It was possible for the woman to draw up her legs after the wound, but she could not have turned over. The wound was inflicted by drawing the knife across the throat. A short knife, such as a shoemaker's well-ground knife, would do the same thing. My reason for believing that deceased was injured when on the ground was partly on account of the absence of blood anywhere on the left side of the body and between it and the wall.

A JUROR: Was there any trace of malt liquor in the stomach?—There was no trace.

**Dr. Blackwell** (who assisted in making the post-mortem examination) said: I can confirm Dr. Phillips as to the appearances at the mortuary. I may add that I removed the cachous from the left hand of the deceased, which was nearly open. The packet was lodged between the thumb and the first finger, and was partially hidden from view. It was I who spilt them in removing them from the hand. My impression is that the hand gradually relaxed while the woman was dying, she dying in a fainting condition from the loss of blood.

I do not think that I made myself quite clear as to whether it was possible for this to have been a case of suicide. What I meant to say was that, taking all the facts into consideration, more especially the absence of any instrument in the hand, it was impossible to have been a suicide. I have myself seen many equally severe wounds self-inflicted. With respect to the knife which was found, I should like to say that I concur with Dr. Phillips in his opinion that, although it might possibly have inflicted the injury, it is an extremely unlikely instrument to have been used. It appears to me that a murderer, in using a round-pointed instrument, would seriously handicap himself, as he would be only able to use it in one particular way. I am told that slaughterers always use a sharp-pointed instrument.

THE CORONER: No one has suggested that this crime was committed by a slaughterer.—WITNESS: I simply intended to point out the inconvenience that might arise from using a blunt-pointed weapon.

THE FOREMAN: Did you notice any marks or bruises about the shoulders?—They were what we call pressure marks. At first they were very obscure, but subsequently they became very evident. They were not what are ordinarily called bruises; neither is there any abrasion. Each shoulder was about equally marked.

A JUROR: How recently might the marks have been caused?—That is rather difficult to say.

Did you perceive any grapes near the body in the yard?—No.

Did you hear any person say that they had seen grapes there?—I did not.

**Mr. Sven Ollsen** deposed: I live at No. 23, Prince's-square, St. George's-in-the-East, and am clerk of the Swedish Church there. I have examined the body of the deceased at the mortuary. I have seen her before.

THE CORONER: Often?—Yes.

For how many years?—Seventeen.

Was she a Swede?—Yes.

What was her name?—Her name was Elizabeth Stride, and she was the wife of John Thomas Stride, carpenter. Her maiden name was Elizabeth Gustafdotter. She was born at Torlands, near Gothenburg, on Nov. 27, 1843.

How do you get these facts?—From the register at our church.

Do you keep a register of all the members of your church?—Of course. We register those who come into this country bringing a certificate and desiring to be registered.

When was she registered?—Her registry is dated July 10, 1866, and she was then registered as an unmarried woman.

Was she married at your church?—No.

Then how do you know she was the wife of John Thomas Stride?—In the registry I find a memorandum, undated, in the handwriting of the Rev. Mr. Palmayer, in Swedish, that she was married to an Englishman named John Thos. Stride. This registry is a new one, and copied from an older book. I have seen the original, and it was written by Mr. Frost, our pastor, until two years ago. I know the Swedish hymn book produced, dated 1821. I gave it to the deceased.

When?—Last winter, I think.

Do you know when she was married to Stride?—I think it was in 1869.

Do you know when he died?—No. She told me about the time the Princess Alice went down that her husband was drowned in that vessel.

Was she in good circumstances then?—She was very poor.

Then she would have been glad of any assistance?—Yes.

Did you give her some?—I did about that time.

Do you remember that there was a subscription raised for the relatives of the sufferers by the Princess Alice?—No.

I can tell you that there was, and I can tell you another thing—that no person of the name of Stride made any application. If her story had been true, don't you think she would have applied?—I do not know.

Have you any schools connected with the Swedish Church?—No, not in London.

Did not ever hear [sic] that this woman had any children?—I do not remember.

Did you ever see her husband?—No.

Did your church ever assist her before her husband died?—Yes, I think so; just before he died.

Where has she been living lately?—I have nothing to show. Two years ago she gave her address as Devonshire-street, Commercial-road.

Did she then explain what she was doing?—She stated that she was doing a little work in sewing.

Could she speak English well?—Pretty well.

Do you know when she came to England?—I believe a little before the register was made, in 1866.

**William Marshall**, examined by the Coroner, said: I reside at No. 64, Berner-street, and am a labourer at an indigo warehouse. I have seen the body at the mortuary. I saw the deceased on Saturday night last.

Where?—In our street, three doors from my house, about a quarter to twelve o'clock. She was on the pavement, opposite No. 58, between Fairclough-street and Boyd-street.

What was she doing?—She was standing talking to a man.

How do you know this was the same woman?—I recognise her both by her face and dress. She did not then have a flower in her breast.

Were the man and woman whom you saw talking quietly?—They were talking together.

Can you describe the man at all?—There was no gas-lamp near. The nearest was at the corner, about twenty feet off. I did not see the face of the man distinctly.

Did you notice how he was dressed?—In a black cut-away coat and dark trousers.

Was he young or old?—Middle-aged he seemed to be.

Was he wearing a hat?—No, a cap.

What sort of a cap?—A round cap, with a small peak. It was something like what a sailor would wear.

What height was he?—About 5ft. 6in.

Was he thin or stout?—Rather stout.

Did he look well dressed?—Decently dressed.

What class of man did he appear to be?—I should say he was in business, and did nothing like hard work.

Not like a dock labourer?—No.

Nor a sailor?—No.

Nor a butcher?—No.

A clerk?—He had more the appearance of a clerk.

Is that the best suggestion you can make?—It is.

You did not see his face. Had he any whiskers?—I cannot say. I do not think he had.

Was he wearing gloves?—No.

Was he carrying a stick or umbrella in his hands?—He had nothing in his hands that I am aware of.

You are quite sure that the deceased is the woman you saw?—Quite. I did not take much notice whether she was carrying anything in her hands.

What first attracted your attention to the couple?—By their standing there for some time, and he was kissing her.

Did you overhear anything they said?—I heard him say, "You would say anything but your prayers."

Different people talk in a different tone and in a different way. Did his voice give you the idea of a clerk?—Yes, he was mild speaking.

Did he speak like an educated man?—I thought so. I did not hear them say anything more. They went away after that. I did not hear the woman say anything, but after the man made that observation she laughed. They went away down the street, towards Ellen-street. They would not then pass No. 40 (the club).

How was the woman dressed?—In a black jacket and skirt.

Was either the worse for drink?—No, I thought not.

When did you go indoors?—About twelve o'clock.

Did you hear anything more that night?—Not till I heard that the murder had taken place, just after one o'clock. While I was standing at my door, from half-past eleven to twelve, there was no rain at all. The deceased had on a small black bonnet. The couple were standing between my house and the club for about ten minutes.

DETECTIVE-INSPECTOR REID: Then they passed you?—Yes.

A JUROR: Did you not see the man's face as he passed?—No; he was looking towards the woman, and had his arm round her neck. There is a gas lamp at the corner of Boyd-street. It was not closing time when they passed me.

**James Brown:**[56] I live in Fairclough-street, and am a dock labourer. I have seen the body in the mortuary. I did not know deceased, but I saw her about a quarter to one on Sunday morning last.

---

[56]See Commentary 1 regarding Brown's testimony.

THE CORONER: Where were you?—I was going from my house to the chandler's[57] shop at the corner of the Berner-street and Fairclough-street, to get some supper. I stayed there three or four minutes, and then went back home, when I saw a man and woman standing at the corner of the Board School. I was in the road just by the kerb, and they were near the wall.

Did you see enough to make you certain that the deceased was the woman?—I am almost certain.

Did you notice any flower in her dress?—No.

What were they doing?—He was standing with his arm against the wall; she was inclined towards his arm, facing him, and with her back to the wall.

Did you notice the man?—I saw that he had a long dark coat on.

An overcoat?—Yes; it seemed so.

Had he a hat or a cap on?—I cannot say.

You are sure it was not her dress that you chiefly noticed?—Yes. I saw nothing light in colour about either of them.

Was it raining at the time?—No. I went on.

Did you hear anything more?—When I had nearly finished my supper I heard screams of "Murder" and "Police." This was a quarter of an hour after I had got home. I did not look at any clock at the chandler's shop. I arrived home first at ten minutes past twelve o'clock, and I believe it was not raining then.

Did you notice the height of the man?—I should think he was 5ft. 7in.

Was he thin or stout?—He was of average build.

Did either of them seem the worse for drink?—No.

Did you notice whether either spoke with a foreign accent?—I did not notice any. When I heard screams I opened my window, but could not see anybody. The cries were of moving people going in the direction of Grove-street. Shortly afterwards I saw a policeman standing at the corner of Christian-street, and a man called him to Berner-street.

**William Smith**, 452 H Division: On Saturday last I went on duty at ten p.m. My beat was past Berner-street, and would take me twenty-five minutes or half an hour to go round. I was in Berner-street about half-past twelve or twenty-five minutes to one o'clock, and having gone round my beat, was at the Commercial-road corner of Berner-street again at one o'clock. I was not called. I saw a crowd outside the gates of No. 40, Berner-street. I heard no cries of "Police." When I came to the spot two constables had already arrived. The gates at the side of the club were not then closed. I do not remember that I passed any person on my way down. I saw that the woman was dead, and I went to the police-station for the ambulance, leaving the other constables in charge of the body. Dr. Blackwell's assistant arrived just as I was going away.

THE CORONER: Had you noticed any man or woman in Berner-street when you were there before?—Yes, talking together.

Was the woman anything like the deceased?—Yes. I saw her face, and I think the body at the mortuary is that of the same woman.

Are you certain?—I feel certain. She stood on the pavement a few yards from where the body was found, but on the opposite side of the street.

Did you look at the man at all?—Yes.

What did you notice about him?—He had a parcel wrapped in a newspaper

---

[57]A chandler was a retail dealer in provisions or groceries.

in his hand. The parcel was about 18in. long and 6in. to 8in. broad.

Did you notice his height?—He was about 5ft. 7in.

His hat?—He wore a dark felt deerstalker's hat.

Clothes?—His clothes were dark. The coat was a cutaway coat.

Did you overhear any conversation?—No.

Did they seem to be sober?—Yes, both.

Did you see the man's face?—He had no whiskers, but I did not notice him much. I should say he was twenty-eight years of age. He was of respectable appearance, but I could not state what he was. The woman had a flower in her breast. It rained very little after eleven o'clock. There were but few about in the bye [*sic*] streets. When I saw the body at the mortuary I recognised it at once.

**Michael Kidney**, the man with whom the deceased last lived, being recalled, stated: I recognise the Swedish hymn-book produced as one belonging to the deceased. She used to have it at my place. I found it in the next room to the one I occupy—in Mrs. Smith's room. Mrs. Smith said deceased gave it to her when she left last Tuesday—not as a gift, but to take care of. When deceased and I lived together I put a padlock on the door when we left the house. I had the key, but deceased has got in and out when I have been away. I found she had been there during my absence on Wednesday of last week—the day after she left—and taken some things.

THE CORONER: What made you think there was anything the matter with the roof of her mouth?—She told me so.

Have you ever examined it?—No.

Well, the doctors say there is nothing the matter with it?—Well, I only know what she told me.

**Philip Krantz** (who affirmed) deposed: I live at 40, Berner-street, and am editor of the Hebrew paper called "The Worker's Friend." I work in a room forming part of the printing office at the back of the International Working Men's Club. Last Saturday night I was in my room from nine o'clock until one of the members of the club came and told me that there was a woman lying in the yard.

Had you heard any sound up to that time?—No.

Any cry?—No.

Or scream?—No.

Or anything unusual?—No.

Was your window or door open?—No.

Supposing a woman had screamed, would you have heard it?—They were singing in the club, so I might not have heard. When I heard the alarm I went out and saw the deceased, but did not observe any stranger there.

Did you look to see if anybody was about—anybody who might have committed the murder?—I did look. I went out to the gates, and found that some members of the club had gone for the police.

Do you think it possible that any stranger escaped from the yard while you were there?—No, but he might have done so before I came. I was afterwards searched and examined at the club.

**Constable Albert Collins**, 12 H. R.,[58] stated that by order of the doctors, he, at half-past five o'clock on Sunday morning, washed away the blood caused by the murder.

---

[58]"H.R." refers to H Division "Reserve" force; specially selected constables used for processions, demonstrations, etc., with a corresponding increase in allowances. Collins is confusingly listed in H Division records as *both* PC 426H and PC 12HR (personal correspondence, Bernard Brown).

**Detective-Inspector Reid** said: I received a telegram at 1:25 on Sunday morning last at Commercial-street Police-office. I at once proceeded to No. 40, Berner-street, where I saw several police officers, Drs. Phillips and Blackwell, and a number of residents in the yard and persons who had come there and been shut in by the police. At that time Drs. Phillips and Blackwell were examining the throat of the deceased. A thorough search was made by the police of the yard and the houses in it, but no trace could be found of any person who might have committed the murder. As soon as the search was over the whole of the persons who had come into the yard and the members of the club were interrogated, their names and addresses taken, their pockets searched by the police, and their clothes and hands examined by the doctors. The people were twenty-eight in number. Each was dealt with separately, and they properly accounted for themselves. The houses were inspected a second time and the occupants examined and their rooms searched. A loft close by was searched, but no trace could be found of the murderer. A description was taken of the body, and circulated by wire around the stations. Inquiries were made at the different houses in the street, but no person could be found who had heard screams or disturbance during the night. I examined the wall near where the body was found, but could detect no spots of blood. About half-past four the body was removed to the mortuary. Having given information of the murder to the coroner I returned to the yard and made another examination and found that the blood had been removed. It being daylight I searched the walls thoroughly, but could

discover no marks of their having been scaled.

I then went to the mortuary and took a description of the deceased and her clothing as follows: Aged forty-two; length 5ft. 2in; complexion pale; hair dark brown and curly; eyes light grey; front upper teeth gone. The deceased had on an old black skirt, dark-brown velvet body, a long black jacket trimmed with black fur, fastened on the right side, with a red rose backed by a maidenhair fern. She had two light serge petticoats, white stockings, white chemise with insertion, side-spring boots, and black crape [*sic*] bonnet. In her jacket pocket were two handkerchiefs, a thimble, and a piece of wool on a card. That description was circulated. Since then the police have made a house-to-house inquiry in the immediate neighbourhood, with the result that we have been able to produce the witnesses who have appeared before the Court. The investigation is still going on. Every endeavour is being made to arrest the assassin, but up to the present without success.

The inquiry was adjourned to Tuesday fortnight, at two o'clock.

The sketches,[59] on the next page, are presented not, of course, as authentic portraits, but as a likeness which an important witness[60] has identified as that of the man who was seen talking to the murdered woman in Berner-street and its vicinity until within a quarter of an hour of the time when she was killed last Sunday morning. Three men, William Marshall, James Brown, both labourers, and Police-constable Smith, have already stated before the coroner that a man and woman did stand in Fairclough-street, at the corner of Berner-street, for some time—that

[59]This is one of the few *Telegraph* articles where the reporter can be identified; in this case, Joseph Hall Richardson (Sugden, p. 502). For the difficulties this particular story caused, see Sugden, pp. 223–224, and Evans and Skinner, *Letters From Hell*, pp. 169–176 for more on Richardson.
[60]Matthew Packer. The police later refuted the publication of these sketches as "unauthorised."

**"Sketch Portraits of the Supposed Murderer"** from the *Telegraph* of 6 October (courtesy Evans/ Skinner Crime Archive).

is, from a quarter to twelve o'clock, as stated by Marshall, to a quarter before one a.m., the hour mentioned by Brown. The policeman appears to have seen the same pair in Berner-street at half-past twelve.

The evidence of another witness has yet to be taken, and this man seems to have had a better opportunity of observing the appearance of the stranger than any other individual, for it was at his shop that the grapes which other witnesses saw near the body were bought. This witness, Mathew Packer, has furnished information to the Scotland-yard authorities, and it was considered so important that he was examined in the presence of Sir Charles Warren himself.[61] He has also identified the body of Elizabeth Stride as that of the woman who accompanied the man who came to his shop, not long before midnight on Saturday. In accordance with the general description furnished to the police by Packer and others, a number of sketches were prepared, portraying men of different nationalities, ages, and ranks of life. These were submitted to Packer, who unhesitatingly selected one of these here reproduced—the portrait of the man without the moustache, and wearing the soft felt or American hat. Further, in order to remove all doubt, and, if possible, to obtain a still better visible guidance, Packer was shown a considerable collection of photographs, and from these, after careful inspection, he picked out one which corresponded in all important respects to the sketch. It was

---

[61]There is no doubt that Warren reviewed and annotated Packer's statement (MEPO 3/140, ff. 215–216), but it is questioned whether the Commissioner personally spoke with him. Packer was ultimately interviewed seven times between 30 September and 6 October. See Commentary 1 regarding his differing statements.

noticed that Packer, as also another important witness, presently to be mentioned, at once rejected the faces of men of purely sensuous type, and that they thus threw aside the portraits of several noted American criminals. Both witnesses inclined to the belief that the man's age was not more than thirty, in which estimate they were supported by the police-constable, who guessed him to be twenty-eight. If the impressions of two men, who, it may be supposed, have actually conversed with the alleged murderer, be correct, and their recollection of his features can be relied upon, then, in their opinion, at all events, the above sketches furnish a reasonably accurate representation of his general appearance as described and adopted by them. It is possible that, with the aid of these drawings, many persons who may also have met the man may be able to recognise him more easily than by reading the bare particulars of his height, dress, &c., and it is for this reason that we publish them.

A man like the one without the moustache, and wearing the soft black felt deerstalker hat, as drawn, was seen by Mathew Packer, of 44, Berner-street, two doors from the scene of the murder, late on Saturday night, and Packer, as above stated, attests the general accuracy of the likeness given. He describes the incident which brought the man to his notice as follows: On Saturday night about half-past eleven o'clock, this man and the woman he has identified as the deceased came to the fruiterer's shop which he keeps. It was not necessary for them to enter it, as customers usually stand upon the pavement, and make their purchases through the window, which is not a shop front of the ordinary kind. Packer is certain that the woman, who wore a dark jacket and a bonnet with some crepe stuff in it, was playing with a white flower which she carried. The man was square-built, about 5ft. 7in. in height, thirty years of age, full in the face, dark complexioned, without moustache, and alert-looking. His hair was black. He wore a long black coat and soft felt hat. It seemed to Packer that he was a clerk, and not a working man. He spoke in a quick, sharp manner, and stood in front of the window. The man purchased half a pound of black grapes, which were given to him in a paper bag, and he paid threepence in coppers. The couple then stood near the gateway of the club for a minute of so, and afterwards crossed the road and remained talking by the Board School for some time. They were still there when Packer had had supper and when he went to bed; and Mrs. Packer remarked it as strange that they should remain, for rain was falling at the time.

In connection with the Whitechapel murders a black bag has been repeatedly mentioned. Mrs. Mortimer said: "The only man I had seen pass through Berner-street previously was a young man who carried a black shiny bag.[62] He walked very fast down the street from the Commercial-road. He looked up at the club, and then went round the corner by the Board school." This was on the morning of the murder in Berner-street.

---

# THE DAILY TELEGRAPH
Monday, October 8, 1888

Page 3
THE LONDON TRAGEDIES.
*[Letters from Jack the Ripper]*

Communications from all parts of the country, in ever-varying handwritings,

---

[62]Leon Goldstein. The bag was filled with empty cigarette boxes (HO 144/221/A49301C [8a] f. 148–159).

signed "Jack the Ripper," continue to be received in large numbers by the East-end police, and it is obvious that the vast majority of them are forwarded in joke. That a telegram, however, bearing the same signature should be accepted and despatched by the postal authorities without the sender being detained or even watched has naturally caused some astonishment. We are informed that on Friday night the following telegraphic message, transmitted from the chief office of the eastern district in Commercial-road, was received at Scotland-yard: "Charles Warren, head of the Police News, Central Office.—Dear Boss— If you are willing enough to catch me, I am now in City-road, lodging, but number you will have to find out, and I mean to do another murder to-night in Whitechapel.—Yours, Jack the Ripper." The circumstances under which the telegram was sent are the subject of police investigation.[63]

# THE DAILY TELEGRAPH
Friday, October 19, 1888

Page 3
*[A House to House Search]*

The force of police, dressed in private clothes, who have been told off to make a house-to-house search in Whitechapel and Spitalfields, were busily engaged yesterday. At every house or tenement visited they left a copy of the subjoined police notice: "To the Occupier.—On the mornings of Friday, Aug. 31, Saturday, 8th, and Sunday, Sept. 30, 1888, women were murdered in or near Whitechapel, supposed by some

one residing in the immediate neighbourhood. Should you know of any person to whom suspicion is attached, you are earnestly requested to communicate at once with the nearest police-station." The police have everywhere been received with the greatest good-feeling, even in the poorest districts, and have had no difficulty in obtaining information.[64]

# THE DAILY TELEGRAPH
Wednesday, October 24, 1888

Page 3
THE WHITECHAPEL TRAGEDY.
*[Fifth and Final Session of Stride Inquest]*

At the Vestry Hall of St. George-in-the-East yesterday, Mr. Wynne Baxter, coroner for East Middlesex, resumed the inquest concerning the death of Elizabeth Stride, who, early on the morning of Sunday, Sept. 30, was found with her throat cut in a yard adjoining the International Working Men's Club, Berner-street, Commercial-road East.

**Detective-Inspector Reid** deposed that since the last sitting he had found in the books of the Poplar and Stepney Sick Asylum at Bromley an entry recording the death of John Thomas Stride, carpenter, of Poplar, on Oct. 4, 1884.

**Walter Stride**, constable 385 W, stated that he had seen the photograph of the deceased, and recognised it as that of the woman who was married to his uncle, John Thomas Stride, a carpenter, either in 1872 or 1873. They lived in East India

---

[63]The flood of phony "Ripper" correspondence and the headaches it caused the police is a topic too extensive to be discussed in these pages. The interested reader is directed to Evans & Skinner, *Jack the Ripper: Letters from Hell*, for a comprehensive overview of the subject.

[64]This is a good indication that rancor against the police, as put forth by the more radical elements of the press, was not wholly prevalent.

Dock-road the last time he saw them, which was soon after their marriage.[65]

**Mrs. Elizabeth Stokes**, who shed tears bitterly, said: I live at 5, Charles-street, Tottenham, and am the wife of Joseph Stokes, a brickmaker. I was first married to Mr. Watts, a wine merchant, of Bath. Mrs. Mary Malcolm, of 50, Red Lion-square, Eagle-street, Holborn, who gave evidence early in this inquiry, is my sister. Her testimony is all false. I have not seen her for years, and it is untrue that she allowed me 2s per week for five years.[66]

A juror suggested whether Mrs. Malcolm could have referred to another sister.

Inspector Reid thought not, because Mrs. Malcolm identified the deceased as a person with crippled feet, and Mrs. Stokes had crippled feet.

MRS. STOKES (EXCITEDLY): She knows me well enough, and my crippled feet could not pass away in death, as she suggested might be the case. Her evidence was infamy and lies, and I am sorry that I have a sister who can tell such dreadful falsehoods. She has put me, a poor woman, to terrible trial, and I want to know if she is to be allowed to take my character away in such a cruel manner. She said that I had been the curse of many families.

THE CORONER: I think that will do, Mrs. Stokes. Is Mrs. Malcolm present?[67]

INSPECTOR REID: No, sir, and that is all the evidence I can produce.

The coroner having summed up, the jury returned a verdict of wilful murder against some person or persons unknown.[68]

# THE DAILY TELEGRAPH
Wednesday, October 31, 1888

Page 3
*[Upkeep Costs for
Vigilance Committees]*

The East-end Murders.—In appealing for funds to enable the Whitechapel Vigilance Committee to carry on their investigations into the recent murders in the East-end, the hon. secretary, writing from 74, Mile-end-road, points out the services his colleagues have already rendered; the payment of men to patrol the streets by night, the first offer of a reward which was made by any organised body, and many important pieces of information communicated to the police. Owing to the outlay entailed by their work the committee feel themselves unable to continue it unless assisted by subscriptions from the public.[69]

---

[65]PC Stride viewed the mortuary photos on 1 October, rather than the body, which was not buried until 6 October. Elizabeth Stride is buried in grave 15509, square 37 of the East London Cemetery, Plaistow, London (*Ripperana* No. 14, October 1995).

[66]For whatever reason, Mary Malcolm was convinced—or managed to convince herself—that her sister was the Berner Street victim. She viewed the body three times and had "not a shadow of doubt" about its identity, yet she was demonstrably wrong.

[67]It would seem that after the lengthy time Baxter spent hearing out Malcolm—which he was legally obliged to do—he did not wish to revisit the somewhat awkward episode. History is silent on the ultimate fates of Mary Malcolm and the wronged Elizabeth Stokes.

[68]It is unknown why the *Telegraph* did not report Baxter's summary, as they had with the other inquests (ref. *Times*, 24 October, and Evans and Skinner, pp. 170–177).

[69]This is an indication that public enthusiasm for the wearying work of patrolling East End streets and donating money to help in the hunt for the Whitechapel killer was on the wane, which is also indicated by a decline in *Telegraph* articles and reports on the murders since early to mid October. An invaluable examination of fluctuations in newspaper coverage of the Whitechapel Murders can be found in Curtis, *Jack the Ripper and the London Press.*

# *Elizabeth Stride— Commentary*

## DAVE YOST

### 1. Stride Sightings

*—Matthew Packer:*

Had Matthew Packer testified at the inquest, he would have added little except to state before a jury that a man with Stride bought grapes and that he identified her body. Yet, had Packer testified, Coroner Baxter most likely would have whittled down his testimony on certain points because of Packer's inconsistency. Essentially, the following would have remained—the man Packer saw stood 5'7", wore dark clothes, had a quick way of talking and appeared to be a clerk. These are the points on which Packer remained consistent once he mentioned the grape-buyer. However, the man's role—beyond that provided by Packer—cannot be ascertained without a host of assumptions, considering the other events which led up to Stride's death. Hence, Packer's real value as a witness lies not in the hope of determining Stride's killer, but in the hope of better understanding the events of 30 September as they might have occurred.

Packer was interviewed seven times within six days. The initial interview was with Sergeant Stephen White on 30 September:

> I asked him what time he closed his shop on the previous night. He replied Half past twelve [*Note in margin reads:—*? Half past 11.] in consequence of the rain it was no good for me to keep open. I asked him if he saw anything of a man or woman going into Dutfield's Yard, or saw anyone standing about the street about the time he was closing his shop. He replied "No I saw no one standing about neither did I see anyone go up the yard. I never saw anything suspicious or heard the slightest noise and know nothing about the murder

until I heard of it in the morning["] [MEPO 3/140/221/A49301C, ff. 212–214].

This is perhaps Packer's more accountable statement, since White did not lead Packer to any conclusion and because Packer was not potentially biased either by other interviews or the first day of the Stride inquest, all of which occurred or were published on 1 October:

—PC Smith's description of the man with Stride was published on 1 October (*Telegraph*, 1 October, p. 5).

—Mortimer's interviews were published on 1 October (*Telegraph*, 1 October, p. 5, *Evening News*, 1 October, pp. 2–3, *Daily News*, 1 October).

—Diemschütz's interview was published on 1 October (*Telegraph*, 1 October, p. 5).

—The inquest's first day was 1 October (*Telegraph*, 2 October, p. 3).

Although Sergeant White did not necessarily ask every possible question, the interview was understandably brief since Packer stated he closed up at 12:30am. Hence, Packer would have no direct knowledge of Stride's murder. This and his inconsistency are the main reasons for his not testifying at the inquest:

> Packer who is an elderly man, has unfortunately made different statements so that apart from the fact of the hour at which he saw the woman (and she was seen afterwards by the P.C. & Schwartz as stated) any statement he made would be rendered almost valueless as evidence [HO 144/221/A49301C (8a) ff. 148–159].

Despite the above, however, Packer was singularly *inconsistent* on "the hour at which he saw the woman," altering his time for closing up shop with nearly each successive interview, from 12:30am, to shortly after midnight, to midnight and then to 11:30pm. Yet despite this time shifting, Packer neglected one very important event in all of his statements—the discussion at the International Working-men's Educational Club (IWEC), just three doors north from his shop. There were ninety to one hundred people attending the discussion, which ended between 11:30 and 11:45pm with approximately sixty to eighty people leaving at that time, using the street door. This is not an event that would have been missed by even the most casual observer, especially a shopkeeper hoping to sell his wares. Therefore, Packer could not have closed up shop at any time after the discussion ended.

Packer originally stated "half past twelve" for closing up shop, because he most likely assumed that the exiting IWEC members were people leaving a pub after it closed. He had already closed up shop and was preparing for bed, so he would not necessarily have any direct visual confirmation of the people in the street. It seems that he erroneously discerned the hour from a commonly occurring event, just as someone today might note the hour from when the nightly news comes on TV. This would explain why Packer originally stated 12:30, and possibly why he readily adjusted his time at each successive interview.

Another indication that Packer closed up no later than 11:30pm is the weather. He informed Sergeant White that he closed up because of the rain. Per various testimonies at Stride's inquest, we know it rained very little after 11:00pm, with the rain stopping around 11:30pm. While the official weather records state, "Sudden heavy R. 9:5p.m. lasting till after midnight," the testimonies of those who were outside indicate that the weather front was moving inland. Additionally, Dr. Blackwell noted at the inquest that Stride's clothes were "not wet with rain" (Meteorological Library & Archives, September 1888 weather records for London area).

When the foregoing is combined with the following:

—Best and Gardner saw Stride and a man leave the Bricklayer's Arms pub just before 11:00pm (BFS, p. 42);

—Marshall saw Stride and a man near Boyd & Berner Streets around 11:45pm (*Telegraph*, 6 October, p. 3);

—Packer identified the body (HO 144/221/A49301C [8a], ff. 148–159; MEPO 3/140, f. 211–212)

it can be ascertained that Packer's most accurate statement was that first given on 4 October. Relating that statement back to Packer's initial comments to Sergeant White, it can be asserted that Stride and her man moved on prior to Packer closing up shop. There are other minor disparities between Packer's Scotland Yard statement and those made by other witnesses, but not knowing the exact time (*i.e.*, some of the times were a guess) would account for the differences in minutes. This official statement would also serve to indicate that Packer did sell grapes, which Mortimer, Batchelor and Grand and several others corroborate.

The question of Packer's grapes and the existence of a grape-stalk are mini-mysteries within the Stride case, even though they have no bearing on her death. But in acknowledging that Packer sold the grapes, the medical testimony of Drs. Blackwell and Phillips cannot be ignored. The medicos explicitly stated that no stalk was seen near her body when examined *in situ*. No one mentioned grapes or grape-stalk during the exam, whilst approximately thirty people stood in the yard. The autopsy clearly showed that Stride swallowed neither skin nor seed of any grape within several hours prior her death. Witnesses like Edward Spooner, who put his hand under Stride's chin, saw nothing of grapes or grape-stalk near her body, let alone in her hand. Witness Israel Schwartz also never noted Stride carrying anything larger than that which could have been concealed in the palm of a hand, *e.g.*, cachous. And no witness claimed to have touched a grape-stalk. Yet these conflicts do not necessarily contradict each other.

After Stride and her man left the Bricklayer's Arms, just before 11:00pm, Packer sold the man some grapes, noted that Stride and the man stayed in the area for a while, and then closed shop no later than 11:30pm. The couple eventually moved on and were seen by Marshall at 11:45pm. During this time, Stride and her man would have consumed the grapes, albeit Stride herself did not actually swallow any of them. It is very doubtful that Stride would have retained possession of a bare stalk for nearly one hour! Had the stalk found by Batchelor and Grand been the one sold by Packer to the man with Stride, it most likely would have been simply tossed into Dutfield's Yard after the grapes were consumed. The statements claiming that Stride's lifeless hand still clutched grapes (or grape-stalk), are most likely newsman exaggeration (ref. PC Lamb and Diemschütz's statements to the press as compared to their inquest testimonies, *Telegraph*, 1 October, p. 5, 2 October, p. 3, and 3 October, p. 3).

As a final comment on Packer, the "Yankee hat" placed by MEPO 3/140, f. 215–216 on the grape-buyer's head could very possibly be a residual effect of an interview with the *Evening News* from the day before. During that interview, the reporter led Packer into stating that his grape-buyer spoke with an American accent by attempting to imitate the American "twang." Reviewing the interviews which followed (Scotland Yard statement and J Hall Richardson *Telegraph* article), the "American" venue is sustained in one fashion or another. While it is certain that Packer was not led to any conclusion during his interview at Scotland Yard, Richardson most likely led Packer into asserting the grape-buyer was an American (HO 144/221/A49301C [8a], ff. 148–159;

MEPO 3/140, ff. 215–216; *Ripperana* No. 15, pp. 6–7, No. 16, pp. 4–9).

—*Israel Schwartz:*

Among all the testimonies within the Stride case, Schwartz's statement has greater bearing on the events because he viewed an assault on Stride approximately *fifteen minutes* before her body was discovered:

> 12:45 a.m. 30th Israel Schwartz of 22 Helen [Ellen] Street, Backchurch Lane, stated that at this hour, turning into Berner Street from Commercial Road, and having gotten as far as the gateway where the murder was committed, he saw a man stop and speak to a woman, who was standing in the gateway. He tried to pull the woman into the street, but he turned her round and threw her down on the footway and the woman screamed three times, but not very loudly. On crossing to the opposite side of the street, he saw a second man lighting his pipe. The man who threw the woman down called out, apparently to the man on the opposite side of the road, "Lipski," and then Schwartz walked away, but finding that he was followed by the second man, he ran as far as the railway arch, but the man did not follow so far. Schwartz cannot say whether the two men were together or known to each other. Upon being taken to the mortuary, Schwartz identified the body as that of the woman he had seen. He thus describes the first man who threw the woman down:—age, about 30; ht, 5ft 5in[s]; comp., fair; hair, dark; small brown moustache, full face, broad shouldered; dress, dark jacket and trousers, black cap with peak, and nothing in his hands. Second man: age, 35; ht., 5ft 11in[s], comp., fresh; hair, light brown; dress, dark overcoat, old black hard felt hat, wide brim; had a clay pipe in his hand [HO 144/221/A49301C (8a), ff. 148–159].

The greatest point of confusion in Schwartz's statement is how the narrative is being relayed. Inspector Swanson wrote the above as part of his 19 October report to the Home Office in the third person, yet the statement is still from Schwartz's point of view. Because of this atypical narrative style, the following statement has conveyed some confusion: "On crossing to the opposite side of the street, he saw a second man lighting his pipe. The man who threw the woman down called out, apparently to the man on the opposite side of the road."

Prior this particular incident, Schwartz was crossing from the western side of Berner Street (Dutfield's Yard side) to the eastern side of the street (board school side). Hence, it was Schwartz who was in the act of crossing to the opposite side of the street, when he saw a man light a pipe. When the first man yelled "Lipski," Schwartz was already heading toward the school; therefore, the man with the pipe was, at that point, on the *opposite side* (Dutfield's Yard side) of the street with respect to Schwartz. This view is corroborated by the only other known version of Schwartz's statement, in the *Star* of 1 October:

> Information which may be important was given to the Leman Street police yesterday by an Hungarian concerning this murder. The foreigner [Schwartz] was well dressed, and had the appearance of being in the theatrical line. He could not speak a word of English, but came to the police station accompanied by a friend, who acted as interpreter. He gave his name and address, but the police have not disclosed them. A Star man, however, got wind of his call, and ran him to earth in Backchurch Ln. The reporter's Hungarian was quite as imperfect as the foreigner's English, but an interpreter was at hand, and the man's story was retold as he had given it to the police. It is, in fact, to the effect that he saw the whole thing.
>
> When he first came homewards about a quarter before one he first walked down Berner St to see if his wife had moved. As he turned the corner from Commercial Rd he noticed some distance in front of him a

man walking as if partially intoxicated. He [Schwartz] walked on behind him, and presently he noticed a woman standing in the entrance to the alleyway where the body was found. The half-tipsy man halted and spoke to her. The Hungarian saw him put his hand on her shoulder and push her back into the passage, but feeling rather timid of getting mixed up in quarrels, *he crossed to the other side of the street. Before he had gone many yards, however, he heard the sound of a quarrel, and turned back to learn what was the matter, but just as he stepped from the kerb a second man came out of the doorway of a public house a few yards off* [italics added], and shouting some sort of warning to the man who was with the woman, rushed forward as if to attack the intruder. The Hungarian states positively that he saw a knife in the second man's hand, but he waited to see no more. He fled incontinently to his new lodgings.

He described the man with the woman as about 30 years of age, rather stoutly built, and wearing a brown moustache. He was dressed respectably in dark clothes and felt hat. The man who came at him with a knife he also describes, but not in details. He says he was taller than the other but not so stout, and that his moustaches were red. Both men seemed to belong to the same grade of society. The police have arrested one man answering the description the Hungarian furnishes. The prisoner has not been charged, but is held for inquiries to be made. The truth of the man's statement is not wholly accepted.

The *Star*'s version better clarifies the event with the added detail that the second man "came out of the doorway of a public house a few yards off." This has been identified as The Nelson at 46 Berner Street, on the northwest corner of Berner and Fairclough Streets and three doors south of Dutfield's Yard. However, the *Star*'s version does add some confusion of its own by stating that the second man had a knife and yelled to the first man, whereas in Swanson's report, the second man lit a pipe and it was the first man who yelled.

And while the *Star* might not have fully accepted Schwartz's statement, a review of official records clearly shows that the police took him seriously.

Schwartz voluntarily made his initial statement at the Leman Street Police Station on Sunday evening, 30 September, the day before the opening of Stride inquest. He then viewed Stride's body, positively identifying it as the woman he saw. Hence, Schwartz's official statement would be the more accurate of the two versions, even though the *Star*'s version provides some detail not available within Swanson's report.

With respect to the word "Lipski," it has been questioned whether or not Schwartz correctly heard the word (*i.e.*, "Lizzy" or "Lipski"). It has been opined that because Schwartz was a Hungarian, he might have misunderstood an English shout. Considering that we are discussing a two-syllable word with a labial distinction between "zz" and "psk," it is doubtful that Schwartz misheard, especially since the word was "yelled."

Discussing Schwartz's statement also involves on some level trying to determine *why* "Lipski" was yelled. Israel Lipski was a Polish Jew who, in 1887, poisoned Miriam Angel, a fellow-lodger at 16 Batty Street. Following Angel's death, Lipski unsuccessfully attempted to poison himself and was eventually hung for the murder. In 1888, the term "Lipski" was used as an anti–Semitic remark. After Schwartz gave his statement to the police, the subject of "Lipski" was the topic of numerous official memos, including one from Dr. Robert Anderson:

> With ref. to the letter ... that the opinion arrived at in this office upon the evidence given by Schwartz at the inquest of Eliz Stride's case is that the name Lipski ... was used by a man whom he saw assaulting the woman in Berner St on the night of the murder, was not addressed to the supposed accomplice but to Schwartz himself. Dated "5/11/8" [MEPO 3/140 f207, as given in BFS, pp. 249–250].

Reviewing the events leading up to the first man yelling, "Lipski," Schwartz was already crossing over to the eastern side of the street. The first man, who by account was still facing towards Dutfield's Yard, was occupied with Stride and no other person was known to be around. A second man exits the pub and lights his pipe. The sudden appearance of light would have attracted the first man's attention, as it did Schwartz's. Given that a Socialist Jews' club was right next door, the first man most likely assumed that this second man was a Jew. Wanting this second man to stay out of the situation, which Schwartz was already avoiding, the first man yells "Lipski" to the second man. At that point, Schwartz and the second man left the area.

After Schwartz left the area, it has been supposed that the second man returned, which is essential for the team killers concept (which Anderson expressed in his memo). Yet there is no information to support it, and at least circumstantial evidence to discount it. In all probability, Schwartz's second man was the man seen with Stride between 11:00pm and 12:35am. Additionally, Anderson's comment about "Lipski" being yelled at Schwartz does not seem to follow the events, since the word was not yelled until after the second man exited the pub and lit his pipe and Schwartz already crossing the street to avoid the situation.

The final question regarding Schwartz is why he did not testify at the inquest, considering the importance of his statement. According to Anderson, Schwartz *did* testify, yet his previously-quoted memo is the only evidence to date indicating that Schwartz testified either openly or behind closed doors. Sadly, the official inquest transcripts which might answer this particular question no longer exist. Some researchers have accepted Anderson's statement because his memo was written less than three weeks after the Stride inquest concluded, because of Schwartz's importance, and because Coroner Baxter would not let such testimony go unrecognized. Nevertheless, the police had Schwartz's statement and did accept it as accurate, whether or not he testified (ref. BFS, p. 388).

*—James Brown:*

James Brown testified on 5 October that he saw Stride and a man standing at the corner of the board school at 25–41 Berner Street, on the northeast corner of Berner and Fairclough streets. He timed this sighting as "about a quarter to one," which is when the Schwartz incident occurred. Yet Brown never noted anything unusual happening, and obviously the woman he saw could not have been Stride if Schwartz saw Stride being assaulted at the gateway. The reconciliation between Schwartz's timing and Brown's can only be accomplished with Brown's description of the situation as he saw it.

Momentarily ignoring Brown's timing, the most singular aspect of his testimony is where he was.

> I was going from my house to the *chandler's shop at the corner of the Berner-street and Fairclough-street*, to get some supper. I stayed there three or four minutes, and then went back home, when I saw a man and woman standing at the corner of the Board School. *I was in the road just by the kerb* [northeast corner of Berner and Fairclough streets], and *they were near the wall.*
> When I had nearly finished my supper I heard screams of "Murder" and "Police." This was a quarter of an hour after I had got home. I did not look at any clock at the chandler's shop. I arrived home first at ten minutes past twelve o'clock, and I believe

it was not raining then [*Telegraph*, 6 October, p. 3; emphasis added].

The chandler shop at 48 Berner Street was owned by Henry Norris and stood at the southwest corner of Berner and Fairclough streets, and James Brown lived at 35 Fairclough Street, east of Berner Street, near the corner of Christian and Fairclough streets. Hence, Brown had to pass through the junction of Berner and Fairclough in order to return home. Had he travelled through this junction at 12:45am, he could not have missed seeing four people in the street—especially while travelling from southwest to northeast—with one person yelling "Lipski," and two people heading south. Also, Brown's uncertainty about the woman's identification casts doubt on his reliability: "Did you see enough to make you certain that the deceased was the woman?—I am almost certain" (*Telegraph*, 6 October, p. 3).

Additionally, the *Evening News* of 1 October located a couple who, by all accounts, were the couple seen by Fanny Mortimer (see below) and would have been the couple seen by Brown. This couple never noted seeing the Schwartz incident, and Schwartz never noted passing anyone when leaving the area. The timing Brown gives for seeing this couple by the board school cannot be correct, and his testimony shows that he was not very observant. So when did Brown leave the chandler shop? Mortimer never saw anyone pass through the junction of Berner and Fairclough streets (except for the couple) while she stood outside of her house. Diemschütz never noted seeing anyone in the junction as he approached Dutfield's Yard. Brown stated, "When I had nearly finished my supper I heard screams of 'Murder' and 'Police.'" Brown could only have heard those "screams" at about or shortly after 1:00am when Diemschütz and another club member ran for help

(Mortimer and Marshall also heard the "cries" at this time). This fixes Brown's time for being in the junction between Mortimer and Diemschütz (*Telegraph*, 1 October, p. 5; Sugden, p. 169; *Manchester Guardian*, 1 October).

*— Fanny Mortimer:*

To help pin down the events as they might have occurred, Mrs. Fanny Mortimer also comes into play. She lived on the same side of the street as and only three doors north of Dutfield's Yard. On 1 October, her statement was published in the *Daily Telegraph*:

> Mrs. Mortimer, living at 36, Berner-street, four doors from the scene of the tragedy, states: "I was standing at the door of my house nearly the whole time between half-past twelve and one o'clock this (Sunday) morning, and did not notice anything unusual. I had just gone indoors and was preparing to go to bed when I heard a commotion outside, and immediately ran out, thinking that there was another row at the Socialists' Club close by. I went to see what was the matter, and was informed that another dreadful murder had been committed in the yard adjoining the club-house, and on going inside I saw the body of a woman lying huddled up just inside the gates, with her throat cut from ear to ear. A man [Edward Spooner] touched her face, and said it was quite warm, so that the deed must have been done while I was standing at the door of my house. There was certainly no noise made, and I did not observe any one enter the gates. It was just after one o'clock when I went out, and the only person whom I had seen pass through the street previously was a young man [Leon Goldstein] carrying a black shiny bag, who walked very fast from the direction of Commercial-road. He looked up at the club, and then went round the corner by the Board School. I was told that the manager or steward of the club had discovered the woman on his return home in his pony-cart. He drove through the gates, and my opinion is that he interrupted the

murderer, who must have made his escape immediately, under cover of the cart. If a man had come out of the yard before one o'clock I must have seen him.

Mortimer gives every indication that she was standing outside her door between 12:30 and 1:00am and saw nothing; however, there are other individuals to consider when reviewing her comments:

—Charles Letchford walked up Berner Street on his way home at about 12:30am, seeing nothing unusual (BFS, p. 247).

—Joseph Lave exited the IWEC at about 12:30am, going to the street via Dutfield's Yard, seeing nothing unusual. Lave re-entered the club between 12:35–12:40am. Some books erroneously list Lave as a witness at the Stride inquest (*Telegraph*, 1 October, p. 5).

—Morris Eagle returned to the IWEC at about 12:40am, first trying the front door, which was "closed" (locked), then entering the club via Dutfield's Yard, noticing nothing unusual (*Telegraph*, 2 October, p. 3).

—PC Smith saw Stride with a man near Dutfield's Yard as he patrolled his beat southward down Berner Street at about 12:30–12:35am (*Telegraph*, 6 October, p. 3).

Mortimer only saw Leon Goldstein walking down Berner Street. She never saw Letchford, PC Smith, Eagle—who went to the front door of the IWEC—or Lave, who stood in the gateway of Dutfield's Yard. Additionally, she missed the entire Schwartz incident. Had Mortimer factually been outside her door between 12:30 and 1:00am, she could not have missed many, let alone all, of these occurrences. Hence, she could not have been standing outside her door for a half-hour.

Fortunately, Mortimer's statement to the *Evening News* sheds additional light:

> When the alarm of murder was raised a young girl had been standing in a bisecting

thoroughfare not fifty yards from the spot where the body was found. She had, she said, been standing there for about twenty-minutes, talking with her sweetheart, but neither of them heard any unusual noises. A woman [Mortimer] who lives two doors from the club has made an important statement. It appears that shortly before a quarter to one o'clock she heard the measured, heavy tramp of a policeman passing the house on his beat. Immediately afterwards she went to the street-door, with the intention of shooting the bolts, though she remained standing there ten minutes before she did so. During the ten minutes she saw no one enter or leave the neighbouring yard, and she feels sure that had any one done so she could not have overlooked the fact. The quiet and deserted character of the street appears even to have struck her at the time. Locking the door, she prepared to retire to bed, in the front room on the ground floor, and it so happened that in about four minutes' time she heard Diemschitz's [Diemschütz] pony cart pass the house, and remarked upon the circumstance to her husband.

Mortimer never claimed to see the person who passed by with a "measured heavy tramp." He was only *assumed* to be a constable. If Mortimer had gone outside immediately after hearing the footsteps, she could not have missed seeing PC Smith. But the timing is incorrect for PC Smith, who traveled southward through Berner Street at approximately 12:30–12:35am. Schwartz or his first man could not have made these footsteps when they first traveled down Berner Street, otherwise Mortimer would have witnessed the assault on Stride. Nor could it have been Letchford, Lave or Eagle for similar reasons. Neither could it have been Schwartz or his second man when they left the area, because they traveled south—*away* from Mortimer's house. Obviously the time of "shortly before a quarter to one o'clock" cannot be directly accepted. This estimated time could only have occurred after

the Schwartz incident and before Diemschütz's arrival. This corresponds with the other events that took place, as well as with Mortimer's statements to the *Evening News*. The *Daily News* of 1 October reported a story similar to that in the same day's *Telegraph*, both of which, in all probability, based their times on the "measured heavy tramp" being PC Smith. As well, the *Evening News'* "young girl" and her "sweetheart" could not have been in the junction of Berner and Fairclough for twenty minutes, or else they would have witnessed the Schwartz incident; hence, they would have to have entered the area after the assault on Stride.

Interestingly, Mortimer never testified at the inquest, even though three newspapers published statements that she was outside at about the time of the murder. The police most likely viewed her variations, like those of Packer, as unreliable, even though her information has a bearing on the chain of events, as discussed below.

## 2. The Time of Death

Stride's death is usually timed at about one o'clock, with Diemschütz's arrival possibly disturbing the killer. Inspector Swanson's suggestion (HO 144/221/A49301C [8a], ff. 148–159) that Stride might have left Dutfield's Yard after the Schwartz incident only to return again and be killed does not have much merit because of the other witnesses:

1. After the Schwartz incident, Mortimer went outside.
2. Mortimer returned indoors after Goldstein passed by, but the young couple was by the Board School—they saw nothing unusual.
3. This would be the approximate time that Brown left the chandler shop (ref. Commentary 1).

4. Diemschütz came upon the body after driving his pony cart down Berner Street from Commercial Road.

At no time could Stride have departed the area and then returned without being seen, which would also negate the possibility of Schwartz's second man returning to the area.

After the Schwartz incident, however, Mortimer heard a "measured heavy tramp" of someone passing her house. This timing corresponds with the medicos' estimated time of death. On 2 October, Dr. Blackwell testified at the inquest that Stride would have been dead between 20 and 30 minutes before he arrived at 1:16am. This would place the time of death between 12:46 and 12:56am. Additionally, on 3 October, Dr. Phillips testified that Stride died within an hour of his arrival. But when did *he* arrive at the scene? Blackwell arrived at 1:16am and believed that Phillips was at the scene 20–30 minutes later; hence, Phillips arrived between 1:36 and 1:46am. At approximately 1:45am, however, Inspector Reid arrived at Dutfield's Yard and Phillips was already with the body. So it can be safely estimated that Dr. Phillips arrived between 1:36 and 1:44am. This would mean that he estimated that Stride died no earlier than between 12:36 and 12:44am. And on 5 October, Phillips stated that the injury to Stride's throat could have been accomplished in about two seconds.

Obviously, Stride did not die prior to 12:45am, but the doctors' timing corresponds to when Mortimer heard the footfalls passing her house. Because Stride and Schwartz's first man are the only known people to have been in the area between the times of the Schwartz incident and Mortimer standing outside, it is conclusive that Schwartz's first man killed Elizabeth Stride. This discussion provides us with the following chain of events:

5. Best and Gardner saw Stride with a man at the Bricklayers' Arms pub (c. 11:00pm).
6. Packer sold grapes to the man with Stride (11:00–11:30pm).
7. Packer closed up shop (c. 11:30pm).
8. Discussion ended at the IWEC (c. 11:30pm).
9. Marshall saw Stride with a man near Boyd and Berner streets (11:45–11:55pm).
10. PC Smith saw Stride with a man near Dutfield's Yard (12:30–12:35am).
11. Lave was in Dutfield's Yard at the gateway (12:30–12:35 / 12:40am).
12. Eagle returned to the IWEC (c. 12:40am).
13. Brown at Norris' chandler shop (c. 12:43am).
14. Schwartz saw Stride assaulted by the first man at Dutfield's yard (12:45am).
15. Schwartz and the second man left the area (12:46–12:47am).
16. Schwartz's first man killed Stride (c. 12:47am).
17. Mortimer heard a "measured, heavy tramp" (12:47–12:48am).
18. Young couple moved into area (c. 12:48am).
19. Mortimer went outside (c. 12:48am).
20. Mortimer saw Goldstein pass by (c. 12:54am).
21. Mortimer went back inside (c. 12:55am).
22. Brown left Norris' chandler shop (c. 12:56am).
23. Diemschütz discovered the body (c. 12:58am).
24. Alarm raised at IWEC (c. 1:00am).
25. Shouts heard by Marshall, Mortimer and Brown (just after 1:00am).

## 3. Was She a Ripper Victim?

While Elizabeth Stride may always be viewed as the third canonical victim, is it prudent to ask if she actually fell victim to Jack the Ripper? Is she accepted in his tally merely because of the "Double Event," or because of the information at hand? In addressing this, the pertinent question is, "How did she die?"

At the inquest on 3 October, Dr. Phillips provided the following details:

> The carotid artery on the left side and the other vessels contained in the sheath were all cut through, save the posterior portion of the carotid, to a line about 1-12th of an inch in extent, which prevented the separation of the upper and lower portion of the artery. The cut through the tissues on the right side of the cartilages is more superficial, and tails off to about two inches below the right angle of the jaw. It is evident that the haemorrhage which produced death was caused through the partial severance of the left carotid artery.

Additionally, Stride's jacket was plastered with mud on its left side with a "slight amount of mud" on the right side and no mud on the back. Her right hand was "smeared with blood." Stride's scarf was turned to the left and "pulled very tight"; its "slightly frayed" lower border corresponded with the throat wound. There were "pressure marks" about the shoulders. The wound could have been inflicted in about "two seconds." Stride bled to death "comparatively slowly." And she was in the fetal position when found (ref. *Telegraph*, 3 October, p. 3, 4 October, p. 5, and 6 October, p. 3).

Phillips' statement, in accordance with the chain of events proposed in Commentary 2, indicates the following scenario: the "pressure marks" were produced when Schwartz's first man pushed Stride to the ground. After Schwartz and his second man left the area, the first man took Stride into the yard. She was on her feet, with the killer behind her. Instead of grabbing her chin, the man pulled the scarf with his left hand. Stride's right hand went to her throat out of reflex (the left hand spilling some of her cachous), and her throat was then slit from her left to right. Stride fell or was pushed onto her left side, at which time, the killer fled. Lying on her left side, Stride curled into the fetal position while she bled to death.

This scenario could happen within a minute or two. The lack of blood on the jacket is explained by the left carotid artery not being separated, the scarf's border infringing on the throat wound and Stride's right hand being at her throat—which accounts for it being mysteriously smeared in blood. The quickness in which the injury was produced and the severance of the windpipe account for the lack of noise.

If we ignore the lulling certainty of the "Double Event" and compare Stride's murder to the typical manner of death for the other canonical victims, several distinctions are noted:

—Stride was in the fetal position when she died, instead of on her back.

—She was not killed while lying down.

—There was a single throat wound, instead of two.

—Stride's throat wound did not encircle the neck, let alone traverse down to the spinal column.

—There was no attempt to render Stride unconscious, as there had been with the others.

—The other victims were not publicly assaulted by their killer prior to death.

—There was no attempt to disembowel.

—A different type of knife was used— short bladed versus long bladed.

Of course, arguments exist against the inclusion of some of these points. The use of a different knife may not be as significant if Martha Tabram (who was attacked with two weapons) is considered to be part of the Whitechapel Murderer's tally. The man seen by Schwartz assaulting Stride may not have thought it prudent to remain in the area as he had been observed by two witnesses, either of whom might have returned with a policeman. And there is also the oft-proposed possibility that Diemschütz might have disturbed Stride's killer. However, the information we have strongly indicates that the killer was not disturbed, but merely contented himself with slitting her throat. Stride's attacker—Schwartz's first man—was, thus, likely not the serial killer Jack the Ripper, and her death should be classified as an aggravated assault turned murder instead of one in a series of murders.

*Chapter 4*

# CATHERINE EDDOWES

—*found murdered Sunday, 30 September 1888*

The last words addressed to her were a caution to beware of the "knife," an allusion to the Whitechapel murderer. She replied, "Oh, don't fear for me; I'll take care," and went off.
— *Daily Telegraph*, Thursday, 4 October 1888

The second victim of the "double event" of 30 September was 46-year-old Catherine Eddowes, a cheery, well-liked but somewhat feckless woman who had just returned to London after an unsuccessful hopping excursion to Kent. She was murdered in Mitre Square within the "City," which is that part of London situated within the ancient boundaries and governed separately from the greater metropolis of London itself. So a second police force was now engaged in the Ripper hunt.

The City Police came into being almost despite themselves. Previously, London had been guarded by a haphazard group of thief-takers, informants and watchmen who had evolved into the Bow Street Runners, a somewhat systematic grouping of constables who were charged with keeping watch, arresting felons and investigating crimes. The creation of a formal police force within London had been warily regarded by those fearful of abuses of power. By the 1790s, however, the Run-

ners had proven worthy of the confidence of both law-and-order and civil liberties types, and so it was proposed that a professional city-wide body supervised and directed by paid magistrates be created. This was opposed, however, by the city fathers, who did not wish to give up their own magistrates' courts and the monies these generated. They fought for years against the formation of a London force; it was only after the Metropolitan Police were established in 1829 and the Lord Mayor and aldermen were faced with the possibility of losing all their independence in the name of public safety that a city Police Force with jurisdiction over the one square mile of the City of London came into being. They would carry out an admirably thorough investigation into Eddowes' death, but would be no more successful in this endeavour than their Met counterparts.

In contrast to the multi-day inquests of Wynne Baxter, coroner Samuel Langham took only two days to hear testimony.

Although it was not stated explicitly by either police or medical men, the press and public believed that, frustrated in his attempt to mutilate Stride, the killer had crossed over into the City to slaughter Eddowes.

In addition to the Stride and Eddowes inquests, which kept the story of the Whitechapel Murders current, the months of September and October saw the delivery of three macabre missives, all purporting to be from the mysterious fiend stalking the East End.

On 29 September, the Central News Agency gave the police a letter they had received, which had been held back because the editors believed it to be a joke. Opening with the cheeky salutation, "Dear Boss," the penman took credit for the murders, while at the same time blithely dismissing the various guesses as to his identity. As people were regularly claiming to have killed Nichols or Chapman, there was nothing particularly special about this communication to make anyone take notice; but, in what was a stroke of blood-curdling genius, the macabre calligrapher closed with the most famous signature in criminal history—*"Jack the Ripper."*

This letter, and a follow-up postcard in similar handwriting from "saucy Jacky" claiming responsibility for the Stride and Eddowes murders, now had the country talking about "Jack" or "The Ripper." The police distributed hundreds of posters featuring these epistles, in an ultimately fruitless effort to find someone who recognised the writing. As anyone might have predicted, however, the only result was a flood of parchment, all of it inked with the killer's new name. With a few lines in red and a brilliantly-chosen pseudonym, someone gave the Whitechapel Murders to the public and propelled them into legend. Anyone might now call himself "Jack the Ripper." Anyone might now make himself part of the story of the century.

One who did was 21-year-old Maria Coroner. She sent letters to the chief constable of Bradford and to her local paper, adopting the *nom de guerre* of the Ripper while threatening to come and "do a little business." She was found out, and charged with a breach of the peace. Just an act of immature deviltry, perhaps, and yet ... at a time when even such a socially-crusading newspaper as the *Pall Mall Gazette* would stoop at this time to headline a story with the words "Another Murder— and More to Follow," who can say with certainty what Miss Coroner's darker motives might have been?

Then came 16 October. George Lusk, head of the Whitechapel Vigilance Committee, opened his evening mail to discover a small package containing a human kidney, with a letter "From hell" boasting that it had been torn from the body of Catherine Eddowes. Was it real? Probably not, but no matter. Until the Ripper could be caught, any villainy might be ascribed to him, and no one knew what he could be capable of. He might do anything...

Except murder again. There was, for the first time, a break in the pattern of death at the beginning and end of each month. The first and last weeks of October came and went bloodlessly, and as autumn began to fade to early winter, once more the hope arose that Jack the Ripper had at last ended his spree.

November would shatter that hope.

## THE DAILY TELEGRAPH
Monday, October 1, 1888

Page 4
TWO MORE WOMEN
MURDERED IN WHITECHAPEL
AND ALDGATE

Church Passage, Aldgate (courtesy of Evans/Skinner Crime Archive).

Two more murders of the same cold-blooded character as those recently perpetrated in Whitechapel were committed early yesterday morning, one in that district, and the other in the eastern part of the City, both the victims being unfortunate women. The former outrage was committed just within the entrance to a badly lighted courtyard opening off a narrow thoroughfare named Berner-street, and the dead body, not yet cold, was discovered, shortly before one a.m., with the throat cut. In the other case the scene of the tragedy was Mitre-square, a retired and dark locality near Aldgate. The corpse in this instance also was still warm when it was discovered at a quarter to two in the morning, but was much more mutilated, the throat being cut, the abdomen gashed and the right ear slashed off.[1] The murderer left no trace.

On behalf of the inhabitants of the East-end of London a petition was forwarded to her Majesty on Saturday, urging that a reward should be offered for the detection of the murderer or murderers of the four women who up to that date had been killed in Whitechapel, and expressing the conviction that the offender, if undiscovered, would sooner or later commit other crimes of a like nature.[2]

SAVAGE BUTCHERY
AND MUTILATION
PUBLIC TERROR
PETITION TO THE QUEEN

Again this vast metropolis has been horror-stricken by a repetition of the hideous murders and mutilations of which the East-end of London, four times in succession, has already been the scene during the past few months. On this occasion a double crime, in all its leading characteristics so closely resembling its predecessors as to leave little doubt that it was committed by the same merciless hand which deliberately slaughtered and mangled Mary Ann Smith [*sic*], Ann Tabram [*sic*], Mary Ann Nicholls, and Annie Chapman, has been added to the dread list of assassinations perpetrated with impunity in the chief city of the civilised world. The latest victims to the incredible blood-lust of an unknown malefactor, or gang of malefactors, have not as yet been identified with certainty, but their appearance, the hour at which they were barbarously slain, and the obscure, sordid character of the localities in which their bodies were discovered, justify the presumption that they belonged to the class of poor and pitiable "unfortunates" upon whom the ruthless and wily assassin had previously wreaked his homicidal fury. Yesterday morning's twofold murder only differs from those preceding it in the respect that its victims were done to death at an hour when the streets of the populous district in which the crimes were committed had by no means lapsed into the stillness of early morn, but were still frequented by a considerable number of persons belonging to the Whitechapel district. In the East-end, as in the majority of poor London neighbourhoods, a good deal of open-air business is transacted on Saturday nights, with the effect of keeping up buyers and sellers alike to a later hour than that on which they seek their homes on ordinary week-nights. In Berner-street, St. George's, within hearing of the woman murdered there shortly after midnight, the

---

[1]The lobe and auricle of the right ear had been cut off, probably by accident rather than design; the cut portion later dropped from Eddowes' clothing when her body was being disrobed in the mortuary.

[2]As the petition was forwarded on Saturday, September 29, the "four women" mentioned here are obviously Emma Smith, Martha Tabram, Mary Ann Nichols and Annie Chapman.

members of a working-men's club were singing songs and indulging in other convivial recreations whilst the assassin was doing his deadly work. Mitre-square, the scene of another crime perpetrated, in all probability, about half-an-hour later than that of Berner-street,[3] is an open space surrounded by warehouses and accessible by three thoroughfares. During daytime it is a busy spot, much occupied by vendors of fruit, porters, and miscellaneous idlers. Yet within its small precincts, approachable from Mitre-street, Duke-street and St. James's-place, a woman was butchered in cold blood, not fifty yards from the quarters of a night watchman,[4] who heard no sound of a struggle or even of footsteps, although he has alleged that, "as a rule, he can hear the tread of the policeman passing on his beat every quarter of an hour."[5]

Thus, between midnight and one o'clock,[6] two murders were effected at places half a mile distant from one another, without hindrance, noise, or detection, and obviously by one and the same hand.[7] It seems probable that the assassin, having cut the throat of his first victim in Berner-street, was alarmed by the sound of some approaching footstep, possibly that of a member of the club above alluded to, and took to flight, foregoing his ghastly purpose of mutilation for the moment. Having reached the purlieus of Mitre-square on his homeward way, and being unsated with the blood he had already shed, he found another opportunity of carrying out his revolting resolve to its uttermost atrocity of detail, induced a second luckless waif of the night to accompany him into the still, deserted little enclosure hard at hand, and there slaugh-

tered her with more than the savagery of a wild beast, hacking her face to pieces, and mutilating her lifeless body in a manner that is all but indescribable.

## THE CRIME IN ALDGATE.

It is the general belief that the murderer, in the case of the Berner-street tragedy, above described, also committed the following still more frightful deed in Aldgate; but there is no actual evidence to support that supposition. Still there are remarkable circumstances which appear to justify the assumption that the same hand not only perpetrated the atrocities yesterday, but was also guilty of two, if not of more, of the recent Whitechapel murders. It would have been quite possible for the miscreant, who has become the terror of East London, to have made his way from the Commercial-road East, to Mitre-square, Aldgate, in less than ten minutes. His clothing, even if bloodstained, would probably have escaped notice, for his road would have led him through a neighbourhood habitually frequented by slaughterers. The theory which the authorities entertain is that shortly after half-past one a.m. yesterday, the individual who had been disturbed in Berner-street, with his deadly weapon concealed about him, had with deliberate intention, and with the recklessness of a maniac, proceeded to carry out a second horrible crime without delay. The plan differed in no way from that which was successfully practised first in Osborne Street, then in George-yard, next in Buck's-row, again in Hanbury-street, and finally in Berner-street. A woman of the lowest class was to be accosted, and she

[3]Actually about 45 minutes.
[4]George James Morris, an ex-policeman employed by Kearley & Tonge, wholesale grocers (BFS, p. 306).
[5]This ties in with PC Watkins' account later in this news story that he entered Mitre Square at 1:30am and then again at 1:45.
[6]Actually between 12:45 and 1:45am.
[7]The issue of Stride's canonicity, as mentioned earlier, is a contentious point among Ripper scholars.

**Mitre Square, Aldgate. The site of the Eddowes murder was in the corner between the van and motorcycles (courtesy of Evans/Skinner Crime Archive).**

was either to be lured, or suffered to lead the way, into a dark spot; there she was to be cruelly done to death and mutilated. The whole of the hideous programme appears to have been carried out in an incredibly short space of time. Where the man encountered his victim there is no testimony to show; but he would have had many opportunities in the vicinity of the Church of St. Botolph, Aldgate, which is close to the scene of the latest horror. This quarter of London is just within the City police boundaries, and is not comprised in the area over which the Metropolitan police jurisdiction extends. Houndsditch, Aldgate-street, and Leadenhall-street form three sides of a quadrangle, of which the forth side is bounded by a nest of courts and passages, terminating in St. Mary-axe. In the centre of this locality there is Mitre-square, which has three approaches.

On the Houndsditch side there is Church-passage, which is 85 ft. long and 6 ft. wide, and it runs between Mitre-square and Duke-street. In the other corner of the square on the same side—the north-eastern—there is an archway, opening into a passage, 55 ft. long and 5 ft. wide, which leads into a little open market known as St. James's-place. The third entry is, perhaps, 30 ft. wide, and consists of a short piece of roadway and pavements, which connects Mitre-square with Mitre-street, a narrow turning off Aldgate. Thus, any person familiar with the square and its surroundings might have entered it without being perceived. Since the recurrence of the mysterious deaths in Whitechapel and Spitalfields, however, the City police have, acting under special orders from headquarters, directed particular attention to the low class of women of whom six have now been killed; and they have been accustomed to observe them closely, if accompanied by men.[8] No one noticed any such couple pass along either of the streets named. It is therefore imagined that the man having made an appointment with the woman,[9] left her to find her own way to Mitre-square, and that he took the first opportunity of rejoining her unperceived. The Acting-Commissioner of City Police, Major Henry Smith, has courteously afforded every assistance in his power, in order that the true facts might be stated. This gentleman puts the fullest confidence in the account which Police-constable Watkins, 881, has given. This officer says that at half-past one o'clock yesterday morning he went round the square and saw nothing unusual. The place is ill-lighted, for there is only one lamp-post and a lantern lamp which projects from the corner of the buildings on one side of Church-passage.[10]

In the City, where the police supervision is as perfect as could possibly be expected, the beats are short, and it is the testimony of the residents that the constables diligently perform their duty. The constables are under supervision of a sergeant, who is constantly on the alert, and unexpected surveys of the beats are also made by the inspector and the superintendent. There is no reason to doubt that Watkins went into the square at the hour mentioned, and further that a quarter of an hour later, that is, at 1:45a.m., he re-entered it and then made the fearful discovery. As he was walking near to the south-west corner, quite twenty-five yards

removed from the nearest gaslight, he saw the body of a woman, with the clothes disarranged, and with dreadful injuries to the abdomen and to the face. Watkins immediately summoned assistance, and Sergeant Jones, 92, and other policemen were at once on the scene. As showing the promptitude with which the City police acted it may be mentioned that a message despatched to Bishopsgate-street Without Police-station, to Inspector Collard, was, within a quarter of an hour, answered by the officer in person, and he at once took charge of the case until the arrival, shortly afterwards, of Major Henry Smith, from Cloak-lane, and Superintendent Foster, from Old Jewry, to whom messengers had been sent. The authorities in the City at once determined that no clue should be sacrificed by ill-considered haste. Every step of the inquiry, which was straightaway commenced, was carefully and systematically taken. Strangely enough, with the exception of one witness, the whole of the testimony thus far collected is that of the police. The exception referred to is that of a watchman, George James Morris, who was employed by Messrs. Kearley and Tongue [sic], general merchants, of Mitre-square. Part of their premises extend between Church-passage and the arched exit which leads into St. James's-place. They are newly-erected buildings, occupying land formerly belonging to the Jews' Synagogue in Duke-street. On the ground floor, in the counting-house block, the watchman was on duty, his light burning brightly. Directly Watkins found the

[8]This order was given by Major Henry Smith (1835–1921), Acting Commissioner of the City of London Police (BFS, pp. 417–420).

[9]The theory that Eddowes arranged an assignation with her killer is occasionally aired in order to explain her repeated questioning of PC George Hutt as to the correct time when she was released from police custody (see 12 October), as well as to explain her traveling in the direction of Aldgate rather than back to her previous lodgings at the Shoe Lane workhouse, or to join her paramour John Kelly at Cooney's lodging house. Of present authors, only Hinton and Wolf have endorsed this theory in print.

[10]There was also a lamppost at the Mitre Street entrance; this, however, did not throw much light into the square itself, and none at all into the corner where Eddowes' body lay.

body of the murdered woman he went over to the watchman and called his attention to it. Morris immediately responded, and the following is his account of what then passed:

> About a quarter to two o'clock the policeman upon the beat came and knocked at the door of the warehouse. I answered. He said, "For God's sake, man, come out and assist me; another woman has been ripped open!" I said, "All right, keep yourself cool while I light a lamp." Having done so, he led me to the south-west corner, where I saw a woman lying stretched upon the pavement with her throat cut, and horribly mutilated. I then left the constable Watkins, with the body while I went into Aldgate and blew my whistle, and other police officers soon made their appearance. The shape of the woman was marked out in blood upon the pavement. In addition to her throat being cut, there were two slashes across the face, one almost completely severing the nose. The woman was so mutilated about the face I could not say what she was like. She wore a dark skirt and a black bonnet. Altogether her appearance was exceedingly shabby. The strangest part about the whole thing is that I heard no sound. As a rule I can hear the policeman as he passes by every quarter of an hour, so the woman could not have uttered any cry without my detecting it. It was only last night I made the remark to some policeman that I wished the butcher would come round Mitre-square, and I would soon give him a doing, and here, to be sure, he has come, and I was perfectly ignorant of it.

Photograph of Catherine Eddowes in the shell at the Golden Lane mortuary on 30 September, 1888, prior to her autopsy (courtesy of Evans/Skinner Crime Archive).

Morris was asked to knock up Mr. Sequira,[11] of 34, Jewry-street, Aldgate, the nearest surgeon, but, before the body was allowed to be touched, Mr. Gordon

---

[11]Dr. George William Sequeira (1859–1926) (BFS, p. 407).

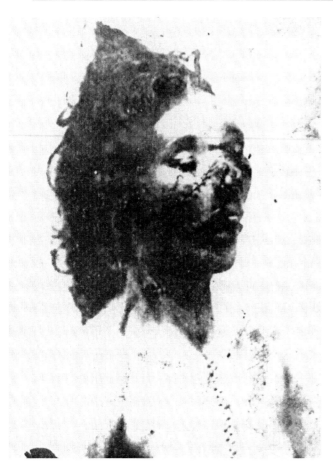

**Three-quarters face view (courtesy of Evans/Skinner Crime Archive).**

square were closed to the public, the constables having orders to admit no one. The intelligence from Berner-street was reported and it made the City police doubly careful in their researches; but nothing which would afford a tangible clue was discovered. Motive of every kind appeared to be absent. There was nothing to denote that robbery was the object; and, on the other hand, there were so many signs of savage ferocity that the idea was strongly entertained that the murderer was a maniac. The injuries to the body surpassed in their hideousness every preceding attack ascribed to the same operator.[14]

The throat had been cut half-way round, with great force, and the knife had severed the carotid artery. From this wound the blood which covered the upper part of the body had evidently proceeded. There were no stains upon the lower members. Apparently the knife had been plunged deep into the chest, and jagged downwards through the soft tissues of the abdomen, to the pelvis. The intestines were torn from the body and thrown towards the chest, and some were found twisted into the gaping wound on the right side of the neck. The thighs were cut across, deeply on the right side. A handkerchief which the woman wore round her throat was saturated with blood.

Brown,[12] of 17, Finsbury-circus, who is the divisional surgeon of police, was also in attendance.

By this time Superintendent Foster[13] had also arrived, and every detail was carefully noted. The news of the murder had scarcely spread, but to guard against disturbances, the three approaches to the

---

[12]Dr. Frederick Gordon Brown (1843–1928). City Police surgeon, 1886–1914. He would perform Eddowes' post-mortem examination (BFS, pp. 62–68).

[13]City Police Detective Superintendent Alfred Lawrence Foster, 1826–1897 (BFS, p. 138).

[14]Eddowes' injuries described here are generally consistent with Gordon Brown's post-mortem notes (ref. Coroner's inquest [L], 1888, No. 135, Catherine Eddowes inquest, 1888 [Corporation of London Record Office]). The post-mortem was carried out on the afternoon of September 30, and the detail here appears to indicate that the *Telegraph*'s source was someone in attendance at the time—possibly Gordon Brown himself, who granted an interview to *Lloyd's Weekly Newspaper* on the morning of the 30th and may have done so later on for the *Telegraph*.

Although there was no sign of a struggle, the murderer, alarmed by some movement, or, perhaps, with the intention of rendering identification difficult, had hacked at the nose of the woman, and the gash extended to the right ear, which was sliced off. Subsequently it was disentangled from the clothing.

The appearances of the body were carefully recorded, and Dr. Brown sketched its exact position. In the opinion of Mr. Sequiera, the first surgeon who saw the corpse—whose opinion may be qualified by fuller examination—the weapon employed must have been a large one and sharp. In order to describe the exact spot where the woman was lying it will be necessary to give some particulars of the size of the square. The measurements are those of Mr. Foster,[15] son of the Superintendent, whose artistic services were immediately requisitioned. By his aid the police will be prepared with every detail to assist the inquiry of the coroner. A line drawn from the passage leading into Duke-street to the opposite corner of the square is 110 ft. long, whereas from the archway opening into St. James's-place a diagonal line stretching from the spot where the body was found is not more than 90 ft. in length. Around the square there is a pavement averaging 10 ft. wide, and in the cor-

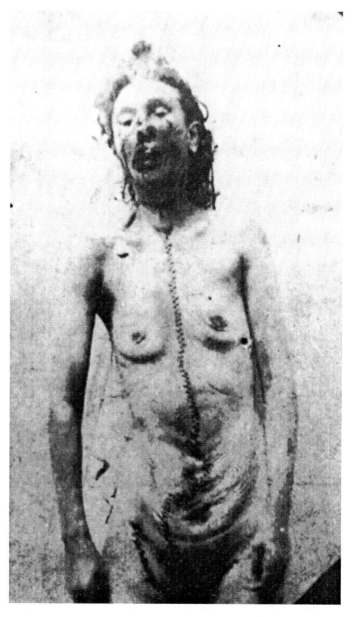

Front view of Catherine Eddowes, photographed at the mortuary after the autopsy. Note the post-mortem stitching (courtesy of Evans/Skinner Crime Archive).

ners the width increases to at least 15 ft. The south-west corner is the one which is on the right hand when the square is entered from Mitre-street. On this side,

---

[15]Frederick Foster, City surveyor (BFS, p. 138). His sketch and measurements of the murder scene are held by the Department of Forensic Medicine, London Hospital Medical College (Begg, illustration 10).

separated from the open public space by a low wall and fence, there is a private yard, which is for the most part roofed in, and is used as a lumber room. This yard, which is some 40 ft. to 50 ft. in depth and about 30 ft. wide, intervenes between a tall pile of warehouses, six stories high, occupied by Messrs. Horner and Sons, drug merchants, and a block of dwelling houses, with shops on the ground floor, the backs of which look upon the square, and the fronts face Mitre-street. The corner house only is occupied, the tenant being Mr. Taylor, a picture-frame maker, who was absent from home. Therefore, the premises, together with those adjoining, were quite empty. In the fence above-mentioned there is a door, which opens into the private yard, but it was locked. Near to the door is a coal shoot [sic], and at a distance of a few feet a couple of arched gratings, giving light to the cellars of the corner houses in Mitre-street. Above these gratings there are two windows, provided with green shutters, which were closed. The woman was lying on the pavement, with her head about eighteen inches from the door in the fence and the coal shoot, and with her legs towards the roadway. Inspector Collard gives this further description:

> The head was inclined to the left; the arms were extended; the left leg was extended straight; and the right flexed. The clothes were drawn up as far as the chest, and the abdomen was ripped open downwards, in a zigzag fashion.

The inspector, of course, observed the other injuries already indicated, but he could not give an opinion whether any anatomical knowledge had been displayed, or whether any attempt had been made to extract any portion of the body.[16]

Both Mr. Sequeira and Mr. Gordon Brown found that the body was still warm, and the blood had not coagulated. The warmth was still present when it was removed to the mortuary in Golden-lane, whither it was taken in a shell upon an ambulance. Major Smith, Superintendent Foster, and other eye-witnesses concur in the description of a singular mark which was apparent upon the flagstones after the body of the woman had been lifted. The form of the legs and feet were there vividly impressed, as it were, in a white tint. This effect was so striking that it was determined, if possible, to obtain a permanent representation of it; but in the course of a short time it disappeared, the explanation of the peculiarity being that the warmth of the body had absorbed the moisture from the wet pavement. Major Smith went to the mortuary, as also did Mr. Foster, the latter for the purpose of sketching the bloodstains, which drawing will be produced before the coroner.

Appended is the official description of the body, which was fully examined at the mortuary by the surgeons mentioned. Major Smith decided that Mr. Phillips, divisional surgeon of Metropolitan Police, who had had the Berner-street murder and the Hanbury-street murder in hand, should be asked to view the latest victim to the assassin's knife. Mr. Phillips accordingly came, and he has, it is said, expressed the opinion that the Mitre-square murder had the same author as the rest. There was considerable discussion as to the manner in which the throat had been cut, and it was agreed that there was nothing to indicate that it had been done in a peculiar way; but it is not clear at present whether the windpipe was severed from left to right, or from right to left; and this is one of the points which will be definitively settled at the inquest. Under the direction of

---

[16]Eddowes' left kidney and a portion of her uterus had been removed.

the doctors the mortuary keeper undressed the body, which is described as that of a woman of the lowest class; but, although the clothing was old and dirty, and the pockets were empty, with the exception of five pieces of soap and some bits of string and such trifles,[17] it was noticed that the hands were small and of a delicate cast, indicating that the deceased had known at one time better conditions of life than her present calling. This was only supposition, as there is nothing directly bearing out the inference. The full official description is as follows:

Age forty;[18] length, 5 ft.; dark auburn hair; hazel eyes; dressed in black jacket, with imitation fur collar and three large metal buttons; brown bodice; dark green chintz skirt, of Michaelmas and Gordon lily pattern, and with three flounces, thin white vest, light drab linsey skirt, dark green alpaca petticoat, white chemise; brown ribbed stockings, mended at foot with piece of white stocking; black straw bonnet, trimmed with black beads and green and black velvet; large white handkerchief round neck. She wore a pair of men's old lace-up boots, and a piece of coarse white apron. The letters "T.C." were tattooed on the left fore-arm in blue ink.[19]

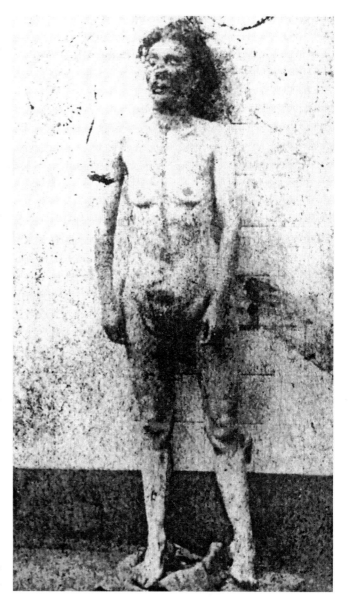

**The body of Catherine Eddowes photographed at the mortuary, propped against the wall after the autopsy (courtesy of Evans/Skinner Crime Archive).**

No time was lost in communicating the news to Mr. S. F. Langham, the City Coroner, whose officer found him at church. An order for a post-mortem was forthwith

---

[17]Six pieces of soap and a ball of hemp, according to the official police inventory (Evans & Skinner, pp. 203–204).

[18]Eddowes was actually 46, born 14 April 1842 (Shelden, p. 25).

[19]The initials of Thomas Conway, from whom Eddowes separated in 1880 or 1881. Though she claimed they were married, no certificate has been found. Press reports of these initials would later be one of the identifiers alerting Eddowes' lover John Kelly to the fact of her death.

signed, and accordingly later in the day the examination was commenced. It lasted from half-past two o'clock until six p.m. Dr. Gordon Brown was assisted by Mr. Sequeira, and the services of Mr. Phillips were also retained. The Metropolitan police were represented by Mr. M'Kellar. All the doctors resolved not to divulge the conclusions to which they had come; but there does not appear reason to suppose that there will be any sensational disclosures at the inquest. The murderer had no time, even if that were his object, to perform a difficult operation such as has been suggested in connection with the murder of Annie Chapman in Hanbury-street.

Who the unfortunate woman who died in Mitre-square really is had not, until a late hour last night, been cleared up.[20] In the course of the day a number of persons called at the mortuary to view the body and gave information which it was hoped would lead to its identification. A thorough investigation was made in each instance but, so far, the inquiries have failed to establish the identity of the deceased.

One of the most extraordinary features of the murder is the fact that not a sound was heard by any resident or passerby. Most unusual risks were run, as will presently appear. It is assumed that it was the woman, and not the man, who selected the place of rendezvous, for women of her class must necessarily know of the most secluded places and the chances of police interference. Mitre-square has not, however, a bad name; at the most at night it seems a deserted spot, avoided by everybody except those whose business takes them there. One of these persons is the night watchman, whose story has been told; the other is the constable on the beat; and the third is a City policeman, who actually lives in the square.[21] He and his family are the only people who do so.

The cottage he occupies is one of two tenements which are squeezed between the blocks of warehouses, one of which fronts upon Mitre-street and the other abuts the archway leading into St. James's-place. The house next to the policeman's is in a tumble-down state, with broken windows, and a waste piece of garden, or yard, insecurely railed in. Pearse, the constable, occupies, with his wife, the front room on the first floor. He says he is a light sleeper, and he did not go to bed until half-past twelve. During the night he heard no noise whatever, and neither did his wife. There was another great risk, Messrs. Heydemann and Co., general merchants, 5, Mitre-street, have three-storeyed premises, the back windows of which are those between Messrs. Horner's warehouse and the opposite block of empty dwelling houses. To Messrs. Heydemann belongs the yard, which is divided from the square by the fencing, near to which the murder was committed. The windows on the second and third floors command an uninterrupted view of a great portion of the public space. They face the policeman's house, from whose room a still better view can be obtained of the spot. Messrs. Heydemann's caretaker, George Clapp, and his wife retired to rest in the second floor apartment soon after eleven p.m. on Saturday night, and throughout they heard nothing. Similarly an old lady who is acting as nurse, and who is sleeping above, was not disturbed. Too much stress must, however, not be laid upon these circumstances, as it appears that a

---

[20]Although this wording suggests that Eddowes' body had been identified late on the evening of September 30, what is meant is that *by* a late hour she had still not been identified. Kelly would perform this sad duty the evening of October 2.

[21]PC 922 Richard Pearce, living at No. 3 Mitre Square (BFS, p. 343).

great many people in the neighbourhood slept on, until long after the removal of the body by the police, without noticing the noise they must have occasioned. Some of the inhabitants of Duke-street were awakened between five and six a.m. by some quarrelling, in the course of which a foreigner was accused of being the guilty man. The cry of "Murder!" was raised, but there it ended. There is a good deal of negative evidence to show that nothing of an unusual character had occurred, as people living in all the adjacent streets declare that they had heard no cry during the night. Mr. Levy, the custodian of the Great Synagogue, who resides in the house next to that building, came home past midnight, and saw nothing then to attract attention. There is a general expression of opinion that the police do their duty well. A club in Duke-street[22] was not closed until two a.m., but no member can add to the information. In St. James's-place there is a fire-station in the centre, and there is another club, but nobody saw or heard anything. The neighbourhood is occupied chiefly by Russians, Germans and Austrians, who get their living as clothiers and cigarette-makers. It has the character of being a respectable quarter of the City.

Throughout yesterday the City Detectives under Inspector M'William,[23] were making inquiries, but, so far, without result. Mr. Langham is expected to open the inquest to-morrow.[24] Major Smith had an interview with Sir Charles Warren at Scotland-yard to intimate that the City force were prepared to co-operate with the Metropolitan. A conference of the detectives of each body took place. Among others who inspected the scene in Mitre-square during the day was Mr. Wynne Baxter, the coroner, who inquired into the previous murders. Until a plan was prepared the police kept all approaches to the square, but, about five p.m., the public were allowed admission.

---

# THE DAILY TELEGRAPH
Tuesday, October 2, 1888

Page 3
## THE TRAGEDIES IN ALDGATE AND WHITECHAPEL
*[Further Investigation Into the Murders]*

As we have already regretfully observed, nothing new of any grave import transpired in the course of yesterday with relation to the hideous tragedies of Berner-street and Mitre-square. A portion of the apron worn by the unfortunate woman done to death in the latter locality was picked up at a distance there from of 500 yards, in the direction of the scene of the first murder.[25]

This is an indication that the assassin, after completing his second butchery, retraced his steps for a little more than a third of a mile; but it affords no clue to his subsequent itinerary, for, having dropped the tatter of bloodstained apron within hail of Berner-street, he vanished as completely as though the earth had swallowed him up. Yesterday was a day of rumours and arrests; the rumours have all proved unfounded on fact, and the arrested persons, having satisfactorily proved their innocence, were all liberated. The only steps

---

[22]The Imperial Club at 16–17 Duke's Place. Witnesses Harry Harris, Joseph Lawende and Joseph Levy left here about 1:35am on 30 September.

[23]Inspector James McWilliam, head of the City Police detective department (Evans & Skinner, p. 678).

[24]The inquest would begin Thursday, 4 October.

[25]The apron swatch was found in the doorway of Nos. 108–119 Goulston Street by PC Alfred Long at 2:56am on 30 September (ref. 12 October).

of potential efficacy taken towards pluck-ing out the heart of this ghastly mystery were those due to the Corporation of the City of London,[26] which offers a reward of £500 for "such information as shall lead to the discovery and conviction of the mur-derer or murderers"; to Colonel Kirby and the officers of the Tower Hamlets Engi-neers, who have generously subscribed £100 for the same purpose, and have offered the services of fifty of their men to assist the police in the persecuted district; and to other public-spirited gentlemen, including Mr. Montagu, M.P., who have made up a sum of about £400, also offered as a reward, £300 of which have been ten-dered as above to Mr. Matthews, and by him rejected. Nearly £1,100 now, therefore, awaits acceptance at the hands of any man or woman who, knowing where the assas-sin is to be found, will disclose his place of concealment to the authorities; and it may be hoped that so great a temptation will prove irresistible to his accomplices or har-bourers, if indeed he stand "within the danger" of any such.

The inquest on the body of the woman slaughtered in Mitre-square will be held in Golden-lane on Thursday next, by Mr. Langham, the City Coroner, and a jury of London citizens.[27]

The Commissioner of the City Police (Colonel Sir James Fraser) has decided to offer a reward of £500 for the detection of the murderer of the woman found in Mitre-square, which is within the City boundaries. This determination was ar-rived at yesterday, after consultation among the City authorities, and the placards con-taining the announcement will be imme-diately issued. It will be remembered that a reward of £300 was offered by Mr. Samuel Montagu, M.P., for the detection

of the perpetrator of the Whitechapel out-rages. This still remains open, while other sums have been subscribed in the locality. The decision of the City authorities there-fore brings the total reward now offered to over £1,000, despite the fact that the Home Secretary has declined to take any steps in the same direction. The terms of the reward offered by the City Police are set forth in the subjoined:

To the editor of "The Daily Telegraph."
Sir.—I beg to enclose you a copy of bills about to be issued, offering a reward of £500 in this case.—I am, Sir, your obedi-ent servant,
Jas, M'William, Inspector.
City of London Police, Detective Depart-ment,
26, Old Jewry, E.C., Oct. 1.

Murder.—£500 Reward.—Whereas, at 1:45 a.m. on Sunday, Sept. 30 last, a woman, name unknown, was found bru-tally murdered in Mitre-square, Aldgate, in this City, a reward of £500 will be paid by the Commissioner of Police of the City of London, to any person (other than a person belonging to a police-force in the United Kingdom) who shall give such in-formation as shall lead to the discovery and conviction of the murderer or murderers.

Information to be given to the Inspec-tor of the Detective Department, 26, Old Jewry, or at any police-station.

JAMES FRASER, Colonel,
Commissioner.

City of London Police-office, 26, Old Jewry.

Oct. 1

## THE ALDGATE MURDER.

City police detectives, under the di-rection of Mr. M'William, continued their researches yesterday with a view to the

---

[26]The mayor, aldermen and common-councilmen of the City of London.

[27]Not Thursday, 11 October, as the wording might suggest, but the Thursday of the same week—4 Octo-ber.

identification of the woman who was found murdered and mutilated in Mitre-square on Sunday, between half-past one a.m. and a quarter to two o'clock. The difficulties which have been experienced have been unusually great. On Sunday, and again yesterday, systematic inquiry was pursued in the common lodging-houses of Spitalfields and Whitechapel. Considerable reluctance was shown by the deputies and others to visit the mortuary in Golden-lane to see the remains. The fact was established that in the East-end of London there are hundreds of degraded women enduring a wretched existence, known to one another by nickname merely. Little attention is paid to their doings, or their comings and goings. If they possess the fourpence they can get a bed at a common lodging-house; if they have not the money they sleep anywhere. As many as thirty in one shed were observed yesterday morning. Such people can disappear from their haunts, and their departure is not noted. When wanted they cannot be found, and they seem to think more of the "price of a pint" than of any consideration of truth.

Nevertheless, under the terror of a common danger these women speak honestly and are drawn together for the time. As they themselves admit, "their turn may come next"; for they make no secret of their dreadful trade. Yet, for perfectly natural reasons, they will not willingly associate themselves with the investigation of the murders. They have their own theories about them; and they speak freely about the risks they run when they believe themselves to be out of the hearing of strangers, but they resort to their customary prevarication when taxed either by detectives or reporters. They seem to fear that public-

ity will imperil their own safety. Thus it has been no easy matter to sift the truth of the stories which have been going the round of the kitchens in Whitechapel. Mary Price, of 36, Flower and Dean-street, having seen the body, was of opinion that the woman was a certain Jane Kelly; but subsequent inquiries showed that this person was alive. Then information was obtained from George Smith, 15, Great Pearl-street, that the deceased was called "Phoebe the Jewess," but this was also negatived.

It is not unreasonable to suppose that there are scores of women in Whitechapel whose general description might tally with that of the deceased. The City Police had one clue to work upon. A few feet from the spot where the body was discovered in the south-west corner of Mitre-square was picked up a tin box, such as is usually sold full of mustard for a penny. In this box there were two pawntickets, issued by a Spitalfields firm whose shop is near Commercial-street. The first ticket was made out in the name of Jane Kelly, 6, Dorset-street, and dated Sept. 28. It was for a man's pair of boots, which were pawned for 2s 6d. The other ticket had the name Emily Burrell [*sic*], of 52, White's-row, and it was for a man's flannel shirt, upon which 9d was lent on Aug. 31 last.[28] Reference being made to the pawnbrokers, it was ascertained that the woman who pledged these articles was unknown to them. They could not recollect what she was like. Hundreds of poor women make it a regular rule to pawn their clothing and redeem it when they can. Further inquiry proved that a Jane Kelly was not known at 6, Dorset-street, and that the address in White's-row was purely fictitious, as there

---

[28]The boots were those of John Kelly and were pawned the morning of 29 September. "Jane Kelly" was an alias of Eddowes, though there is a remote possibility it may have here been a scrawled "*John* Kelly" on the ticket. Emily Birrell was a woman met while the couple were hop-picking in Kent. As Birrell was going on to Cheltenham and they returning to London, Birrell gave the pawnticket and use of the man's shirt to them (ref. 4 October).

is no such number. Of course there is no actual proof that the box belonged to the deceased, for it might have been dropped by some other woman in the corner of the square where it was found; but if it was deceased's property the fact that she had pledged man's clothing was taken as evidence that, like many others of her class, she had been living with a man. This individual has not at present come forward. Should the pawntickets have been lost by someone, the owner, if living, will probably in the usual course lodge an affidavit with the pawnbroker in order not to forfeit the property. Notification of the loss has not been received, and in the absence of such intimation it may be assumed that the pawntickets really did belong to the woman by whose body they were lying.

In support of this idea the following circumstances have been reported to the police: Two women yesterday afternoon, whilst engaged in pledging various articles, were drawn into conversation by a pawnbroker. They stated that they were sure that the body at Golden-lane mortuary was that of a woman known as "Annie," who lived at a shop in a court near to Dorset-street. When asked if they would communicate this belief to the police they refused. A little later the importance of their doing so was urged upon them. They still declined, saying that the shopkeeper would know more of Annie than they did. They could not bear to look upon the mutilated body of a person with whom they had associated. No attempt was made to conceal the fact that they belonged to the same class; and both women expressed a fear that they might be attacked. Shame for their calling they had none; but, on the other hand, they were righteously indignant that their nightly trade should be subjected to such risks. One woman ad-

mitted that fair-haired "Annie" had met her late on Saturday night, a couple of hours before the murder, and they had had a drink together in the City-road. Whatever the tale may be worth, partial corroboration was obtained from other sources, and it seems clear that, by common consent of women of her rank in Spitalfields, the dead woman at the mortuary in Golden-lane is regarded as none other than the missing Annie. Nevertheless, no one will come forward to testify to that belief, or to view the body so as to negative it, if wrong.

Inquiry into the incident above related was delayed somewhat by an extraordinary coincidence. In the afternoon Inspector Collard at Bishopsgate-street Station, who has charge of the clothes of the deceased, conducted a respectable woman, her son-in-law, and another to the mortuary in Golden-lane. These people, who came from Rotherhithe, had observed in the papers that the letters "T.C." were tattooed upon the left forearm of the deceased in blue ink, and they had arrived at the conclusion that it was that of a relative. The woman for many years had lost sight of a sister, who was living with a man named Kelly, in a street leading from Bishopsgate. This sister had "T.C." tattooed upon her arm by her husband, whose initials they were. Kelly was the name, it will be remembered, which figured on one of the pawntickets supposed to belong to the deceased. Thus, when all three witnesses, upon viewing the body, appeared to recognise the features, the detectives thought that they had obtained a clue to identification; but their next step was to escort the party of three persons from Rotherhithe to the address which their relative had last given them. There Sergeant Outram discovered that the woman was alive and well. The "identification," therefore, fell to the ground.[29]

---

[29]Though not identical, this story in many ways parallels the affair of Elizabeth Stokes and Mary Malcolm in Chapter 3.

As throwing a light upon the movements of the murderer after he quitted Mitre-square, an important piece of evidence was obtained yesterday. When the body was examined there was a piece of white coarse apron still attached to it. The missing portion was discovered yesterday in Goulston-Street by a policeman in the Metropolitan force.[30] In the opinion of the doctors who compared the two parts there is no room for doubt that they had formed one apron. It is assumed from certain bloodstains upon the portion which was torn away that the murderer had taken it for the purpose of wiping his hands upon it, and had thrown it aside when at some distance from the scene of the crime. The measurement from Goulston-street to Mitre-square is 1,550 feet. Two routes would have been open to him—one by Duke-street, and thence via Aldgate and Whitechapel High-street, which is the open thoroughfare; and the other route, of a more secluded character, lies across Duke-street, along Gravel-lane, Stoney-lane and New Goulston-street. Either route is based on the assumption that the man made his exit from Mitre-square by Church-passage. There are circumstances, however, which indicate that he may have passed into Mitre-street, without crossing the square. On the doorway and window of one of the houses there have been noticed stains, believed to be of blood, and the inference is that someone had wiped his fingers on the window ledge and drawn a blood-stained knife down a part of the doorway.[31]

The other point is contained in the statement of Frank Radway, horsekeeper to Mr. Bull, livery stableman, whose office abuts upon Church-passage. The entrance to the stables is in Duke-street. Hansom cabs are let out, and Radway says that the last to get back on Sunday morning arrived at twenty minutes to one a.m. Immediately he put the horse up, and then, in three or four minutes, went to the gates. According to his custom, he lingered there for fully a quarter of an hour, and did not go to bed before two o'clock. Thus, during the whole time that the murder was being enacted in the adjacent square Radway was looking up and down Duke-street. He saw neither man nor woman pass, and no one came out of the passage. When he retired to his room, which overlooks the passage, his attention was attracted by no sound; but he also failed to notice the noise subsequently caused by the police in removing the body.[32]

# THE DAILY TELEGRAPH

Wednesday, October 3, 1888
THE ALDGATE MURDER.
*[More on Eddowes'
Immediate History]*

---

[30]It was actually discovered on Sunday morning, 30 September.

[31]These bloodstains are also described in the *Advertiser* of 6 October, which noted that a Sergeant Dudman saw bloodstains "upon the doorway and underneath the window" of 36 Mitre Street. The *Star* of 2 October, however, reported the stains to be only candle grease.

[32]This story seems to have no connection with Eddowes' murder, which took place sometime between 1:35 and 1:45am. It is possible that the time of "twenty minutes to one" is a misprint for "twenty minutes to *two*," which would explain why Radway was insistent he did not go to bed before 2:00am. But even were we to accept this as a misprint, his testimony poses problems. If the last hansom cab returned at about 1:40am, it is reasonable to assume Radway might have been at the gates a few minutes beforehand. If he were (and if the *Telegraph* did misreport the stated time), then he missed seeing Eddowes and her companion at the entrance to Church Passage, never saw Lawende, Harris and Levy passing by, did not see PC Harvey enter Church Passage from Duke Street, did not hear the watchman Morris' whistle for help at approximately 1:45 and did not hear any City police rushing to Mitre Square under what might be considered "alarm conditions." Radway was not called to testify at the Eddowes inquest despite his statement, and so perhaps we should put this story aside.

Although the woman who was murdered in Mitre-square has not been fully identified, important information was obtained yesterday which throws some light upon her immediate past history. It appears that Detective-Sergeant Outram,[33] of the City Police, came to the mortuary in Golden-lane, with a party of six women and a man. Some of the former had, it is said, described the clothing of the deceased so accurately that they were allowed to confirm their belief by viewing it at the Bishopsgate-street Police-station. Subsequently they were taken to the chief office in Old Jewry, and thence conducted to the mortuary. Here two of the women positively identified the deceased as an associate, but they did not know her by name. She does not seem to have borne a nickname.[34]

They were ignorant of her family connections or her antecedents, and did not know whether she had lived with any man. The dead woman had, in fact, belonged to the lowest class, and frequently was without the money to obtain admission to the common lodging-houses. Whenever she was in this impecunious state she had, in the company of the woman who now identified her body, slept in a shed off Dorset-street, which is the nightly refuge of some ten to twenty houseless creatures who are without the means of paying for their beds.

Probably further information from people who were better acquainted with her will be forthcoming before the inquest opens to-morrow, as the City police are pursuing active inquiries in Spitalfields and neighbourhood. There is scarcely any doubt, however, as to her doings on Saturday night. Two City policemen at that time took her into custody at Aldgate for being drunk. She was sober enough to give the name of Kelly, with the address 6 Fashion-street. Kelly was the name upon one of the pawntickets contained in the tin box which was found near the body in the square on Sunday; but the address on the pasteboard was 6, Dorset-street, which was fictitious. The constables are sure that the deceased was the woman they had in charge.[35] She was detained at Bishopsgate-street Station until one a.m. on Sunday, the morning of the murder, when she had sufficiently recovered to be released.[36]

Apparently she then walked straight to her doom in Aldgate, the nearest way to which would be along Houndsditch. The mutilated corpse was discovered three-quarters of an hour after she had left the police-station. Kelly was not known at any of the addresses she gave. She was accustomed to live on the streets from hand to mouth, and did no honest work whatever.

Among the many unfounded rumours in circulation yesterday was one to the effect that Sir Charles Warren, on visiting the yard of the Working Men's International Constitutional Club [sic] on Sunday morning, had discovered some chalk writing on the wall beside where the body was found which was of a very objectionable character, and was supposed to have been the work of the murderer. This was alleged to have given such great offense that Sir Charles, fearing a disturbance in the neighbourhood, directed the writing to be washed out—an order said to have been very promptly complied with by the police.

---

[33]Detective Sergeant Robert Outram, with the City Police from 1865 to 1895 (BFS, p. 345).

[34]Eddowes' family gave her the nickname of "Chick," but everyone else who knew her appears to have called her "Kate" (Sugden, p. 233).

[35]PC 931 Louis Robinson and PC George Simmons (BFS, p. 375).

[36]The City Police generally let people arrested for drunkenness go once they had sufficiently sobered up. Had Eddowes been arrested on Metropolitan territory, ironically, she would have been kept in the cells overnight and later brought up before a magistrate on charges.

There is not an iota of truth in the story. It is pure fiction from beginning to end, and as no writing was ever discovered, it follows that it could not have been washed out by Sir Charles Warren or anybody else.[37]

During the day the description of a man, who is supposed to have been seen in company of the deceased late on Saturday night was circulated. It states that he was apparently about twenty-eight years of age, 5 ft. 7 in. in height, of dark complexion, and no whiskers. He wore dark clothes, and a felt hat somewhat stained.

Wednesday Morning (1:30 A.M.)

Upon inquiry this morning no further information pointing to the detection of the murderer or leading to the identification of the victim of the Mitre-square tragedy was to be obtained from the Metropolitan or City authorities.[38]

# THE DAILY TELEGRAPH
Thursday, October 4, 1888

Page 5
THE LONDON TRAGEDIES
ALDGATE AND
WHITEHALL CRIMES.
WHITECHAPEL MURDER.
A KNIFE FOUND.
LETTER FROM
SIR CHAS. WARREN.
THE CRIME IN ALDGATE.
*[Eddowes Identified; The First Letter
from Jack the Ripper]*

All doubt as to the identification of the victim of the Mitre-square murder has now been removed. Her real name is Catherine Edowes [*sic*], but she was better known as Catherine Kelly. The publicity which was given in this paper to the particulars of the pawntickets, found near the body on Sunday, furnished the clue to the solution of the mystery concerning the antecedents of the deceased. John Kelly, an inmate of a common lodging-house, 55, Flower and Dean-street, whilst reading a newspaper, had his attention attracted to the name Emily Burrell, which was stated to be attached to one of the tickets in question, and to the fact that a pair of boots was also mentioned. Some women coming in at the moment said they had been to the mortuary, and it then occurred to Kelly that the dead woman was known to him intimately. At a late hour on Tuesday night he went to the Bishopsgate-street station, and there he was able to describe minutely the clothing which the deceased had worn, particularly the boot which, as it happened, he had repaired himself with a piece of leather. Major Smith, the Acting-Commissioner of City Police, and Superintendent Foster were at once informed of the circumstances, and Kelly's frank explanations were heard by them.

He spoke without reserve, and he was conducted to the mortuary in Golden-lane. Here he was able to at once identify the remains, which have not undergone noticeable change. That he was accustomed with the customs of such women as the deceased he showed by searching for the pawnticket and for money in the bonnet, a place of concealment which would probably escape the notice of the uninitiated. Kelly was very much affected. He

---

[37]This appears to be an account of the "Juwes" graffiti found in Goulston Street, though unaccountably transferred to Berner Street. See 12 October and Commentary 2.

[38]The *Telegraph* of 4 October would carry full particulars of Eddowes' antecedents, as John Kelly identified her late on the night of 2 October. However, as we have seen that twice Eddowes was purportedly identified and both identifications proved dead-ends, it is possible that the police would not release the details of Kelly's identification until it could be verified.

stated that he had become acquainted with the deceased seven years ago, when she took up her abode in the common lodging-house where she had continued, more or less regularly, to stay ever since. They had never married, and he understood from her that she had a husband living, by name Tom Conway, and it was this man's initials, T.C., which were tattooed upon her arm, and she had had two children, one of them a daughter, Annie, aged 21, married to Louis Phillips, supposed to live in the neighbourhood of Bermondsey, and to be employed at a gun factory. This daughter had two children, whom Kelly had seen, but he had never met the father. Deceased also had a son, George, a labourer.[39]

Tom Conway was a discharged soldier, and supposed to belong to the Connaught Rangers.[40] He had fallen out with deceased, and they had separated and Kelly had never encountered him or heard that the woman had any reason to fear this pensioner. The couple passed their lives together getting odd jobs, the woman at charring and the man in Spitalfields Market. Every year they went hopping, and this season they were in the vicinity of Maidstone. Whilst there Kelly bought of Mr. Arthur Pash, in the High-street, a pair of boots, and his companion purchased at a shop nearby a jacket, and this garment was the one which she wore at the time of her death, and which Kelly has identified. The pair of boots, too, were the ones which were recently pawned in Spitalfields, the ticket being made out on Sept. 28 for half-a-crown in the name of Jane Kelly.

To account for the possession of the other ticket Kelly stated that whilst they were walking from Kent back to London a fortnight ago they met a woman named Emily Burrell, who had also been hopping, and she gave them a pawn-ticket for a flannel-shirt, pledged for 9d. Both tickets were put in the tin box which Kelly has recognised. On returning to London work failed them both, and on Friday last they were without money. Deceased wished to pawn some of her own clothing; but Kelly refused to allow her, and took off his boots, which were those upon which 2s 6d was lent.[41]

Their last meal together was on Saturday, and they parted in the afternoon at about two p.m., the woman then expressing the intention of visiting her daughter in Bermondsey.[42] The last words addressed to her were a caution to beware of the "knife," an allusion to the Whitechapel murderer. She replied, "Oh, don't fear for me; I'll take care," and went off. Kelly, when she did not return, paid no attention to the matter, as he believed she was with her friends. On Sunday he even visited Mitre-square, and looked on the scene of the murder, without knowing that he had reason to be deeply interested in the awful event.[43] It was not until Tuesday night that he guessed the truth.

Yesterday corroboration was obtained from the sister of the deceased, Eliza Gold, of 6, Thrawl-street, who was taken

[39]There was also a second son, Alfred, born 1873 (Shelden, p. 28).
[40]Conway had actually been in the 18th Royal Irish Foot (Begg, p. 114).
[41]Kelly's discarding of his boots rather than allowing Eddowes to pawn her clothing is occasionally used as support for the argument that she was not a regular prostitute, theorists pointing out that if she were, it would be far more likely that Kelly would have turned her out on the streets rather than walk barefoot. See esp. Hinton, pp. 109–111.
[42]Annie Phillips last saw her mother in 1886 and had moved at least twice since that time. In September 1888 she was living at 12 Dilston Grove, Southwark Park Road. These changes of address appear to have been deliberately kept from Eddowes, in order to frustrate her asking Annie for money, and it appears no forwarding address from Bermondsey was left (Sugden, p. 238).
[43]This anecdote is also reported in an interview with Kelly in the *Star* of 3 October.

to the mortuary, and identified the body. She stated that her sister was not married to Tom Conway. The deputy of the lodging-house, Frederick Wilkinson, also bore out Kelly's story, which is not inconsistent with the belief of the two constables, that she was in custody for being drunk at Bishopsgate-street Police-station on Saturday night until one a.m. on Sunday.

Sergeant Outram prosecuted the fullest researches in the neighbourhood of the Old Kent-road, yesterday, assisted by Kelly, with the object of discovering the daughter Annie Phillips, but without success. It is not known what has become of Tom Conway, or whether he is still living.[44]

It is understood that the deceased was born in Wolverhampton forty years since, and that soon afterwards her parents moved to London, where she was educated at the Dowgate Charity School and where she has since lived. It was when she was about twenty years of age that she became acquainted with the soldier Thomas Conway—whose initials, "T.C.," are tattooed on her arm—and subsequently joined him. No marriage ceremony was gone through, but they continued to live as man and wife for about twelve years, during which time she bore him two children. Ten years ago, however, Conway deserted the woman, and neither she nor her relatives had heard anything of him since.[45]

It is not now believed that the unhappy woman belonged to the class from which the five other victims appear to have been selected. She has, on the other hand, the character of having been a decent woman, doing work whenever she could get it.[46]

The following page has the full text of the letter and post-card.[47] The letter, which had the E.C. post-mark and was directed in red ink, ran:

Sept. 25

Dear Boss—I keep on hearing the police have caught me, but they won't fix me just yet. I have laughed when they look so clever and talk about being on the right track. That joke about Leather Apron gave me real fits. I am down on whores, and I shan't quit ripping them till I do get buckled. Grand work, the last job was. I gave the lady no time to squeal. How can they catch me now? I love my work, and want to start again. You will soon hear of me with my funny little games. I saved some of the proper red stuff in a ginger-beer bottle over the last job to write with, but it went thick like glue and I can't use it. Red ink is fit enough, I hope. Ha! ha! The next job I do I shall clip the lady's ears off, and send to the police-officers, just for jolly, wouldn't you? Keep this letter back till I do a bit more work, then give it out straight. My knife's so nice and sharp, I want to get to work right away if I get a chance. Good luck—Yours truly, Jack the Ripper—Don't mind me giving the trade name.—Wasn't good enough to post this before I got all the red ink off my hands; curse it. No luck yet. They say I'm a doctor now. Ha! ha!

The post-card bearing the stamp "London, E., Oct. 1," was received on Monday morning. It was as follows: "I was not codding, dear old Boss, when I gave

---

[44]Conway was still alive (ref. 5 and 16 October).

[45]Conway and Eddowes separated in either 1880 or 1881. One of Eddowes' sisters claimed that Conway drank and beat her, another averred that Eddowes' tippling offended the teetotaller Conway. A 27 October report from Inspector McWilliam (HO 144/221/A49301C, ff. 162–170), after interviewing Conway, noted he "…was eventually compelled to leave her on account of her drunken and immoral habits."

[46]This is quite a change from the previous day's portrait of her as "accustomed to live on the streets from hand to mouth, and [who] did no honest work whatever."

[47]The transcriptions given here of what are known as the "Dear Boss" letter and "saucy Jacky" postcard are accurate, though some unknown hand at the *Telegraph* has added punctuation and capitalizations not found in the originals as well as removing selected underscorings. The *Telegraph* first published a transcription of the letter on 1 October.

*Above and opposite:* The "Dear Boss" letter dated 25 Sept. 1888, sent to the Central News Agency on 27 September 1888 and signed "Jack the Ripper" (courtesy of Evans/Skinner Crime Archive).

you the tip. You'll hear about Saucy Jacky's work to-morrow. Double event this time. Number One squealed a bit; couldn't finish straight off. Had not time to get ears for police. Thanks for keeping last letter back till I got to work again.—Jack the Ripper."

As we have already announced, the Central News received the above letter on Thursday morning last, and it therefore must have been posted on the Wednesday. The writer uses this threat: "The next job I do I shall cut the lady's ears off and send police officers just for jolly wouldnt you. Keep this letter back till I do a bit more work. then give it out straight. My knife's so nice and sharp I want to get to work right away if I get a chance, good luck.

yours truly
Jack the Ripper

Dont mind me giving the trade name

[sideways text in left margin:] wasnt good enough to post this before I got all the red ink off my hands curse it. No luck yet. They say I am a doctor now ha ha

to the police-officers."[48] The Central News did not attach importance to this document, and it was regarded in the light of a practical joke, perpetrated for idle

---

[48]Several authors have suggested that the threat to cut the ears off combined with the actual portion of right ear cut from Eddowes supports the authenticity of the letter and postcard. A close reading of both communications does not appear to justify this. Though the letter promises a ghoulish trophy, the postcard backs away from the promise by noting that "Number One [presumably Stride] squealed a bit," and so there was no time for the killer to carry out his plan. Eddowes, however, is not mentioned beyond the laconic "double event this time"; when the extensive injuries to her head and face are taken into consideration, it is difficult to believe that her murderer had no time to remove her ears had he wished so to do. Additionally, it is rather odd to imagine a killer so fastidious that when he finds he cannot carry out his promise of removing a relic from his "next job" he does not perform the surgery on a later victim because she is not, technically, his "next" job.

The "saucy Jacky" postcard sent to the Central News Agency on 1 October 1888 signed "Jack the Ripper" (from an original 1888 facsimile owned by Stewart P. Evans).

papers of Monday, and was, therefore, known to a very few persons on the Sunday. On Monday morning, by the first post, the Central News received a post-card in the same handwriting and much blood-besmeared. The writer observes "double event this time. Number One squealed a bit; couldn't finish straight off. Had not time to get ears for the police." The letter and the post-card were handed to the Scotland-yard authorities, and, although they do not profess to attach any great importance to them, still they thought it well to have facsimiles prepared, and to send them to the Press, in the possibility that the handwriting may be recognised by some one.[49]

Some part of the post-card is to a great extent undecipherable, but the reproductions above given, with the opening and concluding sentences of the letter, will give an absolutely correct idea of the whole. The post-card appears to have been scribbled hastily, and the hand is not so firm as that of the letter, but there is very little doubt that both are from the same pen. The writer is probably an American or an Englishman, who has mixed with our cousins on the other side of the Atlantic. "Bos," [sic] "Fix me," "shan't quit," and "Right away" are American forms of expression.

amusement; but, curiously enough, the Mitre-square victim did have a portion of the ear cut off. This particular fact escaped observation until it was published in the

---

[49]Posters reproducing the letter and card were outside police stations on 3 October; several papers (including the *Telegraph*) published the text of both communications on 4 October. No one was ever conclusively identified as the author, but the "Littlechild Letter" points the finger at Charles Moore and T.J. Bulling of the Central News Agency (Evans & Gainey, pp. 99–103).

## FACSIMILES OF "JACK THE RIPPER'S" LETTER AND POST CARD.

25 Sept. 1888

Dear: Boss

I keep on hearing the police have caught me but they wont fix me just yet I have laughed when they look so clever and talk about being on the right track That joke about Leather Apron gave me real fits.———(PART OF LETTER OMITTED)————

Keep this letter back till I do a bit more work then give it out straight My knife's so nice and sharp I want to get to work right away if I get a chance Good luck

yours truly
Jack the Ripper

Dont mind me giving the trade name

I was not codding dear old Boss when I gave you the tip you'll hear about Saucy Jacky's work tomorrow double event this time number one squealed a bit couldn't finish straight off. had not time to get ears for police thanks for keeping last letter back till I got to work again
Jack the Ripper

The following is the full text of the letter and post-card. The letter, which had the E.C. post-mark and was directed in red ink, ran:

Sept. 25.

Dear Boss—I keep on hearing the police have caught me, but they won't fix me just yet. I have laughed when they look so clever and talk about being on the right track. That joke about Leather Apron gave me real fits. I am down on whores, and I shan't quit ripping them till I do get buckled. Grand work, the last job was. I gave the lady no time to squeal. How can they catch me now? I love my work, and want to start again. You will soon hear of me with my funny little games. I saved some of the proper red stuff in a ginger-beer bottle over the last job, to write with, but it went thick like glue, and I can't use it. Red ink is fit enough, I hope. Ha! ha! The next job I do I shall clip the lady's ears off, and send to the police-officers, just for jolly, wouldn't you? Keep this letter back till I do a bit more work, then give it out straight. My knife's so nice and sharp, I want to get to work right away if I get a chance. Good luck.—Yours truly, JACK THE RIPPER.—Don't mind me giving the trade name.—Wasn't good enough to post this before I got all the red ink off my hands; curse it. No luck yet. They say I'm a doctor now. Ha! ha!"

The post-card bearing the stamp " London, E., Oct. 1," was received on Monday morning. It was as follows : "I was not codding, dear old Boss, when I gave you the tip. You'll hear about Saucy Jacky's work to-morrow. Double event this time. Number One squealed a bit; couldn't finish straight off. Had not time to get ears for police. Thanks for keeping last letter back till I got to work again.—JACK THE RIPPER."

"Facsimiles of 'Jack the Ripper's' Letter and Post Card" as printed in the *Telegraph* of 4 October (courtesy of Evans/Skinner Crime Archive).

# THE DAILY TELEGRAPH
Friday, October 5, 1888

Page 3
LONDON TRAGEDIES.
ARRESTS AND SEARCHES.
THE ALDGATE CRIME.
*[First Session of Inquest]*

Every effort to find Annie Phillips, the married daughter of Catherine Eddowes, the Mitre-square victim, has been unsuccessful. A Tom Conway has been discovered, but he is not the man who ten years since lived with the deceased, and it is believed that this man is dead. It has been ascertained that Kate Eddowes, as she was called in early life, was the daughter of a tin-plate worker at Wolverhampton, her mother having been a cook at an hotel in that town. Some years ago the family removed to London, where the parents died, leaving twelve children. When the deceased was twenty years of age she ran away to Birmingham, where she became acquainted with the pensioner, and she lived and travelled with him. She reappeared at the residence of her aunt, who had brought her up as a child, in a destitute condition. She went back to London subsequently. An uncle of the dead woman lives in Birmingham.[50]

She appears to have been estranged from her relatives by reason of her mode of life. In connection with the risk which her murderer ran of detection on Sunday morning last, it is mentioned that the foreman of the sewer works in Aldgate is positive that he was standing within a short distance of the spot where the body was found by the constable Watkins at the time when it is supposed the crime was committed. He heard no cries for help.[51]

THE INQUEST.

At the Coroner's Court, Golden-lane, yesterday, Mr. S.F. Langham, coroner for the City of London, opened the inquest into the death of Catherine Eddowes, or Conway, or Kelly, who was murdered in Mitre-court, Aldgate, about half-past one o'clock on Sunday morning last. The court was crowded, and much interest was taken in the proceedings, many people standing outside the building during the whole of the day. Mr. Crawford, City solicitor, appeared on behalf of the Corporation, as responsible for the police; Major Smith and Superintendent Forster [*sic*] represented the officers engaged in the inquiry. After the jury had viewed the body, which was lying in the adjoining mortuary, Mr. Crawford, addressing the coroner, said: I appear here as representing the City police in this matter, for the purpose of rendering you every possible assistance, and if I should consider it desirable, in the course of the inquiry, to put any questions to witnesses, probably I shall have your permission when you have finished with them.

THE CORONER: Oh, certainly.

The following evidence was then called—

**Eliza Gold** deposed: I live at 6, Thrawl-street Spitalfields. I have been married, but my husband is dead. I recognise the deceased as my poor sister (witness here commenced to weep very much, and for a few moments was unable to proceed with her story). Her name was Catherine Eddowes. I cannot exactly tell where she was living. She was staying with a gentleman, but she was not married to him. Her age last birthday was about 43 years, as far as I can remember. She has

---

[50]This account of Eddowes' life is accurate (Shelden, pp. 25–27). The "aunt" referred to is probably Elizabeth Eddowes of Wolverhampton. The "uncle" is Thomas Eddowes.
[51]This account has not been corroborated.

been living for some years with Mr. Kelly. He is in court. I last saw her alive about four or five months ago. She used to go out hawking for a living and was a woman of sober habits. Before she went to live with Kelly, she had lived with a man named Conway for several years, and had two children by him. I cannot tell how many years she lived with Conway. I do not know whether Conway is still living. He was a pensioner from the army, and used to go out hawking also. I do not know on what terms he parted from my sister. I do not know whether she had ever seen him from the time they parted. I am quite certain that the body I have seen is my sister.

BY MR. CRAWFORD: I have not seen Conway for seven or eight years. I believe my sister was living with him then on friendly terms.

Was she living on friendly terms with Kelly?—I cannot say. Three or four weeks ago I saw them together, and they were then on happy terms. I cannot fix the time when I last saw them. They were living at 55, Flower and Dean-street—a lodging-house. My sister when staying there came to see me when I was very ill. From that time, until I saw her in the mortuary, I have not seen her.

A Juryman pointed out that witness previously said she had not seen her sister for three or four months, whilst later on she spoke of three or four weeks.

THE CORONER: You said your sister came to see you when you were ill, and that you had not seen her since. Was that three or four weeks ago?

MRS. GOLD: Yes.

So that your saying three or four months was a mistake?—Yes. I am so upset and confused.[52]

Witness commenced to cry again. As she could not write she had to affix her mark to the deposition.

**John Kelly**, a strong-looking labourer, was then called and said: I live at a lodging-house, 55, Flower and Dean-street. Have seen the deceased and recognise her as Catherine Conway. I have been living with her for seven years. She hawked a few things about the streets and lived with me at a common lodging-house in Flower and Dean-street. The lodging-house is known as Cooney's. I last saw her alive about two o'clock on the afternoon of Saturday in Houndsditch. We parted on very good terms. She told me she was going over to Bermondsey to try and find her daughter Annie. Those were the last words she spoke to me. Annie was a daughter whom I believe she had had by Conway. She promised me before we parted that she would be back by four o'clock, and no later. She did not return.

Did you make any inquiry after her?—I heard she had been locked up at Bishopsgate-street on Saturday afternoon.[53] An old woman who works in the lane told me she saw her in the hands of the police.

Did you make any inquiry into the truth of this?—I made no further inquiries. I knew that she would be out on Sunday morning, being in the City.

Did you know why she was locked up?—Yes, for drink; she had had a drop of drink, so I was told. I never knew she went out for any immoral purpose.[54] She occa-

---

[52]Eddowes and Kelly returned from Kent on 28 September. It would seem that Gold saw them last just before they went hop-picking.

[53]This is likely a slip of the tongue; Eddowes was not arrested until 8:30pm.

[54]Kelly may here be anticipating an additional question about the likelihood of Eddowes being arrested for prostitution in order to stop any inquiry along that line. This claim, and the statement of Frederick Wilkinson further on that he had never heard of Eddowes being intimate with anyone but Kelly, are, depending upon the author, used either as support for the argument that Eddowes was not a prostitute (Hinton), (*cont.*)

sionally drank, but not to excess.[55] When I left her she had no money about her. She went to see and find her daughter to get a trifle, so that I shouldn't see her walk about the streets at night.

What do you mean by "walking the streets?" I mean that if we had no money to pay for our lodgings we would have to walk about all night. I was without money to pay for our lodgings at the time. I do not know that she was at variance with anyone—not in the least. She had not seen Conway recently not that I know of. I never saw him in my existence. I cannot say whether Conway is living. I know of no one who would be likely to injure her.

THE FOREMAN OF THE JURY: You say you heard the deceased was taken into custody. Did you ascertain, as a matter of fact, when she was discharged?—No. I do not know when she was discharged.

What time was she in the habit of returning to her lodgings?—Early.

What do you call early?—About eight or nine o'clock.

When she did not return on this particular evening, did it not occur to you that it would be right to inquire whether she had been discharged or not?—No, I did not inquire. I expected she would turn up on the Sunday morning.

MR. CRAWFORD: You say she had no money. Do you know with whom she had been drinking that afternoon?—I cannot say.

Do you know anyone who paid for drink for her?—No.

Had she on a recent occasion absented herself from you at night?—No.

This was the only time?—Yes.

But had not she left you previously?—Yes, a long time ago—some months ago.

For what purpose?—We had a few words, and she went away, but came back in a few hours.

Had you any angry conversation with her on Saturday afternoon?—No, not in the least.

No words about money?—No.

Have you any idea where her daughter lives?—She told me in King-street, Bermondsey, and that her name was Annie.

Had she been previously there for money?—Yes, once last year.[56]

How long have you been living in this lodging-house together?—Seven years in the self-same house.

Previous to this Saturday had you been sleeping there each evening during the week?—No; I slept there on Friday night, but she didn't.

Did she not sleep with you?—No.

Was she walking the streets that night?—She had the misfortune to go to Mile-end.

What happened there?—She went into the casual ward.

What was the evening you two slept at the lodging-house during that week?—Not one.

Where did you sleep?—On Monday, Tuesday, and Wednesday, we were down at the hop-picking, and came back to London on Thursday. We had been unfortunate at the hop-picking, and had no money. On Thursday night we both slept in the casual ward. On the Friday I earned 6d at a job, and I said, "Here, Kate, you

---

or to claim that neither man could freely admit to profiting from her prostitution (Sugden). It is impossible at this distance to be certain, but the fact that Eddowes had no money on parting from Kelly yet managed somehow to get incapacitatingly drunk seems to favor the theory of at least occasional prostitution (ref. HO 144/221/A49301C, ff. 162–170).

[55]A claim belied both by Eddowes' state the night of her death, and by the fact that she was charged with being "drunk and disorderly and using obscene language" on 21 September 1881 (Shelden, p. 29).

[56]Eddowes and her daughter last saw each other in 1886, one week after the birth of Annie's child, so Kelly may be misremembering here (Shelden, p. 29).

take 4d and go to the lodging-house and I will go to Mile-end," but she said, "No, you go and have a bed and I will go to the casual ward," and she went.[57] I saw her again on Saturday morning early.

At what time did you quit one another on Friday?—I cannot tell, but I think it would be about three or four in the afternoon.

What did she leave you for?—To go to Mile-end.

What for?—To get a night's shelter in the casual ward.

When did you see her next morning?—About eight o'clock. I was surprised to see her so early. I know there was some tea and sugar found on her body. She bought that out of some boots we pawned at Jones's for 2s 6d. I think it was on Saturday morning that we pawned the boots. She was sober when she left me. We had been drinking together out of the 2s 6d. All of it was spent in drink and food. She left me quite sober to go to her daughter's. We parted without an angry word. I do not know why she left Conway. In the past seven years she only lived with me. I did not know of her going out for immoral purposes at night. She never brought me money in the morning after being out at night.

A JURYMAN: Is not eight o'clock a very early hour to be discharged from a casual ward?—I do not know. There is some tasks—picking oakum—before you can be discharged.[58] I know it was very early.

MR. CRAWFORD: Is it not the fact that the pawning took place on the Friday night?—I do not know. It was either Friday night or Saturday morning. I am muddled up. (The tickets were produced, and were dated the 28th, Friday).

She pawned the boots, did she not?—Yes; and I stood at the door in my bare feet.

Seeing the date on the tickets, cannot you recollect when the pawning took place?—I cannot say, I am so muddled up. It was either Friday or Saturday.

THE CORONER: Had you been drinking when the pawning took place?—Yes.[59]

**Frederick William Wilkinson** deposed: I am the deputy of the lodging-house at Flower and Dean-street.[60] I have known the deceased and Kelly during the last seven years. They passed as man and wife, and lived on very good terms. They had a quarrel now and then, but not violent. They sometimes had a few words when Kate was in drink, but they were not serious. I believe she got her living by hawking about the streets and cleaning amongst the Jews in Whitechapel.[61] Kelly paid me pretty regularly. Kate was not often in drink. She was a very jolly woman, always singing. Kelly was not in the habit of drinking, and I never saw him the worse for drink. During the week the first time I saw the deceased at the lodging-house was on Friday afternoon. Kelly was not with her then. She went out and did not return until Saturday morning, when I saw

---

[57]As a woman, Eddowes would only have to perform menial tasks in return for her bed in the casual ward. Kelly, however, would be required to perform a grinding day's work at the Mile End Workhouse, which is presumably why Eddowes allowed him the lodging-house bed.

[58]Picking apart old ropes for their hemp content.

[59]Crawford and Langham here are attributing Kelly's error as to when his boots were pawned to his having been drunk, but it may not be so cut-and-dried. Had the boots been pawned on Friday, the money given for them would easily have paid for both Kelly and Eddowes to stay at the lodging house. As they did not—and Kelly noted that the 6d he earned on Friday was not enough for them both—it seems logical to presume the boots really were pawned on Saturday, 29 September, and the "28th" was a clerical error.

[60]Cooney's lodging-house, 55 Flower and Dean Street (Eddleston, p. 193).

[61]This may also have been the mysterious source of Eddowes' money on 29 September.

her and Kelly in the kitchen together having breakfast. I did not see her go out, and I do not know whether Kelly went with her. I never saw her again.

Did you know she was in the habit of walking the streets at night?—No; she generally used to return between nine and ten o'clock. I never knew her to be intimate with any particular individual except Kelly; and never heard of such a thing. She use [sic] to say she was married to Conway; that her name was bought and paid for—meaning that she was married. She was not at variance with anyone that I know of. When I saw her last, on Saturday morning, between ten and eleven, she was quite sober. I first heard from Kelly on Saturday night that Kate was locked up, and he said he wanted a single bed. That was about 7:30 in the evening. A single bed is 4d, and a double 8d.

BY A JURYMAN: I don't take the names of my lodgers, but I know my "regulars." If a man comes and takes a bed I put the number of the bed down in my book, but not his name. Of course I know the names of my regular customers.

MR. CRAWFORD: When was the last time Kelly and the deceased had slept together in your house previous to last week?—The last time the two slept at the lodging-house was five or six weeks ago, before they went to the hop-picking. Kelly slept there on Friday and Saturday, but not Kate. I did not make any inquiry about her not being there on Friday. I could not say whether Kate went out with Kelly on Saturday, but I saw them having their breakfast together. I saw Kelly in the house about ten o'clock on Saturday morning. I am positive he did not go out again. I cannot tell when he got up on Sunday. I saw him about dinner time. I believe on Saturday morning Kate was wearing an apron. Nothing unusual struck me about her dress. The distance between our place and the scene of the murder is about 500 yards.

SEVERAL JURYMEN: Oh, more than that.[62]

MR. CRAWFORD: Did anyone come into your lodging-house and take a bed between one and two o'clock on the Sunday morning?—No stranger came in then.

Did any one come into your lodging-house about that hour?—No; two detectives came about three, and asked if I had any women out.[63]

Did anyone come into your lodging-house about two o'clock on Sunday morning whom you did not recognise?—I cannot say; I could tell by my book, which can soon be produced.

BY A JURYMAN: Kelly and the deceased were at breakfast together between ten and eleven on Saturday morning. If they had told me the previous day that they had no money I would have trusted them. I trust all lodgers I know.[64] The body was found half a mile from my lodging-house.

The deputy was dispatched for his book, with which after an interval he returned. It merely showed, however, that there were fifty-two beds occupied in the house on Saturday night. There were only

---

[62]The distance from Cooney's to Mitre Square was approximately 650 yards as the crow flies. By the most direct walking route, it was about 1,050 yards between the two locations (personal correspondence, Adrian Phypers).

[63]It is not known who these detectives were. They may have been men sent by Inspector McWilliam after Eddowes' body was discovered, or perhaps detectives Daniel Halse, Robert Outram or Edward Marriott.

[64]If this statement and Wilkinson's claim that Kelly paid "pretty regularly" can be believed, it would appear that neither Eddowes nor Kelly cared to presume upon the deputy's kindness, or that they had doubts about their ability to repay him. However, as Kelly earlier noted that without money he and Eddowes would be forced to "walk about all night," it may be Wilkinson was not quite as generous as he presented himself.

six strangers. He could not say whether any one took a bed about two o'clock on Sunday morning. He had sometimes over 100 persons sleeping in the house at once. They paid for their beds and were asked no questions.

**Edward Watkin** [Watkins], No. 881 of the City Police, said: I was on duty at Mitre-square on Saturday night. I have been in the force seventeen years. I went on duty at 9:45 upon my regular beat. That extends from Duke-street, Aldgate, through Heneage-lane, a portion of Bury-street, through Cree-lane,[65] into Leaden-hall-street, along eastward into Mitre-street, then into Mitre-square, round the square again into Mitre-street, then into King-street to St. James's-place, round the place, then into Duke-street, where I started from. That beat takes twelve or fourteen minutes. I had been patrolling the beat continually from ten o'clock at night until one o'clock on Sunday morning.

Had anything excited your attention during those hours?—No.

Or any person?—No. I passed through Mitre-square at 1:30 on the Sunday morning. I had my lantern alight and on—fixed to my belt. According to my usual practice, I looked at the different passages and corners.

At half-past one did anything excite your attention?—No.

Did you see anyone about?—No.

Could any people have been in that portion of the square without your seeing them?—No. I next came into Mitre-square at 1:44, when I discovered the body lying on the right as I entered the square. The woman was on her back, with her feet towards the square. Her clothes were thrown up. I saw her throat was cut and the stomach ripped open. She was lying in a pool of blood. I did not touch the body. I ran across to Kearley and Long's [*sic*] warehouse. The door was ajar, and I pushed it open, and called on the watchman Morris, who was inside. He came out. I remained with the body until the arrival of Police-constable Holland.[66] No one else was there before that but myself. Holland was followed by Dr. Sequeira. Inspector Collard arrived about two o'clock, and also Dr. Brown, surgeon to the police force.[67]

When you first saw the body did you hear any footsteps as if anybody were running away?—No. The door of the warehouse to which I went was ajar, because the watchman was working about. It was no unusual thing for the door to be ajar at that hour of the morning.

By Mr. Crawford: I was continually patrolling my beat from ten o'clock up to half-past one.[68] I noticed nothing unusual up until 1:44, when I saw the body.

By the Coroner: I did not sound an alarm. We do not carry whistles.

By a Juror: My beat is not a double but a single beat. No other policeman comes into Mitre-street.

**Frederick William Foster**, of 26, Old Jewry, architect and surveyor, produced a plan which he had made of the place where the body was found, and the district. From Berner-street to Mitre-street is three-quarters of a mile, and a

---

[65]Watkins' signed statement in the official coroner's inquest papers gives this as "Cree Church Lane."
[66]PC 814 James Holland, who also arrived with City PC 964 James Harvey (BFS, pp. 158 and 164).
[67]City Police Inspector Edward Collard (1846–1892) (BFS, p. 85).
[68]Although earlier Watkins stated he was walking his beat until 1:00am, he here amends this to 1:30am. It is possible he may have taken a short break during that half hour; it is also possible his earlier statement of time was a slip of the tongue.

man could walk the distance in twelve minutes.

**Inspector Collard**, of the City Police, said: At five minutes before two o'clock on Sunday morning last I received information at Bishopsgate-street Police-station that a woman had been murdered in Mitre-square. Information was at once telegraphed to headquarters. I dispatched a constable[69] to Dr. Gordon Brown, informing him, and proceeded myself to Mitre-square, arriving there about two or three minutes past two. I there found Dr. Sequeira, two or three police officers, and the deceased person lying in the south-west corner of the square, in the position described by Constable Watkins. The body was not touched until the arrival shortly afterwards of Dr. Brown. The medical gentlemen examined the body, and in my presence Sergeant Jones picked up from the foot way by the left side of the deceased three small black buttons, such as are generally used for boots, a small metal button, a common metal thimble, and a small penny mustard tin containing two pawn-tickets. They were handed to me. The doctors remained until the arrival of the ambulance, and saw the body placed in the conveyance. It was then taken to the mortuary, and stripped by Mr. Davis, the mortuary keeper, in presence of the two doctors and myself. I have a list of articles of clothing more or less stained with blood and cut.

Was there any money about her?—No; no money whatever was found. A piece of cloth was found in Goulston-street, corresponding with the apron worn by the deceased. When I got to the square I took immediate steps to have the neighbourhood searched for the person who committed the murder. Mr. M'Williams, chief of the Detective Department, on arriving shortly afterwards sent men to search in all directions in Spitalfields, both in streets and lodging-houses. Several men were stopped and searched in the streets, without any good result. I have had a house-to-house inquiry made in the vicinity of Mitre-square as to any noises or whether persons were seen in the place; but I have not been able to find any beyond the witnesses who saw a man and woman talking together.[70]

MR. CRAWFORD: When you arrived was the deceased in a pool of blood?—The head, neck, and, I imagine, the shoulders were lying in a pool of blood when she was first found, but there was no blood in front. I did not touch the body myself, but the doctor said it was warm.[71]

Was there any sign of a struggle having taken place?—None whatever. I made a careful inspection of the ground all round. There was no trace whatever of any struggle. There was nothing in the appearance of the woman, or of the clothes, to lead to the idea that there had been any struggle. From the fact that the blood was in a liquid state I conjectured the murder had not been long previously committed. In my opinion the body had not been there more than a quarter of an hour. I endeavoured to trace footsteps, but could find no trace whatever. The backs of the empty houses adjoining were searched, but nothing was found.

**Dr. Frederick Gordon Brown** was then called and deposed: I am surgeon to the City of London Police. I was called shortly after two o'clock on Sunday morning, and reached the place of the murder about twenty minutes past two. My

---

[69]This policeman has not been identified.
[70]These "witnesses" were Lawende, Harris and Levy.
[71]This may refer to either Sequeira or Brown; Brown does testify later that Eddowes' body was "quite warm."

attention was directed to the body of the deceased. It was lying in the position described by Watkins, on its back, the head turned to the left shoulder, the arms by the side of the body, as if they had fallen there. Both palms were upwards, the fingers slightly bent. A thimble was lying near. The clothes were thrown up. The bonnet was at the back of the head. There was great disfigurement of the face. The throat was cut across. Below the cut was a neckerchief. The upper part of the dress had been torn open. The body had been mutilated, and was quite warm—no rigor mortis. The crime must have been committed within half an hour, or certainly within forty minutes from the time when I saw the body. There were no stains of blood on the bricks or pavement around.

BY MR. CRAWFORD: There was no blood on the front of the clothes. There was not a speck of blood on the front of the jacket.

BY THE CORONER: Before we removed the body Dr. Phillips was sent for, as I wished him to see the wounds, he having been engaged in a case of a similar kind previously.[72] He saw the body at the mortuary. The clothes were removed from the deceased carefully. I made a post-mortem examination on Sunday afternoon. There was a bruise on the back of the left hand, and one on the right shin, but this had nothing to do with the crime. There were no bruises on the elbows or the back of the head. The face was very much mutilated, the eyelids, the nose, the jaw, the cheeks, the lips, and the mouth all bore cuts. There were abrasions under the left ear. The throat was cut across to the extent of six or seven inches.

Can you tell us what was the cause of death?—The cause of death was haemorrhage from the throat.[73] Death must have been immediate.

There were other wounds on the lower part of the body?—Yes; deep wounds, which were inflicted after death. (Witness here described in detail the terrible mutilation of the deceased's body.)[74]

MR. CRAWFORD: I understand that you found certain portions of the body removed?—Yes. The uterus was cut away with the exception of a small portion, and the left kidney was also cut out. Both these organs were absent and have not been found.

Have you any opinion as to what position the woman was in when the wounds were inflicted?—In my opinion the woman must have been lying down. The way in which the kidney was cut out showed that it was done by somebody who knew what he was about.[75]

Does the nature of the wounds lead you to any conclusion as to the instrument that was used?—It must have been a sharp-pointed knife, and I should say at least 6 in. long.

Would you consider that the person who inflicted the wounds possessed anatomical skill?—He must have had a good deal of knowledge as to the position of the abdominal organs, and the way to remove them.

---

[72]Brown is likely referring to the murder of Annie Chapman, though Phillips was also called to the scene of Elizabeth Stride's death.

[73]That is, from loss of blood after the throat had been cut. Pathologists Dr. Francis Camps and Professor James Cameron as well as Begg, Fido and Skinner believe the Ripper first throttled his victims to induce unconsciousness before slitting their throats.

[74]See Coroner's inquest (L), 1888, No. 135, Catherine Eddowes inquest, 1888 (Corporation of London Records Office) for the details omitted here, also Evans and Skinner, pp. 204–207.

[75]As Brown points out later on, the kidney is a somewhat difficult organ for the layman to extract, though this opinion is qualified when he imparts the same knowledge to slaughtermen. Dr. Sequeira, however, disagreed with Brown's attribution of skill when he testified on 11 October.

Would the parts be of any use for professional purposes?—None whatever.

Would the removal of the kidney, for example, require special knowledge?—It would require a good deal of knowledge as to its position, because it is apt to be overlooked, being covered by a membrane.

Would such a knowledge be likely to be possessed by some one accustomed to cutting up animals?—Yes.

Have you been able to form any opinions as to whether the perpetrator of this act was disturbed?—I think he had sufficient time, but it was in all probability done in a hurry.

How long would it take to make the wounds?—It might be done in five minutes.[76] It might take him longer, but that is the least time it could be done in.

Can you, as a professional man, ascribe any reason for the taking away of the parts you have mentioned?—I cannot give any reason whatever.

Have you any doubt in your own mind whether there was a struggle?—I feel sure there was no struggle. I see no reason to doubt that it was the work of one man.

Would any noise be heard, do you think?—I presume the throat was instantly severed, in which case there would not be time to emit any sound.

Does it surprise you that no sound was heard?—No.

Would you expect to find much blood on the person inflicting these wounds?—No, I should not. I should say that the abdominal wounds were inflicted by a person kneeling at the right side of the body.[77] The wounds could not possibly have been self-inflicted.

Was your attention called to the portion of the apron that was found in Goulston-street?—Yes. I fitted that portion which was spotted with blood to the remaining portion, which was still attached by strings to the body.

Have you formed any opinion as to the motive for the mutilation of the corpse?—It was done to disfigure the corpse, I should imagine.

A JUROR: Was there any evidence of a drug being used?—I have not examined the stomach as to that. The contents of the stomach have been preserved for analysis.[78]

Mr. Crawford said he was glad to announce that the Corporation had unanimously approved the offer by the Lord Mayor of a reward of £500 for the discovery of the murderer.

Several jurymen expressed their satisfaction at the promptness with which the offer was made.

The inquest was then adjourned until next Thursday [October 11].

---

# THE DAILY TELEGRAPH

Monday, October 8, 1888
*[Burial of Catherine Eddowes]*

The body of the Mitre-square victim—Catherine Eddowes, alias Conway, alias Kelly—still lies in the City Mortuary, Golden-lane. At half-past-one o'clock to-day, it will be removed for burial in the Ilford Cemetery.[79]

---

[76]In fact, the murder and mutilations were almost certainly done in a time window of no more and probably less than five minutes, when eyewitness sightings and police testimony are considered.

[77]This was also the opinion of pathologist Professor James Cameron (BFS, p. 75).

[78]See Dr. William Sedgwick Saunders' testimony, 12 October.

[79]Eddowes is buried in public grave 49336, square 318, City of London Cemetery, Manor Park, London. The plaque marking her grave misspells her surname as "Eddows," and gives the incorrect age of 43 (*Ripperana* No. 14, October 1995).

# THE DAILY TELEGRAPH
Friday, October 12, 1888

Page 2
## THE LONDON TRAGEDIES.
## MITRE-SQUARE INQUEST.
*[Second and Final Session
of Eddowes' Inquest]*

Yesterday, at the City Coroner's Court, Golden-lane, Mr. S.F. Langham resumed the inquest respecting the death of Catherine Eddowes, who was found murdered and mutilated in Mitre-square, Aldgate, early on the morning of Sunday, Sept. 30.

Mr. Crawford, City Solicitor, again watched the case on behalf of the police.

**Dr. G.W. Sequeira**, surgeon, of No. 34, Jewry-street, Aldgate, deposed: On the morning of Sept. 30 I was called to Mitre-square, and I arrived at five minutes to two o'clock, being the first medical man on the scene of the murder. I saw the position of the body, and I entirely agree with the evidence of Dr. Gordon Brown in that respect.

BY MR. CRAWFORD: I am well acquainted with the locality and the position of the lamps in the square. Where the murder was committed was probably the darkest part of the square, but there was sufficient light to enable the miscreant to perpetrate the deed.[80]

I think that the murderer had no design on any particular organ of the body. He was not possessed of any great anatomical skill.

Can you account for the absence of noise?—The death must have been instantaneous after the severance of the windpipe and the blood-vessels.

Would you have expected the murderer to be bespattered with blood?—Not necessarily.

How long do you believe life had been extinct when you arrived?—Very few minutes—probably not more than a quarter of an hour.

**Mr. William Sedgwick Saunders**, medical officer of health for the City, said: I received the stomach of the deceased from Dr. Gordon Brown, carefully sealed, and I made an analysis of the contents, which had not been interfered with in any way. I looked more particularly for poisons of the narcotic class, but with negative results, there being not the faintest trace of any of those or other poisons.

**Annie Phillips** stated: I reside at No. 12, Dilston-road, Southwark Park-road, and am married, my husband being a lamp-black packer. I am daughter of the deceased, who formerly lived with my father. She always told me that she was married to him, but I have never seen the marriage lines. My father's name was Thomas Conway.

THE CORONER: Have you seen him lately?—Not for the last fifteen or eighteen months.

Where was he living then?—He was living with me and my husband, at No. 15, Acre-Street, Southwark Park-road.[81]

What calling did he follow?—That of a hawker.

What became of him?—I do not know.

---

[80]What did Sequeira mean by "sufficient light?" Theories as to precisely when Eddowes were killed are generally predicated on how much light was thrown towards the spot where she lay and whether the site could be seen by a passing policeman. Did "sufficient light" mean enough for the murderer to kill but not be seen otherwise, or was Sequeira speaking only of Eddowes' injuries without consideration of outside visibility? Hinton dismisses this statement entirely, believing that the lamps of policemen surrounding Eddowes' body misled the doctor as to the actual amount of light in Mitre Square.

[81]"Anchor" Street, according to the official inquest papers.

Did he leave on good terms with you?—Not on very good terms.

Did he say that he would never see you again, or anything of that sort?—No.

Was he a sober man?—He was a tee-totaller.

Did he live on bad terms with your mother?—Yes, because she used to drink.

Have you any idea where Conway is now?—Not the least. He ceased to live with Eddowes entirely on account of her drinking habits.

Your father was in the 18th Royal Irish Regiment?—So I have been told. He had been a pensioner ever since I was eight years old. I am twenty-three now. They parted about seven or eight years ago.

Did your mother ever apply to you for money?—Yes.

When did you last see her?—Two years and one month ago.

Where did you live when you last saw her?—In King-street, Bermondsey.

Have you any brothers or sisters by Conway?—Two brothers.

Did your mother know where to find either of you?—No.

Were your addresses purposely kept from her?—Yes. To prevent her applying for money.

THE FOREMAN: Was you father aware when he left you that your mother was living with Kelly?—Yes.

MR. CRAWFORD: Are you quite certain that your father was a pensioner of the 18th Royal Irish?—I was told so, but I not sure whether it was the 18th or the Connaught Rangers. It may have been the latter.

THE CORONER: That is the 88th.—I do not know.

MR. CRAWFORD: That is so. It so happens that there is a pensioner of the name of Conway belonging to the Royal Irish, but that is not the man.[82] To witness: When did your mother last receive money from you?

WITNESS: Just over two years ago. She waited upon me in my confinement, and I paid her for it.

Did you ever get a letter from her?—No.

Do you know anything about Kelly?—I have seen him two or three times at the lodging-house in Flower and Dean-street, with my mother.

When did you last see them together?—About three years and a half ago.

You knew they were living together as man and wife?—Yes.

Is it the fact that your father is living with your two brothers?—He was.

Where are your brothers residing now?—I do not know. He was always with them. One was fifteen and the other eighteen years of age.

When did you last see them?—About eighteen months ago. I have not seen them since.

Are we to understand that you had lost all trace of your mother, father, and two brothers for at least eighteen months?—That is so.

**Detective-Sergeant John Mitchell**, of the City police, said: I have, under instructions, and with other officers, made every endeavour to find the father and brothers of the last witness, but without success up to the present.

THE CORONER: Have you found a pensioner named Conway belonging to the 18th Royal Irish?—I have. He has not been identified as the husband of the deceased.

**Detective Baxter Hunt**: Acting under instructions, I discovered the pensioner, Conway, of the Royal Irish, and have

---

[82]The difficulty in locating Conway was that he was drawing his pension under the name of "Thomas Quinn" in an attempt to frustrate Eddowes importuning him for money (ref. 16 October).

confronted him with two sisters of the deceased, who, however, failed to recognise him as the man who used to live with the deceased. I have made every endeavour to trace the Thomas Conway in question and the brothers of Annie Phillips, but without success.

A JUROR: Why did you not confront this Conway with the daughter of the deceased, Annie Phillips?—That witness had not been found then.

MR. CRAWFORD: The theory has been put forward that it was possible for the deceased to have been murdered elsewhere, and her body brought to where it was found. I should like to ask Dr. Gordon Brown, who is present, what his opinion is about that.

DR. GORDON BROWN: I do not think there is any foundation for such a theory. The blood on the left side was clotted, and must have fallen at the time the throat was cut. I do not think that the deceased moved the least bit after that.

THE CORONER: The body could not have been carried to where it was found?—Witness: Oh, no.

**City-constable Lewis [*sic*] Robinson**, 931, deposed: At half-past eight, on the night of Saturday, Sept. 29, while on duty in High-street, Aldgate, I saw a crowd of persons outside No. 29, surrounding a woman whom I have since recognised as the deceased.

THE CORONER: What state was she in?—Drunk.

Lying on the footway?—Yes. I asked the crowd if any of them knew her or where she lived, but got no answer. I then picked her up and sat her against the shut-

ters, but she fell down sideways. With the aid of a fellow-constable[83] I took her to Bishopsgate Police-station. There she was asked her name, and she replied "Nothing." She was then put into a cell.

Did anyone appear to be in her company when you found her?—No one in particular.

MR. CRAWFORD: Did any one appear to know her?—No.

The apron being produced, torn and discoloured with blood, the witness said that to the best of his knowledge it was the apron the deceased was wearing.

THE FOREMAN: What guided you in determining whether the woman was drunk or not?

WITNESS: Her appearance.

THE FOREMAN: I ask you because I know of a case in which a person was arrested for being drunk who had not tasted anything intoxicating for eight or nine hours. You are quite sure this woman was drunk?—She smelt very strongly of drink.

**Sergeant James Byfield**, of the City Police: I remember the deceased being brought to the Bishopsgate Station at a quarter to nine o'clock on the night of Saturday, Sept. 29.

In what condition was she?—Very drunk. She was brought in supported by two constables and placed in a cell, where she remained until one o'clock the next morning, when she had got sober. I then discharged her, after she had given her name and address.

What name and address did she give?—Mary Ann Kelly, No. 6, Fashion-street, Spitalfields.[84]

Did she say where she had been, or

[83]PC George Simmons (BFS, p. 413).
[84]The name and address are both false, but it is a curious coincidence for theorists who believe Mary *Jane* Kelly was the Ripper's intended victim all along, and Eddowes was killed through mistaken identity. See Knight, p. 149.

what she had been doing?—She stated that she had been hopping.[85]

**Constable George Henry Hutt**, 968, City Police: I am gaoler at Bishopsgate station. On the night of Saturday, Sept. 29, at a quarter to ten o'clock, I took over our prisoners, among them the deceased. I visited her several times until five minutes to one on Sunday morning. The inspector, being out visiting, I was directed by Sergeant Byfield to see if any of the prisoners were fit to be discharged. I found the deceased sober, and after she had given her name and address, she was allowed to leave. I pushed open the swing-door leading to the passage and said, "This way, missus." She passed along the passage to the outer door. I said to her, "Please, pull it to." She replied, "All right. Good night, old cock." (Laughter). She pulled the door to within a foot of being close [*sic*], and I saw her turn to the left.

THE CORONER: That was leading towards Houndsditch?—Yes.

THE FOREMAN: Is it left to you to decide when a prisoner is sober enough to be released or not?—Not to me, but to the inspector or acting inspector on duty.

Is it usual to discharge prisoners who have been locked up for being drunk at all hours of the night?—Certainly.

How often did you visit the prisoners?—About every half-hour. At first the deceased remained asleep; but at a quarter to twelve she was awake and singing a song to herself, as it were. I went to her again at half-past twelve, and she then asked when she would be able to get out. I replied: "Shortly." She said, "I am capable of taking care of myself now."

MR. CRAWFORD: Did she tell you where she was going?—No. About two minutes to one o'clock, when I was taking her out of the cell, she asked me what time it was. I answered, "Too late for you to get any more drink." She said, "Well, what time is it?" I replied, "Just on one." Thereupon she said, "I shall get a ____ fine hiding when I get home, then."[86]

Was that her parting remark?—That was in the station yard. I said, "Serve you right; you have no right to get drunk."

You supposed she was going home?—I did.

In your opinion is that the apron the deceased was wearing?—To the best of my belief it is.

What is the distance from Mitre-square to your station?—About 400 yards.

Do you know the direct route to Flower and Dean-street?—No.

A JUROR: Do you search persons who are brought in for drunkenness?—No, but we take from them anything that might be dangerous. I loosened the things round the deceased's neck, and I then saw a white wrapper[87] and a red silk handkerchief.

**George James Morris**, night watchman at Messrs. Kearley and Tonge's tea warehouse, Mitre-square, deposed: On Saturday, Sept. 29, I went on duty at seven o'clock in the evening. I occupied most of my time in cleaning the offices and looking about the warehouse.

THE CORONER: What happened about a quarter to two in the morning?—Constable Watkins, who was on the Mitre-square beat, knocked at my door, which was slightly ajar at the time. I was then

---

[85]Many East End poor went to Kent to pick hops during the summer as a respite from the filth of London slums.

[86]The word omitted in deference to the sensitivities of the *Telegraph*'s readers was "damned." (Evans & Skinner, p. 210).

[87]This may be the "large white handkerchief" in the official listing of Eddowes' belongings (Evans & Skinner, pp. 203–204).

sweeping the steps down towards the door. The door was pushed when I was about two yards off. I turned round and opened the door wide. The constable said, "For God's sake, mate, come to my assistance." I said, "Stop till I get my lamp. What is the matter?" "Oh dear," he exclaimed, "here is another woman cut to pieces."

I asked where, and he replied, "In the corner." I went into the corner of the square and turned my light on the body. I agree with the previous witnesses as to the position of the body. I ran up Mitre-street into Aldgate, blowing my whistle all the while.

Did you see any suspicious persons about?—No. Two constables came up and asked what was the matter.[88]

I told them to go down to Mitre-square, as there was another terrible murder. They went, and I followed and took charge of my own premises again.

Before being called by Constable Watkins, had you heard any noise in the square?—No.

If there had been any cry of distress, would you have heard it from where you were?—Yes.

BY THE JURY: I was in the warehouse facing the corner of the square.

BY MR. CRAWFORD: Before being called I had no occasion to go into the square, I did not go there between one and two o'clock; of that I am certain. There was nothing unusual in my door being open and my being at work at so late an hour. I had not seen Watkins before during the night. I do not think my door had been ajar more than two or three minutes when he knocked.

**James Harvey**, City constable, 964: On the night of Saturday, Sept. 29, I was on duty in the neighbourhood of Houndsditch and Aldgate. I was there at the time of the murder, but did not see any one nor hear any cry. When I got into Aldgate, returning towards Duke-street, I heard a whistle and saw the witness Morris with a lamp. I asked him what was the matter, and he told me that a woman had been ripped up in Mitre-square. Together with Constable Hollins [*sic*] I went to Mitre-square, where Watkins was by the side of the body of the deceased. Hollins went for Dr. Sequeira, and a private individual[89] was despatched for other constables, who arrived almost immediately, having heard the whistle.

I waited with Watkins, and information was sent to the inspector.

At what time previous to that were you in Aldgate?—At twenty-eight minutes past one o'clock I passed the post-office clock.

**George Clapp**, caretaker at No. 5, Mitre-street, deposed: The back part of the house looks into Mitre-square. On the night of Saturday week last I retired to rest in the back room on the second floor about eleven o'clock.

THE CORONER: During the night did you hear any disturbance in the square?—No.

When did you first learn that a murder had been perpetrated?—Between five and six o'clock in the morning.

BY MR. CRAWFORD: A nurse, who was in attendance upon my wife, was sleeping at the top of the house. No person slept either on the ground floor or the first floor.

**Constable Richard Pearce**, 922 City: I reside at No. 3, Mitre-square. There are only two private houses in the square.[90] I

---

[88]PCs James Harvey and James Holland (BFS, pp. 158 and 164).

[89]It is not known who this may have been.

[90]Where Pearce lived and an empty house between his dwelling and the Kearley & Tonge warehouse (Sugden, p. 174).

retired to rest at twenty minutes past twelve on the morning of last Sunday week.

Did you hear any noise in the square?—None at all.

When did you first hear of the murder?—At twenty past two, when I was called by a constable.

From your bedroom window could you see the spot where the murder was committed?—Yes, quite plainly.

BY MR. CRAWFORD: My wife and family were in no way disturbed during the night.

**Joseph Lawende**: I reside at No. 45, Norfolk-road, Dalston, and am a commercial traveller. On the night of Sept. 29, I was at the Imperial Club, Duke-street, together with Mr. Joseph Levy and Mr. Harry Harris. It was raining, and we sat in the club till half-past one o'clock, when we left. I observed a man and a woman together at the corner of Church-passage, Duke-street, leading to Mitre-square.

THE CORONER: Were they talking?— The woman was standing with her face towards the man, and I only saw her back. She had one hand on his breast. He was the taller. She had on a black jacket and bonnet. I have seen the articles at the police-station, and believe them to be those the deceased was wearing.

What sort of man was this?—He had on a cloth cap with a peak of the same.

MR. CRAWFORD: Unless the jury wish it, I do not think further particulars should be given as to the appearance of this man.

THE FOREMAN: The jury do not desire it.

MR. CRAWFORD (TO WITNESS): You have given a description of the man to the police?
—Yes.[91]

Would you know him again?—I doubt it.[92] The man and woman were about nine or ten feet away from me.[93] I have no doubt it was half-past one o'clock when we rose to leave the club, so that it would be twenty-five minutes to two o'clock when we passed the man and woman.

Did you overhear anything that either said?—No.

Did either appear in an angry mood?— No.

Did anything about their movements attract your attention?—No. The man looked rather rough and shabby.

When the woman placed her hand on the man's breast, did she do it as if to push him away?—No; it was done very quietly.

You were not curious enough to look back and see where they went.—No.

**Mr. Joseph Hyam Levy**, the butcher in Hutcheson [*sic*]-street, Aldgate, stated: I was with the last witness at the Imperial Club on Saturday night, Sept. 29. We got up to leave at half-past one on Sunday morning, and came out three or four minutes later. I saw a man and a woman standing at the corner of Church-passage, but I did not take any notice of them. I passed on, thinking they were up to no good at so late an hour.

---

[91]Lawende's full description of the man he saw with Eddowes was printed in the *Police Gazette* of 19 October: "…age 30, height 5ft. 7 or 8in., complexion fair, moustache fair, medium build; dress, pepper-and-salt colour loose jacket, grey cloth cap with peak of same material, reddish neckerchief tied in knot; appearance of a sailor."

[92]Despite Lawende's demurral, the police used him again in February 1891 in an effort to identify Ripper suspect Thomas Sadler (ref. *Telegraph*, 18 February 1891).

[93]In contrast, Lawende's official inquest statement says it was "15 or 16 feet" from the Imperial Club to the couple he saw. Given that the *Times* transcribes Lawende's estimate as "nine or ten yards," the *Telegraph*'s measurement is probably a misprint.

What height was the man?—I should think he was three inches taller than the woman, who was, perhaps, 5ft high.[94] I cannot give any further description of them. I went down Duke-street into Aldgate, leaving them still talking together.

BY THE JURY: The point in the passage where the man and woman were standing was not well lighted. On the contrary, I think it was badly lighted then, but the light is much better now.

BY MR. CRAWFORD: Nothing in what I saw excited my suspicion as to the intention of the man. I did not hear a word that he uttered to the woman.

Your fear was rather about yourself?—Not exactly. (Laughter.)

**Constable Alfred Long**, 254A, Metropolitan police: I was on duty in Goulston-street, Whitechapel, on Sunday morning, Sept. 30, and about five minutes to three o'clock I found a portion of a white apron (produced). There were recent stains of blood on it. The apron was lying in the passage leading to the staircase of Nos. 106 to 119, a model dwelling-house. Above on the wall was written in chalk, "The Jews are the men that will not be blamed for nothing." I at once searched the staircase and areas of the building, but did not find anything else. I took the apron to Commerical-street and reported to the inspector on duty.[95]

Had you been past that spot previously to your discovering the apron?—I passed about twenty minutes past two o'clock.

Are you able to say whether the apron was there then?—It was not.

MR. CRAWFORD: As to the writing on the wall, have you not put a "not" in the wrong place? Were not the words, "The Jews are not the men that will be blamed for nothing?"—I believe the words were as I have stated.

Was not the word "Jews" spelt "Juwes?"—It may have been.

Yet you did not tell us that in the first place. Did you make an entry of the words at the time?—Yes, in my pocket-book.

Is it possible that you have put the "not" in the wrong place?—It is possible, but I do not think that I have.

Which did you notice first—the piece of apron or the writing on the wall?—The piece of apron, one corner of which was wet with blood.

How came you to observe the writing on the wall?—I saw it while trying to discover whether there were any marks about.

Did the writing appear to have been recently done?—I could not form an opinion.

Do I understand that you made a search in the model dwelling-house?—I went into the staircases.

Did you not make inquiries in the house itself?—No.

THE FOREMAN: Where is the pocket-book in which you made the entry of the writing?—At Westminster.

Is it possible to get it at once?—I dare say.

MR. CRAWFORD: I will ask the coroner to direct that the book be fetched.

THE CORONER: Let that be done.

**Daniel Halse**,[96] detective officer, City police: On Saturday, Sept. 29, pursuant to instructions received at the central office

---

[94]This was, in fact, Eddowes' height.

[95]The testimony given here by Long and Halse provides the outline of the discovery and removal of what is known to Ripper researchers as the "Goulston Street Graffito." A discussion of the writing and its various interpretations may be found in Commentary 2.

[96]Detective Constable Daniel Halse (b. 1839), member of the City Police from 1863–1891 (BFS, p. 154).

in Old Jewry, I directed a number of police in plain clothes to patrol the streets of the City all night. At two minutes to two o'clock on the Sunday morning, when near Aldgate Church, in company with Detectives Outram and Marriott, I heard that a woman had been found murdered in Mitre-square. We ran to the spot, and I at once gave instructions for the neighbourhood to be searched and every man stopped and examined. I myself went by way of Middlesex-street into Wentworth-street, where I stopped two men, who, however, gave a satisfactory account of themselves. I came through Goulston-street about twenty minutes past two, and then returned to Mitre-square, subsequently going to the mortuary. I saw the deceased, and noticed that a portion of her apron was missing. I accompanied Major Smith back to Mitre-square, when we heard that a piece of apron had been found in Goulston-street. After visiting Leman-street police station, I proceeded to Goulston-street, where I saw some chalk writing on the black facia of the wall.[97] Instructions were given to have the writing photographed, but before it could be done the Metropolitan police stated that they thought the writing might cause a riot or outbreak against the Jews, and it was decided to have it rubbed out, as the people were already bringing out their stalls into the street. When Detective Hunt returned inquiry was made at every door of every tenement of the model dwelling-house, but we gained no tidings of anyone who was likely to have been the murderer.

BY MR. CRAWFORD: At twenty minutes past two o'clock I passed over the spot where the piece of apron was found, but I did not notice anything then. I should not necessarily have seen the piece of apron.[98]

As to the writing on the wall, did you hear anybody suggest that the word "Jews" should be rubbed out and the other words left?—I did. The fear on the part of the Metropolitan police that the writing might cause riot was the sole reason why it was rubbed out. I took a copy of it and what I wrote down was as follows: "The Juwes are not the men who will be blamed for nothing."

Did the writing have the appearance of having been recently done?—Yes. It was written with white chalk on a black facia.

THE FOREMAN: Why was the writing really rubbed out?—Witness: The Metropolitan police said it might create a riot, and it was their ground.

MR. CRAWFORD: I am obliged to ask this question. Did you protest against the writing being rubbed out?—I did. I asked that it might, at all events, be allowed to remain until Major Smith had seen it.

Why do you say that it seemed to have been recently written?—It looked fresh, and if it had been done long before, it would have been rubbed out by the people passing. I did not notice whether there was any powdered chalk on the ground, though I did look to see if a knife could be found. There were three lines of writing in a good schoolboy's round hand. The size of the capital letters would be about ¾ in., and the other letters were in proportion. The writing was on the black bricks,

---

[97]A fascia is any flat member with a small projection; Halse here applies the term to the black-painted bricks below the white ones which together made up the doorway and wall.

[98]It seems reasonable to assume—as Halse infers—that the apron swatch was at Goulston Street when he and Long passed through at about 2:30am. The alternative explanations—that the Ripper hung about unnoticed for 45 minutes before dropping the incriminating cloth, or that he returned to his lodgings, cleaned up and then carried the bloodstained trophy back to where it was found—are rather unlikely. We might also take into account Long's admission that 30 September was the first time he had been on duty in Goulston Street when determining the time the cloth was dropped before leaping to a fanciful hypothesis.

which formed a kind of dado, the bricks above being white.[99]

MR. CRAWFORD: With the exception of a few questions to Long, the Metropolitan police constable, that is the whole of the evidence I have to offer at the present moment on the part of the City police. But if any point occurs to the coroner or the jury I shall be happy to endeavour to have it cleared up.

A JUROR: It seems surprising that a policeman should have found the piece of apron in the passage of the buildings, and yet made no inquiries in the buildings themselves. There was a clue up to that point, and then it was altogether lost.

MR. CRAWFORD: As to the premises being searched, I have in court members of the City police who did make diligent search in every part of the tenements the moment the matter came to their knowledge. But unfortunately it did not come to their knowledge until two hours after. There was thus delay, and the man who discovered the piece of apron is a member of the Metropolitan police.

A JUROR: It is the man belonging to the Metropolitan police that I am complaining of.

At this point Constable **Long** returned, and produced the pocket-book containing the entry which he made at the time concerning the discovery of the writing on the wall.

MR. CRAWFORD: What is the entry?—Witness: The words are, "The Jews are the men that will not be blamed for nothing."

Both here and in your inspector's report, the word "Jews" is spelt correctly?—Yes, but the inspector remarked that the word was spelt "Juwes."

Why did you write "Jews" then?—I made my entry before the inspector made the remark.

But why did the inspector write "Jews?"—I cannot say.

At all events, there is a discrepancy?—It would seem so.

What did you do when you found the piece of apron?—I at once searched the staircases leading to the buildings.

Did you make inquiry in any of the tenements of the buildings?—No.

How many staircases are there?—Six or seven.

And you searched every staircase?—Every staircase to the top.

You found no trace of blood or of recent footmarks?—No.

About what time was that?—Three o'clock.

Having examined the staircase, what did you next do?—I proceeded to the station.

Before going did you hear that a murder had been committed?—Yes.

It is common knowledge that two murders have been perpetrated. Which did you hear of?—I heard of the murder in the City. There were rumours of another, but not certain.

When you went away, did you leave anybody in charge?—Yes; the constable on the next beat—190, H Division—but I do not know his name.[100]

Did you give him instructions as to what he was to do?—I told him to keep observation on the dwelling house, and see if any one entered or left.

When did you return?—About five o'clock.

Had the writing been rubbed out then?—No; it was rubbed out in my presence at half-past five.

---

[99]The exact order of the Graffito is in dispute. Other than that the first line contained the word "Juwes," we are unsure of its precise layout. In a report to the Home Office (HO 144/221/A49301C, f. 183), Warren includes a transcription of the writing, laid out in an apparent attempt to replicate the original.

[100]PC 190H Henry Bate (personal correspondence, Bernard Brown).

Did you hear any one object to its being rubbed out?—No. It was nearly daylight when it was rubbed out.

A JUROR: Having examined the apron and the writing, did it not occur to you that it would be wise to search the dwelling?—I did what I thought was right under the circumstances.

THE JUROR: I do not wish to say anything to reflect upon you, because I consider that altogether the evidence of the police redounds to their credit; but it does seem strange that this clue was not followed up.

WITNESS: I thought the best thing to do was to proceed to the station and report to the inspector on duty.

THE JUROR: I am sure you did what you deemed best.

MR. CRAWFORD: I suppose you thought it more likely to find the body there than the murderer?—Witness: Yes, and I felt that the inspector would be better able to deal with the matter than I was.

THE FOREMAN: Was there any possibility of a stranger escaping from the house?—Not from the front.

Did you not know about the back?—No, that was the first time I had been on duty there.

**The coroner** said he considered a further adjournment unnecessary, and the better plan would be for the jury to return their verdict and then leave the matter in the hands of the police. In summing up it would not be at all necessary for him to go through the testimony of the various witnesses, but if the jury wanted their memories refreshed on any particular point he would assist them by referring to the evidence on that point. That the crime was a most fiendish one could not for a moment be doubted, for the miscreant, not satisfied with taking a defenceless woman's life, endeavoured so to mutilate the body as to render it unrecognisable. He presumed that the jury would return a verdict of willful murder against some person or persons unknown, and then the police could freely pursue their inquiries and follow up any clue they might obtain. A magnificent reward had been offered, and that might be the means of setting people on the track and bringing to speedy justice the creature who had committed this atrocious crime. On reflection, perhaps it would be sufficient to return a verdict of willful murder against some person unknown, inasmuch as the medical evidence conclusively demonstrated that only one person could be implicated.

The jury at once returned a verdict accordingly.

The coroner, for himself and the jury, thanked Mr. Crawford and the police for the assistance they had rendered in the inquiry.

MR. CRAWFORD: The police have simply done their duty.

THE CORONER: I am quite sure of that.

The jury having presented their fees to Annie Phillips, daughter of the deceased, the proceedings terminated.[101]

---

[101]The term "presenting a fee" in England refers to a bill being submitted for payment; however, the cost of a coroner's jury was not borne by the deceased's survivors and so this cannot be the meaning of the sentence. It seems more likely that the jury, touched by the plight of Annie Phillips, donated their monies to her after the manner of a *deodand*, defined in the OED as "spec. in Eng. Law, a personal chattel which, having been the immediate occasion of the death of a human being, was given to God as an exemplary offering, i.e., forfeited to the Crown to be applied to private uses, e.g., to be distributed in alms," though the practice had been abolished in 1846. Such an occurrence, however, is unique in the annals of the Whitechapel Murders, and more research is needed here (personal correspondence, Bernard Brown).

# THE DAILY TELEGRAPH
Tuesday October 16, 1888

Page 3
## THE WHITECHAPEL MURDERS.
*[Eddowes' Husband Discovered]*

The City police have succeeded in discovering Thomas Conway, who some years ago lived with Catherine Eddowes, the woman murdered in Mitre-Square.[102] Up to yesterday, the efforts of the detectives had been at fault, owing, as was suggested by the City solicitor at the inquest, to the fact that Conway had drawn his pension from the 18th Royal Irish Regiment under another name—that of Thomas Quinn. Apparently, he has not read the papers, for he was ignorant till the last few days that he was being sought for. Then, however, he learned that the City detectives were inquiring after him, and yesterday afternoon he and his two sons went to the detective office of the City police, in Old Jewry, and explained who they were. Conway was at once taken to see Mrs. Annie Phillips, Eddowes's daughter, who recognised him as her father. He states that he left Eddowes in 1880 in consequence of her intemperate habits, which prevented them from living comfortably together. He knew that she had been living with Kelly, and had once or twice seen her in the streets, but had, as much as possible, kept out of her way.

# THE DAILY TELEGRAPH
Friday, October 19, 1888

Page 3
## MITRE-SQUARE MURDER.
## AN EXTRAORDINARY PARCEL.[103]
*[A Letter "from Hell"]*

Mr. George Lusk, the chairman of the Whitechapel Vigilance Committee, has been the recipient of some extraordinary communications from a person who is supposed to be connected with the recent murders in Whitechapel. A few days ago, a postman delivered at Mr. Lusk's residence in Alderney-road, Globe-road, Mile-end, a postcard, which read as follows:

Say Boss—

You seem rare frightened, guess I'd like to give you fits, but can't stop time enough to let you box of toys play copper games with me, but hope to see you when I don't hurry to [*sic*] much.

Bye-bye, Boss.

The card was addressed "Mr. Lusk, Head Vigilance Committee, Alderney-street, Mile-end." As Mr. Lusk has received other communications of the same kind since he has been connected with the Whitechapel Vigilance Committee he paid no attention to the communication; but on Tuesday evening there reached him through the post a small parcel, similarly addressed, which on examination proved to contain some meaty substance that gave off a very offensive odour. A closer inspection showed that the article was a portion of a kidney. Enclosed in the box with it was a letter worded in revolting terms, the writer stating that he had eaten "tother piece," and threatening to send Mr. Lusk

---

[102]At the time of this report, Conway was living at 43 York Street, Westminster (Shelden, p. 31). He is mentioned as bringing his sons to the police station with him, so it is possible that they were still living together, as per Annie Phillips' earlier inquest testimony.

[103]Fuller particulars surrounding the *bona fides* of what is known as the Lusk Kidney can be found in Commentary 1. The reader is also referred to Warren, "A Postal Kidney," *Criminologist*, Spring 1989, DiGrazia, "Revisiting the Lusk Kidney," *Ripperologist* No. 29, June 2000, pp. 4–9 and Evans and Skinner, *Letters from Hell*, pp. 54–71.

The "From hell" letter sent to George Lusk of the Whitechapel Vigilance Committee on 16 October 1888 along with a portion of human kidney (an 1888 copy photographed by Stewart P. Evans).

the matter before the Vigilance Committee, which met at the Crown, Mile-end-road, at a late hour on Wednesday evening. It was then agreed to investigate the subject next day, and yesterday morning Mr. J. Aarons, the treasurer; Mr. W. Harris, the secretary; and Messrs. Reeves and Lawton, members of the Vigilance Committee, proceeded to Mr. Lusk's home to inspect the strange parcel.

There they examined the post-card, letter, and kidney, the latter of which had evidently been immersed in spirits of wine. As no definite conclusion could be arrived at, it was decided to call upon Dr. Wiles, of 56, Mile-end-road. In his absence, however, Mr. F.S. Reed, his assistant, examined the contents of the box, and at once expressed an opinion that the article formed the half of a human kidney, which had been divided longitudinally. He thought it best, however, to submit the kidney to Dr. Openshaw, the pathological curator at the London Hospital, and this was at once done.[105] By the use of the microscope, Dr. Openshaw was able to determine

the knife "that took it if you only wate whil longer." The letter was dated "From Hell," and signed "Catch me when you Can."[104]

Mr. Lusk was naturally much exercised in his mind over receiving this extraordinary parcel, and decided to bring

---

[104]See Commentary 1 for the full text of the letter.

[105]Thomas Horrocks Openshaw (1856–1929), curator of the London Hospital anatomical museum from 1887 (BFS, pp. 339–340). His actions here encouraged someone to send him a "Ripper" letter beginning "Old boss you was rite it was the left kidny…" (ref. Evans & Skinner, *Letters From Hell*, p. 67).

that the kidney had been taken from a full-grown human being, and that the portion before him was part of the left kidney. It at once occurred to the Vigilance Committee that at the inquest on the body of the woman Eddowes, who was murdered at Mitre-square, Aldgate, it was stated that the left kidney was missing, and in view of this circumstance it was deemed advisable to at once communicate with the police. Accordingly the parcel and the accompanying letter and post-card were at once taken to Leman-street Police-station, and the matter placed in the hands of Inspector Abberline. Subsequently, the City police were communicated with, as the discovery relates to a crime occurring within their jurisdiction.

The card-board box which Mr. Lusk received is about 3 in square, and was wrapped in paper. The cover bears a London postmark, but the stamping is not sufficiently clear to enable it to be stated from what postal district of the metropolis the article was sent. On this point it is expected that the assistance of the Post Office officials will be invoked.[106] The portion of the kidney which it enclosed has, according to the medical experts, been preserved for some time in spirits of wine. The person from whom it was taken was probably alive some three weeks since, a circumstance which fits in with the suggestion that the organ may have been taken from the body of the deceased woman, Eddowes, murdered in Mitre-square. Another fact is that the kidney is evidently that of a person who had been a considerable drinker, as there were distinct marks of disease.[107]

The handwriting of the postcard and letter differs altogether from that of "Jack the Ripper," specimens of whose calligraphy were recently published. The writing is of an inferior character, evidently disguised, while the spelling, as will be seen, is indifferent.

Mr. J. Aarons, the treasurer of the Whitechapel Vigilance Association, made the following statement last evening: "Mr. Lusk, our chairman, came over to me last (Wednesday) night in a state of considerable excitement. I asked him what was the matter, when he replied, 'I suppose you will laugh at what I am going to tell you, but you must know that I had a little parcel come to me on Tuesday evening, and to my surprise it contains half a kidney and a letter from "Jack the Ripper." To tell you the truth, I did not believe in it, and I laughed and said I thought somebody had been trying to frighten him. Mr. Lusk, however, said it was no laughing matter to him. I then suggested that, as it was late, we should leave the matter over till the morning, when I and other members of the committee would come round. This morning, at about half-past nine, Mr. Harris, our secretary, Mr. Reeves, Mr. Lawton, and myself went across to see Mr. Lusk, who opened his desk and pulled out a small square cardboard box, wrapped in brown paper. Mr. Lusk said, "Throw it away; I hate the sight of it." I examined the box and its contents, and being sure that it was not a sheep's kidney, I advised that, instead of throwing it away, we should see Dr. Wills [*sic*] of 56, Mile-end-road.

We did not, however, find him in, but Mr. Reed, his assistant, was. He gave an

---

[106]Postal officials later determined that as the mysterious package had only one postmark, it was probable the kidney was posted in the same district in which it was delivered.

[107]There may be some truth in these medical statements, but there are also improbabilities as well. Both this story and one in the 19 October *Star* are almost identically worded, suggesting a common pen rather than different reporters, and it would be interesting to know who the "medical experts" referred to were. A careful reading would suggest them to be Reed and Openshaw, in which case this news report needs to be taken with a grain of salt. See Commentary 1.

opinion that it was a portion of a human kidney which had been preserved in spirits of wine; but, to make sure, he would go over to the London Hospital, where it could be microscopically examined. On his return Mr. Reed said that Dr. Openshaw, at the Pathological Museum, stated that the kidney belonged to a female, that it was part of the left kidney, and that the woman had been in the habit of drinking.[108] He should think that the person had died about the same time the Mitre-square murder was committed. It was then agreed that we should take the parcel and the letter to Leman-street Police-station, where we saw Inspector Abberline. Afterwards some of us went to Scotland-yard, where we were told that we had done quite right in putting the matter into Mr. Abberline's hands. Our committee will meet again to-night, but Mr. Lusk, our chairman, has naturally been much upset."

The force of police, dressed in private clothes, who have been told off to make a house-to-house search in Whitechapel and Spitalfields, were busily engaged yesterday. At every house or tenement visited they left a copy of the subjoined police notice: "To the Occupier.—On the mornings of Friday, Aug. 31, Saturday, 8th, and Sunday, Sept. 30, 1888, women were murdered in or near Whitechapel, supposed by someone residing in the immediate neighbourhood. Should you know of any persons to whom suspicion is attached, you are earnestly requested to communicate at once with the nearest police-station." The police have everywhere been received with the greatest good feeling, even in the poorest districts, and have had no difficulty in obtaining information.[109]

## Catherine Eddowes— Commentary

### CHRISTOPHER-MICHAEL DIGRAZIA

#### 1. The Lusk Kidney

When discussion turns to the subject of letters purporting to come from the pen of Jack the Ripper, most credence is usually given to that delivered to George Lusk on 16 October, which is known to scholars as the "From hell" letter because of its superscription. Enclosed within was a piece of flesh said to be half of a human kidney. It is because of this grisly item that the letter has drawn sustained attention, supporters pointing to the very act of mailing an internal organ as beyond the purview of a hoaxer, while detractors enumerate the points of evidence which speak against the kidney's *bona fides*.

The case in favor of the kidney rests primarily on an intriguing passage from the 1910 memoirs of Major Henry Smith, Acting Commissioner of the City Police. In brief, he stated that medical experts consulted by him pronounced the offal to be a left human kidney infected with Bright's Disease which had been placed in spirits within hours of extraction from the body and which still had one inch of renal artery attached to it; all, Smith crowed, factors which proved the artifact to be real beyond doubt. Commentary by the contemporary press is also used to bolster the claims for the "Lusk Kidney," and popular histories of the Ripper murders usually accept it as genuine, while more sober tomes either dismiss it outright or treat it with guarded acceptance.

[108]The opinions Reed puts in the mouth of Openshaw are medical nonsense, and Openshaw himself, in the 19 October *Star*, disavowed everything except the observation that the Lusk Kidney was half of a left human kidney. Did Openshaw really say these things, did Reed trick up the diagnosis himself, or did Aarons misunderstand what he was told? At this remove, it is impossible to say.

[109]This may be only journalistic boilerplate, but it is a useful corrective to keep in mind against the frequently-expressed view that Jack the Ripper was not caught because of suspicion of, and hostility to, the police.

Press reports can be easily dealt with. Early news stories (such as those in the *Telegraph* and *Star* of 19 October) put forth the same limited amount of information and conjecture: the kidney was a left kidney, it was from a human female, it was a "ginny" kidney (meaning that it came from an alcoholic), was from the body of a person aged about 45 and had been extracted within three weeks of its receipt. None of these statements save the first would turn out to be true, but the cumulative effect of such official-sounding reportage would be to plant in the public mind the certainty that the Ripper had sent Lusk a ghastly souvenir of his latest kill. All of these reports, moreover (as has been pointed out in earlier footnotes), can be traced back to the imaginations or misreporting of four people—Dr. Openshaw, F.S. Reed, Joseph Aarons or an anonymous reporter. There is no need to take them seriously, particularly as Openshaw himself (and later, Dr. Gordon Brown) would emphatically deny the extravagant gilding of Lusk's package as being more than just half of a common human kidney.

We now turn to Smith. While active in the Eddowes investigation and an able policeman, his memoirs are, in the words of Philip Sugden, "repeatedly inaccurate." His reminiscences cannot be taken entirely at face value, especially as he is writing from memory long after the events he describes. We must also remember that what Smith has told us previously about the Lusk Kidney is not supported by outside evidence. Dr. Gordon Brown prepared a report on the kidney for the City Police, but this has been lost. Smith said an unnamed "police surgeon" also prepared a report for his use, but this too has vanished and Smith admits only to giving his readers its "substance." As well, he tells us that London Hospital senior surgeon Henry Sutton "pledge[d] his reputation" that the kidney had been placed in spirits within hours of its presumed removal from the ravaged corpse of Eddowes; alas, no trace of Sutton's pronouncements can now be located.

And so, if neither the press nor Major Smith can be fully believed, are there any reasons for thinking the Lusk Kidney real beyond the gross boasting of its covering letter? There are, in fact, two reasons, though each requires a good dose of supposition.

The first is simply receipt of the kidney itself. Could it really have been easy, as the police believed, for a hoaxer to have procured a human kidney, taken it away and sent it through the mail? The modern era of precise medical care with endless reams of records and strict, obsessive control makes it impossible to imagine a time where a medical student might easily stroll away with a human organ safely secreted on his person. And yet, that the Lusk Kidney was a medical student's prank was the general police consensus by the end of October. City Police Inspector McWilliam noted that such a person would have "no difficulty in obtaining the organ in question" (HO 144/221/A49301C, ff. 162–170). The Metropolitan Police were even more dismissive; in their opinion, a kidney could easily be obtained after a post-mortem by a student or even a lowly dissecting room porter (HO 144/221/A49301C, ff. 184–94).

The reader who believes the police too ready to accept this convenient explanation might consider the medical response when Coroner Wynne Baxter advanced his "mad medico" theory on 26 September. Sir James Risdon Bennett, President of the Royal College of Physicians, informed the press that uteri could be obtained almost for the asking at any public hospital, "where there are always many paupers or unclaimed persons who are made the subjects of experiments" (*Evening News*, 1 October).

Obviously, it would be hard to imagine

a civilian or even a medical student simply walking into a hospital and out again with a human kidney without exciting some comment. Even Victorian medicine was not quite that informal. If the Lusk Kidney was a hoax, then it almost certainly came from someone within the medical profession who knew how to slip away with such an item, or at the least from someone with medical connections who would not be unduly questioned about their request. It might be useful in this particular context to consider the thoughts in a 1966 letter to the *London Hospital Gazette* from Leonard Archer, Lusk's grandson, who noted that his grandfather had at one time done some work in the Hospital or for some of its staff, and so later came to believe the eponymous kidney was a "practical joke" sent to him by someone there (*Letters from Hell*, pp. 70–71).

A second reason for considering that the kidney might have been real stems from two things Smith noted about its condition; that it had one inch of renal artery attached and that both it and the remaining right kidney in Eddowes' body evidenced symptoms of "Bright's Disease," an ailment known today by the more specific term "chronic glomerulonephritis." Newspapers in 1888 did not provide pathologic comments on the kidney save to note that it was visibly affected by some sort of condition, offering us only frustrating and fragmentary descriptions such as "ginny kidney" or "distinct marks of disease." The rediscovery of Dr. Brown's postmortem notes aided this line of research, as in them he labeled Eddowes' remaining kidney as being "pale, bloodless with slight congestion of the base of the pyramids." N.P. Warren, FRCS (editor of *Ripperana* and a practicing surgeon), opined that this description clearly indicates Bright's Disease, and his diagnosis is now commonly received wisdom. And yet, we must bear in mind that not all nephritic opinion is in

agreement with Warren and no comprehensive, contemporary description of the Lusk Kidney exists to enable us to state definitively that it, too, had Bright's Disease.

What of the renal artery, then? True, there is usually about three inches of such in the human body, but again, we have no witness other than Smith to a corresponding bit of vessel being attached to the Lusk Kidney. In fact, when interviewed by the *Sunday Times* of 21 October, Dr. Brown himself stated that the renal artery had been "trimmed up," so again, Smith's memory and conclusions cannot be corroborated.

Eddowes had *some* kidney ailment; this much is evident, even if its exact nature cannot be agreed upon. The Lusk Kidney showed "distinct marks of disease." As tempting as it might be to put the two propositions together and claim "From hell" as an authentic communication from the Ripper, we simply do not have enough evidence to move beyond a guarded "perhaps."

It may be that the Lusk Kidney floats in a jar in some dark anteroom of the London Hospital, uncataloged and unrecognised, and the definitive answer to this puzzle may yet be written. Until that day, however, its authenticity must remain in tantalising doubt.

## 2. The Juwes Are the Men...

It is to be pondered what the reaction of PC Alfred Long would have been were he told that his discovery of a short chalked message would become the inspiration for years of theorising, conspiracy-mongering and outright looniness. Certainly the patient reader who has digested the *Telegraph*'s short account of the "Goulston Street Graffito" might be forgiven for wondering why an item which caused so little comment in 1888 has become a near-obsessive puzzle for some researchers and why modern documentary films invest this slight, grammatically obscure message with such a freight of meaning. Was the graffiti the great lost clue—the *Mary Celeste* of Ripperology? Was its erasure a prudent act or crass stupidity? Most singularly, would its preservation have led to the capture of Jack the Ripper himself? Important questions, all. And to answer them, a review of the scanty available evidence must prevail before we wander into the misty realm of endless possibility.

To begin with, *what*, exactly, was written on the wall? PC Long testified on 12 October that the words were *The Jewes are the men that will not be blamed for nothing.* City Solicitor Crawford challenged this phrasing, asking if it were not actually written as, *The Jews are not the men that will be blamed for nothing.* Long averred that his phrasing was correct, and it was written as such in his notebook. Detective Daniel Halse, however, the third person to see the writing, testified that the words ran as Mr. Crawford had them, adding that "Jewes" was spelt *"Juwes"* (Coroner's Inquest [L], 1888, No. 135, Catherine Eddowes Inquest, 1888 [Corporation of London Public Record Office], pp. 37–42, and *Telegraph*, 12 October, p. 2). Nevertheless, Sir Charles Warren, Superintendent Thomas Arnold, PC Long, Chief Inspector Donald Swanson and Inspector James McWilliam argued for putting the word "not" further along in the phrase. Warren himself, in a report to the Home Office, not only endorsed PC Long's transcription, but also apparently tried to reproduce the Graffito's layout (HO 144/221/A49301C, f. 183):

> The Juwes are
> The men That
> Will not
> be Blamed
> for Nothing

This brings us neatly on to another quandary regarding the phrase; exactly what was the troublesome second word? No one at the time seems to have doubted that "Juwes" referred to the Hebrew race, but the precise spelling was in dispute. Of eyewitnesses, Warren and Halse rendered it JUWES, with Long and Arnold opting for JUEWES. Halse's spelling is the more widely accepted today, but it should in fairness be pointed out that at least six spelling variations exist within the official records themselves—"Jewes," "Jeuwes," "Juwes," "Jeuws," "Juewes" and "Juews" (HP 144/221/A46301C, ff. 164, 195, 197 and Catherine Eddowes Inquest Papers).

Contemporary thought generally took the writing at face value. While the syntax might be obscure, it seemed to police, press and public that the elusive author was referring in some way to Jews. But in what manner? Were they being blamed for the killings? Was this an admission of culpability? Or was it merely an everyday anti–Semitic comment, having nothing at all to do with the murders? In any case, "Juwes" undisputedly alluded to Jews in general but to no one—and apparently nothing—in particular. That view changed in 1976, however, when Stephen Knight, author of *Jack the Ripper: The Final Solution*, expanded on a startling explanation first aired by the BBC in the 1973 Barlow and Watt series *Jack the Ripper*. "Juwes" was, in reality, a secret code word, revealing a Freemason conspiracy responsible for the Ripper murders! According to Knight, "Juwes" referred collectively to "Jubela," "Jubelo" and "Jubelum," legendary assassins of Hiram Abiff, the architect of Solomon's Temple and figures in Masonic ritual. In Knight's tale, the Goulston Street Graffito was a message to those "in the know" that Jack the Ripper had Masonic connections; as Freemasonry was inclusive of some of England's most powerful men, a revelation that the killer was a member of their fraternity could destroy the ruling class. Therefore, the graffiti had to be removed at all costs before its significance could be realized. This explained, according to Knight, why Sir Charles Warren—one of England's highest-ranking Masons—personally visited Goulston Street and ensured that the writing was destroyed.

Anti-Semitism turned conspiracy. A provoking theory, and one so sufficiently persuasive that books, documentaries and films trailing in *The Final Solution*'s wake have invested the graffiti with an almost mystical significance, portraying its erasure as misguided at best and sinister at worst. And yet the theory is a castle built on sand.

A casual reading of Knight would lead one to believe that the legend of Hiram Abiff and his killers is common Masonic knowledge, whatever an initiate's rank. In fact, as Scott Palmer, author of *Jack the Ripper: A Reference Guide* (and himself a Master Mason), points out, the three names are mentioned only in the ceremony of the third, final Masonic degree, when one becomes a Master Mason—the highest level in Masonry. The names are more widely known now, of course, since the publication of Knight's book as well as the films *Murder by Decree* and *From Hell*, whose plots are heavily drawn from it, but the knowledge would not have been so common in 1888.

But what of that niggling word "Juwes?" With respect to Knight's sinister meaning, Paul Begg, author of *Jack the Ripper: The Uncensored Facts*, demurs:

> "Juwes" is supposed to be the collective name for Jubelo, Jubela and Jubelum, who, during the building of Solomon's Temple, murdered the Grand Master, Hiram Abiff. They featured in British Masonic rituals until 1814, but they were dropped during the major revision of the ritual between 1814 and 1816. By 1888 it is doubtful if many British Masons would even have known their names. In the United States, however, the names were and are used. But in neither country were Jubelo, Jubela and Jubelum known officially or colloquially as the "Juwes." They were always referred to as "the ruffians." "Juwes" is not and has never been a Masonic word, nor has "Juwes" or any word approximating to it ever appeared in British, Continental or American Masonic rituals. It is a mystery why anyone ever thought that "Juwes" was a Masonic word [pp. 127–128].

And although John Robinson's 1989 Masonic history *Born in Blood* suggests the word "Juwes" might be derived from misunderstood mediaeval French and have originally been the collective term *Jubes*, Begg and Palmer's facts provide the simplest explanation—the word *Juwes*, with respect to Freemasonry, does not exist. Whatever the intended meaning of the Goulston Street Graffito, it is definitely *not* a secret Masonic message.

What, then, of Sir Charles Warren? Knight stated that the very act of the Chief Commissioner of the Metropolitan Police visiting a Ripper crime scene was in itself highly suspicious, and could only have been in order to control knowledge of the incriminating scrawl. Many writers have considered Warren's actions ill-judged, but do they deserve the epithet "sinister?"

To begin with, Warren was perfectly within his rights to go to Goulston Street. Even Major Smith—Acting Commissioner of the City Police—took to the alleys of the East End that night after learning of the Eddowes murder (but then, he has always had easier treatment at the hands of Ripperologists!). During an early-morning briefing from Superintendent Arnold, Warren learned of the "double event" and the concomitant discovery of Eddowes' apron piece and the mysterious writing. Arnold also noted that he had himself posted a policeman on the scene ready to sponge away the message. Warren could have let his subordinate proceed, but allowing a Superintendent to take responsibility for the destruction of a possible clue without his personally examining it would have been a cowardly, buck-passing measure and Sir Charles—despite his faults—was known to be loyal to his men.

The Home Office report earlier referenced preserves Warren and Arnold's explanations for their actions that morning, and it is instructive. Arnold feared that the same anti–Semitic outcry which happened after the Chapman killing could well break out again more forcefully in the wake of the "double event," were a Jewish connection made public. Warren took into account his subordinate's familiarity with Whitechapel emotion, and quite evidently agreed with him:

> The writing was on the jamb of the open archway or doorway visible to anybody in the street and could not be covered up without danger of the covering being torn off at once.
>
> A discussion took place whether the writing could be left covered up or otherwise or whether any portion of it could be left for an hour until it could be photographed; but after taking into consideration the excited state of the population in London generally at the time, the strong feeling which had been excited against the Jews, and the fact that in a short time there would be a large concourse of people in the streets, and having before me the report that if it was left the house was likely to be wrecked I considered it desirable to obliterate the writing at once, having taken a copy.
>
> I do not hesitate to say that if the writing had been left there would have been an onslaught upon the Jews, property would have been wrecked, and lives would probably have been lost... [HO 144/221/A49301C, f. 183].

With respect to the grand conspiracy, Sir Charles' "having taken a copy" of the Graffito and directing several policemen around him to copy the message as well is decidedly curious behavior for someone desperate to erase all traces of a blackmailing missive! Additionally, a decent photograph would not have been possible until sunrise, which did not occur until almost 5:59am—nearly one half hour after the message was removed from the bricks and approximately one hour after the Spitalfields Market opened. In view of the crowd that would normally attend a market day as well as the overwhelming masses of humanity which would crowd Berner Street and Mitre Square once news of the Ripper's latest atrocities became public, it seems Warren and Arnold wanted to avoid even a hint of police interest in a "clue" which might at best be nothing at all and at worst a catalyst for a pogrom.

Would a riot have broken out were the writing preserved? One answer serves as well as the other. Public opinion was muted when the graffiti text became public, but whether this resulted from sober consideration or from Warren's handling of the situation is impossible to say. It is highly unlikely that preserving the Graffito would have brought the police any closer to catching the killer than did their possession of the bloodstained swatch of Catherine Eddowes' apron. At most, it might have allowed a comparison between the penmanship of the shadowy author and that of the numerous jokers who sent "Ripper" letters to press and police.

We only know Warren acted as he thought best. We may deplore his decision to only copy the writing and wash it away before it could be photographed, but we are not justified in tarring him as a frantic Masonic stooge bent on a cover-up.

# Chapter 5

# MARY JANE KELLY

*—found murdered Friday, 9 November 1888*

About the last thing she said to me was, "Whatever you do, don't you do wrong and turn out as I have." She had often spoken to me in this way, and warned me against going on the streets, as she had done. She told me, too, she was heartily sick of the life she was leading, and wished she had money enough to go back to Ireland, where her people lived.
*—Daily Telegraph*, Monday, 12 November 1888

The morning of 9 November saw the discovery of the body of Mary Jane Kelly, generally considered to be the last of the Ripper's victims. At 25, she was the youngest, by most accounts the prettiest, and certainly the most horribly butchered. The phantom killer surpassed his catalogue of horrors in the destruction wreaked on her; she had been savagely slaughtered and disembowelled, her face so ravaged by the Ripper's depredations that at the inquest on 12 November, Kelly's lover Joseph Barnett testified he could only recognise her ear and eyes.

Surprisingly, in view of this latest atrocity, there were fewer scenes of antic hysteria or emotion such as had attended both the Chapman murder and the "double event." It was as though the inhuman ferocity of Kelly's murder made open excitement and speculation almost obscene. In contrast to the earlier murders, where taunts, threats and theories coursed freely through the streets, the removal of Kelly's razored remains to the Shoreditch mortuary produced a solemn atmosphere, as the *Times* noted on 10 November: "The crowd … was of the humblest class, but the demeanour of the poor people was all that could be desired. Ragged caps were doffed and slatternly-looking women shed tears as the shell, covered with a ragged-looking cloth, was placed in the van…"

The brief, business-like Kelly inquest was chaired by Dr. Roderick MacDonald, who concluded the proceedings in a single day. Later writers have tended to view his actions with suspicion, but this shows a misunderstanding of Victorian inquests, which typically ran only for one or two sessions.

The muted proceedings were, for once, echoed by much of the press. The *Times'* report of it was relegated to page 10, rather than the standard page 3 occupied by Ripper stories. The *Telegraph* and *Star* expressed only a cynical resignation that the police would be unable to catch Kelly's murderer; gone were the extravagant limnings of editorials speculating on the nature of the fiend or when he might—no, *would*—strike again. There was, it appeared, an unspoken acknowledgement that the death of Mary Kelly went far beyond all that had preceded it; a sense that some invisible, dreadful line in murder news had been crossed. A reconsideration and assessment of the past few weeks' ink-stained grotesqueries was needed.

On 19 November, the body of Mary Kelly was laid to rest in Saint Patrick's Roman Catholic Cemetery in Leytonstone. A sombre crowd of several thousand, bare-headed and weeping, followed her to the grave, where the penniless Irish prostitute was buried with all the dignity of a state funeral.

Police crime-scene photograph of 13 Miller's Court, Spitalfields, on 9 November 1888 (courtesy of Evans/Skinner Crime Archive).

## THE DAILY TELEGRAPH

London, Saturday,
November 10, 1888[1]

Page 5
THE EAST-END TRAGEDIES.
A SEVENTH MURDER.
ANOTHER CASE OF
HORRIBLE MUTILATION.

Yesterday a seventh murder, the most horrible of the series of atrocities attributed to the same hand, was committed in Whitechapel.[2] As in all the previous instances, the victim was a woman of immoral character and humble circumstances, but she was not murdered in the open street, her throat having been cut and the subsequent mutilations having taken place in a room which the deceased rented at No. 26, Dorset-street. She has been identified as Mary Jane Kelly, and is

---

[1]Concurrent with coverage of Kelly's murder were lengthy reports on Warren's tenure as Commissioner of the Metropolitan Police Force and his resignation, which are impracticable to include here. It is worth noting, however, that his resignation, tendered on 8 November 1888, was occasioned not by Whitechapel murder but by a dispute over authority in day to day police administration between Warren and Home Secretary Henry Matthews. The interested reader is directed to Sugden, pp. 342–343.

[2]Despite classifying Kelly here as the seventh victim, this same edition later discounted the earlier murders of Smith and Tabram, saying: "The two earlier murders—the one in George-yard and the other in Osborne-street—are not believed to have been the work of the miscreant who is still at large."

believed to be the wife of a man from whom she is separated, and the daughter, it is said, of a foreman employed at an iron foundry in Carnarvon, in Wales. The unfortunate woman was twenty-four years of age, tall, slim, fair, of fresh complexion, and of attractive appearance. The room, which she occupied at a weekly rental of 4s, was on the ground floor of a three-storeyed house in Dorset-street, which is a short thoroughfare leading off Commercial-street, and in the shadow of Spital-fields Church and Market. Kelly was last seen alive on Thursday night;[3] but as late as one a.m. yesterday morning she was heard by some lodgers in the house singing "Sweet Violets." No other noise appears to have been distinguished, and it was not suspected that she was at that time accompanied by a man.[4] Entrance to her apartment was obtained by means of an arched passage, opposite a large lodging-house, and between Nos. 26, and 28, Dorset-street, ending in a *cul de sac* known as Miller's-court. In this court there are six houses let out in tenements, chiefly to women, the rooms being numbered. On the right-hand side of the passage there are two doors. The first of these leads to the upper floors of the house in which Kelly was living. It has seven rooms, the first-floor front, facing Dorset-street, being over a shed or warehouse used for the storage of costers' barrows. A second door opens inwards, direct from the passage, into Kelly's apartment, which is about 15ft. square, and is placed at the rear

corner of the building. It has two windows, one small, looking into a yard, which is fitted with a pump. The opposite side of the yard is formed by the side wall of houses, which have whitewashed front-ages, and are provided with green shutters. From some of these premises, on the left-hand side of the court, it is possible to secure a view, in a diagonal direction, of the larger window, and also the doorway belonging to the room tenanted by the deceased. In this room there was a bed placed behind the door, and parallel with the window. The rest of the furniture consisted of a table and two chairs.

It was at a quarter to eleven o'clock yesterday morning that the discovery of the latest tragedy was made. The rents of the tenements in Miller's-court are collected by John McCarthy, the keeper of a provision and chandler's shop, which is situated on the left-hand side of the entrance to the court in Dorset-street. McCarthy instructed his man, John Bowyer, a pensioned soldier, to call for the money due, the deceased woman having been 29s in arrear. Accordingly Bowyer knocked at the door of Kelly's room, but received no answer. Having failed to open the door, he passed round the angle of the house and pulled the blind of the window, one of the panes being broken.[5] Then he noticed blood upon the glass,[6] and it immediately occurred to him that another murder had been committed. He fetched M'Carthy, who, looking through the window, saw upon the bed, which was against the wall,

---

[3]See Commentary 2 for a discussion of various Kelly sightings.

[4]Both these claims were later refuted. For reported cries of "Oh Murder!" being heard see 10 November, Mrs. Kennedy's reported account, 12 November, the inquest testimony of Elizabeth Prater and Sarah Lewis, and the contrary testimony of Mary Ann Cox, 13 November. For sightings of a man with Kelly see 13 November and testimony of Mary Cox.

[5]Two panes in one window were broken. The window covering was variously described as a blind or curtain, but also included the man's coat, which Maria Harvey claimed to have left behind in Kelly's room. See 12 November and Dr. Phillips' inquest testimony, 13 November.

[6]No official record or other main newspaper report makes reference to blood on the window glass. This potentially significant piece of information therefore remains merely uncorroborated comment.

the body of a woman, without clothing, and terribly mutilated. The police at Commercial-street and at Leman-street, both stations being within five minutes' walk, were instantly informed, and in response to the summons Inspector Beck[7] arrived. This officer despatched a message for Inspector Abberline and Inspector Reid, both of the Detective department. Nothing, however, was done until the arrival of Mr. T. Arnold, the Superintendent of the H Division of Metropolitan Police, who, shortly after eleven o'clock, gave orders for the door of the room to be broken open.[8] The last person to have left the place must have closed the door behind him, taking with him the key from the spring lock, as it is missing.[9]

A most horrifying spectacle was presented to the officers' gaze, exceeding in ghastliness anything which the imagination can picture. The body of the woman was stretched on the bed, fearfully mutilated. Nose and ears had been cut off, and, although there had been no dismemberment, the flesh had been stripped off, leaving the skeleton. The nature of the other injuries was of a character to indicate that they had been perpetrated by the author of the antecedent crimes in the same district; and it is believed that once more there are portions of the organs missing.[10] That the miscreant must have been some time at his work was shown by the deliberate

manner in which he had excised parts, and placed them upon the table purposely to add to the horror of the scene. Intelligence was promptly conveyed to Scotland-yard, and personally to Sir Charles Warren. Meanwhile the street was as far as possible closed to traffic, a cordon of constables being drawn across each end, and the police took possession of Miller's-court, refusing access to all comers in the expectation that bloodhounds would be used. Acting upon orders, the detectives and inspectors declined to furnish any information of what had occurred, and refused permission to the press to inspect the place. Every precaution was taken to preserve any trace of evidence which might be existing. Mr. Phillips, the divisional surgeon, was called, and he shortly afterwards received the assistance of other experts, among them being Dr. Bond, who came from Westminster in obedience to special instructions,[11] and Dr. Gordon Browne [*sic*], the City Police surgeon, who conducted the post-mortem in the case of the Mitre-square murder. Dr. J. R. Gabe, who viewed the body, said he had seen a great deal in dissecting rooms, but he had never witnessed such a horrible sight as the murdered woman presented. Before anything was disturbed a photograph was taken of the interior of the room. There was comparatively little blood, death having been due to the severing of the throat, the

---

[7]Inspector Walter Beck (b. 1852), with the Metropolitan Police from 1871 to 1896. Duty Inspector at the time of the Kelly murder (Evans and Skinner, p. 676).

[8]The door of Kelly's room was not forced open until 1:30 pm (ref. Phillips' inquest testimony).

[9]The *Star* of 12 November reported: "The key of the murdered woman's door has been found, so that her murderer did not carry it away with him, as was at first supposed." But Abberline confirmed at the inquest that the key had been missing for sometime and was not required to either open or bolt the door. See 13 November.

[10]This surmise was contradicted later in the article, but in fact, it appears Kelly's heart was taken by her killer (ref. MEPO 3/3153, ff. 10–18 and Yost, "Did Kelly Have a Heart?" *Ripper Notes*, May 1999, pp. 8–11).

[11]Dr. Thomas Bond (1841–1901) was the A (Westminster) division police surgeon who had given expert medical opinion in the case of the recently discovered Whitehall torso (BFS, pp. 44–50 and 480–481). On 28 October, in light of the varying opinions on the degree of surgical skill evidenced in previous Whitechapel murders, Met Assistant Commissioner Dr. Robert Anderson requested him to review and offer an opinion on the past medical evidence (HO 144/221/A49301C f. 217). It was while engaged on this review that, with Kelly's demise, Bond was afforded his first opportunity to view the handiwork of Jack the Ripper.

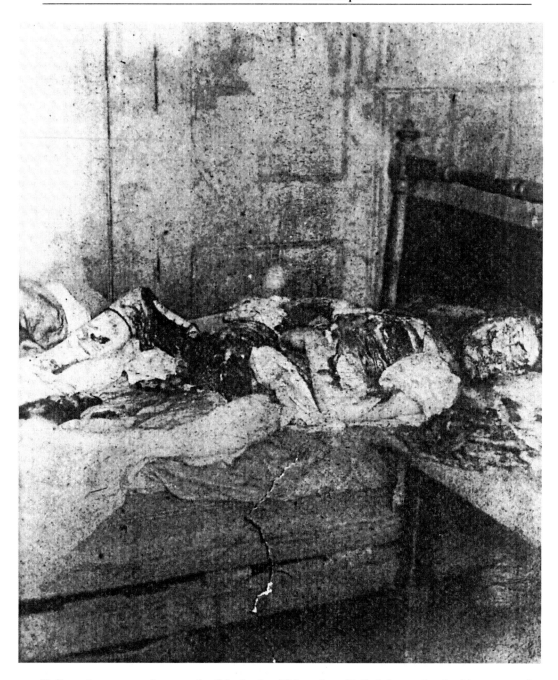

**Police crime-scene photograph of the body of Mary Jane Kelly lying on her bed (courtesy of Evans/Skinner Crime Archive).**

mutilations having been subsequently per- formed. It was evident that a large and keen knife had been used by a hand pos- sessed of some knowledge and practice. That the woman had had no struggle with her betrayer was shown by her position and the way in which her garments, in- cluding a velvet bodice, were arranged by the fireplace. The medical men were engaged until past four p.m. in their

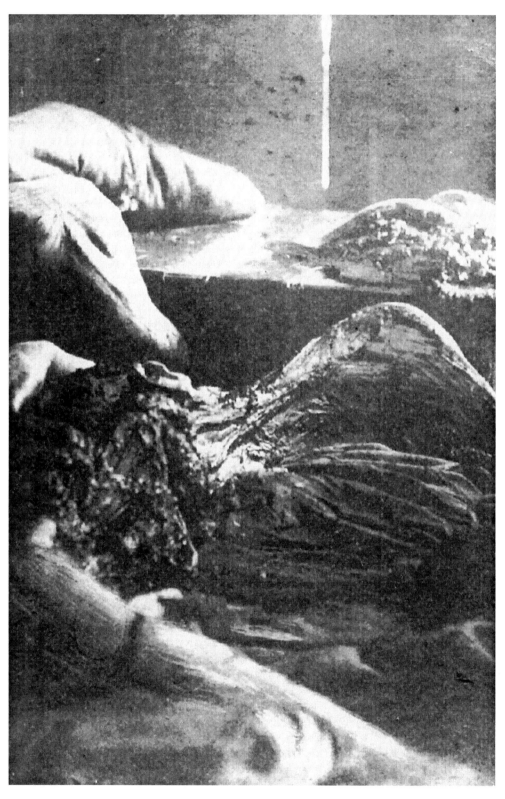

**Second police crime-scene photograph of the lower half of the body of Mary Kelly (courtesy of Evans/Skinner Crime Archive).**

examination upon the spot, the police, having satisfied themselves that no weapon had been left, reserving a complete investigation of the contents of the room for a later opportunity. Mr. Anderson, the recently-appointed Assistant-Commissioner,[12] had driven up in a cab at ten minutes to two o'clock, and he remained for some time. Detectives searched all the adjacent houses for suspicious characters, but without result. All the inmates were able satisfactorily to account for their whereabouts. Not one of them had heard any sound to point to the hour when the woman must have been attacked by her assailant.[13] The walls are of thin match lining, which makes this circumstance the more unaccountable, and the couple in the room overhead had slept soundly without being awakened by scuffling in the room beneath them.

Elizabeth Prater, the occupant of the first floor front room, was one of those who saw the body through the window. She affirms that she spoke to the deceased on Thursday. She knew that Kelly had been living with a man, and that they had quarrelled about ten days since. It was a common thing for the women living in these tenements to bring men home with them. They could do so as they pleased. She had heard nothing during the night,[14] and was out betimes in the morning, and her attention was not attracted to any circumstances of an unusual character. Kelly was, she admitted, one of her own class, and she made no secret of her way of gaining a livelihood. During the day the police

succeeded in finding John [Joseph] Barnett, the man with whom the deceased had cohabited until a week ago, when they separated in consequence of a quarrel, in the course of which the window was broken. Barnett is a porter at the market close by, and he was able to answer the police that on Thursday night he was at a lodging-house in New-street, Bishopsgate-street, and was playing whist there until half-past twelve, when he went to bed. Another witness states that she met the deceased near the church in Commercial-street on Thursday night about seven o'clock. As far as the statements furnished to the police go, there is no actual evidence forthcoming that a man entered the room in Miller's-court.[15] No one was seen to go there with the deceased, and there is still no clue to the identity of the mysterious and crafty assassin who has again become the terror of Whitechapel. In Dorset-street, however, the fact of a man having been in the company of a woman would probably attract no notice from those who are accustomed to such an incident. The street is fairly lighted, and, late at night especially, is pretty well frequented. It is one of those spots where a good deal of street gambling may be detected at times. Deceased was observed in the company of a man at ten p.m. on Thursday, of whom no description can be obtained. She was last seen, as far as can be ascertained, in Commercial-street, about half-past eleven. She was then alone, and was probably making her way home. It is supposed that she met the murderer in Commercial-street. The

---

[12]Dr. [later Sir] Robert Anderson [1841–1918], Assistant Commissioner of the Metropolitan Police CID and in charge of the Whitechapel Murder Investigation from October 1888 until the shelving of the files in 1892. Best known to modern researchers for his repeated confident declarations that the identity of Jack the Ripper was a "definitely ascertained fact" (BFS, pp. 19–25).

[13]This statement is contradicted later in the same report.

[14]This report is directly contradicted by Prater's statement to the police on 9 November (Kelly Inquest Papers), a report in the 12 November *Telegraph* and Prater's inquest testimony. See also Commentary 1.

[15]For contradiction of this see Mary Ann Cox's inquest testimony, 12 November, and Hutchinson's statement, 13 November.

pair would have reached Miller's-court about midnight, but they were not seen to enter the house. The street-door was closed, but the woman had a latchkey. A light was seen shining through the window of the room for some time after the couple must have entered it.

Shortly after four o'clock yesterday a covered van was driven to Miller's-court, and in a few minutes the remains were placed in a shell and quietly removed to the mortuary adjoining Shoreditch Church to await the inquest, at the Shoreditch Town Hall, on Monday. The room was then closed, the window being boarded up and the door padlocked. There were at times considerable numbers of spectators in the vicinity of Dorset-street, but when the police cordon was withdrawn the bystanders grew fewer. Dorset-street is made up principally of common lodging-houses, which provide not less than 600 registered beds. In one of these establishments Annie Chapman, the Hanbury-street victim lived. Curiously enough, the warehouse at No. 26, now closed by large doors, was until a few weeks ago the nightly resort of poor homeless creatures, who went there for shelter. One of these women was Catherine Eddowes, the woman who was murdered in Mitre-square.[16]

As yet the murderer is at large, and if the police have any clue they have dissembled their knowledge with absolute success. Up to the present moment, beyond the strange coincidence of dates and the very vague and unfortunately conflicting descriptions given by witnesses at the inquests already held, scarce a vestige of evidence exists on which to base a search.

It has always been the belief of East-end residents that these foul deeds were not the work of a landsman—and this mainly on account of what may be called their periodicity. "They've been done by some short voyage man" was the expression of an opinion which is widespread. There was time, it is thought, for a sailor to have made short voyages to the Continent, and to have committed the murders either immediately on landing or just before sailing. There may be no value underlying the suggestion, and it may be next to impossible to synchronise the arrival and departure of certain ships with the dates we have given, still less to ascertain the composition of their crews, and most difficult of all to bring guilt home to any individual; but in the absence of any better trace it might be worth while to make the investigation. In this connection attention has been drawn to the following fact. It appears that the cattle boats bringing live freight to London are in the habit of coming into the Thames on Thursdays or Fridays, and leave again for the Continent on Sundays or Mondays. It has already been a matter of comment that the recent revolting crimes have been committed at the end of the week, and hence the opinion shared by some of the detectives that the murderer is a drover or butcher employed on one of these boats—of which there are many—and that he periodically appears and disappears with one of the steamers. It is thought, therefore, that the criminal may be a person either employed upon one of these boats or having occasion to travel by them.[17] It is pointed our that at the inquests on the previous victims the coroners

---

[16]Before using this passage to advance a theory that all the Ripper's victims knew each other, it is useful to recall the *Telegraph* report of 3 October, where Eddowes' body was viewed in the mortuary by two women who knew neither her name nor nickname, were ignorant of her family connections, antecedents, or whether or not she lived with a man, yet still claimed her as an associate who sometimes shared accommodation with them in a shed off Dorset Street. It seems doubtful these women knew Eddowes at all, and this reported "warehouse" connection seems virtually worthless.

[17]Although perhaps coincidental, 10 November was the day E. K. Larkins, a clerk in the UK Customs (*cont.*)

had expressed the opinion that the knowledge of physiology possessed by a butcher would have been sufficient to enable him to find and cut out the parts of the body which in several cases were abstracted.

Some of the reported clues must be received with caution. No end of stories are rife in the neighbourhood, told with an air of circumstantiality, which on examination prove to be utterly baseless. Almost the sole testimony which seems to have any bearing on the affair is that given by a young woman named Pannier [Paumier], who sells roasted chestnuts at the corner of Widegate-street, a narrow thoroughfare about two minutes' walk from the scene of the crime. Mrs. Pannier is reported to have stated that shortly after noon yesterday a man, dressed like a gentleman, said to her, "I suppose you have heard about the murder in Dorset-street?" and that when she replied that she was aware of it he said, "I know more about it than you." He then proceeded down Sandy's-row, a narrow thoroughfare which cuts across Widegate-street, looking back as if to see whether he was watched. Mrs. Pannier described this person as a man about 5ft 6in high, with a black moustache, and wearing a black silk hat, dark coat, and speckled trousers. He carried a black shiny bag about eighteen inches long and a foot deep. It will be remembered that this description agrees fairly well with a personage previously described, and that the black bag has more than once figured in the evidence given. It may be worth while to recall that at the inquiry into the Berner-street murder Mrs. Mortimer said, "The only man I had seen pass through

Berner-street previously was a young man who carried a black shiny bag."

Similarly Arthur Bachert deposed: "On Saturday night, at about seven minutes to twelve, I entered the Three Nuns Hotel, Aldgate.[18] While in there an elderly woman, very shabbily dressed, came in and asked me to buy some matches. I refused, and she went out. A man who had been standing by me remarked that these persons were a nuisance, to which I responded 'Yes.' He then asked me to have a glass with him, but I refused, as I had just called for one myself. He then asked a number of questions about the women of the neighbourhood, and their ages &c. He asked if I could tell him where they usually visited. He went outside and spoke to the woman, and gave her something, I believe. He was a dark man, height about 5ft 6in or 5ft 7in. He wore a black felt hat, dark clothes, morning coat, black tie, and carried a black shiny bag." But the point in Mrs. Pannier's statement which engaged the greatest amount of attention, and which, if corroborated, might unquestionably possess real significance was her further averment that she had seen the same man on the previous evening, and that he had accosted three young unfortunates in Dorset-street, who chaffed him, and asked what he had in the bag, and he replied, "Something that the ladies don't like." It remains to be seen at Monday's inquest whether this statement, and especially the latter portion of it, upon which its significance really depends, is confirmed.[19]

The following are additional statements: A young woman, named Harvey, who had slept with the woman Kelly on

---

Statistical Dept., first presented his detailed theory that the murderer could be a crewmember of Portuguese cattle-boats to Inspector Moore at Leman Street Police Station. By 11 January 1889, Larkins had been branded a "troublesome faddist" and his theory deemed "untenable" by Anderson (HO 44/221/A49301C, ff. 235–245).

[18]This location has also been reported as the Three Tuns Hotel (Evans & Skinner, *Letters from Hell*, p. 99).

[19]Paumier was not called to give evidence at the inquest.

several occasions, said she had been on good terms with the deceased, whose education was much superior to that of most persons in her position of life. Harvey, however, took a room in New-court, off the same street, but remained friendly with the unfortunate woman, who visited her in New-court on Thursday night. After drinking together they parted at half-past seven o'clock, Kelly going off in the direction of Leman-street, which she was in the habit of frequenting. She was perfectly sober at the time. Harvey never saw her alive afterwards. Upon hearing that a murder had been committed she said, "I'll go and see if it's any one I know," and to her horror found that it was her friend.

Joseph Barnett, an Irishman, at present residing in a common lodging-house in New-street, Bishopsgate, stated that he had occupied his present lodgings since Tuesday week. Previous to that he had lived in Miller's-court, Dorset-street, for eight or nine months, with the murdered woman, Mary Jane Kelly. They were very happy and comfortable together until an unfortunate came to sleep in their room, to which he strongly objected. Finally, after the woman had been there two or three nights, he quarrelled with his "wife" and left her. The next day, however, he returned and gave Kelly money. He called several other days, and gave her money when he had it. On Thursday night he visited her, between half-past seven and eight, and told her he was sorry he had no money to give her. He saw nothing more of her. He was indoors yesterday morning when he heard that a woman had been murdered in Dorset-street, but he did not know at first who the victim was. He voluntarily went to the police, who, after questioning him, satisfied themselves that his statements were correct. Barnett believed Kelly, who was an Irishwoman, was an "unfortunate" before he made her acquaintance, and she had never had any children. She used occasionally to go to the Elephant and Castle district to visit a friend.[20]

The poor woman who has been thus foully done to death was by no means among the lowest of her fallen class. For a considerable part of the twelve months during which she was Mr. M'Carthy's tenant she was to all appearance fairly well conducted. It was supposed that the man with whom she lived was her husband. He was employed about the fish and fruit markets, and when work was plentiful the pair seem to have paid their way honourably; but earnings were often irregular, and then it is to be feared the woman resorted to the streets. The landlord emphatically disowns any knowledge of his tenement having been used for improper purposes. Moreover, the room which she occupied—which was on the ground floor—and for which she paid 4s a week, was part of the adjoining shop—now used as a ware-room. It was separated from the other dwellings in the narrow court, and strangers could not easily frequent it without being observed. Formerly the woman, who was of a fair complexion, with light hair, and possessing rather attractive features, dressed pretty well. Usually she wore a black silk dress, and often a black jacket, looking shabby genteel in her attire, but generally neat and clean. Latterly, it was confessed, she had been much given to drink, and had rapidly gone from bad to worse. This, it is supposed, led to the quarrel, a few days ago,[21] between her and the man with whom she had been living, and

---

[20]A neighborhood in the present-day South Bank area of London, east of Lambeth. The origin of the name is uncertain.

[21]According to his inquest testimony, Barnett ceased to live with Kelly on 30 October 1888.

to the arrears of 29s in the rent. Dorset-street abounds in women whose features, language, and behaviour are such that the smallest vestige of self-respect, if any remained in Mary Jane Kelly, would be sufficient to distinguish her from the more degraded of her associates. This short thoroughfare and the adjoining Paternoster-row, leading direct to the Spitalfields vegetable market, have now been given up to common lodging-houses at 4d and 6d a night, or "6d for a single bedded cabin," and to women who have lost every trace of womanliness. The street and the row are places which the police state are hardly safe for any respectable person by day and certainly not at night. In such a neighbourhood it was impossible to rise; to sink lower was inevitable. Evidence tends to show that when Kelly first made its acquaintance respectable friends still looked after and wrote to her. It is the uniform testimony of local authorities that these evil surroundings are only remedied by wholesale demolitions, and that while they exist moral agencies are almost hopeless. They are whirlpools, and the poor and the wretched are dragged into them. Though the police report that Kelly's father lives in Wales, there seems no doubt that she is Irish, and McCarthy states that the letters for her used to come from some part of Ireland.

In the naturally intense excitement and indignation prevailing over the whole of East London there is a danger of innocent persons becoming suspected and suffering maltreatment. Last night a young man respectably dressed appeared in Dorset-street, and by his anxious inquiries, especially in regard to the possible employment of bloodhounds, drew upon himself the unpleasant attentions of bystanders, some of whom determined to watch his movements. On leaving the spot the young man—a clerk, it was subsequently ascertained—found himself followed by three men. As it was quite certain that he was the object of their regards, he became somewhat alarmed, while his agitation only served to strengthen their suspicions. In the end he would have suffered from the hands of the mob, but for police protection. Fortunately Bishopsgate-street Police-station was near, and thither he was conveyed for safety.

The Scotland-yard authorities shortly after midday telegraphed the following notification of the crime to the various police-stations: "Found at 10:30 a.m., a woman cut to pieces in a room on the ground floor at 26, Dorset-street, Spitalfields."

During the course of last evening Dr. G. B. Phillips visited the House of Commons, where he had a conference with the Under-Secretary of the Home Office, Mr. Stuart-Wortley.

The Central News states, upon what is described as indisputable authority, that no portion of the murdered woman's body was taken away by the murderer.[22] The post-mortem examination was of the most exhaustive character, and the surgeons did not quit their work until every organ had been accounted for and placed as nearly as possible in its natural position.

Some residents in the court declare that about a quarter to two they heard a faint cry of murder, which would seem to fix with tolerable exactitude the time at which the crime was committed; but against this must be set the statement of a woman residing at 26, Dorset-street, a house the

---

[22]Despite this confident statement, it appears that Kelly's heart was removed by her killer, as noted earlier. However, the partial news blackout imposed by the police during this series of crimes and the pressure of deadlines coupled with unreliable statements from witnesses should be kept in mind when encountering contradictory statements about the presence or absence of Kelly's viscera. See also Curtis, p. 188.

back rooms of which abut upon the court, according to which a cry of murder was heard at three o'clock. It is characteristic of the locality that no one thought anything of the incident, which, indeed, is of too common occurrence to cause interest or alarm. A man engaged as a market porter and living at 3, Miller's-court, stated that, although his rooms face the scene of the murder, he heard nothing of it until he went out in the morning at half-past ten to get some milk; and was stopped by the police. A man's pilot-coat has been found in the murdered woman's room, but whether it belonged to the murderer has not been ascertained.[23] Late last evening a man was arrested near Dorset-street on suspicion of being concerned in the murder. He was taken to Commercial-street Police-station, followed by a howling mob, and is still detained there. Another man, respectably dressed, wearing a slouch hat, and carrying a black bag, was arrested and taken to Leman-street Station. The bag was examined, but its contents were perfectly harmless, and the man was liberated.

# THE DAILY TELEGRAPH
Monday, November 12, 1888

Page 5
THE MURDER AND MUTILA-
TION IN DORSET-STREET.
*[Kelly's History;
A Queen's Pardon]*

Throughout Saturday and yesterday the police, under Inspectors Abberline and Reid, of the Criminal Investigation Department, were busy in making exhaustive inquiries at lodging-houses and in every place where information could be gleaned,

but their efforts were without material result. As a matter of fact that the last murder committed by the maniac has not yielded any fresh clue to his whereabouts, nor provided a title of evidence which would serve to connect him with the crime. Nevertheless, a large amount of investigation has had to be undertaken. Since Friday evening until six o'clock yesterday four men had been detained for some time on suspicion, two at Commercial-street Police-station and one each at Leman-street and Arbour-square, but in each case the suspects were liberated, having fully satisfied the police of their doings upon the night of the crime. Various statements have had to be sifted, but no great reliance is to be placed upon them, although the persons who have made them will be called before the coroner, Dr. Macdonald, who opens the inquest this morning at the Shoreditch Town Hall. One of these depositions relates to the hour at which the crime was probably perpetrated, and if the deponent is not mistaken the deed must have been done in broad daylight.

Mrs. Maxwell, who lives at 14, Dorset-street, but who assists her husband in the care of a common lodging house opposite Miller-court, says: "We stay up all night, and yesterday (Friday) as I was going home, carrying my lantern and other things with me, I saw the woman Kelly standing at the entrance of the court. It was then half-past eight, and as it was unusual for her to be seen about at that hour, I said to her, 'Hallo! what are you doing up so early?' She said, 'Oh, I'm very bad this morning. I have had the horrors. I have been drinking so much lately.' I said to her, 'Why don't you go and have half a pint of beer. It will put you right.' She replied, 'I've just had one, but I'm so bad I

---

[23]Maria Harvey, a laundress and friend of Kelly, later claimed ownership of the coat.

couldn't keep it down.' I didn't know then that she had separated from the man she had been living with, and I thought he had been 'paying' her. I then went out in the direction of Bishopsgate to do some errands, and on my return I saw Kelly standing outside the public-house talking to a man. That was the last I saw of her." Mrs. Maxwell is very positive as to this statement. Inquiry, however, tends to show that the deceased woman did not go to the public-house at the corner, nor was she served at any other in the neighbourhood on the morning of her death. The story also is inconsistent with the medical opinion, Mr. Phillips, the divisional police-surgeon, having thought that life had been extinct for five or six hours when the body was first examined between eleven a.m. and midday.[24] This account of Mrs. Maxwell has naturally attracted a large amount of attention, and the woman has been severely cross-examined, without, however, in any way disturbing the confidence with which she makes her narrative. There is no question whatever of her having known the deceased most intimately, and it is not obvious what motive she could have for making a false representation. Yet there are many difficulties in the way of its acceptance. Mr. John M'Carthy and the police-officer who entered poor Mary Janet [sic] Kelly's room aver that the body was quite cold, and the blood coagulated, and it is understood the professional opinion will be to the effect that several hours must have elapsed before the discovery of the crime was made. Further, it has been objected that the witness, though living opposite Miller's-court, did not make any disclosure till long after the already published facts had been made known. To this, however, she replied, reasonably, that as her husband is the night watchman at

Crossingham's lodging-house, they have to sleep in the daytime, and it was only in the afternoon that they heard what had happened; and even then, it appears, a long interval elapsed before she thought that her evidence could be of any material importance, and it was only after it had been given to a reporter that the police paid any attention to it. Mrs. Maxwell states that she took no particular notice of the young man with whom she observed Kelly conversing. She saw him at a distance; there was nothing in his appearance to arrest attention; and she supposed he was one of the many hands employed about the adjoining Spitalfields market. It is stated that a tailor, named Morris [Maurice] Lewis, has also affirmed that he saw Kelly between eight and nine in the morning.[25] The question has arisen whether Mrs. Maxwell might not have confounded one morning with another, but when questioned on this point she avers that there were circumstances connected with her own work to enable her to fix it as Friday morning without any doubt or misgiving whatever. Against one portion of this statement the landlady of the public-house referred to declares that Kelly was not in their bar at the hour mentioned, and as they were not busy at the time she is quite confident as to her recollection.

Another tale of a neighbour will also be told to the coroner, who will no doubt closely inquire into its veracity. A woman, whose parents live in Miller's-court, in the house opposite the room where the tragedy took place, declares that at about three o'clock on Friday morning she entered Dorset-street on her way home, and she noticed three persons at the corner of the street, near the Britannia Public-house. There was a young man, respectably dressed, and with a dark moustache, talking

---

[24]See Commentary 1 for a discussion of time of death.
[25]See Commentary 2 for a discussion of Maxwell and Lewis' sightings.

to a woman whom she did not know, and also another woman, poorly clad, and without any head covering. The man and woman appeared to be the worse for liquor, and she heard the former say, "Are you coming?" whereupon the woman, who seemed to be obstinate, turned in an opposite direction to which the man apparently wished her to go. Mrs. Kennedy went on her way, and nothing unusual occurred until about half an hour later. She explains that she did not retire to rest immediately she reached her parents' abode, but sat up, and between half-past three and a quarter to four she heard a cry of "murder" in a woman's voice proceed from the direction in which Mary Kelly's room was situated. As the cry was not repeated she took no further notice of the circumstance until the morning, when she found the police in possession of the place. Upon being questioned by them as to what she had heard throughout the night, she made a statement to the above effect, which she has since supplemented by the following: "On Wednesday evening, about eight o'clock, I and my sister were in the neighbourhood of Bethnal-green-road, when we were accosted by a very suspicious-looking man about forty years of age. He was about 5ft 7in high, wore a short jacket, over which he had a long top-coat. His moustache was black, and he wore a billycock hat.[26] He invited us to accompany him into a lonely spot, as he was known about there, and there was a policeman looking at him. No policeman was, however, in sight. The man made several

strange remarks and appeared to be agitated. He was very white in the face, and prevented them looking him straight in the face, and he carried a black bag. He avoided walking with them, and led the way into a very dark thoroughfare at the back of the workhouse, inviting them to follow, which they did. Pushing open a small door in a pair of large gates, requested one of them to follow him, remarking, "I only want one of you," whereupon his companions became suspicious. He refused to leave his bag in possession of either of the women, and acted in a very strange manner. Both of them became alarmed at his behaviour, and escaped, at the same time raising a cry of "Jack the Ripper." A gentleman who was passing is stated to have intercepted the man, while the women ran off. The witness asserts that the individual whom she saw on Friday morning with the woman at the corner of Dorset-street resembled very closely the person who caused such alarm on the night in question, and that she would be able to recognise him.[27]

Apart from the foregoing, there seems to be no reason to doubt that the woman was heard in her room as late as one a.m., singing, "Sweet Violets"[28]—at times the poor creature helped to earn her living by selling flowers. Whether a cry of "Murder" was raised is open to question. A woman named Prater, an occupant of the same house, says there was such a call at about three a.m.,[29] but the word "Murder" is so commonly used in Spitalfields that it does not attract attention. The two people

[26]A low-crowned felt hat; what Americans know as a "derby."

[27]The strong similarities between this account and that given by Sarah Lewis at the inquest (ref. 13 November) suggest that Mrs. Kennedy and Lewis were one and the same. Slight differences between the accounts, however, leave the possibility that these were two separate individuals who happened to witness the same scenes.

[28]Both here and in the *Pall Mall Gazette* of 10 November, Kelly is said to have sung "Sweet Violets" the night of her death. Almost all other references contemporary and modern, however, assign the song "Only a Violet I Plucked from Mother's Grave" to Kelly on that cold evening.

[29]See Commentary 1.

who can speak definitely as to the deceased's antecedents and her doings on the evening of Thursday are Joseph Barnett and Lizzie Allbrook, whose statements are appended. Barnett was the man who passed as Kelly's husband until last week, and he supplies the following full particulars:

I first met the deceased last Easter twelve-month, and lived with her from that time until last Tuesday week. I was in decent work in Billingsgate Market when I first encountered her, and we lived quite comfortably together. She was then twenty-two years of age, fresh-looking and well-behaved, though she had been walking the streets for some three years previously. She told me that her maiden name was Marie Jeanette Kelly, and that she was born in Limerick. Her parents, who were fairly well off, removed when she was a child to Wales, and they lived in Carmarthenshire. When she was but little over sixteen years of age she married a collier, but I do not remember his name. He was killed in an explosion in the mine, and then Marie went to Cardiff with her cousin, living as best she could. Thence she went to France, but remained only a short time. Afterwards she lived in a fashionable house of ill-fame in the West-end of London, but drifted from the West to the East-end, where she took lodgings in Pennington-street. Her father came from Wales and tried to find her there; but, hearing from her companions that he was looking for her, Marie kept out of the way. A brother in the 2nd Battalion Scots Guards came to see her once, but beyond that she saw none

of her relations, nor did she correspond with them. When she was in Pennington-street a man named Morganstone lived with her, and subsequently a man named Joseph Fleming passed as her husband. She lived with me first of all in George-street, then in Paternoster-row, Dorset-street, but we were ejected from our lodgings there because we got drunk and did not pay our rent. We took lodgings afterwards in Brick-lane, and finally, about four months ago, in Miller's-court, where the murder occurred.[30] We lived comfortably until Marie allowed a woman named Julia to sleep in the same room.[31] I objected, and, as Mrs. Harvey afterwards came and stayed there, I left her, and took lodgings elsewhere.[32] I told her I would come back if she would go somewhere else. I used to call there nearly every day, and if I had any money I gave her some. I last saw her alive at 7:30 on Thursday night, when I stopped about a quarter of an hour, and told her I had no money. Next day I heard there had been a murder in Miller's-court, and on my way there I met my sister's brother-in-law, and he told me Marie had been murdered.[33] I went to the court, and there saw the police-inspector, and told him who I was, and where I had been the previous night. I was kept about for hours,[34] and the constables examined my clothes for blood-stains, and finally, finding the account I gave of myself to be correct, let me go free. Marie never went on the streets when she lived with me. She would never have gone wrong again, and I should never have left her, if it had not been for the bad women stopping with her. She only let them in the room because she was good-hearted, and

---

[30]Barnett's statements in the press and at the inquest are the only source we have for Kelly's past history. Unfortunately, it has proven almost impossible for researchers to verify in all its particulars, and there is suspicion that she deliberately lied. The search for the "real" Mary Kelly could fill an entire chapter; at this writing, researcher Mark King tentatively identifies her with a Mary Jane Kelly born 24 January, 1864, at Fermoy, Co. Cork, Ireland (ref. *Ripperologist* 31, October 2000, pp. 11–13).

[31]"Julia" is presumed by Ripperologists to be Julia Venturney, but in neither her police statement nor inquest testimony did Venturney ever speak of staying with Kelly. Who Barnett's "Julia" really was, therefore, is not entirely certain. See also Sugden, p. 513.

[32]For a comparison of Barnett's various statements of his reason for leaving, see 13 November.

[33]This statement appears to have a bearing on Barnett's identification of Kelly by suggesting that even before reaching Miller's Court he was expecting to view her remains.

[34]This statement appears abridged in many newspapers. In those where this portion is included, the words "for hours" are sometimes replaced with "four hours."

did not like to refuse them shelter on a cold, bitter night.

Lizzie Allbrook, a young woman of twenty, who resides in Miller's-court, and works at a lodging-house in Dorset-street, says: "I knew Mary Jane Kelly very well, as we were near neighbours. The last time I saw her was on Thursday night, about eight o'clock, when I left her in her room with Joe Barnett, the man who had been living with her. About the last thing she said to me was, 'Whatever you do, don't you do wrong and turn out as I have.' She had often spoken to me in this way, and warned me against going on the streets, as she had done. She told me, too, she was heartily sick of the life she was leading, and wished she had money enough to go back to Ireland, where her people lived. I don't believe she would have gone out as she did if she had not been obliged to do so in order to keep herself from starvation. She had talked to me about her friends several times, and on one occasion told me she had a female relation in London who was on the stage."

## SCENE OF THE MURDER

A somewhat important investigation was made on Saturday in the room in Miller's-court in which the crime was perpetrated. There was reason to believe that the murderer had burnt something before leaving the place after the deed, and accordingly the ashes and other matter in the grate were carefully preserved. On Saturday afternoon Dr. Phillips and Dr. Macdonald, M.P., the coroner for the district, visited Miller's-court, and after the refuse had been passed through a sieve it was subjected to the closest scrutiny by the medical gentlemen. Nothing, however, was found which is likely to afford any as-

sistance or clue to the police. The doctors were engaged some hours at the Mortuary, Shoreditch-churchyard, in making a post-mortem examination. Every portion of the body was fully accounted for, and at the conclusion of the investigation the various portions were sewn together and placed in a coffin.[35] The furniture of the room consisted of the bed upon which the body was stretched, which was placed next to a disused washstand in the corner behind the door, and opposite the two windows, in the smaller one of which there were two panes of glass broken. A man's coat was put across these to keep out the draught. Close to the larger window stood a table, and another table of smaller size was placed between it and the bed, and it was upon this that the flesh stripped from the body was heaped. This article of furniture, when the door was opened, was partly hidden by it. Next to the fireplace was a cupboard. Means of observation were abundant in this small courtyard. A gas lamp is fixed on the opposite side of the passage, and from several windows a view could have been obtained of the room. From M'Carthy's back shop a small window looks into the narrow court, through which any one passing into the doorway could have been seen. In addition to this there is another small window in the next house, while the tenants of at least two of the three tenements on the left-hand side could have overlooked from their apartments the room rented by Kelly.

The Scotland-yard authorities have issued the following proclamation:

> Murder.—Pardon.—Whereas, on November 8th or 9th, in Miller-court, Dorset-street, Spitalfields, Mary Janet Kelly was murdered by some person or persons unknown, the Secretary of State will

---

[35]The confusion as to whether Kelly's corpse was complete in all its disparate parts may, as earlier noted, have been a result of contradictory statements from police and medical men; alternatively, it may have been part of a police plan to hold back evidence in case the real killer was ever questioned.

## SCENE OF THE MURDER.

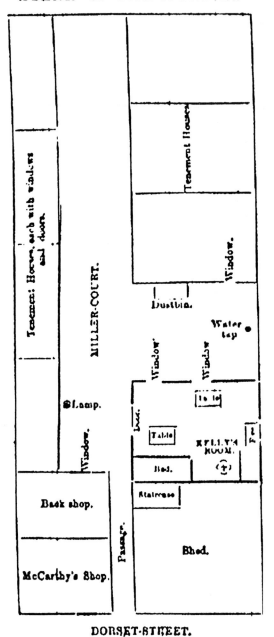

DORSET-STREET.

*Left:* "Scene of the Murder" of Mary Kelly, as printed in the *Telegraph* of 12 November (courtesy of Evans/Skinner Crime Archive).

advise the grant of her Majesty's gracious pardon to any accomplice not being a person who contrived or actually committed the murder, who shall give such information and evidence as shall lead to the discovery and conviction of the person or persons who committed the murder.—(Signed) CHARLES WARREN, the Commissioner of Police of the Metropolis. Metropolitan Police Office, 4, Whitehall-place, Nov. 10, 1888.[36]

Several arrests have been made, but all the persons taken into custody were released after short periods of detention, having been able to give the police satisfactory explanations of their movements.

A most minute search has been conducted by the police and medical gentlemen in the room where the crime was perpetrated, but practically nothing in the nature of a clue has been obtained. The man's coat discovered there belonged to Mrs. Harvey, who had lived with the woman Kelly; whilst the ashes, which have been carefully sifted, reveal no traces of burnt human flesh.[37]

Yesterday the constabulary made a complete census of Dorset-street, having especial reference to the persons within it on Thursday night. Although it is but a short thoroughfare there are, it is stated, no fewer than 1,200 men who sleep every night in the common lodging-houses with which it abounds.

# THE DAILY TELEGRAPH
Tuesday, November 13, 1888

---

[36]The offer of a pardon had been discounted by the Home Office. This apparent policy change was explained by the Home Secretary to Parliament on 23 November 1888. The *Telegraph* of 24 November reported Matthews claiming, "In the case of the woman Kelly there were certain circumstances which were wanting in the earlier cases, which made it more probable that other persons—at any rate after the crime—had assisted the murderer." Exactly what these "certain circumstances" were remains unknown.

[37]This seems to confirm that some portion of the body was being looked for amid the ashes.

## Page 5
## DORSET-STREET MURDER.
## INQUEST AND VERDICT.
## DESCRIPTION
## OF THE ASSASSIN.

Comparatively little that was new was elicited by the coroner's inquiry into the death of Marie Jeanette Kelly. Going beyond the statements that have already appeared in these columns, the principal evidence was that of Mary Ann Cox, residing in Miller's-court, who described a man she had seen entering the court with the deceased. It is stated that the police attach weight to her description, and will circulate it in the usual manner. The account of the man and his attire agrees with some of those statements previously given, and disagrees with others. The Berner-street suspect was described as a very dark man. The Hanbury-street victim was seen in company with a dark foreign-looking man, and a similar description was given of a suspected individual at the time of the Buck's-row murder. It is noteworthy, however, that there were two descriptions given of the suspected Mitre-square and Hanbury-street murderers, which agree in some respects with that furnished by the witness Cox of the man seen in Kelly's company on Thursday night. About ten minutes before the body of Catherine Eddowes was found in Mitre-square, a man about thirty years of age, of fair complexion, and with a fair moustache, was said to have been seen talking to her in the covered passage leading to the square. On the morning of the Hanbury-street murder, a suspicious looking man entered a public-house in the neighbourhood. He was of shabby-genteel appearance and had a sandy moustache. The first of these descriptions was given by two persons who were in the Orange Market and closely observed the man. The City police have been making inquiries for this man for weeks past, but

without success, and they do not believe that he is the individual described by Cox. On the other hand the Metropolitan authorities are inclined to attach significance to it. Cox stated that the man who accompanied Kelly to her home carried a can or pot of beer. No trace of this beer has been found in the room, nor of the pewter in the ashes of the grate. Inquiry has equally failed to obtain evidence of Kelly or any person similar to the man described having bought beer at any of the neighbouring public-houses. Considering the amount of drinking on and off the premises of these establishments near midnight the mere absence of evidence on this point would not be surprising in any case.

By design, the medical testimony adduced at the inquest was limited to that which was absolutely required to enable the jury to find respecting the cause of death. We are enabled to state, on good authority, that notwithstanding all that has been said to the contrary, a portion of the bodily organs was missing. The police, and with them the divisional surgeon, have arrived at the conclusion that it is in the interest of justice not to disclose the details of the professional inquiry. On all hands the evidence of the witness who declares that she saw Kelly between eight and nine o'clock on Friday morning, is put down to error, the common impression being that the witness is thinking of what happened on probably the previous day. Those who have charge of the case are most of all surprised that the huge blaze in the unfortunate's woman's room— which the murderer kept up by burning his victim's clothes, in order, as it is supposed, to give him light to execute his appalling work—did not attract the attention of residents of the adjoining tenements.

Yesterday Mrs. McCarthy, the wife of the landlord of the house where the murder was enacted, received a post-card bearing the Folkestone post-mark, and signed "Jack Sheridan, the Ripper." In bad spelling and writing were the words, "Don't be alarmed. I am going to do another; but this time it will be a mother and daughter." The missive, which, unlike many of the previous communications to a similar effect, was written in black ink, was handed over to the detectives. The handwriting was carefully compared with similar letters, and found to be of a different character.[38]

It was stated late last night that the persons taken in custody on the previous day had been liberated, and it is doubtful if the constabulary have obtained new clues to assist their search. A circumstantial statement was made last night by a labouring man[39] who knew the deceased, which was very minute in its particulars regarding a man seen in company with the woman Kelly early on the morning of the 9th inst. According to this description the individual in question was of respectable appearance, about 5ft 6in in height, and 34 or 35 years of age, with dark complexion and dark moustache curled up at the ends. He wore a long dark coat trimmed with astrachan [sic],[40] a white collar with black necktie, in which was affixed a horse-shoe pin, and he had on a pair of dark gaiters with light buttons over button boots, and

displayed from his waistcoat a massive gold chain. It has not been ascertained why the witness did not make this statement—so much fuller and so different from the others that have been given—immediately after the murder was discovered.

Yesterday, at the Shoreditch Town Hall, Dr. Macdonald, M.P., the coroner for the North-Eastern District of Middlesex,[41] opened his inquiry relative to the death of Marie Jeanette Kelly, the woman whose body was discovered on Friday morning, terribly mutilated, in a room on the ground floor of 26, Dorset-street, entrance to which was by a side door in Miller's-court.

Superintendent T. Arnold, H Division[42]; Inspector Abberline, of the Criminal Investigation Department; and Inspector Nairn[43] represented the police. The deputy-coroner, Mr. Hodgkinson, was present during the proceedings.

The jury having answered to their names, one of them said: I do not see why we should have the inquest thrown upon our shoulders, when the murder did not happen in our district, but in Whitechapel.

THE CORONER'S OFFICER (MR. HAMMOND): It did not happen in Whitechapel.

THE CORONER (TO THE JUROR,

[38]The *Evening News* of 12 November also repeated this story, only to pronounce it false a few paragraphs later.

[39]George Hutchinson. His full statement, taken by Sergeant Badham on 12 November, was believed to be true by Inspector Abberline (MEPO 3/140 ff. 227–232). He is the preferred Ripper suspect of Eddleston, Hinton and Wright.

[40]Astrakhan: in 1888, a curly wool taken from sheep in the Russian province of Astrakhan or from Persia or Syria; also fur with a pile in imitation of true astrakhan.

[41]Roderick MacDonald (1841–1894). The loser to Wynne Baxter in a dirty electoral campaign for the coronership of the East London and Tower of London district in 1887, he was given his post when the district was, ironically, partitioned the next year (BFS, pp. 265–266). His dispatch in conducting the Kelly inquest has been seen by Knight and others as evidence of an official cover-up. This, however, is a misunderstanding of 19th century inquests, which were generally held in the space of one or two days. It was Baxter with his expansive, multi-day proceedings who was the anomaly, not MacDonald.

[42]Superintendent Thomas Arnold (b. 1835), head of H Division at the time of the Whitechapel Murders (Evans and Skinner, p. 741).

[43]Inspector James William Nearn, warrant no. 61557, with the Metropolitan Police from 1877 to 1902 (BFS, p. 314).

SEVERELY): Do you think that we do not know what we are doing here, and that we do not know our own district? The jury are summoned in the ordinary way, and they have no business to object. If they persist in their objection I shall know how to deal with them. Does any juror persist in objecting?

THE JUROR: We are summoned for the Shoreditch district. This affair happened in Spitalfields.

THE CORONER: It happened within my district.

ANOTHER JURYMAN: This is not my district. I come from Whitechapel, and Mr. Baxter is my coroner.

THE CORONER: I am not going to discuss the subject with jurymen at all. If any juryman says he distinctly objects, let him say so. (After a pause): I may tell the jurymen that jurisdiction lies where the body lies, not where it was found, if there was doubt as to the district where the body was found.[44]

The jury having made no further objection, they were duly sworn, and were conducted by Inspector Abberline to view the body, which, decently coffined, was at the mortuary adjoining Shoreditch Church, and subsequently the jury inspected the room, in Miller's-court, Dorset-street, where the murder was committed. This apartment, a plan of which was given in yesterday's *Daily Telegraph*, is poorly furnished, and uncarpeted. The position of the two tables was not altered. One of them was placed near the bed, behind the door, and the other next to the largest of the two windows which look upon the yard in which the dustbin and water-tap are situated.

The Coroner (addressing the reporters) said a great fuss had been made in some papers about the jurisdiction of the coroner, and who should hold the inquest. He had not had any communication with Dr. Baxter upon the subject. The body was in his jurisdiction; it had been taken to his mortuary; and there was an end of it. There was no foundation for the reports that had appeared. In a previous case of murder which occurred in his district the body was carried to the nearest mortuary, which was in another district. The inquest was held by Mr. Baxter, and he made no objection. The jurisdiction was where the body lay.

**Joseph Barnett** deposed: I was a fish-porter, and I work as a labourer and fruit-porter. Until Saturday last I lived at 24, New-street, Bishopsgate, and have since stayed at my sister's, 21, Portpool-lane, Gray's Inn-road. I have lived with the deceased one year and eight months. Her name was Marie Jeanette Kelly, with the French spelling as described to me.[45] Kelly was her maiden name. I have seen the body, and I identify it by the ear and eyes,[46] which are all that I can recognise; but I am positive it is the same woman I knew. I lived with her in No. 13 room, at Miller's-court, for eight months. I separated from her on Oct. 30.

---

[44]See BFS, pp. 186–187, for further discussion of this dispute.

[45]Of all Kelly's associates, only Barnett seems to have called her "Marie Jeanette"; other than her reported sojourn in France, there seems no reason for this affectation. As Barnett noted he had to have the French spelling "described to me," it may be that he is the source for newspaper reports which name Kelly as Mary *Janet*.

[46]It has been proposed that this identification was misheard and that Barnett actually said "hair and eyes." Given that "ear and eyes" are the means of identification recorded in the *Telegraph*, the *Star* of 12 November and the official inquest notes, the possibility of at least three independent recorders of proceedings suffering identical mishearing seems highly unlikely. Robinson describes Barnett as noting "the peculiar shape of the ears"; it is a possibility this aspect of the identification was mentioned at the inquest but not so recorded.

Why did you leave her?—Because she had a woman of bad character there, whom she took in out of compassion, and I objected to it. That was the only reason.[47] I left her on the Tuesday between five and six p.m. I last saw her alive between half-past seven and a quarter to eight on Thursday night last, when I called upon her. I stayed there for a quarter of an hour.

Were you on good terms?—Yes, on friendly terms; but when we parted I told her I had no work, and had nothing to give her, for which I was very sorry.

Did you drink together?—No, sir. She was quite sober.

Was she, generally speaking, of sober habits?—When she was with me I found her of sober habits, but she has been drunk several times in my presence.

Was there any one else there on the Thursday evening?—Yes, a woman who lives in the court. She left first, and I followed shortly afterwards.

Have you had conversation with deceased about her parents?—Yes, frequently. She said she was born in Limerick, and went when very young to Wales. She did not say how long she lived there, but that she came to London about four years ago. Her father's name was John Kelly, a "gaffer" or foreman in an iron works in Carnarvonshire, or Carmarthen. She said she had one sister, who was respectable, who travelled from market place to market place. This sister was very fond of her. There were six brothers living in London, and one was in the army. One of them was named Henry. I never saw the brothers to my knowledge. She said she was married when very young in Wales to a collier. I think the name was Davis or Davies. She said she had lived with him until he was killed in an explosion, but I cannot say how many years since that was. Her age was, I believe, 16 when she married. After her husband's death deceased went to Cardiff to a cousin.

Did she live there long?—Yes, she was in an infirmary there for eight or nine months. She was following a bad life with her cousin, who, as I reckon, and as I often told her, was the cause of her downfall.

After she left Cardiff did she come direct to London?—Yes. She was in a gay house in the West-end, but in what part she did not say. A gentleman came there to her and asked her if she would like to go to France.

Did she go to France?—Yes; but she did not remain long. She said she did not like the part, but whether it was the part or purpose I cannot say. She was not there more than a fortnight, and she returned to England, and went to Ratcliffe-highway. She must have lived there for some time. Afterwards she lived with a man opposite the Commercial Gas Works, Stepney. The man's name was Morganstone.[48]

Have you seen that man?—Never. I don't know how long she lived with him.

Was Morganstone the last man she lived with?—I cannot answer that question, but she described a man named Joseph Fleming, who came to Pennington-street, a bad house, where she stayed. I don't

---

[47]Among the many slight discrepancies between official inquest notes, newspaper inquest coverage and statements give to the police on 9 November, this example is worth noting as it is sometimes seen to cast doubt on Barnett's honesty. In his statement to Abberline on 9 November, Barnett claimed his reason for leaving Kelly was "in consequence of not earning sufficient money to give her and her resorting to prostitution." The official inquest notes record, "I left her because she had a person who was a prostitute whom she took in and I objected to her doing so, that was the only reason, not because I was out of work" (Official Kelly Inquest Papers—Ref. MJ/SPC, NE1888, Box 3, Case Paper 19 [London Metropolitan Archives]).

[48]"Morganstone" has been tentatively identified as either Dutch gas stoker Adrienus Morgestern or his brother Maria (Connell & Evans, p. 59).

know when this was. She was very fond of him. He was a mason's plasterer, and lodged in the Bethnal-green-road.[49]

Was that all you knew of her history when you lived with her?—Yes. After she lived with Morganstone or Fleming—I don't know which one was the last—she lived with me.

Where did you pick up with her first?—In Commercial-street. We then had a drink together, and I made arrangements to see her on the following day—a Saturday. On that day we both of us agreed that we should remain together. I took lodgings in George-street, Commercial-street, where I was known. I lived with her, until I left her, on very friendly terms.

Have you heard her speak of being afraid of any one?—Yes; several times. I bought newspapers, and I read to her everything about the murders, which she asked me about.

Did she express fear of any particular individual?—No, sir. Our own quarrels were very soon over.

THE CORONER: You have given your evidence very well indeed. (To the Jury): The doctor has sent a note asking whether we shall want his attendance here to-day. I take it that it would be convenient that he should tell us roughly what the cause of death was, so as to enable the body to be buried. It will not be necessary to go into the details of the doctor's evidence; but he suggested that he might come to state roughly the cause of death.

The jury acquiesced in the proposed course.

**Thomas Bowyer** stated: I live at 37, Dorset-street, and am employed by Mr. McCarthy. I serve in his chandler's shop, 27, Dorset-street. At a quarter to eleven

a.m., on Friday morning, I was ordered by McCarthy to go to Mary Jane's room, No. 13. I did not know the deceased by the name of Kelly. I went for rent, which was in arrears. Knocking at the door, I got no answer, and I knocked again and again. Receiving no reply, I passed round the corner by the gutter spout, where there is a broken window—it is the smallest window.

Charles Ledger, an inspector of police, G Division, produced a plan of the premises.

Bowyer pointed out the window, which was the one nearest the entrance. He continued: There was a curtain. I put my hand through the broken pane and lifted the curtain. I saw two pieces of flesh lying on the table.

Where was this table?—In front of the bed, close to it. The second time I looked I saw a body on this bed, and blood on the floor. I at once went very quietly to Mr. McCarthy. We then stood in the shop, and I told him what I had seen. We both went to the police-station, but first of all we went to the window, and McCarthy looked in to satisfy himself. We told the inspector at the police-station of what we had seen. Nobody else knew of the matter. The inspector returned with us.

Did you see the deceased constantly?—I have often seen her. I knew the last witness, Barnett. I have seen the deceased drunk once.

BY THE JURY: When did you see her last alive?—On Wednesday afternoon, in the court, when I spoke to her. McCarthy's shop is at the corner of Miller's-court.

**John McCarthy**, grocer and lodging-house keeper, testified: I live at 27, Dorset-street. On Friday morning, about a quarter to eleven, I sent my man Bowyer to

---

[49]Researcher Mark King has proposed a "Joseph Fleming otherwise James Evans" who died in Claybury Mental Hospital in August 1920 as Kelly's erstwhile lover (BFS, p. 137).

Room 13 to call for rent. He came back in five minutes, saying, "Guv'nor, I knocked at the door, and could not make any one answer; I looked through the window and saw a lot of blood." I accompanied him, and looked through the window myself, saw the blood and the woman. For a moment I could not say anything, and I then said: "You had better fetch the police." I knew the deceased as Mary Jane Kelly, and had no doubt at all about her identity. I followed Bowyer to Commercial-street Police-station, where I saw Inspector Beck. I inquired at first for Inspector Reid. Inspector Beck returned with me at once.

How long had the deceased lived in the room?—Ten months. She lived with Barnett. I did not know whether they were married or not; they lived comfortably together, but they had a row when the window was broken. The bedstead, bed-clothes, table, and every article of furniture belonged to me.

What rent was paid for this room?— It was supposed to be 4s 6d a week. Deceased was in arrears 29s. I was to be paid the rent weekly. Arrears are got as best you can. I frequently saw the deceased the worse for drink. When sober she was an exceptionally quiet woman, but when in drink she had more to say. She was able to walk about, and was not helpless.

**Mary Ann Cox** stated: I live at No. 5 Room, Miller's-court. It is the last house on the left-hand side of the court. I am a widow, and get my living on the streets. I have known the deceased for eight or nine months as the occupant of No. 13 Room. She was called Mary Jane. I last saw her alive on Thursday night, at a quarter to twelve, very much intoxicated.

Where was this?—In Dorset-street. She went up the court, a few steps in front of me.

Was anybody with her?—A short, stout man, shabbily dressed. He had on a longish coat, very shabby, and carried a pot of ale in his hand.

What was the colour of the coat?—A dark coat.

What hat had he?—A round hard billycock.

Long or short hair?—I did not notice. He had a blotchy face, and full carrotty moustache.

The chin was shaven?—Yes. A lamp faced the door.

Did you see them go into her room?— Yes; I said "Good night, Mary," and she turned round and banged the door.

Had he anything in his hands but the can?—No.

Did she say anything?—She said "Good night, I am going to have a song." As I went in she sang "A violet I plucked from my mother's grave when a boy." I remained a quarter of an hour in my room and went out. Deceased was still singing at one o'clock when I returned. I remained in the room for a minute to warm my hands as it was raining, and went out again. She was singing still, and I returned to my room at three o'clock. The light was then out and there was no noise.

Did you go to sleep?—No; I was upset. I did not undress at all. I did not sleep at all. I must have heard what went on in the court. I heard no noise or cry of "Murder," but men went out to work in the market.

How many men live in the court who work in Spitalfields Market?—One. At a quarter-past six I heard a man go down the court. That was too late for the market.

From what house did he go?—I don't know.

Did you hear the door bang after him?—No.

Then he must have walked up the court and back again?—Yes.

It might have been a policeman?—It might have been.

What would you take the stout man's age to be?—Six-and-thirty.

Did you notice the colour of his trousers?—All his clothes were dark.

Did his boots sound as if the heels were heavy?—There was no sound as he went up the court.

Then you think that his boots were down at heels?—He made no noise.

What clothes had Mary Jane on?—She had no hat; a red pelerine[50] and a shabby skirt.

You say she was drunk?—I did not notice she was drunk until she said good night. The man closed the door.

BY THE JURY: There was a light in the window, but I saw nothing, as the blinds were down. I should know the man again, if I saw him.

BY THE CORONER: I feel certain if there had been the cry of "Murder" in the place I should have heard it; there was not the least noise. I have often seen the woman the worse for drink.

**Elizabeth Prater**, a married woman, said: My husband, William Prater, was a boot machinist, and he has deserted me. I live at 20 Room, in Miller's-court, above the shed. Deceased occupied a room below. I left the room on the Thursday at five p.m., and returned to it at about one a.m. on Friday morning. I stood at the corner until about twenty minutes past one. No one spoke to me. McCarthy's shop was open, and I called in, and then went to my room. I should have seen a glimmer of light in going up the stairs if there had been a light in deceased's room, but I noticed none. The partition was so thin I could have heard Kelly walk about in the room. I went to bed at half-past one and barricaded the door with two tables. I fell asleep directly and slept soundly. A kitten

disturbed me about half-past three o'clock or a quarter to four. As I was turning round I heard a suppressed cry of "Oh—murder!" in a faint voice. It seemed to proceed from the court.

Do you often hear cries of "Murder?"—It is nothing unusual in the street. I did not take particular notice.

Did you hear it a second time?—No.

Did you hear beds or tables being pulled about?—None whatever. I went asleep, and was awake again at five a.m. I passed down the stairs, and saw some men harnessing horses. At a quarter to six I was in the Ten Bells.

Could the witness, Mary Ann Cox, have come down the entry between one and half-past one o'clock without your knowledge?—Yes, she could have done so.

Did you see any strangers at the Ten Bells?—No. I went back to bed and slept until eleven.

You heard no singing downstairs?—None whatever. I should have heard the singing distinctly. It was quite quiet at half-past one o'clock.

**Caroline Maxwell**,[51] 14, Dorset-street, said: My husband is a lodging-house deputy. I knew the deceased for about four months. I believe she was an unfortunate. On two occasions I spoke to her.

THE CORONER: You must be very careful about your evidence, because it is different to other people's. You say you saw her standing at the corner of the entry to the court?—Yes, on Friday morning, from eight to half-past eight. I fix the time by my husband's finishing work. When I came out of the lodging-house she was opposite.

Did you speak to her?—Yes; it was an unusual thing to see her up. She was a young woman who never associated with

---

[50]A long cloak whose ends taper in front to points; synonym for a shawl or shoulder-cape.
[51]See Commentary 2.

any one. I spoke across the street, "What, Mary, brings you up so early?" She said, "Oh, Carrie, I do feel so bad."

And yet you say you had only spoken to her twice previously; you knew her name and she knew yours?—Oh, yes; by being about in the lodging-house.

What did she say?—She said, "I've had a glass of beer, and I've brought it up again"; and it was in the road. I imagined she had been in the Britannia beer-shop at the corner of the street. I left her, saying that I could pity her feelings. I went to Bishopsgate-street to get my husband's breakfast. Returning I saw her outside the Britannia public-house, talking to a man.

This would be about what time?—Between eight and nine o'clock. I was absent about half-an-hour. It was about a quarter to nine.

What description can you give of this man?—I could not give you any, as they were at some distance.

INSPECTOR ABBERLINE: The distance is about sixteen yards.

WITNESS: I am sure it was the deceased. I am willing to swear it.

THE CORONER: You are sworn now. Was he a tall man?—No; he was a little taller than me and stout.

INSPECTOR ABBERLINE: On consideration I should say the distance was twenty-five yards.

THE CORONER: What clothes had the man?—Witness: Dark clothes; he seemed to have a plaid coat on. I could not say what sort of hat he had.

What sort of dress had the deceased?—A dark skirt, a velvet body, a maroon shawl, and no hat.

Have you ever seen her the worse for drink?—I have seen her in drink, but she was not a notorious character.

BY THE JURY: I should have noticed if the man had had a tall silk hat, but we are accustomed to see men of all sorts with women. I should not like to pledge myself to the kind of hat.

**Sarah Lewis**[52] deposed: I live at 24, Great Pearl-street, and am a laundress. I know Mrs. Keyler, in Miller's-court, and went to her house at 2, Miller's-court, at 2:30a.m. on Friday. It is the first house. I noticed the time by Spitalfields' Church clock. When I went into the court, opposite the lodging-house I saw a man with a wideawake.[53] There was no one talking to him. He was a stout-looking man, and not very tall. The hat was black. I did not take any notice of his clothes. The man was looking up the court; he seemed to be waiting or looking for some one. Further on there was a man and woman—the later being in drink. There was nobody in the court. I dozed in a chair at Mrs. Keyler's, and woke at about half-past three. I heard the clock strike.

What woke you up?—I could not sleep. I sat awake until nearly four, when I heard a female's voice shouting "Murder" loudly. It seemed like the voice of a young woman. It sounded at our door. There was only one scream.

Were you afraid? Did you wake anybody up?—No, I took no notice, as I only heard the one scream.

You stayed at Keyler's house until what time?—Half-past five p.m. on Friday. The police would not let us out of the court.

Have you seen any suspicious persons in the district?—On Wednesday night I

---

[52]Compare with Mrs. Kennedy's statement, 12 November.
[53]A "wideawake" was a soft felt hat with a low crown and wide brim, said to be punningly so named because its material would not "take a nap." It is generally considered that the man Lewis saw was George Hutchinson (ref. MEPO 3/140, ff. 227–232).

was going along the Bethnal-green-road, with a woman, about eight o'clock, when a gentleman passed us. He followed us and spoke to us, and wanted us to follow him into an entry. He had a shiny leather bag with him.

Did he want both of you?—No; only one. I refused. He went away and came back again, saying he would treat us. He put down his bag and picked it up again, saying, "What are you frightened about? Do you think I've got anything in the bag?" We then ran away, as we were frightened.

Was he a tall man?—He was short, pale-faced, with a black moustache, rather small. His age was about forty.

Was it a large bag?—No, about 6in to 9in long. His hat was a high round hat. He had a brownish overcoat, with a black short coat underneath. His trousers were a dark pepper-and-salt.

After he left you what did you do?—We ran away.

Have you seen him since?—On Friday morning, about half-past two a.m., when I was going to Miller's-court, I met the same man with a woman in Commercial-street, near Mr. Ringer's public-house (the Britannia). He had no overcoat on.

Had he the black bag?—Yes.

Were the man and woman quarrelling?—No; they were talking. As I passed he looked at me. I don't know whether he recognised me. There was no policeman about.

**Mr. George Bagster Phillips**, divisional surgeon of police, said: I was called by the police on Friday morning at eleven o'clock, and on proceeding to Miller's-

court, which I entered at 11:15, I found a room, the door of which led out of the passage at the side of 26, Dorset-street, photographs of which I produce.[54] It had two windows in the court. Two panes in the lesser window were broken, and as the door was locked I looked through the lower of the broken panes and satisfied myself that the mutilated corpse lying on the bed was not in need of any immediate attention from me, and I also came to the conclusion that there was nobody else upon the bed, or within view, to whom I could render any professional assistance. Having ascertained that probably it was advisable that no entrance should be made into the room at that time, I remained until about 1:30p.m., when the door was broken open by McCarthy, under the direction of Superintendent Arnold.[55] On the door being opened it knocked against a table which was close to the left-hand side of the bedstead, and the bedstead was close against the wooden partition. The mutilated remains of a woman were lying two-thirds over, towards the edge of the bedstead, nearest the door. Deceased had only an under-linen garment upon her, and by subsequent examination I am sure the body had been removed, after the injury which caused death, from that side of the bedstead which was nearest to the wooden partition previously mentioned. The large quantity of blood under the bedstead, the saturated condition of the palliasse, pillow, and sheet at the top corner of the bedstead nearest to the partition leads me to the conclusion that the severance of the right carotid artery,[56] which was the immediate cause of death, was inflicted while the deceased was lying at

---

[54]Only three photographs of the Miller's Court crime scene are known to exist. Antiquarian book dealer Eric Barton was said to have possessed a full set, but these have vanished (*Ripper Notes*, November 1999, p. 3).

[55]This confirmation of the time of entry contradicts earlier reports. See 10 November.

[56]Previous Ripper victims were deemed to have died from the severance of the left carotid artery.

the right side of the bedstead and her head and neck in the top right-hand corner.

The jury had no questions to ask at this stage, and it was understood that more detailed evidence of the medical examination would be given at a future hearing.

An adjournment for a few minutes then took place, and on the return of the jury the coroner said: It has come to my ears that somebody has been making a statement to some of the jury as to their right and duty of being here. Has any one during the interval spoken to the jury, saying that they should not be here to-day?

Some jurymen replied in the negative.

THE CORONER: Then I must have been misinformed. I should have taken good care that he would have had a quiet life for the rest of the week if anybody had interfered with my jury.

**Julia Vanturney** [Venturney, Van Teurney, Van Turney], 1, Miller's-court, a charwoman, living with Harry Owen, said: I knew the deceased for some time as Kelly, and I knew Joe Barnett, who lived with her. He would not allow her to go on the streets. Deceased often got drunk. She said she was fond of another man, also named Joe. I never saw this man. I believe he was a costermonger.

When did you last see the deceased alive?—On Thursday morning, at about ten o'clock. I slept in the court on Thursday night, and went to bed about eight. I could not rest at all during the night.

Did you hear any noises in the court?—I did not. I heard no screams of "Murder," nor any one singing.

You must have heard deceased singing?—Yes; I knew her songs. They were generally Irish.

**Maria Harvey**, 3, New-court, Dor-

set-street, stated: I knew the deceased as Mary Jane Kelly. I slept at her house on Monday night and on Tuesday night. All the afternoon of Thursday we were together.

Were you in the house when Joe Barnett called?—Yes. I said, "Well, Mary Jane, I shall not see you this evening again," and I left with her two men's dirty shirts, a little boy's shirt, a black overcoat, a black crêpe bonnet with black satin strings, a pawn-ticket for a grey shawl, upon which 2s had been lent, and a little girl's white petticoat.

Have you seen any of these articles since?—Yes; I saw the black overcoat in a room in the court on Friday afternoon.

Did the deceased ever speak to you about being afraid of any man?—She did not.

**Inspector Beck**, H Division, deposed that, having sent for the doctor, he gave orders to prevent any person leaving the court, and he directed officers to make a search. He had not been aware that the deceased was known to the police.

**Inspector Frederick G. Abberline**, inspector of police, Criminal Investigation Department, Scotland-yard, stated: I am in charge of this case. I arrived at Miller's-court about 11:30 on Friday morning.

Was it by your orders that the door was forced?—No; I had an intimation from Inspector Beck that the bloodhounds had been sent for, and the reply had been received that they were on the way. Dr. Phillips was unwilling to force the door, as it would be very much better to test the dogs, if they were coming. We remained until about 1:30 p.m., when Superintendent Arnold arrived, and he informed me that the order in regard to the dogs had been countermanded, and he gave orders for the door to be forced.[57] I agree with the medical evidence as to the condition of the room. I subsequently took an inventory of the contents of the room. There were traces of a large fire having been kept up in the grate, so much so that it had melted the spout of a kettle off. We have since gone through the ashes in the fireplace; there were remnants of clothing, a portion of a brim of a hat, and a skirt, and it appeared as if a large quantity of women's clothing had been burnt.

Can you give any reason why they were burnt?—I can only imagine that it was to make a light for the man to see what he was doing. There was only one small candle in the room, on the top of a broken wine-glass. An impression has gone abroad that the murderer took away the key of the room. Barnett informs me that it has been missing some time, and since it has been lost they have put their hand through the broken window, and moved back the catch. It is quite easy.[58] There was a man's clay pipe in the room, and Barnett informed me that he smoked it.

Is there anything further the jury ought to know?—No; if there should be I can communicate with you, sir.

**The Coroner** (to the jury): The question is whether you will adjourn for further evidence. My own opinion is that it is very unnecessary for two courts to deal with these cases, and go through the same evidence time after time, which only causes expense and trouble. If the coroner's jury can come to a decision as to the cause of death, then that is all that they have to do. They have nothing to do with prosecuting a man and saying what amount of penalty he is to get. It is quite sufficient if they find out what the cause of death was. It is for the police authorities to deal with the case and satisfy themselves as to any person who may be suspected later on. I do not want to take it out of your hands. It is for you to say whether at an adjournment you will hear minutiae of the evidence, or whether you will think it is a matter to be dealt with in the police-courts later on, and that, this woman having met with her death by the carotid artery having been cut, you will be satisfied to return a verdict to that effect. From what I learn the police are content to take the future conduct of the case. It is for you to say whether you will close the inquiry to-day; if not, we shall adjourn for a week or fortnight, to hear the evidence that you may desire.

The Foreman, having consulted with his colleagues, considered that the jury had had quite sufficient evidence before them upon which to give a verdict.

THE CORONER: What is the verdict:

THE FOREMAN: Wilful murder against some person or persons unknown.

---

# THE DAILY TELEGRAPH
Thursday, November 15, 1888

Page 5
THE EAST-END MURDERS.
EXTRAORDINARY STATEMENT.

---

[57]In the wake of the "double event" and after several trials with bloodhounds, Warren issued orders that in the event of another murder, nothing was to be disturbed until dogs arrived. As no one at the Kelly murder scene knew the Chief Commissioner had resigned, the order remained in force until Arnold countermanded it (ref. HO 144/221/A49301E and Sugden, pp. 292–296).

[58]This statement should clarify any confusion over the key to Kelly's room. It is occasionally claimed that the official inquest notes having no reference to ease of operation of the catch negates this newspaper report. All *Telegraph* inquest coverage, however, clearly contains considerably more detail than the official notes, and as it is unlikely any inquest reporter would simply invent testimony, Abberline's reported claim that the operation of the catch was "quite easy" strongly suggests this was something the police had tested.

*[George Hutchinson and
Matthew Packer]*

Arrests of suspected persons continue to be made in the district of Whitechapel and Spitalfields, but the prisoners are invariably discharged upon the result of inquiries set on foot by the police. Hitherto it has been customary for the officers of the Criminal Investigation Department, from the chief to the lowest grade, to assist reporters in the performance of their duties; and the latter have in return respected their confidence. Under the new regulations there is distrust on both sides. Difficulties are put in the way of the press, whilst, on the other hand, the police assert that their labours are hindered by interviewers. One result of this want of harmony has been the publication of the description of a man, who is said to have accompanied Kelly into Miller's-court between two and three a.m. on the day of the murder. Absolute reliance was not placed in this story, but Hutchinson, the man who tells it, has accompanied detectives in their search for the dark-complexioned, middle-aged, foreign-looking bushy-eyebrowed gentleman, with the dark moustache turned up at the ends, who wore the soft felt hat, the long dark coat, trimmed with astrakhan, the black necktie, with horseshoe pin, and the button boots, and displayed a massive gold watch chain, with large seal and a red stone attached. The authorities anticipate that this full description having been given, the culprit will take pains to change his personal appearance, but it is to be remembered that the description itself is totally at variance with that of the stout fair man, with blotchy face and carroty moustache, who, according to testimony taken upon oath, was seen to go with Kelly into her room on the morning of her death.[59]

Mr. Matthew Packer, the fruiterer who sold some grapes to a man in company with the murdered woman just before the Berner-street murder, has made the following extraordinary statement:

On Tuesday evening two men came to my house and bought 12s worth of rabbits of me. They then asked me if I could give an exact description of the man to whom I sold the grapes, and who was supposed to have committed the Berner-street and Mitre-square murders, as they were convinced they knew him and where to find him. In reply to some questions, one of the men then said: "Well, I am sorry to say that I firmly believe it is my own cousin. He is an Englishman by birth, but some time ago he went to America, stayed there a few years, and then came back to London about seven or eight months ago. On his return he came to see me, and his first words were, 'Well, Boss, how are you?' He asked me to have some walks out with him, and I did round Commercial-street and Whitechapel. I found that he was very much altered on his return, for he was thorough harem scarem. We met a lot of Whitechapel women, and when we passed them he used to say to me, 'Do you see those—? How do you think we used to serve them where I came from? Why, we used to cut their throats and rip them up. I could rip one of them up and get her inside out in no time.' He said, 'We Jack Rippers killed lots of women over there. You will hear of some of it being done over here soon, for I am going to turn a London Jack Ripper.'" The man added "I did not take much notice then of what he said as he had had a drop of drink, and I thought it was only his swagger and bounce of what he had been doing in America, at some place which he mentioned, but I forget the name; but," continued the man, "when I heard of the first

---

[59]It appears that once Hutchinson went to the police, further search for the "blotchy faced man" was given up in favor of Hutchinson's extraordinarily detailed report, the very thoroughness of which has led some theorists to believe Hutchinson was the Ripper (ref. esp. Eddleston, Hinton and Wright).

woman being murdered and stabbed all over I then began to be very uneasy, and to wonder whether he really was carrying out his threats. I did not, however, like to say anything about him, as he is my own cousin. Then, as one murder followed after another, I felt that I could scarcely rest. He is a perfect monster towards women, especially when he has a drop of drink. But in addition to what he said to me about these murders in America, and what was going to be done here, I feel certain it is him, because of the way these Jack Ripper letters which have appeared in the papers begin. They all begin 'Dear Boss,' and that is just the way he begins his letters. He calls everybody 'Boss' when he speaks to them. I did not want to say anything about him if I could help it, so I wrote to him, but he did not answer my letter. Since this last murder I have felt that I could not remain silent any longer, for at least something ought to be done to put him under restraint."

Packer states he feels sure the men are speaking the truth, as they seemed very much concerned, and hardly knew what to do in the matter. He knows where to find the men. One is employed at some ironworks and the other at the West India Docks, and the man they allude to lives somewhere in the neighbourhood of Whitechapel.

The reporter to whom the above statement was made at once sent off a copy of it to the Home Secretary, and also to Sir William Fraser, the Chief Commissioner of the City Police. Sir William Fraser immediately acted on the information, and sent Detective-sergeants White and Mitchell to investigate it. They read the letter to Packer, who said it was true, and then took the detectives to the man's house. On being questioned by the police he stated where his cousin was generally to be found. It transpired that he is sometimes engaged on the Thames, and late last night a search was, it is said, being made for him upon the river.

On inquiring early this morning we were officially informed that the above statement had not led to any satisfactory result.[60]

---

# THE DAILY TELEGRAPH
Tuesday, November 20, 1888

Page 3
## THE WHITECHAPEL MURDER.
*[Burial of Mary Kelly]*

The remains of Mary Janet [*sic*] Kelly, who was murdered on Nov. 9 in Miller's-court, Dorset-street, Spitalfields, were brought yesterday morning from Shoreditch mortuary to the cemetery at Leytonstone, where they were interred.[61]

[With this, the *Daily Telegraph* coverage of Kelly's murder, which had itself seemed to be in terminal decline since 15 November, was also laid to rest. Brief accounts of the arrest and release of drunken, self-professed "Jack the Rippers" would occasionally surface, and 22 November saw a superficial attack on prostitute Annie Farmer reported under the heading "Alarming Outrage in Whitechapel." For all practical purposes, however, what are known as the "canonical" Ripper murders—and what is remembered as banner coverage of them—came to an end with Mary Kelly's death.]

---

[60]It seems almost superfluous to point out that no useful lead ever came of Packer's story, and it should be relegated to the fiction bin.

[61]Mary Jane Kelly is buried in (public) grave 16, row 67 of St. Patrick's Cemetery, Leytonstone, London (*Ripperana* No. 14, October 1995). A garish headstone proclaiming her the "Prima Donna of Spitalfields" was erected in 1986 by theorist John Morrison. It was later removed amidst public complaint and revelation that it was in the wrong location. A small marble block now marks the proper site.

# Mary Jane Kelly— Commentary

## ALEX CHISHOLM

### 1. Time of Death

The centrality of time of death to any murder investigation is obviously beyond dispute. But in the case of Mary Kelly's murder, any attempt to determine even an approximate time of death is hampered by both the paucity of extant evidence and the contradictory nature of that evidence. Even at the time uncertainty reigned, as the *Star* neatly summed up: "There have been many conflicting statements as to the time at which Kelly was last seen. Some women have said they saw her between half-past eight and nine on Friday morning. But medical opinion goes against this" (*Star*, 12 November, p. 3).

The only medical opinion on time of death now known to exist is provided by Dr. Thomas Bond in official files, and brief comments from Dr. George Bagster Phillips reported in some newspapers.

Dr. Bond opined:

> In the Dorset Street case the body was lying on the bed at the time of my visit, 2 o'clock ... Rigor Mortis had set in, but increased during the progress of the examination. From this it is difficult to say with any degree of certainty the exact time that had elapsed since death as the period varies from 6 to 12 hours before rigidity sets in. The body was comparatively cold at 2 o'clock and the remains of a recently taken meal were found in the stomach and scattered about over the intestines. It is therefore, pretty certain that the woman must have been dead about 12 hours and the partly digested food would indicate that death took place about 3 or 4 hours after the food was taken, so one or two o'clock in the morning would be the probable time of the murder [HO 144/221/A49301C, ff. 217–232].

In his post-mortem notes, Bond elaborated on the partly digested food: "In the abdominal cavity was some partly digested food of fish & potatoes & similar food was found in the remains of the stomach attached to the intestines" (MEPO 3/3153, ff. 12–18).

Clearly, techniques in forensic pathology have advanced almost immeasurably since 1888, and modern methods can cast considerable doubt on the accuracy of Bond's estimate. In a recent article on this topic, Bond's assessment of the body as "comparatively cold," being unsatisfactory for modern evaluation of algor mortis, is discounted as "worthless." Similarly, Bond's view that the "partly digested food would indicate that death took place about 3 or 4 hours after the food was taken" is countered by assuming Kelly's last meal was "not a large banquet," and drawing on the modern generality that "the stomach will empty a small meal or sandwich in one or two hours." The onset of rigor mortis, varying, according to Bond, "from 6 to 12 hours before rigidity sets in" is challenged with the "fairly constant" time frame in "several medical/legal textbooks" of "2 to 4 hours after death" within which rigor mortis "generally commences." (Vanderlinden, W., "Screams of Murder," *Ripper Notes*, July 2001.) Against this, however, his 21 years' experience as a police surgeon, his first-hand examination of the body in question, and—ironically—the very vagueness of the account he has left all allow the possibility that Dr. Bond remains better placed to provide informed opinion on the time of Mary Kelly's demise than present-day pathology. In which case, Bond's estimated time of death of one or two o'clock, while certainly open to considerable question, cannot be wholly dismissed.

Dr. Phillips, on the other hand, reportedly thought: "...that life had been extinct for five or six hours when the body was first examined between eleven a.m.

and midday" (*Telegraph*, 12 November, p. 5). Other newspapers elaborated:

> There is no doubt that the body of a person who, to use Dr. Phillips' own words, was "cut all to pieces" would get cold far more quickly than that of one who had died simply from the cutting of the throat; and the room would have been very cold, as there were two broken panes of glass in the windows. Again, the body being entirely uncovered would very quickly get cold [*Times*, 12 November].

An alternative impression of room temperature in relation to Phillips' observations was offered in the *Star*: "Owing to the loss of blood the body would have got cold quickly, but a big fire seems to have been kept up, and the police say that when they entered the room it was quite warm" (*Star*, 12 November, p. 3).

Despite such slight discrepancies, Phillips, who confirmed at the inquest having entered Miller's Court at 11:15am, appeared to be estimating a time of death of between approximately 5:30 and 6:30am. This, of course, is assuming that the examination of the body, on which Phillips based his estimate, took place almost immediately after his arrival, an assumption apparently supported by the following report:

> Dr. Phillips, on his arrival, carefully examined the body of the dead woman, and later on again made a second examination in company with Dr. Bond, from Westminster, Dr. Gordon Brown, from the City, Dr. Duke, from Spitalfields, and Dr. Phillips's assistant.... After the examination of the body it was placed in a shell, which was put into a van and conveyed to the Shoreditch mortuary to await an inquest [*Star*, 10 November, p. 2].

Such a view, however, appears to have been conclusively contradicted by various inquest testimonies. Inspector Abberline, who arrived on the scene at 11:30am, testified:

> Dr. Phillips was unwilling to force the door, as it would be very much better to test the dogs, if they were coming. We remained until about 1:30 p.m., when Superintendent Arnold arrived, and he informed me that the order in regard to the dogs had been countermanded, and he gave orders for the door to be forced [*Telegraph*, 13 November, p. 5].

While Dr. Phillips himself confirmed:

> ...as the door was locked I looked through the lower of the broken panes and satisfied myself that the mutilated corpse lying on the bed was not in need of any immediate attention from me, and I also came to the conclusion that there was nobody else upon the bed, or within view, to whom I could render any professional assistance. Having ascertained that probably it was advisable that no entrance should be made into the room at that time, I remained until about 1:30p.m., when the door was broken open by McCarthy, under the direction of Superintendent Arnold [*Telegraph*, 13 November, p. 5].

Unless he felt capable of estimating time of death from a cursory glance through the broken window, it seems certain Phillips based his conclusion on his first detailed examination of the body, which could not have taken place until after 1:30pm. His estimate that "life had been extinct for five or six hours when the body was first examined" would therefore appear to relate to between 7:30–8:30am. Of course it could be that the doctor simply recalculated his estimate of elapsed time since death, based on his post 1:30pm examination, to accommodate a reporter's question relating time of death to his first arrival on the scene. Indeed, the fact that the doctor's estimate was reported as a corrective to Mrs. Maxwell's disputed claims would seem to support such a conclusion.

Nevertheless, in the absence of further evidence, all that can be determined with any degree of certainty is that Dr. Phillips estimated Kelly's time of death to be either between 5:30–6:30am, or 7:30–8:30am, both of which differ substantially from Dr. Bond's opinion.

Witness claims of hearing cries of "murder" offer yet another possible time of death. According to the *Star*, this story, once aired:

> ...soon became popular, until at last half a dozen women were retailing it as their own personal experience. Each story contradicted the others with respect to the time at which the cry was heard. A *Star* reporter who inquired into the matter extracted from one of the women the confession that the story was, as far as she was concerned, a fabrication; and he came to the conclusion that it was to be disregarded [*Star*, 10 November, p. 2].

The authorities, however, were less prepared to disregard all such stories, and two witnesses, Elizabeth Prater and Sarah Lewis, were called to give evidence at the inquest. Prater, who lived above Kelly's room, first told police on 9 November: "About 3:30 or 4 am I was awakened by a kitten walking across my neck, and just then I heard screams of murder about two or three times in a female voice" (MJ/SPC, NE1888, Box 3, Case Paper 19, p. 26 [London Metropolitan Archives]).

Curiously, the *Telegraph* of 10 November reported that Prater "had heard nothing during the night," and on the same day a vivid account in the *Star* of Prater breaking down as she re-told her story to a reporter makes no mention of any cries heard. These early reports were contradicted, however, by the *Telegraph*'s 12 November edition, which had Prater saying "there was such a call at about three a.m." By the time of the inquest, Prater's "two or three" screams had been diminished to one suppressed cry:

> A kitten disturbed me about half-past three o'clock or a quarter to four. As I was turning round I heard a suppressed cry of "Oh—murder!" in a faint voice. It seemed to proceed from the court.

When asked by the Coroner, "Did you hear it a second time?" Prater replied, "No" [*Telegraph*, 13 November, p. 5].

Sarah Lewis, who had spent the night at 2 Miller's Court, had a more consistent tale to tell: "I sat awake until nearly four, when I heard a female's voice shouting "Murder" loudly. It seemed like the voice of a young woman. It sounded at our door. There was only one scream" (*Telegraph*, 13 November, p. 5).

Against these claims were the testimony of others, including Mary Ann Cox and Julia Venturney, who, despite being awake or passing a restless night, were confident that no cries of murder had been heard. Nevertheless, the claims of Prater and Lewis, however inconsistent and therefore dubious at least one of them appears, remain as possible indicators of one more possible time of death. These claims brought the possible times of death to: Bond—approximately 1:00–2:00 am; Prater and Lewis—approximately 3:45am; Phillips—approximately 5:30–6:30am, or possibly 7:30–8:30am.

## 2. Disputed Sightings

In addition to the above possible times of death, the frequently dismissed witnesses who claimed to have seen Kelly alive and walking the streets later on the morning of Friday, 9 November, must also be considered. On 10 November, the following report appeared:

> A tailor named Lewis says he saw Kelly come out about eight o'clock yesterday morning and go back. Another statement is to the effect that Kelly was seen in a public-house known as the "Ringers," at the corner of Dorset-street and Commercial-street, about ten o'clock yesterday

morning, and that she there met her lover Barnett, and had a glass of beer with him. This statement is not substantiated [*Star*, 10 November, p. 2].

Two days on came reports of Caroline Maxwell's claims in all the leading newspapers, while the *Times* included this addition: "Another young woman, whose name is known, has also informed the police that she is positive she saw Kelly between half-past 8 and a quarter to 9 on Friday morning" (*Times*, 12 November).

Of all these claimed sightings, only the statements of Lewis and Maxwell are known to have survived in any detail. While most leading newspapers carried detailed accounts of Maxwell's testimony, Lewis' statement appears to have been less widely reported:

> Maurice Lewis, a tailor, living in Dorset-street, stated that he had known the deceased woman for the last five years. Her name was Mary Jane Kelly. She was short, stout, and dark; and stood about five feet three inches. He saw her on the previous (Thursday) night, between ten and eleven, at the Horn of Plenty in Dorset-street. She was drinking with some woman and also with "Dan," a man selling oranges in Billingsgate and Spitalfields markets, with whom she lived up till as recently as a fortnight ago. He knew her as a woman of the town. One of the women whom he saw with her was known as Julia. To his knowledge she went home overnight with a man. He seemed to be respectably dressed. Whether or not the man remained all night he could not say. Soon after ten o'clock in the morning he was playing with others at pitch and toss in McCarthy's-court, when he heard a lad call out "Copper," and he and his companions rushed away and entered a beer-house at the corner of Dorset-street, known as Ringer's. He was positive that on going in he saw Mary Jane Kelly drinking with some other people, but is not certain whether there was a man amongst them. He went home to Dorset-street on leaving the house, and

about half an hour afterwards heard that Kelly had been found in her room murdered. It would then be close upon eleven o'clock [*Illustrated Police News*, 17 November, p. 2].

The evident inconsistencies and incredible nature of Lewis' statement have led to a general disregard of his claims. It has to be wondered, however, why Lewis should admit to playing an illegal game of "pitch & toss," if he had nothing of greater substance to offer. Even if he wanted to enhance his status in the eyes of his peers by inventing an involvement in the latest sensation, he had no need to admit to illegal activities. In addition, why, if his story was invention, would he identify others who could contradict him, as appears to have happened?

If the man referred to by Lewis as "Dan" was indeed Joe Barnett, as seems to be suggested, then Barnett's inquest testimony that he last saw Kelly alive "between half-past seven and a quarter to eight on Thursday night" appears to refute Lewis' story. That is, of course, if Barnett was being truthful. In similar vein, if Mrs. Venturney was the "Julia" referred to, as has been suggested, then she too contradicted Lewis by informing the inquest that she "went to bed about eight" on Thursday night, and last saw Kelly alive "on Thursday morning, at about ten o'clock."

If Lewis was mistaken about seeing Kelly with "Dan" and "Julia" on the Thursday night, he could equally be mistaken about seeing Kelly around 10:00am on Friday. The fact that Lewis was not called to give evidence to the inquest, and appears to have plied his statement only to the newspapers, leaves no other source against which to test his evidence. The absence of any official record of his account may also suggest that the authorities placed little faith in his credibility. But perhaps crucially, his claim to have seen

Kelly shortly after ten o'clock, leaving less than forty minutes for the murderer to escort his victim back to her room, and then subdue, kill and mutilate her before making good an escape in broad daylight, seems highly improbable. In the end, being wholly incompatible with any of the possibilities allowed by medical evidence, the claims of Maurice Lewis must be seen as highly dubious.

Caroline Maxwell, on the other hand, appears to be a rather more credible witness. Despite some slight discrepancies, Maxwell's various statements, made in the knowledge and under caution that her evidence differed from that of others and was severely doubted by the authorities, are reasonably consistent. It is questionable whether or not she knew Kelly well enough to recognize her at distance, but if she is believed to have been sincere—and more importantly, sober—it is improbable that she could mistake a woman she talked to and called by name for someone else. Further, as the *Telegraph* reported:

> The question has arisen whether Mrs. Maxwell might not have confounded one morning with another, but when questioned on this point she avers that there were circumstances connected with her own work to enable her to fix it as Friday morning without any doubt or misgiving whatever [*Telegraph*, 12 November, p. 5].

While confounding one morning with another might have been possible had Maxwell first recounted her evidence several days after the event, the fact that she told her tale to Inspector Abberline on the 9th, the very day she claimed to have seen Kelly, makes it unlikely she could have been describing events which took place on another day. In addition, the circumstances which enabled her to fix the day without doubt were confirmed by an independent third party, as the *Times* reported:

> When asked by the police how she could fix the time of the morning, Mrs. Maxwell replied, "Because I went to the milkshop for some milk, and I had not before been there for a long time, and she was wearing a woollen cross-over that I had not seen her wear for a considerable time." On inquiries being made at the milkshop indicated by the woman her statement was found to be correct, and the cross-over was also found in Kelly's room [*Times*, 12 November].

So despite the many valid objections to her testimony, reported in the *Telegraph* and elsewhere, Maxwell's dogged resolution suggests she, at least, believed the accuracy of her tale. And, as her claimed conversation with Mary Jane may just fall within an acceptable margin of Phillips' latest possible estimated time of death, it must remain barely possible that Mrs. Maxwell's account was correct. In which case, a further possibility of sometime after 8:30am could be added to the potential times of Kelly's death.

# AFTERWORD

The murder of Mary Jane Kelly is considered the final "canonical" Whitechapel Murder. It was not the last in the series—the deaths of Alice McKenzie in 1889 and Frances Coles in 1891 were both popularly considered to be his handiwork—but tradition has portrayed Kelly as Jack the Ripper's apotheosis in horror. The extra police patrols drafted into the East End were gradually stepped down and finally discontinued in 1889, concurrent with the disbanding of local vigilance committees, and with the retirement of Inspector Abberline in 1892, the case files were shelved.

Since that time, the search for Jack the Ripper has become a cottage industry, with its own house magazines, websites and experts. But although forensic and psychological advances have added slightly to our meager store of knowledge about what sort of person the Ripper might have been, the central question of his identity remains as unanswerable as ever. Only a handful of suspects—George Hutchinson, Aaron Kosminski, Dr. Francis Tumblety, George Chapman—merit serious investigation, yet the cases against each are hollow at the center, with a final, irrefutable solution forever out of reach.

The Ripper killings were interpreted by newspapers to the reading public as a combination of mystery, gothic horror and morality play. Because "the Ripper" so quickly took on a mythic quality, he could be enlisted as a foot soldier in any cause. He might be used as a screed against decadent aristocracy, or an example of the hatreds brewing in the oppressed poor; perhaps a warning against immigrants with their repulsive customs, or even a cautionary example to the liberated "new woman" of what might be her fate without male protection.

Because the "real" Jack the Ripper was swamped so thoroughly by the myth, it is, perversely, that very myth which has obscured the truth for so many years. Jack the Ripper has been elevated from his actuality as a repulsive thug; he has become the "hero" of the Whitechapel Murders and the trademark name for killers. That is the unsettling legacy the newspapers have left us. Though a century old, by whatever name we call it—the Great Victorian Mystery, the classic whodunit, the first sexual serial killings—the "news from Whitechapel" is still sadly fresh.

*Appendix*

# MONETARY
# CONVERSION TABLE

For those readers who wish to convert some of the sums mentioned in the previous pages to modern-day equivalents, we offer this small approximating chart:

| 1888 | Modern UK | Modern US |
|------|-----------|-----------|
| £1.00 | £53.00 | $80.00 |
| 1 shilling (s) | £ 6.00 | $ 9.00 |
| 1 penny (d) | 53 pence | $ .75 |

Because of fluctuating currency rates and vast differences in purchasing power, however, a strict comparison between 1888 and 2002 monetary values is misleading. For example, Catherine Eddowes and John Kelly received 2s 6d when he pawned his boots, but one would be hard-pressed to find a pawnbroker today who would hand over almost $17.00 for used footwear!

# SOURCES AND BIBLIOGRAPHY

While the *Daily Telegraph* has been the primary source for the text of this book, we have cross-checked the transcripts with other London and British newspapers as well as the official Home Office and Metropolitan Police files. Specific newspaper and file references are given throughout the notes; the following is a full list of the sources we have consulted:

## Files

HO 144/221/A49301B
HO 144/221/A49301C
HO 144/221/A49301E
HO 144/221/A49301F
MEPO 1/55
MEPO 3/140
MEPO 3/141
MEPO 3/142
MEPO 3/3153
Coroner's Inquest (L), 1888, No. 135, Catherine Eddowes inquest, 1888 (Corporation of London Public Record Office).
Kelly inquest papers, MJ/SPC, NE1888, Box 3, Case Paper 19 (London Metropolitan Archives).

## Newspapers

*Daily Chronicle*
*Daily News*
*Daily Telegraph*
*East London Advertiser*
*East London Observer*
*Evening News*
*Illustrated Police News*
*Lloyd's Weekly Newspaper*
*Manchester Guardian*
*Morning Post*
*Pall Mall Gazette*
*Penny Illustrated Paper and Illustrated Times*
*Police Gazette*
*Reynolds's Newspaper*
*The Star*
*The Times*
*Star of the East*
*Weekly Times and Echo*

## Books

All books are hardcover unless otherwise noted.

Anderson, Sir Robert, *The Lighter Side of My Official Life* (London, 1910).
Baring-Gould, William and Ceil, *The Annotated Mother Goose* (New York, 1962).
Beadle, William, *Jack the Ripper: Anatomy of a Myth* (Essex, 1995).
Begg, Paul, *Jack the Ripper: The Uncensored Facts* (London, 1988).
Begg, Paul, Martin Fido and Keith Skinner, *The Jack the Ripper A–Z* [3rd edition, pbk.] (London, 1996).
Bourne, H.R. Fox, *English Newspapers* [2 vols.] (New York, 1966).
Caputi, Jane, *The Age of Sex Crime* (Ohio, 1987).
Connell, Nick, and Stewart Evans, *The Man Who Hunted Jack the Ripper* (Cambridge, 1999).

Curtis, Jr., L. Perry, *Jack the Ripper and the London Press* (New Haven, 2001).

Dew, Walter, *I Caught Crippen* (London, 1938).

Eddleston, John, *Jack the Ripper: An Encyclopedia* (California, 2001).

Evans, Stewart, and Paul Gainey, *The Lodger* (London, 1995).

_____, and Keith Skinner, *The Ultimate Jack the Ripper Sourcebook* (London, 2000).

_____, and _____, *Jack the Ripper: Letters from Hell* (London, 2001).

Fido, Martin, *The Crimes, Detection and Death of Jack the Ripper* (New York: Barnes & Noble, 1993).

_____, *A History of British Serial Killing* (London, 2001).

Friedland, Martin, *The Trials of Israel Lipski* (London, 1984).

Hinton, Bob, *From Hell: The Jack the Ripper Mystery* [pbk.] (Abertillery, 1998).

Jeffers, H. Paul, *Bloody Business* (New York, 1992).

Kelly, Alexander, and David Sharp, *Jack the Ripper: A Bibliography and Review of the Literature* [pbk.] (Kent, 1995).

Knight, Stephen, *Jack the Ripper: The Final Solution* (New York, 1976).

Lane, Brian, *The Encyclopedia of Forensic Science* (London, 1992).

Palmer, Scott, *Jack the Ripper: A Reference Guide* (Lanham, 1995).

Riley, Peter, *The Highways and Byways of Jack the Ripper* [pbk.] (Cheshire, 2001).

Robinson, John, *Born in Blood: The Lost Secrets of Freemasonry* (New York, 1989).

Robinson, Tom, *The Whitechapel Horrors* [pbk. reprint] (Manchester, no date).

Rumbelow, Donald, *Jack the Ripper: The Complete Casebook* (Chicago, 1988).

Shelden, Neal, *Jack the Ripper and His Victims* [pbk.] (Essex, 1999).

_____, *Jack the Ripper Victim Annie Chapman: A Short Biography* [pbk.] (Essex, 2001).

Smith, Anthony, *The Newspaper: An International History* (London, 1979).

Smith, Major Henry, *From Constable to Commissioner* (London, 1910).

Sugden, Philip, *The Complete History of Jack the Ripper* (New York, 1994).

Tully, James, *Prisoner 1167* (New York, 1997).

Turnbull, Peter, *The Killer Who Never Was* (Hull, 1996).

Walkowitz, Judith R., *Prostitution and Victorian Society: Women, Class and the State* [pbk.] (Cambridge, 1982).

_____, *City of Dreadful Delight: Narratives of Sexual Danger in Late-Victorian London* [pbk.] (Chicago, 1992).

Wensley, Frederick Porter, *Detective Days* (London, 1931).

Wolf, A.P., *Jack the Myth* (London, 1993).

## Magazines

*Ripperana*, editor N.P. Warren, 16 Copperfield Way, Pinner, HA5 5RY, England.

*Ripper Notes*, editor Christopher-Michael Di-Grazia, 132 Colby Street, Bradford MA 01835, USA.

*Ripperologist*, editor Paul Begg, PO Box 735, Maidstone, Kent ME17 1JF, England.

## Internet

*Casebook: Jack the Ripper* (http://www.casebook.org)

*Casebook Press Project* (http://www.casebook.org/press_reports)

*Casebook Productions* (http://www.casebook-productions.org)

*Royal Meteorological Society* (http://www.royal-met-soc.org.uk)

## Other

Ordnance Survey Maps (Godfrey edition), 1873, 1893, 1894.

*The Oxford English Dictionary* (Oxford University Press, 1933).

National Census Returns, 1841–1891 (held by the Public Record Office, Chancery Lane).

# INDEX

Individual inquest testimony is delineated by the following initials: N: Nichols; C: Chapman; S: Stride; E: Eddowes; K: Kelly. The letter "n" after a page number indicates where a footnote expands on a text reference.